Cities around the World

Cities around the World

Struggles and Solutions to Urban Life

VOLUME 1

Jing Luo, Editor

An Imprint of ABC-CLIO, LLC
Santa Barbara, California • Denver, Colorado

Copyright © 2019 by ABC-CLIO, LLC

All rights reserved. No part of this publication may be reproduced, stored in a retrieval system, or transmitted, in any form or by any means, electronic, mechanical, photocopying, recording, or otherwise, except for the inclusion of brief quotations in a review, without prior permission in writing from the publisher.

Library of Congress Cataloging-in-Publication Data

Names: Luo, Jing, editor.
Title: Cities around the world : struggles and solutions to urban life / Jing Luo, Editor.
Description: First edition. | Santa Barbara, CA : ABC-CLIO, An Imprint of ABC-CLIO,
  LLC, [2019]– | Includes bibliographical references and index.
Identifiers: LCCN 2018051701 (print) | LCCN 2018052097 (ebook) |
  ISBN 9781440853869 (ebook) | ISBN 9781440853852 (hard copy (set) : alk. paper) |
  ISBN 9781440853876 (hard copy (vol. 1) : alk. paper) | ISBN 9781440853883
  (hard copy (vol. 2) : alk. paper)
Subjects: LCSH: City planning. | Policy sciences.
Classification: LCC HT166 (ebook) | LCC HT166 .C473 2019 (print) |
  DDC 307.1/216—dc23
LC record available at https://lccn.loc.gov/2018051701

ISBN: 978-1-4408-5385-2 (set)
    978-1-4408-5387-6 (vol. 1)
    978-1-4408-5388-3 (vol. 2)
    978-1-4408-5386-9 (ebook)

23 22 21 20 19   1 2 3 4 5

This book is also available as an eBook.

ABC-CLIO
An Imprint of ABC-CLIO, LLC

ABC-CLIO, LLC
147 Castilian Drive
Santa Barbara, California 93117
www.abc-clio.com

This book is printed on acid-free paper ∞

Manufactured in the United States of America

Contents

VOLUME I

Preface   ix

Acknowledgments   xi

Introduction   xiii

Employment and Jobs   1
    Overview   1
    Lagos, Nigeria: Government Reform Is Key to Job Creation   6
    London, United Kingdom: Brexit, the Known Unknown   12
    Mumbai, India: Exploring Employment Solutions in Temporary Jobs   19
    New York City, United States: Economically and Environmentally Friendly   24
    Paris, France: A Locomotive of Job Creation   31
    Riyadh, Saudi Arabia: Creating Jobs in the Post–Oil-Boom Era   36
    San Juan, Puerto Rico, United States: A Stronger Local Government Is Key to Job Creation   41
    Seattle, United States: Have Job, Going Homeless   48
    Shenzhen, China: Struggle to Leave Shanzhai Behind   52
    Stockholm, Sweden: Employers Stress Educational Credentials   58

Energy and Sustainability   65
    Overview   65
    Beijing, China: Battling Water Shortage   70
    Copenhagen, Denmark: Striving to Be Carbon-Neutral by 2025   74
    Frankfurt, Germany: Protecting the City from Climate Changes   79
    London, United Kingdom: Improving Mobility Can Save Energy   86
    Melbourne, Australia: Toward a Greater Reliance on Alternative Energy   92
    Mumbai, India: Providing Energy for a City of 21 Million   97
    Pittsburgh, United States: Air Quality Is a Work in Progress   106
    Rio de Janeiro, Brazil: A City with a Passion for Conservation and Renewable Energy   111

Singapore City, Singapore: Go Solar!   116
Toronto, Canada: A City with a Passion for Energy Conservation   120

Green Spaces   127
Overview   127
Abu Dhabi, United Arab Emirates (UAE): Building a Greener City with a More Open Culture   131
Aguascalientes, Mexico: Returning Industrial Ruin to Green Space   135
Halifax, Canada: Near-Urban Wilderness Protection   140
Hong Kong, China: Adding Green Spaces to Densely Populated Neighborhoods   147
Moscow, Russia: Planting 1 Million Trees   154
New York City, United States: Pursuit of More Green   159
Paris, France: Returning to Nature   164
Rotterdam, The Netherlands: Building an Edible City   169
Tel Aviv, Israel: Community Gardening   173
Tokyo, Japan: Making the City More Livable   178

Housing and Infrastructure   185
Overview   185
Almaty, Kazakhstan: Housing Reform   189
Caracas, Venezuela: Will Informal Settlement Be Forever?   195
Chongqing, China: Chongqing's Ingenuity in Providing Public Housing for a City of 33 Million   200
Dandong, China: One Bridge, Two Islands   206
Detroit, United States: Housing and Infrastructure after the Auto Boom   213
Havana, Cuba: Facing Challenges of Housing and Infrastructure in Economic Transition   220
Munich, Germany: The Munich Wall   226
Sydney, Australia: Struggle for Affordable Housing   233
Touba, Senegal: A Spiritual Solution to Affordable Housing   239
Vienna, Austria: Making Access to Public Housing Equitable   244

Migration and Demographic Changes   249
Overview   249
Buenos Aires, Argentina: Impact of European Migration   254
Guangzhou, China: Foreign Communities Facing Challenges of Adaptation   259
Kinshasa, Democratic Republic of the Congo (DRC): Reaching for Demographic Dividend   264
Lima, Peru: Migration and Demographic Changes Driven by Climate Changes   269
London, United Kingdom: Facing the Challenges of Population Growth   274
Los Angeles, United States: A Dynamic Demographic Mix   279
Tehran, Iran: Toward a More Open and Tolerant Society   283
Tokyo, Japan: Sustainable Growth Calls for Immigration Reform   289

Vancouver, Canada: The Most Asian City in the Western World   294
Williamsport, United States: A Quiet Town in Deep Pennsylvania   299

Index   305

VOLUME 2

Pollution   1
  Overview   1
  Baku, Azerbaijan: A Tainted Reputation   6
  Boston, United States: Cleaning Boston's Waterways—An Overview   11
  Flint, United States: National and Local Politics in the Creation of a Public Health Emergency   16
  Karachi, Pakistan: How Pollution Gets Out of Control   23
  Krakow, Poland: Old Furniture, New Fuel Source   28
  New Delhi, India: Success of Pollution Control Depends on Effective Collaboration   33
  Rome, Italy: Reducing Spatial Segregation Contributes to Pollution Control   39
  Sao Paulo, Brazil: Fighting the Deadly Air Pollution   45
  Seoul, South Korea: When Every Citizen Takes It to Heart   50
  Shiprock, United States: Radioactive from the Inside Out   55

Schools   61
  Overview   61
  Bamako, Mali: Private and Public Sectors of Education   67
  Berlin, Germany: Making the City a Center of Learning   72
  Boston, United States: A Model City of STEM Education   78
  Ouagadougou, Burkina Faso: Investing in Higher Education for the Country's Future   83
  Seoul, South Korea: "Education Fever"   87
  Sydney, Australia: Making International Education a Thriving Sector of the Economy   91
  Taipei, Taiwan: Taipei's K–12 Education and Special Education   96
  Tokyo, Japan: The *Yutori* Educational Reforms   100
  Vologda, Russia: Education in the Russian Federation—A City's Solutions   105
  Xi'an, China: Where China's Private Education Debuts   111

Traffic and Transportation   119
  Overview   119
  Beijing, China: Beijing's War on Traffic Congestion   124
  Casablanca, Morocco: Will a Change in Lunch Habit Improve the Town's Traffic?   130
  Istanbul, Turkey: Building More Tunnels and Bridges Won't Make Congestion Go Away   134
  Kolkata, India: When More People Drive Their Own Cars   140
  Mexico City, Mexico: Improving Governance Is Key to Solving Traffic Challenges   145

New York City, United States: The New York Subway 150
Osaka, Japan: Attracting Private Investments to Public Transportation 154
Saint Petersburg, Russia: Swamped with Traffic 160
Stuttgart, Germany: A City with the Best Mass Transit 165
Zurich, Switzerland: Improving Traffic and Transportation through All Possible Venues 170

Violence, Corruption, and Organized Crime 177
Overview 177
Aleppo, Syria: Drought, Global Warming, and Civil War 182
Baghdad, Iraq: Restitching a Torn Society Isn't Easy 187
Beijing, China: Tight Surveillance and Harsh Punishment 193
Brussels, Belgium: Facing Safety Challenges in the 21st Century 197
Chicago, United States: Stop the Crimes before They Spread 202
Kabul, Afghanistan: What Went Wrong? 207
Mexico City, Mexico: Crime, Corruption, and Violence Have Deep Roots 213
Seoul, South Korea: The Continuing Public Fight for Democracy 220
Sicily, Italy: Fighting Organized Crime in the New Era 226
Tokyo, Japan: Violence, Corruption, and Organized Crime 230

Waste Management 237
Overview 237
Baghdad, Iraq: Hauling Garbage in Hell on Earth 241
Cairo, Egypt: The Zabaleen 246
Calgary, Canada: Waste Management Is a National Effort and Calgary's Priority 251
Dakar, Senegal: Peri-Urban/Urban Agriculture and Urban Waste Management 257
Delhi, India: Current Problems and Opportunities for the Future of the National Capital Territory 262
Kobe, Japan: The Cleanest City in the World 267
Naples, Italy: Coping with a Rubbish Crisis 272
Oslo, Norway: Prevention and Reduction, What Makes Oslo Clean 276
Port-au-Prince, Haiti: Challenges of Waste Management under Poor Governance 281
San Francisco, United States: Becoming a "Zero-Waste City" 288
Singapore City, Singapore: Managing Food Waste 293

Selected Bibliography 299

About the Editor and Contributors 309

Index 315

Preface

From the refugee crisis in Europe down to the nitty-gritty of everyday life in a city, urban problems are commanding more of our attention today. I was first drawn to the study of urban challenges in the early 1980s during my college years at Peking University. A French professor gave an inspiring lecture about urban housing programs in Paris that I recall vividly to this day. While expressing great dismay at the lack of aesthetics of the suburban low-income housing (HLM), he warned that Beijing would not be immune from such housing; a rushed urbanization, he cautioned, could turn Beijing into a congested megacity where HLMs would be a common scene. A student rose to his feet and objected: "Professor, imperialists have developed modern cities. Now it is our turn to catch up!" At that time, Beijing's sky was smog-free; commuters biked to work rain or shine, and traffic jams were unheard of. Three decades later, however, the opposite is true: blue skies, clean air, and congestion-free traffic are so rare that they are celebrated enthusiastically at every ephemeral instance. HLMs sprawl out in the tens of thousands in Beijing's suburbs, occupied by farmers who lost their land to the city. Sadly, the French professor was right.

Beijing is not alone in this regard; most megacities around the world, especially those in emerging economies, struggle with the side effects of rampant growth. With this in mind, one might wonder: why the rush? For most of human history, cities were not the main form of settlement. According to the World Bank, only a third of the global population resided in urban areas until the early 1960s. The landscape of urban-rural population only shifted abruptly in the most recent decades. By 2007, the global urban population had crossed the 50th percentage point. The World Bank and the United Nations anticipate that approximately 70 percent of the global population will be urban dwellers by 2050.

From a social perspective, the urban environment is admittedly intrinsic to the development of human society. Humans have grown to be dependent on the urban environment for access to safety, community, education, productivity, cultural development, and better living conditions overall. However, we have witnessed in recent decades a trend of population influx that often exceeds a city's capacity. Studies have identified two major factors behind this trend: one being the increasing concentration of economic activities in cities driven by the tech boom, and the other, climate change. Climate migration has had an unprecedented impact on cities around the globe. Over the past two decades, climatological events have taken place with increasing frequency and severity. Strong hurricanes, multiyear droughts, rising sea levels, and devastating wildfires have forced a great number of rural communities to give up their traditional ways of living and move into cities. The impact of sudden overpopulation is particularly severe in cities with weak governance where resources in energy, housing, education, and transportation are overwhelmed. Employment opportunities are unable to keep up with spiking demand. Poverty, crime, and increasing social inequality breed instability, and in some cases, outright civil wars. World cities are struggling more than ever in their search for solutions to urban crises.

Cities around the World: Struggles and Solutions to Urban Life is a two-volume collection of 101 articles that introduce the experiences of 84 cities worldwide. These cities were selected based on geography, population, economic status, and the challenges they face. Readers will find well-known megacities such as Beijing, New York, and Mumbai, as well as smaller and lesser-known cities such as Touba, Senegal; Bamako, Mali; and Williamsport, Pennsylvania, in the United States. These volumes focus on ten areas of urban problems:

Employment and Jobs

Energy and Sustainability

Green Spaces

Housing and Infrastructure

Migration and Demographic Changes

Pollution

Schools

Traffic and Transportation

Violence, Corruption, and Organized Crime

Waste Management

Essays within the sections are alphabetical by city, and each includes a bibliography of current print and electronic information resources, as well as cross-references to related entries. Aimed at high school students, college and university undergrads, and interested nonspecialist readers, the essays in this work are authored by scholars from a variety of academic fields, including the natural sciences, social sciences, and the arts and humanities. They strive to provide an objective presentation of the most recent findings, historical trends, ongoing challenges, and future perspectives. Many of the authors are also members of the teaching faculty at universities worldwide. Their expertise in teaching and research contributes to making the complexity of urban reality more relatable to the reader's experience. Views and opinions expressed in these articles are those of the authors. A strong belief shared, however, by these authors is that developing urban awareness is a crucial part of the general education today. It is their hope that these volumes will serve as a catalyst for debate and further exploration.

Jing Luo, Editor

Acknowledgments

This book would not have been possible without the great dedication of each and every contributor. I would like to extend my profound gratitude for their expertise, commitment, and inspiring discussions. I owe a special debt to my colleagues at Bloomsburg University for their strong support. My children, Cong, Jon, and Janice, have been patient reviewers of my writings; I owe them many thanks. Finally, I express my special appreciation to Ms. Kaitlin Ciarmiello, Senior Acquisition Editor, and Mr. John Wagner, Senior Development Editor, of ABC-CLIO, for their guidance throughout the publication process.

Introduction

Those who have read *Bleak House* by Charles Dickens may remember the heavy fogs of London that Dickens painted in these words:

> Fog everywhere. Fog up the river, where it flows among green aits and meadows; fog down the river, where it rolls defiled among the tiers of shipping and the waterside pollutions of a great (and dirty) city. Fog on the Essex marshes, fog on the Kentish heights. Fog creeping into the cabooses of collier-brigs; fog lying out on the yards and hovering in the rigging of great ships; fog drooping on the gunwales of barges and small boats. Fog in the eyes and throats of ancient Greenwich pensioners, wheezing by the firesides of their wards; fog in the stem and bowl of the afternoon pipe of the wrathful skipper, down in his close cabin; fog cruelly pinching the toes and fingers of his shivering little 'prentice boy on deck. Chance people on the bridges peeping over the parapets into a nether sky of fog, with fog all round them, as if they were up in a balloon and hanging in the misty clouds. (Dickens 1997: Chapter I)

Dickens's time was the mid-19th century when industrialization was in full swing. At the time, 2 million coal-dependent residents crowded London; today, there are 8 million. Dickens did not see the worst of the fog. The mother of all London fogs, the Great Smog of London, descended on the city in December 1952. Daytime visibility was reportedly limited to within just a few meters. Over 4,000 Londoners reportedly died of respiratory system infections. Are conditions any better today? A 2013 study by the Great London Authority found that all Londoners were exposed to PM2.5 particle concentrations greater than the World Health Organization's air quality guideline. In January 2017, toxic smog once again battered London. The level of air pollution in London surpassed that of Beijing. Mayor Sadiq Khan issued the highest smog alert, to which he added: "We should be ashamed that our young people—the next generation of Londoners—are being exposed to these tiny particles of toxic dust that are seriously damaging their lungs and shortening their life expectancy" (Taylor 2017). Despite all the progress, London's atmospheric conditions leave the citizens confused.

London's air pollution is only a pixel of the broader picture. Rather than improving, air quality has declined globally. The smog in Beijing, Mumbai, Mexico City, Karachi, and many other world cities today has reached catastrophic levels. In parallel with atmospheric degradation, world cities struggle with population influxes, rising crime rates, slashed funding of education, shortages of affordable housing, increasingly congested traffic, failures in waste management, rising unemployment, shrinking green spaces, and more. More than any other time in history, world cities are desperately searching for solutions for sustainable urban life.

THE WORLD IS GOING URBAN

Accelerated urban growth and excessive use of fossil fuels are two challenges world cities face in the 21st century. We now understand that these two factors are correlated, locked in a spiraling positive feedback loop. A United Nations report found that over 50 percent of the world population already reside in cities today, and three-quarters of the world's population is expected to live in cities by 2050 (United Nations 2014). The same study also found that the number of the world's megacities has reached an all-time high. In 1950, there were only two megacities with populations more than 10 million and five with populations between 5 and 10 million. Today, there are 28 megacities, of which 16 are in developing countries. Urban problems have increased proportionally with population, suggesting that overpopulation could be a major source of urban challenges. Studies have shown that a sudden influx of residents can overwhelm a city's resources, in some cases causing social stress and outright armed conflicts (Denny and Walter 2014; Gleick 2013; Femia and Werrell 2012; Clionadh et al. 2008). These hard facts beg the question: Why has urban-bound migration become noticeably more prevalent today?

WHAT IS DRIVING MASS MIGRATION?

Economic shifts and climate change appear to be two of the most significant factors in urban-bound migration. In recent decades, modern industry has transformed cities into centers of productivity. The jobs, education, health care, and generally better living conditions of cities attract rural populations. Liberalization in central-planning economies has also played an important role. In these societies, as economic reform progresses, migration restrictions have been gradually relaxed, giving rural people more opportunity to become urban dwellers. Take China for example: previously, the country's rural economy had been suppressed under central planning to prioritize urban industries, which created a wide income gap. The resultant income differentials have driven a constant stream of internal migration since the early 1980s. Less than 20 percent of China's population lived in cities in 1979; by 2017, the urban population neared 60 percent (The World Bank 2018). However, China's urban expansion has not always been smooth sailing. A phenomenon known as "village in the city," a widely observed phenomenon of rural dwellings surrounded by high-rises, is an example of how a runaway urban expansion gives rise to shantytowns. These urban villages are abundant in cities such as Guangzhou where the population grew from 2 million in 1980 to 13 million in 2012. The process caused 160 million farmers to lose their land (Sneed 2017). While China's urban-planning efforts appear to have avoided shanty development on the scale seen in India and Venezuela, the ultimate costs of dealing with the pressure of urbanization in terms of energy consumption, motorization, preservation of land for agriculture, and provision of water are unavoidable and will surface one way or another (The World Bank 2008).

However, despite spurts of influx, economic migration tends to be gradual; the availability of employment opportunities serves as a natural break. When China's manufacturing sector was hard hit during the 2008–9 global financial crisis, 20 million out of China's 130 million migrant workers subsequently returned to their home villages and picked up farming again, a record inverse flow by the account of China's official newspaper the *People's Daily* (RenminNet 2009). In Guangzhou and the nearby Pearl River Delta Region, the inflow of migrants had been on a declining path, going from 1.1 million in 2008 to 600,000 by 2016. Factors leading to the trend include competition from Southeast Asian countries and population aging (*Economist* 2017).

The second driving force, climate change, has a shorter track record but carries a more severe impact. The increasing frequency and severity of droughts, flooding, hurricanes, and rising sea levels lead rural populations to abandon their occupations and habitats and migrate to cities. Human rights, climate change, environmental degradation, and migration collectively have been raised to the level of a new paradigm (Fatima et al. 2014). Studies have shown that climate change is closely associated with global temperature. Carbon dioxide (CO_2) is an important heat-trapping (greenhouse) gas, which is released through human activities such as deforestation and burning fossil fuels, as well as natural processes such as respiration and volcanic eruptions. Levels of atmospheric CO_2 levels measured at Mauna Loa Observatory, Hawaii, in recent years, reveal a persistent rising trend in recent years.

The year 2010, for example, was one of the hottest years in the global weather record. Pakistan's temperature reached 128.3 Fahrenheit, the highest in Asia in 145 years. Canada experienced its warmest winter in history; California and Arizona were slammed by tornados, blizzards, and hurricane-force winds exceeding 90 miles per hour rarely seen for centuries; Tennessee was devastated by a record superstorm dumping 11 inches of rain in the single month of May; Russia suffered a record-level heat wave, causing severe damage to agriculture and loss of lives. These abnormalities have become the new normal. More extreme weather events have hit the globe including Hurricane Sandy in 2012 and Hurricane Maria in 2017, two of the deadliest hurricanes that have hit the United States. In 2018, California saw the most devastating wildfires on the state's record. By December 21, 2018, according to the National Interagency Fire Center (NIFC), California had been hit by 8,052 wildfires and lost 1,823,220 acres of wildland to the blaze. Additionally, Texas, North Carolina, South Carolina, and Utah were among the states heavily damaged by wildfires. Overall, the United States lost 8,582,608.5 acres of wildland to 55,911 wildfires (NIFC 2018). Scientists contend that these extreme weather events are evidence of anthropogenic climate change (NOAA 2018; Rigaud et al. 2018; Fountain et al. 2018).

Unlike economic forces, climate change is a different beast. Its devastation drives mass migrations into cities in short periods, catching host cities unprepared. According to the National Centers for Environmental Information (NCEI), the earth's temperature has been on the rise for 33 consecutive years, and 18 of the warmest

19 years occurred between 2000 and 2018. Greenhouse gases, such as carbon dioxide, reached their highest level in 800,000 years. Most strikingly, CO_2 emissions rose 60 percent between 1990 and 2014 (The World Bank 2017). The correlation between CO_2 in the global atmosphere and temperature change was evidenced by data collected from DOME C ice-core studies that were conducted by the European Project for Ice Coring in Antarctica (EPICA).

With respect to its impact on human communities, climate change is recognized as having a "multiplier effect," one that amplifies existing societal tensions and leads to destabilization, armed conflicts, and even wars (Schleussner et al. 2016). Such impacts make cities in developing countries particularly vulnerable (Hegre et al. 2013). Sudden demographic changes could exacerbate societal tensions in several ways:

> Rapid growth in the labour force in slow growing economies, a rapid increase in educated youth aspiring to elite positions when such positions are scarce, unequal population growth rates between different ethnic groups, urbanization that exceeds employment growth and migrations that change the balance between and among major ethnic groups, all appear to increase the risks of violent internal political and ethnic conflicts. (Clionadh et al. 2008)

A few examples may serve to illustrate the formidable multiplier effect of climate change.

"ENVIRONMENTAL REFUGEES"

The term "environmental refugees" is credited to Essam El-Hinnawi, author of a well-known 41-page document by the same title published by the United Nations in 1985. In this report, El-Hinnawi used the term to refer to groups forced to leave their traditional habitats due to marked environmental disruption, natural or anthropogenic, that jeopardizes their existence and/or seriously affects their quality of life (Hinnawi 1985). Scholars have since employed and enriched the term's coverage. The definition by Professor Norman Myers of Oxford University appears to best reflect relevant human experience:

> There is a new phenomenon in the global arena: environmental refugees. These are people who can no longer gain a secure livelihood in their homelands because of drought, soil erosion, desertification, deforestation and other environmental problems, together with associated problems of population pressures and profound poverty. In their desperation, these people feel they have no alternative but to seek sanctuary elsewhere, however hazardous the attempt. Not all of them have fled their countries, many being internally displaced. But all have abandoned their homelands on a semi-permanent if not permanent basis, with little hope of a foreseeable return. (Myers 2005)

In 2015, just one year before European cities were hit by 5 million refugees from Syria, Jean-Claude Juncker, President of the European Commission, warned: "Climate change is even one of the root causes of a new migration phenomenon. Climate refugees will become a new challenge—if we do not act swiftly" (Juncker 2015).

In recent years, the number of climate refugees reached unprecedented levels. According to the UN Food and Agriculture Organization, climate- and weather-related disasters were the cause of the displacement of 244 million international migrants, 40 percent more than in 2000 (UNFCCC 2017). In a message delivered on World Food Day 2017, UN Migration Director General William Lacy Swing had the following to say in addressing the issue of the post-Syrian War migration:

> Climate action is paramount. Climate change is having far-reaching effects on agricultural productivity and food security. It is among the main reasons for the record numbers of people compelled to migrate from rural areas to towns and cities around the world. Importantly, the Paris Climate Change Agreement recognizes the need to protect vulnerable populations, including migrants, and establishes a dedicated task force to advance strategies that avert, minimize and address displacement related to climate change. (UNFCCC 2017)

The trend appears to indicate that due to the growing frequency of tropical storms, hurricanes, droughts, floods, and related conflicts in many parts of the world, the scale of involuntary migration will likely grow even further.

THE SYRIAN WAR

Studies suggest that prolonged natural disasters are potential drivers in the collapse of complex societies; while ethnic divides tend to play a major role in armed conflicts, ethnic tensions can intensify due to disruptive events such as natural disasters (Schleussner et al. 2016).

Several studies on the causes of the 2011 Syrian War have been conducted from multiple perspectives. For example, numerous separate studies conducted by Femia and Werrell (2012), Gleick (2014), and Kelley and collaborators (2015) offer blow-by-blow accounts of the role climate change had in the progression to the civil war. Their research indicates that severe drought attacks in Syria drove a massive rural-to-urban migration prior to the onset of the armed conflict. On the one hand, climate migration further tightened urban employment pressure; on the other hand, corruption and unequal treatment by the regime exacerbated ethnic tensions that ignited the social unrest. Their studies reveal that the repression by the brutal Assad regime and the spread of a political movement known as the Arab Spring, two factors widely believed to have caused Syria's civil war, were only partial causes; climate factors must be considered as well.

Femia and Werrell's report (2012) provides a detailed account of the progression of the most severe drought between 2006 and 2011. According to their report, up to 60 percent of Syria's land experienced the worst long-term drought and the most severe crop failures since the birth of agricultural civilizations in the Fertile Crescent. Nearly 75 percent of farming suffered total crop failure, and herders lost 85 percent of their livestock. By 2011, 3 to 4 million Syrians were affected by food insecurity and extreme poverty, leading to a forced mass exodus of farmers, herders, and agriculturally dependent rural families from the countryside to the cities.

The report indicates that the impact of the drought was further intensified by the Syrian regime's ill-devised agricultural policy under which the government generously subsidized water-intensive wheat and cotton farming. Once surface water was exhausted, farmers turned to drawing groundwater, resulting in the depletion of groundwater as a buffer source (Kelley et al. 2015). Overgrazing further reduced fertile land to dust. The total urban population of Syria in 2002 was 8.9 million. This number approached 13.8 million by the end of 2010, in just eight years (Kelley et al. 2015). Due to the sudden population influx, competition for jobs in Syrian cities was intense, particularly for the poor. Additionally, access to food, water, and other necessities for life was also limited. The distress contributed to social unrest in cities such as Dara'a, Aleppo, Damascus, Deir ez-Zour, Hama, and Homs (Gleick 2013). The escalating pressures on urban areas due to internal migration, increasing food insecurity, and the resultant high rates of unemployment spurred many Syrians to make their political grievances publically known, which made the social tensions all the more flammable (Saleeby 2012).

Kelley et al (2015) further established that anthropogenic activities were essential in the causation of the drought. They describe a link between precipitation changes in Syria and a long-term warming trend in the broader Eastern Mediterranean region that added to the drawdown of soil moisture. Their study indicates that the drying and warming trends in the region are consistent with model studies of increases in the levels of greenhouse gases. The authors argue that even though multiyear droughts occur periodically in the Fertile Crescent due to natural causes, it is unlikely that the recent drought would have reached such an extreme level absent the century-long drying trend. Evidence from climate model simulations supports the view that the observed long-term trends in precipitation and temperature are consequences of human interference. Accordingly, these researchers conclude that addressing climatic disasters will be critical for the restoration of stability in Syria.

OPPOSING VIEWS

A recent study by Selby et al. titled "Climate Change and the Syrian Civil War Revisited" contests the validity of anthropogenic climate change, as well as the link between the multiyear drought and the war. They argue that while Syria experienced a severe drought that was 10 percent drier than average during the five to six years prior to the war's onset, such severity still falls within the natural fluctuation of the regional rainfall pattern when taking into account the multi-decadal variability rather than the inter-annual variability. Hence, they find the argument of anthropogenic drying trend unfounded. Additionally, they argue that with respect to the reported scale of migration, the numbers presented in some studies conflated seasonal agricultural labor and livestock herding with the rural-to-urban influx, resulting in an exaggerated volume. The researchers conclude that the Assad regime's agricultural liberalization was to blame. The economic policy resulted in driving the farmers into cities in great numbers yearly since 2000. They argue that the government's sudden removal of input subsidies was far more likely to cause the massive migration than the drought, since such policy made farming unsustainably costly. The researchers conclude that the argument that global climate change-related drought in Syria was a causal factor in the country's civil war is not backed by valid evidence (Selby et al. 2017).

Contrary to the assertions of Selby and collaborators, however, there is evidence showing that the eventual removal of agricultural subsidies by the Syrian government was more than likely forced by the worsening drought, rather than for the sake of introducing economic liberalization. A World Bank report titled "Agriculture in Syria: Towards the Social Market" published in June 2008 indicated that subsidized agriculture would fail to sustain should the drought intensify. The report recommended removal of subsidies since 1) lower oil revenues made agricultural subsidies at 4 percent of the GDP harder to afford; and 2), during the preceding two decades (1980–2004), Syrian farmers had failed to adjust crop structure, as is done in neighboring countries, by shifting focus to vegetable-growing which is less water-intensive. Specifically, the document states:

> Encouraging agriculture to use more water is unsustainable. By 2000 aquifers were being depleted at a rate of 1.8% per year. Since then, the irrigated area has increased by around 20%. Since 2001, unlicensed installations have accounted for 56% of new wells. Between 2004 and 2005, this rose to 96%. Climate change will reduce rainfall, increase the frequency of droughts and raise temperatures by 2 to 3 degrees during the century. It will also shorten the snow season in Turkey, and thus increase variation in the flow of the Euphrates. Uncertainty over transboundary water agreements makes it difficult for Syria to plan water resource use in the Euphrates basin. (The World Bank 2008: 4)

Introducing free-market mechanisms would presumably have been a viable way to wean Syrian farmers off state subsidies and make the worst outcomes preventable. In hindsight, however, the delayed implementation may indeed have had an adversary effect. However, the backdrop is that the strangling hands of climate change were tightening on the Syrian economy and its destabilized society, thus reducing any room for viable options.

HISTORICAL EVIDENCE OF CLIMATE IMPACT ON SOCIAL TRANSITIONS—THE CASE OF CHINA'S DYNASTIC CYCLES

The multiplier effect of climate change on human society is further evidenced by research on peasant uprisings and dynastic successions in Chinese history. Traditionally, Chinese historians were confined to the Marxist vision of social tensions and transitions in which "class struggle" was key. In such a framework, peasant uprisings and dynastic successions, most of which were violent and resulted in the loss of tens of thousands of lives, were invariably due to exploitation. The solutions to such class struggle reflect that the exploited class representing advanced productivity would prevail over the exploiting class that blocked social progress. What this approach fails to account for, however, is the cyclical pattern of similar violent disruptions and those transitions that were peaceful and prosperous. Today, research on climate changes has shown that major social disruptions in Chinese history synchronized with the climatological cold and warm phases in an almost lock-step manner. Because climate change directly affects agricultural and animal husbandry yield, it understandably exerted a multiplier effect through affecting equality in distribution, and more generally, on the social sentiment.

A study conducted by Zhang and collaborators (2006) of 1,672 wars dating from 1000 CE to 1911 reveals that China's agricultural economy was closely influenced by climate changes as evidenced by cycles of wars and dynastic successions. Their findings indicate that outbreaks of war in Northern China were typically associated with cold phases. Five of the six cold phases in the millennium experienced dynastic collapse. Moreover, peasant rebellions occurred more frequently at the onsets of cold phases. The three highest peaks of war represented three of the most notable peasant rebellion periods in Chinese history during the Yuan and the Ming Dynasties (13th to 15th centuries CE). Additionally, the northern regions of China, where animal herding was the dominant way of life, were more reactive to cold phases than the warmer crop-producing regions in the south. Wars regularly followed onsets of cold periods in the northern regions. With respect to periods of prosperity such as the Song Dynasty (960–1279 CE), the findings indicate that the continuous cooling trend forced north-to-south migration, shifting China's cultural centers to the south of the Yangtze after 960 CE where milder cold phases no longer had devastating economic impacts.

These findings are corroborated by Yin and collaborators' 2016 study on the relationship between agricultural yield and dynastic transition between 210 BCE and 1910 CE. The findings indicate that the average temperature anomaly of all 14 dynastic transitions was only -0.21 degrees Celsius, and that most of the dynastic transitions coincided with a cold climate or relatively cold stages of a warm period. In addition, 12 of 14 dynastic transitions occurred when the climate changed from warm to cold. The study found that the majority of transitions occurred when agricultural production decreased. Among the 34 dynastic prosperity periods from 210 BCE to 1910 CE, 14 lasted for more than 20 years, totaling 480 years or 69.1 percent of all the dynastic prosperity periods. Those prosperity moments coincided with warmer temperature shifts by a mere 0.06 degrees Celsius on average.

THE THREAT OF CLIMATE CHANGE IS REAL

The chain reaction triggered by climate change is a relatively young phenomenon. However, global warming, climate-related natural disasters, massive migration, and crises stemming from overpopulation in world cities have quickly become an undeniable reality. A concerted and dedicated effort in slowing down global warming is what modern societies must pursue because it is a fundamental solution to urban challenges in and of itself. The United States is at the forefront of withstanding the worst of climate change. Five of the world's 10 cities most at risk of sea-level rise are in the United States: Miami, New York City, New Orleans, Tampa, and Boston. The other five are Guangzhou, China; Mumbai, India; Nagoya, Japan; Shenzhen, China; and Osaka, Japan. The mean sea level is expected to rise between 0.2 and 0.4 meters (7.8 to 15.7 inches) by 2050. In addition, about a quarter of the 136 cities are located in deltas and directly impacted by sea-level change (Environment News Service 2013). The scale of the challenges suggests that rather than denying climate change, global cities must do everything within reach to control global warming. It should be abundantly clear that reducing pollution and setting the world on a low carbon emission course is not for luxury, but for sustainability.

ABOUT THIS BOOK

Cities around the World: Struggles and Solutions to Urban Life analyzes 10 kinds of challenges faced by cities worldwide. Each challenge is analyzed in a dedicated section. The contents are briefly introduced as follows:

Employment and Jobs. Creating jobs for the fast-rising urban population is a daunting challenge. This section examines the practices of the following cities: Lagos, Nigeria; London, United Kingdom; Mumbai, India; New York City, United States; Paris, France; Riyadh, Saudi Arabia; San Juan, Puerto Rico; Seattle, United States; Shenzhen, China; and Stockholm, Sweden. Governance, resources, social environment, and opportunities for job training and employment are among the elements analyzed.

Energy and Sustainability. Saving energy and preserving clean air are among the top urban concerns. This section looks into the practices of energy consumption and conservation of the following cities: Beijing, China; Copenhagen, Denmark; Frankfurt, Germany; London, United Kingdom; Melbourne, Australia; Mumbai, India; Pittsburgh, United States; Rio de Janeiro, Brazil; Singapore City, Singapore; and Toronto, Canada.

Green Spaces. A challenge to cities of all sizes is preserving green spaces under the pressure of creating more space for affordable housing and commercial activities. This section examines the challenges and solutions of the follow cities: Abu Dhabi, United Arab Emirates (UAE); Aguascalientes, Mexico; Halifax, Canada; Hong Kong, China; Moscow, Russia; New York City, United States; Paris, France; Rotterdam, The Netherlands; Tel Aviv, Israel; and Tokyo, Japan.

Housing and Infrastructure. Urban crowding can seriously affect a city's functionality. Provision of affordable housing is key to a sustainable urban environment. This section reviews the solutions of the following cities: Almaty, Kazakhstan; Caracas, Venezuela; Chongqing, China; Dandong, China; Detroit, United States; Havana, Cuba; Munich, Germany; Sydney, Australia; Touba, Senegal; and Vienna, Austria.

Migration and Demographic Changes. Today, migration is happening at an unprecedented pace, and megacities are in the frontline to bear the brunt. Major challenges include accommodation and integration. This chapter includes the following cities: Buenos Aires, Argentina; Guangzhou, China; Kinshasa, Democratic Republic of the Congo (DRC); Lima, Peru; London, United Kingdom; Los Angeles, United States; Tehran, Iran; Tokyo, Japan; Vancouver, Canada; and Williamsport, United States.

Pollution. Many cities are dealing with polluted environments, some of the capital cities are homes to tens of millions of residents. This chapter examines the solutions of the following cities: Baku, Azerbaijan; Boston, United States; Flint, Michigan, United States; Karachi, Pakistan; Krakow, Poland; New Delhi, India; Rome, Italy; Sao Paulo, Brazil; Seoul, South Korea; and Shiprock, United States.

Schools. Providing education is one of the fundamental functions of a city. Educational opportunities, however, are not keeping up with the demand of population growth. This chapter examines educational provision in the following cities: Bamako, Mali; Berlin, Germany; Boston, United States; Ouagadougou, Burkina Faso; Seoul, South Korea; Sydney, Australia; Taipei, Taiwan; Tokyo, Japan; Vologda, Russia; and Xi'an, China.

Traffic and Transportation. Mobility is critical for a city to carry out its functions. One of the top challenges today is to alleviate traffic congestion. This section looks at the struggles and strategies of the following cities: Beijing, China; Casablanca, Morocco; Istanbul, Turkey; Kolkata, India; Mexico City, Mexico; New York City, United States; Osaka, Japan; Saint Petersburg, Russia; Stuttgart, Germany; and Zurich, Switzerland.

Violence, Corruption, and Organized Crime. Safety is what makes a city livable. Whether a city is able to reduce its crime rate is critical to its sustainability. This chapter reviews the solutions of the following cities: Aleppo, Syria; Baghdad, Iraq; Beijing, China; Brussels, Belgium; Chicago, United States; Kabul, Afghanistan; Mexico City, Mexico; Seoul, South Korea; Sicily, Italy; and Tokyo, Japan.

Waste Management. World cities manage their waste through a wide range of practices. Some cities have little to no management at all, while others gingerly implement the "3-Rs"—recovery, recycle, and reuse. The differences are astounding. This chapter covers the following cities: Baghdad, Iraq; Cairo, Egypt; Calgary, Canada; Dakar, Senegal; Delhi, India; Kobe, Japan; Naples, Italy; Oslo, Norway; Port-au-Prince, Haiti; San Francisco, United States; and Singapore City, Singapore.

Cities around the World includes a total of 101 articles covering 84 unique cities; some cities are analyzed from multiple perspectives. The writings are contributed by 34 scholars from various academic disciplines. Each article covers history, current status, and future perspectives of a city. A section of "further reading" is provided for each topic. Views and opinions expressed in these articles are those of the authors.

An important message these volumes convey is that sustainable cities are those that are capable of transforming problems into opportunities in which people produce solutions through concerted efforts. The tales of these cities indicate that there is an economic fault line limiting what a city can do. Still, the broader picture is clear: sustainability can't be achieved by just a few; it is crucial for global cities large or small, wealthy or poor, to work together and face some of the toughest challenges. It is hoped that these volumes will raise awareness, foster debate, and serve as a catalyst for exploration.

Jing Luo, Editor

FURTHER READING

Clionadh, Raleigh, Lisa Jordan, and Idean Salehyan. 2008. "Assessing the Impact of Climate Change on Migration and Conflict." The Social Development Department, The World Bank Group. https://environmentalmigration.iom.int/assessing-impact-climate-change-migration-and-conflict.

CNN. 2014. "On China Transcript: Urbanization." CNN, January 22. https://www.cnn.com/2014/01/22/world/asia/on-china-urbanization-transcript/index.html.

Denny, Elaine K., and Barbara F. Walter. 2014. "Ethnicity and Civil War." *Journal of Peace Research* 51, 2. http://journals.sagepub.com/doi/pdf/10.1177/0022343313512853.

Dickens, Charles. 1997. *Bleak House*. The Project Gutenberg eBook. http://www.gutenberg.org/files/1023/1023-h/1023-h.htm.

Economist. 2017. "What China Can Learn from the Pearl River Delta." April 8. https://www.economist.com/special-report/2017/04/08/what-china-can-learn-from-the-pearl-river-delta.

El-Hinnawi, Essam. 1985. *Environmental Refugees*. Nairobi, Kenya: United Nations Environmental Program. http://hdl.handle.net/20.500.11822/2651.

Environment News Service. 2013. "10 Coastal Cities at Greatest Flood Risk as Sea Levels Rise." September 13. http://ens-newswire.com/2013/09/03/10-coastal-cities-at-greatest-flood-risk-as-sea-levels-rise.

Fatima, Rabab, Anita Jawadurovana Wadud, and Sabira Coelho. 2014. "Human Rights, Climate Change, Environmental Degradation and Migration: A New Paradigm." Migration Policy Institute (MPI). https://www.migrationpolicy.org/research/human-rights-climate-change-environmental-degradation-and-migration-new-paradigm.

Femia, Francesco, and Caitlin Werrell. 2012. "Syria: Climate Change, Drought and Social Unrest." Briefing No. 11. Center for Climate and Security, Washington, DC. https://climateandsecurity.files.wordpress.com/2012/04/syria-climate-change-drought-and-social-unrest_briefer-11.pdf.

Fountain, Henry, Hiroko Tabuchi, and Somini Sengupta. 2018. "What's Different about California's Fires This Year?" *New York Times*, August 1. https://www.nytimes.com/2018/08/01/climate/california-fires-heat.html.

Fruen, Lauren, and Gemma Mullin. 2017. "Toxic Smog Alert—London on 'Red Alert' and Residents Warned to Stay Indoors as Toxic Air Pollution from Germany Swamps the Capital." *Sun*, January 19. https://www.thesun.co.uk/news/2651941/london-red-alert-toxic-air-pollution.

Gleick, Peter H. 2013. "Water, Drought, Climate Change, and Conflict in Syria." *Weather, Climate, and Society* 6, 3: 331–40. American Meteorological Society. https://journals.ametsoc.org/doi/abs/10.1175/WCAS-D-13-00059.1.

Greater London Authority. 2013. "PM2.5 Map and Exposure Data." https://data.london.gov.uk/dataset/pm2-5-map-and-exposure-data.

Hegre, Havard, Joakim Karlsen, Harvard Mokleiv Nygard, Harvard Strand, and Henrik Urdal. 2013. "Predicting Armed Conflict, 2010–2050." *International Studies Quarterly* 57, 2: 250–70.

Juncker, Jean-Claude. 2015. "State of the Union 2015: Time for Honesty, Unity and Solidarity," September 9. European Commission Press Release Database. http://europa.eu/rapid/press-release_SPEECH-15-5614_en.htm.

Kelley, Colin P., Shahrzad Mohtadi, Mark A. Cane, Richard Seager, and Yochanan Kushnir. 2015. "Climate Change in the Fertile Crescent and Implications of the Recent Drought." *Proceedings of the National Academy of Sciences of the United States of America (PNAS)*. http://www.pnas.org/content/112/11/3241.

Knapton, Sarah. 2017. "Air Pollution in London Passes Levels in Beijing . . . and Wood Burners Are Making Problem Worse." *Telegraph*, January 27. https://www.telegraph.co.uk/science/2017/01/24/air-pollution-london-passes-levels-beijingand-wood-burners-making.

Myers, Norman. 2005. "Environmental Refugees: An Emergent Security Issue." *13th Economic Forum*, Prague. https://www.osce.org/eea/14851.

National Centers for Environmental Information (NOAA). 2018. "Global Climate Report—April 2018." https://www.ncdc.noaa.gov/sotc/global/201804.

National Interagency Fire Center (NIFC). 2018. "National Year-to-Date Report on Fires and Acres Burned." https://gacc.nifc.gov/sacc/predictive/intelligence/NationalYTDbyStateandAgency.pdf.

RenminNet. 2009. "A Survey Report of Migrant Workers: 20 Million Return to Villages due to Loss of Employment during the Global Financial Crisis" (in Chinese). http://finance.people.com.cn/GB/8889165.html.

Rigaud, Kanta Kumari, Alex de Sherbinin, Bryan Jones, Jonas Bermann, Viviane Clement, Kayly Ober, Jacob Schewe, Susana Adamo, Brent McCusker, Silke Heuser, and Amelia Midgley. 2018. "Groundswell: Preparing for Internal Climate Migration." *World Bank Group.* https://openknowledge.worldbank.org/handle/10986/29461.

Saleeby, Suzanne. 2012. "Sowing the Seeds of Dissent: Economic Grievances and the Syrian Social Contract's Unraveling." http://www.jadaliyya.com/Details/25271/Sowing-the-Seeds-of-Dissent-Economic-Grievances-and-the-Syrian-Social-Contract%E2%80%99s-Unraveling.

Schleussner, Carl-Friedrich, Jonathan F. Donges, Reik V. Donner, and Hans Joachim Schellnhuber. 2016. "Armed-Conflict Risks Enhanced by Climate-Related Disasters in Ethnically Fractionalized Countries." *Proceedings of the National Academy of Sciences* 113, 33: 9216–21. doi: 10.1073/pnas.1601611113. http://www.pnas.org/content/113/33/9216.

Selby, Jan, Omar S. Dahi, Christiane Fröhlic, and Mike Hulme. 2017. "Climate Change and the Syrian War Revisited." *ScienceDirect.* https://doi.org/10.1016/j.polgeo.2017.05.007.

Sneed, Adam. 2017. "Life on the Forgotten Farm of Guangzhou." *CityLab*, April 4. https://www.citylab.com/life/2017/04/guangzhou-farms-and-urbanization/522972.

Taylor, Matthew. 2017. "Revealed: Every Londoner Breathing Dangerous Levels of Toxic Air Particle." *Guardian*, October 4. https://www.theguardian.com/environment/2017/oct/04/revealed-every-londoner-breathing-dangerous-levels-of-toxic-air-particle.

United Nations. 2014. "World's Population Increasingly Urban with More Than Half Living in Urban Areas." http://www.un.org/en/development/desa/news/population/world-urbanization-prospects-2014.html.

United Nations Department of Economics and Social Affairs Population Division. 2011. "Population Distribution, Urbanization, Internal Migration and Development: An International Perspective." http://wedocs.unep.org/bitstream/handle/20.500.11822/18920/Population_Distribution_Urbanization.pdf?sequence=1&isAllowed=y.

United Nations Framework Convention on Climate Change (UNFCCC). 2017. "Climate Change Is a Key Driver of Migration and Food Insecurity." https://unfccc.int/news/climate-change-is-a-key-driver-of-migration-and-food-insecurity.

The World Bank. 2008. "Agriculture in Syria: Towards the Social Market." http://documents.worldbank.org/curated/en/890301468304199912/Syria-Agriculture-in-Syria-towards-the-social-market.

The World Bank. 2017. "Year in Review: 2017 in 12 Charts." http://www.worldbank.org/en/news/feature/2017/12/15/year-in-review-2017-in-12-charts.

The World Bank. 2018. "Urban Population (% of Total)." https://data.worldbank.org/indicator/SP.URB.TOTL.IN.ZS.

Xinhuanet. 2018. "Urbanization Rate of China's Agricultural Province Exceeds 50 pct." *Xinhuanet*. http://www.xinhuanet.com/english/2018-03/05/c_137017957.htm.

Yin, Jun, Xiuqi Fang, and Yun Su. 2016. "Correlation between Climate and Grain Harvest Fluctuations and the Dynastic Transitions and Prosperity in China over the Past Two Millennia." *Holocene* 26, 12: 1914–23. http://journals.sagepub.com/doi/10.1177/0959683616646186.

Zhang, David D., C. Y. Jim, George C-S. Lin, Yuan-Qing He, James J. Wang, and Harry F. Lee. 2006. "Climatic Change, Wars and Dynastic Cycles in China over the Last Millennium." *Climatic Change* 76, 3–4: 459–77. https://link.springer.com/article/10.1007%2Fs10584-005-9024-z.

Employment and Jobs

OVERVIEW

As overpopulation accelerates, urban employment pressure increases measurably. According to the World Bank, 50 percent of the world's population is living in cities, and 50 million more are turning into city dwellers every year. There are multiple forces behind this development. On the one hand, cities are the nexus of a better life, jobs, and education. This pulling force draws people from impoverished regions to cities. On the other hand, sprawling urbanization encroaches on communities, uprooting locals and forcing them to be urban dwellers. Additionally, weather-related disasters have become a serious stressor to rural communities, causing massive displacements. Experts believe that natural disasters have a multiplier effect, amplifying existing conflicts and mismanagement. Faced with the sudden arrival of immigrants, most cities, however, are not ready to provide adequate jobs and resources to accommodate the demographic changes. Whether a city can successfully meet the employment challenges is critical to its sustainability.

Urban Solutions Require Healthy Governance

Lagos, Nigeria, is a densely populated city. The size of its population will be 32 million from today's 15 million by 2050, according to the UN's prediction, and it will become the largest city in the world by 2100. The city has 60 percent of the country's industrial infrastructure and is responsible for more than 50 percent of the national economic development. However, currently, a high influx of immigrants, rising rates of unemployment, crime- and drug- infested slums, and epidemics due to poor health infrastructure may jeopardize the city's sustainability. Fifty percent of the population survive on US$1 a day, and 60 percent of the children do not attend school. Approximately 70 percent of the workforce, mostly women, work in the informal sector, which is not accounted for in the GDP (gross domestic product). This sector is characterized by low wages and lack of legal protection. The formal sector under the government's regulation, however, is plagued with corruption and poor management. A considerable portion of goods is produced by the informal sector and sold on the black market. Recommendations by experts encourage the Lagos government to find ways to integrate the informal sector with the formal sector, and provide financial support to small and medium-size companies. Bigon estimates that economic solutions will not likely be found in a short period due to the government being dysfunctional. Aid programs, such as those provided by the World Bank and the International Monetary Fund, may produce limited benefits in the short term; however, those benefits are unlikely to transform into systemic changes until the local government is efficient. Bigon suggests that weaknesses in governance are a major drag on sub-Saharan countries.

San Juan is the capital city of Puerto Rico, a U.S. commonwealth since 1952. The challenge of Puerto Rico, as well as that of San Juan, is to reduce a very high unemployment rate, which stood at 11.5 percent in 2016. Hurricane damages in 2017 to jobs are yet to be fully assessed. Additionally, Puerto Rico's economy faces debt repayment pressure. Becerra et al. show that the trend of economic dysfunction has historical roots that continue to generate new economic and social disturbances. Essentially, being a commonwealth means Puerto Rico's self-governance is weak, the authors argue, and, as a result, mismanagement tends to be uncontrollable. The authors enumerate a number of historical rulings as well as recent economic events that carry negative impact today: The Jones Act of 1917 restricts Puerto Ricans' options of import; Operation Bootstrap in the 1950s initiated industrialization to the detriment of the local agriculture; the PROMESA Act of 2016 increased U.S. oversight and imposed austerity measures that drained funding from educational and health-care services; the entry of Uber technology has caused local taxi drivers to lose their jobs to on-demand drivers. Economic crisis has led to exodus—those who speak English are migrating to the United States; those who don't are migrating to Caribbean countries. The authors see a rise in resistance among Puerto Rican youth against U.S. oversight, and believe that Puerto Rico's solution to unemployment lies in political engagement of the younger generation.

Bring People to Jobs and Bring Jobs to People

Mumbai is the largest city of the state of Maharashtra located on the west coast of India. It is a powerhouse of India's economy, its economic contribution accounting for 23 percent of the country's GDP. The booming economy attracts an influx of migrant workers from all over India. As a result, traffic conditions and urban waste management deteriorate. A BBC documentary, *Mumbai Railway*, reflects the situation to a certain level. Limited residential space and incessant population inflow constitute a serious urban challenge in Mumbai. Sixty percent of the city's population live in slums, of which Dharavi is known as Asia's largest slum with over 1 million inhabitants. Declining jobs in the manufacturing sector force the majority of the workforce into the informal sector, where wages are low and workers typically do not enjoy legal protection. However, the informal sector contributes a respectable $1 billion in value produced, which has prompted the Mumbai government to seek ways to revamp slum neighborhoods and improve living conditions.

Concerns, however, are raised that potential higher rents hurt the interests of the migrant workers. With the services sector on the rise in areas such as IT, finance, and energy, jobs will become available. However, these areas typically require better education and professional skills. The Mumbai municipality seeks a solution by providing training to its workforce. One of Mumbai's creative strategies to boost employment and training is to provide support for temporary jobs. The rise of flexi-jobs in transportation, banking, and financial services suggests that Mumbai pays attention to protecting the interests of temporary workers. Mumbai is also expected to improve housing conditions to retain skilled laborers.

Riyadh, the capital city of Saudi Arabia, is the kingdom's most populous city, political center, economic hub, and where top decisions are made. The challenge of Riyadh is reflective of Saudi Arabia's general headwind: a stagnant public sector unemployment. That challenge is generated by three sources, according to Kumar: The first one is the kingdom's prolonged dependence on oil. The prolonged dependence on a single source of revenue has limited the diversification of the economy. When oil revenues shrink, jobs in the public sector shrink as well. The second source is the privilege that Saudi nationals have grown to depend on. The average public sector hires Saudi nationals and pays them salaries that are 70 percent higher than the private sector. Private-sector jobs, such as retailers, taxi drivers, etc., are typically occupied by immigrant workers. Because many Saudi nationals are unwilling to acquire skills that allow them to compete in the private sector, they are unprepared for the post–oil-boom era. As a result, most of the 433,000 jobs created annually have been taken by non-Saudi workers. The third source is more linked to cultural tradition—women are not encouraged to work outside the house; and, if they do get a job, they are not allowed to work next to men. In a shrinking economy, limiting women's participation—the current labor participation rate being 20.2 percent—only brings the dependency rate higher. Riyadh meets the challenge by investing in labor training programs and through expansion of tourism, such as making the hajj pilgrimage to Mecca a more frequent event. Additionally, Riyadh will develop economic zones, following the Chinese model, attracting foreign money. Finally, yet importantly, Riyadh intends to ban non-Saudi nationals from working in shopping malls, to allow more Saudi nationals to work in the retail sector. The unemployment rate for Saudis stood at 11.5 percent in 2015. That number could double, if these efforts fail.

In the 21st century, European economies are heading more than ever in the direction of knowledge-based and service-oriented jobs. The dearth of manufacturing jobs means that the key to finding a job is to have the required education and training. Stockholm's economy is concentrated in the service sector, which employs more than four-fifths of the city's workforce. The unemployment rate stood at 6 percent in 2017, better than the national average of 7 percent. Jobs are mostly offered by the service sector, such as banks, insurance, and technology firms, and are mostly taken by highly educated seekers or those with the required skills. In Stockholm, educated people have a much lower unemployment rate, and unemployment is three times higher among foreign workers than the national average. Additionally, because young people in general have lower education and experience, they face a tremendous challenge in finding jobs: youth unemployment has reached

25 percent. To help them overcome their disadvantage, Stockholm's Employer's Union advocates a minimum wage. Trade Union, on the other hand, prefers that the government offer subsidies to employers who provide jobs for young people. Headwinds include international competition. Crafting a good CV and getting a convincing recommendation letter are crucial for getting a job, as Cumo indicates.

Facing the Unknowns

London is a power engine of job creation in the United Kingdom. With a population of 8.63 million, it has a workforce of 5.5 million. Yet, despite its efficient management, London has to resolve challenges in unemployment. The city's unemployment rate was about 6 percent in 2016, which does not include a sizable segment of the workforce that is underemployed. To improve this situation, London sets up programs to match workers with jobs that need their skills. Additionally, the city encourages life learning. To temper the high cost of living in London, the government created the London Living Wage program, which has been adopted by many private and public firms as a contract-bidding condition. To help working mothers improve job participation, London proactively revamps unused buildings and increases child-care subsidies. To resolve high rental costs, London launched the campaign "Fifty Thousand Homes," which features employers' provision of deposit loans and salaries at the London Living Wage. Brexit is expected to affect international-oriented services such as financial, travel, real estate, and scientific research. Banks and airlines, as Jorgensen indicates, may lose tens of thousands of jobs. Lower-level jobs, such as those in construction, may face challenges due to attrition of workers from EU countries. Post-Brexit immigration policies, particularly with respect to mobility, may directly affect the status of London as a city of immigrants. Hence, the future of the city's job market will very much depend on final decisions by the UK government.

Can a city that is at the center of the modern economy have an increasing population living under its bridges, in sprawling homeless camps, and, for some very unlucky folks, even in underground sewers? Johansen points his finger at the city of Seattle. Home to Microsoft, Amazon, and a large number of tech firms whose names are not yet as famous, Seattle's average home price is over $1 million. If one buys a crumbling property at $400,000 and replaces it with a new one, one may triple the investment. Johansen argues that in Seattle, income inequality is a great driving force ousting those who can't afford to stay. In Seattle, the homeless crisis reached such a level of severity that the mayor had to declare a state of emergency. While the challenge of providing additional shelters, camps, and beds was met in a relatively short time, income gaps may not be so easily bridged. Amazon and Google jointly added 24,000 jobs in the area over the years. However, how these efforts might help remedy income inequality is yet to be seen. One implication of Seattle's homeless crisis is that the tech boom is causing a socioeconomic displacement in a way that has not been seen before. Moreover, the disturbance will likely spread. Moving forward, how cities like Seattle address technology-induced unemployment will be important to watch.

Diversity Is a Solution

New York City (NYC) is densely populated with 28,000 people per square mile, which is 300 times the average density of the rest of the United States. Nevertheless, the city has a larger demographic share of ethnicities than anywhere else in the country. Evans shows that diversity may be an important contributor to the city's jobs and eco environment. Foreign-born workers account for the majority of the city's workforce. More than 200 languages are spoken in the city, about half of the residents speaking a different language than English. The garment industry is one of the oldest manufacturing sectors that continues to thrive in NYC, and it employs a sizable portion of the city's manufacturing workforce. Being the fashion capital of the United States, NYC's employment in apparel manufacturing is four times higher than the rest of the country. Moreover, the manufacturing sector as a whole is transforming to catch up with the rapidly growing service sector, such as finance, entertainment, education, and technology. The 3-D printing industry, for example, is transforming the old-fashioned manufacturing model and allowing small businesses to produce niche products. As such, NYC's employment and jobs structure is essentially knowledge based, as Evans shows. The key point is that the city's diverse life and culture generate demand and offer plenty of room for job seekers in all walks of life.

Like NYC, the city of Paris is the most powerful job creator in France and a hub of diverse cultures. Paris is the locomotive to the Metropolis of Greater Paris (MGP) and the industrial belt known as the Seine Valley. In 2014, for example, 9 out of 10 salary-earning jobs offered in the Seine Valley were related to businesses in MGP. MGP not only generates jobs in the Seine Valley, but more importantly, it leads the surrounding regions that depend on its industries. Zooming inside Paris's 20 urban districts, the most prolific job creator is tourism. One in five jobs in Paris is located in an International Touristic Zone or "ZTI" in French. Within the 12 ZTIs, jobs are mostly found in retail sales, government offices, education, restaurant businesses, and railway stations. The economic success of the ZTIs, in a sense, reflects how a country's cultural tradition can benefit directly the well-being of later generations. Abundant job opportunities in Paris have attracted waves of immigrant populations, particularly from North African countries. Of the 5.7 million immigrants that represent roughly 10 percent of the French population, more than half reside in the Parisian Region, in which Paris is the metropolis. A major challenge is the historical mismatch between immigration and job availability. Immigrants arrive not primarily for filling job vacancies, but rather for joining families. As a result, many immigrants are either overqualified for the work they are able to find or short of required skills. In recent years, xenophobia and anti-immigration trends have been on the rise. However, in order to live up to the expectations of being an international city, one that champions equality and diversity, the challenge of Paris is to do more to prepare immigrant labor for employment.

There Is Challenge in Being Innovative

Shenzhen is a booming city connected to Hong Kong. Founded in 1979, Shenzhen was one of the first four cities, also known as "special economic zones," to test Western-style management. In the early 1980s, the city was a fishing village of 300,000 inhabitants; by the next decade it was a megacity. Farmlands have turned into industrial parks and shopping malls. Shenzhen's GDP ranks number four in China, behind Shanghai, Beijing, and Guangzhou. The low concentration of state-owned enterprises made Shenzhen a cradle for tech start-ups. The city's economy is made up almost entirely of private companies. Designers, manufacturers, and marketers work seamlessly to form an ecosystem. A final product can be manufactured in a fraction of the time of the standard process and put on the market at a competitive price. As such, Shenzhen has many names: "The world's tech incubator," "Silicon Valley for hardware," "mecca for makers," "easy China," "a sprawling electronics ecosystem," and where "the digi-Key catalog meets *Blade Runner*," among others. The downside, however, is the city's weak enforcement of intellectual property rights and rampant copycat manufacturing. The production of low-priced and unreliable products, known as "shanzhai" (village-made), has lasted for decades and been a major source of growth. Observers believe, however, that shanzhai is a transient economic phase that will eventually phase out. The younger generation is already shunning fake products. Major retail sites, such as Alibaba, are proactively banning fake products. Shenzhen City's challenge is seen in abandoning the shanzhai economic model and engaging in innovation.

Further Reading
The Department of Economic and Social Affairs of the United Nations. 2014. *World Urbanization Prospects.* https://www.compassion.com/multimedia/world-urbanization-prospects.pdf.
The World Bank. 2018. "3 Big Ideas to Achieve Sustainable Cities and Communities." http://www.worldbank.org/en/news/immersive-story/2018/01/31/3-big-ideas-to-achieve-sustainable-cities-and-communities.

Lagos, Nigeria: Government Reform Is Key to Job Creation

Africa's projected city growth is striking. Lagos, the commercial capital of Nigeria and a heterogeneous megacity of over 15 million residents, is predicted to become the world's largest city by the end of the century, with close to 90 million residents. Facing infrastructure and economic crises, it is currently estimated that about 70 percent of the city's working-age population is unemployed or underemployed. For the urban majority, being informally self-employed in a variety of small-scale enterprises is the only strategy to earn a living. These micro-enterprises have recently been recognized by Nigerian urbanists and economists as a positive, vital force in enhancing the economy of the country. They call for pro-poor monetary and managerial assistance—ideally, to be directed by the state—together with the need to formalize the informal sector and to better integrate between the formal and the informal sectors.

With its growing population of over 170 million, Nigeria is located in West Africa, the second most rapidly urbanizing sub-region in Africa. Globally, Africa's urbanization rate of 1.1 percent per year is second only to Asia's 1.24 percent, and Lagos is one of the largest urban agglomerations in Africa, aside from Cairo and Kinshasa (UN-Habitat 2014, 270–71). The Lagos area was estimated in 2010 to have over 10 million residents and is thus rated 20 out of the 101 largest cities by the United Nations World Urbanization Prospects (WUP). Extrapolating to 2050, Lagos will have a population of over 32 million (the sixth-largest city), and over 57 million by 2075 (the third-largest city). Lagos is predicted by WUP to become the world's largest city in 2100, with over 88 million residents (Hoornweg and Pope 2016, 13).

As an integral part of Lagos State—composed of the 16 urban Local Government Areas of Apapa, Ajeromi-Ifelodun, Alimosho, Agege, Ifako-Ijaiye, Ikeja, Somolu, Eti-Osa, Oshodi-Isolo, Amuwo-Odofin, Kosofe, Ojo, Mushin, Lagos Mainland, Lagos Island, and Surulere—Lagos megacity comprises 75 percent of the population of Lagos State. Originating in island settlements that have developed from farming and fishing villages in the 17th century, Lagos has gradually expanded since the (post-)colonial period toward the mainland in the form of rapidly growing, highly urbanized settlements. In spite of the relocation of Nigeria's capital city from Lagos to Abuja—a move that was completed in the early 1990s (Bigon 2009, 139–41)—Lagos remained Nigeria's economic engine, with a thriving commercial activity. It accommodates over 60 percent of the country's industrial infrastructure and is responsible for more than half of the national economic development (Okunlola 2007).

At the same time, for a variety of economic and political reasons, the city is characterized by an infrastructure crisis due to mass-migration and an unregulated mix of land uses, expanding extra-legal slumming, chronic water shortages, a nonexistent sewerage system, chaotic traffic, violent crime, drug and alcohol use, proliferation of epidemics, and deteriorating public health, de-industrialization, and rising rates of unemployment. It faces immense challenges and is desperately in need of state-directed effective urban government and the promotion of financial investment in social and environmental infrastructure.

Despite its rich endowment with natural and human resources, unemployment remains high in Nigeria, which is ranked among the world's 30 least-developed countries. Commenting in 2011 on the rapid population growth, Nigeria's National Bureau of Statistics stated that unemployment was higher in rural areas and stood at 25.6 percent on average in comparison to urban areas, where it was 17 percent. While it is conservatively estimated that about 70 percent of the working-age population is unemployed or severely underemployed with low returns to labor, the country's unemployment rate continues to grow at 16 percent per year. One of the results of this alarming situation is a dramatic rise in social unrest, crime, and urban violence, caused by a youth unemployment rate of over 50 percent (Ezekiel et al. 2009; Fapohunda 2013, 235–36). Estimations regarding the Lagos metropolis show that more than 50 percent of men and women who reside in the city survive on less than US$1 a day (UNDP 2008); and a recent statistical report revealed that 70 percent of Lagos State's population is poor because of unemployment levels (CIA World Fact 2011). As half of Lagos residents are less than 16 years old, each woman has six children on average, and about 60 percent of the children do not attend

A vendor sells fruits from a wheelbarrow in Lagos, Nigeria. The majority of jobs in Lagos, some 60 to 70 percent, are generated in the informal sector. (Joshua Wanyama /Dreamstime.com)

school—in many ways, just surviving in the city is an everyday challenge (Barredo et al. 2004, 68).

Consequently, similarly to other developing urban centers, some 60 to 70 percent of the potential working-age population in Lagos earns its living in the informal sector. Unlike the formal economy, which is subdivided into the public sector and the organized private sector, the informal sector refers to the part of an economy that is not taxed, nor governmentally monitored, nor included in any gross national product (GNP). Yet while the informal sector is unrecognized, unregulated, and unregistered, it is mostly legal (we do not refer here by definition to an underground economy that drives others to illicit activities such as corruption, prostitution, and drug dealing). The informal sector constitutes the only way to earn a living for people who are self-employed in a large number of small-scale enterprises and service activities outside of the formal economy and beyond the chance to be hired by an employer from the formal sector.

In Nigeria, as a survival strategy, the majority of workers in the informal sector are women. Women not only have limited access to substantial resources such as education, land, technology, and credit, but they have to consider aspects of household maintenance and child care as well. Condemned as "illegal traders" by law-enforcement agents, they are often operating in a hostile environment (Fapohunda 2012; Fapohunda 2013). Together with this, a recent series of case studies conducted by Nigerian scholars in Lagos State reveals a dynamic tapestry of informal occupations that include furniture, tailoring, printing and other workshops, agricultural and food producers, textile traders, and motorcycle taxis. These poverty alleviation ventures are tightly related to gender, age, marital status, education, trainee-master relations, and membership in various community networks (e.g., Oluranti 2011; Akinwale 2012; Lawanson and Olanrewaju 2012; Yusuff 2013; Oduwole 2016).

In Lagos State, the informal sector suffers from governmental and municipal disregard as it is often associated with socioeconomic ills, inadequate access to crucial external finance, official credit and information, competitive pressures, simultaneous taxes and fees, exclusion from social insurance coverage, corrupt practices, and encumbering bureaucracies (Okpala 2012; Okwu et al. 2013). At the same time, the informal economy and its demarcation versus the formal sector became stronger due to further instability and fragility of the Nigerian economy. That is, several development plans (1960–88) to promote employment generation have failed, leading to accumulated debts; foreign economic interests became unprecedented, acting through multinational corporations in oil, construction, and telecommunication; and the crises following Nigeria's adaptation of neoliberal and privatization reforms have worsened. Indeed, not only in Nigeria, evidence in sub-Saharan Africa shows that privatization without proper governmental planning has only aggravated unemployment and job insecurity, and is therefore a controversial policy (Agba et al. 2010). Against this background, some inherent characteristics of the informal sector also contribute to its proliferation, such as an ease of entry, a reliance on indigenous resources, skills acquisition outside the school system, family ownership as a net of social security and other networks of support, and the fact that 60 percent of the small enterprises are home based (Akinwale 2012, 318–22; Lawanson and Olanrewaju 2012).

It has been recently understood by policymakers, economists, and urbanists that small and medium-sized enterprises (SMEs) are a vital force in the economy of developing countries, which they can transform if well managed. In Lagos State, the SMEs are also vital for the survival of youth. Among the SMEs' recognized positive aspects are providing job opportunities for a large number of the labor force; helping to alleviate poverty by offering a safety net for the survival of the poor, though the jobs are meagerly paid and hardly secured; bolstering entrepreneurial activity and innovation; enhancing the food supply since more than 90 percent of the country's agricultural products comes from this sector; and increasing government revenues and private sector development.

Consequently, it is now acknowledged—though less in official state-management circles—that SMEs should be recognized and accepted as a reality of urban life. SME-friendly policy should thus be embraced by the government, with specific focus on encouraging female entrepreneurs. Among the practical recommendations for relevant policymakers and agencies are pro-poor planning to ensure the integration of local communities regionally and globally through a supply of public and private infrastructure; community development in terms of accessibility to resources, education, and training, including an improvement of organization and leadership; reducing taxes and costs of registration, licensing, permits, and signage; and crucially, providing the requisite capital through accessible bank loans (Ogunrinola 1992; Okpala 2012; Fapohunda 2013; Okwu et al. 2013).

Still, a major constraint in developing policymaking and economic management regarding the informal sector in Lagos State is the paucity of reliable statistics and adequate data on this sector, its causes, features, and dynamics. As it falls off the radar of government accounting, the official statistics do not accurately mirror the actual state of Nigeria's informal economy, which in turn remains enigmatic (Ogbuabor and Malaolu 2013).

In addition, it is recommended that efforts should be directed to integrating the informal with the formal sector in Nigeria. Indeed, the distinction between employment in the formal and informal sectors in the country is often unclear because of the reciprocal linkages between them. For instance, a considerable portion of goods marketed by the informal sector come from the formal sector, and the formal sector tends to informally employ workers or to use SMEs to increase its marketing. The result is an unequal and exploitative relationship between these sectors in Nigeria because procurement of inputs, spares, and producer goods is controlled by the formal sector. The state should therefore create an enabling environment for the informal sector to thrive in terms of training, easy registration, safe and flexible credit, managerial assistance, and a linkage to large-scale trading enterprises (Arimah 2001). There is also a growing understanding that sub-Saharan Africa countries can only realize limited socioeconomic benefits with the International Monetary Fund and World Bank models of development and "structural adjustment" programs (Geo-Jaja and Mangum 2001). Rather, economic development depends more crucially on social capital in the form of human resource development, through a provision of practical and quality education, and a wise governmental interference in the economy.

Liora Bigon

See also: Employment and Jobs: Mumbai, India: Exploring Employment Solutions in Temporary Jobs; *Migration and Demographic Changes*: Kinshasa, Democratic Republic of the Congo (DRC): Reaching for Demographic Dividend

Further Reading

Adeyemi, Ezekiel, Adisa Waziri, Atere Akinwole, and Amoo Emmanuel. 2009. "Economic Reforms, Living Conditions and Urban Violence: A Situation Analysis of Metropolitan Lagos." *Ethiopian Journal of Environmental Studies and Management* 2, 2: 36–48.

Agba, Ogaboh, M. Agba, E. Ushie, and N. Festus. 2010. "Privatization, Job Security and Performance Efficiency of Privatized Enterprises in Nigeria." *Journal of Arts Science & Commerce* 1, 1: 95–102.

Akinwale, Akeem Ayofe. 2012. "The Informal Sector as a Catalyst for Employment Generation in Lagos State, Nigeria." *African and Asian Studies* 11: 315–44.

Arimah, Ben. 2001. *Nature and Determinants of the Linkages between Informal and Formal Sector Enterprises in Nigeria.* Oxford and Malden, MA: African Development Bank and Blackwell.

Barredo, José, Luca Demicheli, Carlo Lavalle, Marjo Kasanko, and Niall McCormick. 2004. "Modelling Future Urban Scenarios in Developing Countries: An Application Case Study in Lagos, Nigeria." *Environment and Planning B: Planning and Design* 32: 65–84.

Bigon, Liora. 2009. *A History of Urban Planning in Two West African Colonial Capitals: Residential Segregation in British Lagos and French Dakar (1850–1930).* Lewiston, ME: The Edwin Mellen Press.

CIA World Fact Book Data. 2011. *Demographic Statistics: Calculation from Percentage and Overall Population Count of Nigeria.* http://www.cia.gov/library/publications/the world-factbook/goes/ni.html.

Fapohunda, Tinuke. 2012. "Woman and the Informal Sector in Nigeria: Implications for Development." *British Journal of Arts and Social Sciences* 4, 1: 35–45.

Fapohunda, Tinuke. 2013. "Reducing Unemployment through the Informal Sector in Nigeria." *International Journal of Management Sciences* 1, 7: 232–44.

Geo-Jaja, Macleans, and Garth Mangum. 2001. "Structural Adjustment as an Inadvertent Enemy of Human Development in Africa." *Journal of Black Studies* 32, 1: 30–49.

Hoornweg, Daniel, and Kevin Pope. 2016. "Population Predictions for the World's Largest Cities in the 21st Century." *Environment and Urbanization.* https://doi.org/10.1177/0956247816663557.

Lawanson, T., and D. Olanrewaju. 2012. "The Home as Workplace: Investigating Home Based Enterprises in Low Income Settlements of the Lagos Metropolis." *Ethiopian Journal of Environmental Studies and Management* 5, 4: 397–407.

Oduwole, T. Adebowale. 2016. "Coping Mechanism among Unemployed Graduates in Mushin Local Government Area of Lagos State, Nigeria." *International Journal of Innovative Social Sciences & Humanities Research* 4, 1: 48–53.

Ogbuabor, Jonathan, and Victor Malaolu. 2013. "Size and Causes of the Informal Sector of the Nigerian Economy: Evidence from Error Correction Mimic Model." *Journal of Economics and Sustainable Development* 4, 1: 85–103.

Ogunrinola, Oluranti. 1992. "Determinants of Entrepreneurship Development in the Urban Informal Sector of Lagos." *Africa Development* 17, 4: 81–97.

Ogunrinola, Oluranti. 2011. "Informal Self-Employment and Poverty Alleviation: Empirical Evidence from Motorcycle Taxi Riders in Nigeria." *International Journal of Economics and Finance* 3, 2: 176–85.

Okpala, K. Enoch. 2012. "Venture Capital and the Emergence and Development of Entrepreneurship: A Focus on Lagos State." *International Business and Management* 5, 2: 134–41.

Okunlola, P. 2007. "The Power and the Heartbeat of West Africa's Biggest Urban Jungle." UN-Habitat Feature Paper. http://mirror.unhabitat.org/documents/media_centre/sowc/lagos.pdf.

Okwu, Andy, Bakare Biodun, and Timothy Chidi. 2013. "Business Environment, Job Creation and Employment Capacities of Small and Medium Enterprises in Lagos State, Nigeria." *Business Management Dynamics* 3, 2: 97–110.

UN-HABITAT. 2014. *The State of African Cities 2014: Re-Imagining Sustainable Urban Transitions.* Nairobi: United Nations Human Settlements Programme. https://unhabitat.org/?mbt_book=state-of-african-cities-2014-re-imagining-sustainable-urban-transitions.

United Nations Development Programme (UNDP). 2008. *Human Development Statistical Update.* http://hdr.undp.org/sites/default/files/reports/268/hdr_20072008_en_complete.pdf.

Yusuff, Olabisi. 2013. "The Dynamics of Strategic Entry and Motivations of Yoruba Female Textile Traders in the Balogun Market, Lagos State, Nigeria." *Journal of Development Entrepreneurship* 18, 2: 1–25.

London, United Kingdom: Brexit, the Known Unknown

London is a world city and a major driver of job growth in the United Kingdom. Its economy boomed between the end of the 2008–9 recession and the mid-2010s; between 2010 and 2015 a third of the United Kingdom's job growth—a total of 760,000 jobs—took place in London (Thompson et al. 2016, 3). With a population of about 8.63 million, slightly larger than that of Austria, London runs on the labor of an estimated 5.5 million workers. The city is a center for the financial services sector and home to vibrant creative, technology, and tourism industries.

Despite its might, London's workers and employers face a range of challenges. The rate of participation in the city's labor market is lower than that of the UK as a whole, reflecting obstacles such as lack of access to affordable child care. There is a noticeable gap between the skills of many job seekers and the needs of many positions, particularly for jobs that are considered to be at a middle skill level. London's high cost of living poses a challenge both to workers and to employers seeking to attract and retain employees. Finally, the UK's 2016 decision to withdraw from the European Union (EU), known as Brexit, raised questions about the future shape of London's labor force and ability to participate in international economic activities, creating new uncertainties for both workers and employers.

British transport union members demonstrate outside the Department for Transport in London to demand assurances of fair conditions for workers under ferry contracts created because of Brexit, January 11, 2019. The United Kingdom's 2016 decision to exit the European Union, "Brexit," is causing widespread anxiety among blue-collar workers—especially those employed in international jobs. (Ben Stansall/AFP/Getty Images)

THE SHAPE OF JOBS AND EMPLOYMENT IN LONDON

The London job market has a distinctive profile when compared to the rest of the United Kingdom. Some sectors are comparable in size; London's percentage of jobs in customer service occupations such as hotels, restaurants, and retail is similar to other British cities, and the percentage employed in public-sector jobs in education, health care, and public administration is slightly lower than the UK average. Since the 1990s, however, London has diverged from British norms in its higher proportion of financial and business jobs, consistently about seven percentage points above the rate for the UK as a whole. While jobs in fields like manufacturing and transportation have declined across the country since the mid-20th century, since the beginning of the 1990s these sectors have shrunk much more in London than in other parts of the UK.

The shape of employment in London reflects national and international developments since the end of World War II, when London's largest numbers of job opportunities were found in sectors like manufacturing and commerce. At that time trade was mostly in commodities rather than financial services; as the hub of the British Empire, London and its port were a center for imports and exports. During the 1950s, office and service-sector jobs became a majority for the first time, and during the 1960s, London, like other British cities, began to lose manufacturing jobs. The rapid decline of London's port eliminated another traditional source of employment. Britain's colonies became independent beginning in the late 1940s and continuing during the 1950s and 1960s, ending the imperial practice of funneling colonial products through London's port. The docks and their densely populated surrounding areas were also unable to adapt to the growth of containerized shipping. Between 1960 and 1980, all of London's docks were closed, leading to the loss of some 25,000 jobs as shipping moved to new facilities located closer to the North Sea.

At the same time, however, new industries emerged. Official recognition of London as a tourist destination began in 1963 with the creation of the London Tourist Board; by the 1990s, tourism accounted for 15 percent of London jobs. In 1986, the United Kingdom deregulated its banks and financial markets, leading to the emergence of London as a global financial services capital. In the 1990s, creative and cultural industries, a category that includes advertising, design, software, fashion, music, and electronic publishing, became a force in the London job market. Over the 30 years from 1986 to 2016, London reconnected to the global economy as a hub for finance, insurance, banking, real estate, information and communications, and other professional and technical services. Alongside these service export fields, London's growth also included expansion of locally oriented jobs in fields like health care, retail, education, and customer service.

As of 2014, 6 broad categories of employment from the 11 defined by the 2011 UK Census accounted for 60 percent of London's jobs, and growing. In the professional, real estate, scientific and technical category, which accounted for 15.2 percent of the total, management consulting and corporate management activities (220,000 jobs), legal services (86,000 jobs), real estate (108,000 jobs), and advertising and market research (70,000 jobs) were all significant sources of employment.

Administrative and support services housed 10.4 percent of jobs, including categories like temporary workers (127,000 jobs), buildings, grounds and landscaping staff (143,000 jobs), and security and investigation (56,000 jobs). Health and social work (10.2 percent of the total) included work in hospitals (186,000 jobs) and other medical and dental positions (46,000 jobs), social workers (140,000 jobs), and residential care providers (64,000 jobs). Retail work accounted for 8.6 percent of the total, including 407,000 jobs across a range of retail sales. Jobs in primary, secondary, and higher education were 8.1 percent of the total or 327,000 jobs, and information and communication jobs (7.9 percent of the total) included computer programming and related fields (161,000 jobs), and movies- and television-related jobs (53,000 jobs) (Greater London Authority 2016, 9, 18–20).

CHALLENGES FOR JOBS AND EMPLOYMENT IN LONDON

Within this framework, Londoners seeking employment face a range of challenges. In 2016 the city added jobs at a higher rate than any other area in the UK; even so, however, not all Londoners were able to find the work they sought. At the beginning of 2016, London's unemployment rate was less than 6 percent, but an additional 8.8 percent of workers were underemployed, meaning that they were working fewer hours than they would have preferred. Part time workers, young workers, and those in lower-skilled occupations were more likely than others to face underemployment (Greater London Authority 2016, 412). Additionally, about 6 percent of London's workforce, about 240,000 people, held temporary positions; and about 86,000 temp workers, 35 percent of this group, were pushed into such positions by their inability to find permanent employment (London's Poverty Profile 2016).

One element of this challenge is the problem of matching job seekers' qualifications with the needs of employers. London is often described as a city of economic opposites, with a preponderance of highly skilled, knowledge-based industry on one side and a prevalence of poorly paid, unskilled positions on the other. Traditional mid-skilled areas such as administrative and secretarial work have shrunk in response to technological change. The city's educational profile reflects this surface divide: In 2015, more than two-thirds of working-age adults had a postsecondary degree or its equivalent, and the city's primary and secondary school students outperformed students from other parts of the United Kingdom on achievement tests; yet within the education system there was a major achievement gap between average students and those from disadvantaged backgrounds, and literacy rates in some areas of London were among the lowest in the UK.

Beneath its surface polarization, however, observers identified a skill gap that particularly affects jobs classified as mid-skill level, meaning that they do not require higher education for entry, but do demand some specialization and pay what is considered to be a living wage for London. In 2014, mid-skill jobs, a classification that includes child-care workers, education paraprofessionals, bricklayers, electricians, administrative workers, home-care workers, and telecom engineers, accounted for 27 percent of entry-level openings. It was estimated that these jobs would continue to be about a quarter of available positions through 2022, and that there was a shortage of 22,000 people per year willing and able to fill them (Thompson et al. 2016, 8). In addition, some 15 percent of mid-skill workers were projected to retire over the next decade.

The need for effective and accessible training to equip workers for jobs at this level has been widely recognized. In April 2017, the mayor of Greater London established a new program, "Skills for Londoners," designed to link workers with jobs through strategies including mapping of the gaps, development of apprenticeship programs for young people, and working with schools to encourage instruction in subjects needed by employers, such as coding. Observers who noticed that participation in continuing education and skills training is less common in London than in other parts of the United Kingdom proposed greater accessibility and access to financial aid as additional means of bridging the skills gap by encouraging lifelong learning.

Another challenge facing many workers and employers in London is its cost of living. Since the 2008–9 recession, London wages on the whole have failed to keep pace with expenses. The city's cost of living is higher than the UK average, meaning that national-level programs do not provide significant relief. One local response has been the creation of the London Living Wage program by the Greater London Assembly (GLA), London's city government. The London Living Wage for 2016–17 was £9.75 per hour; in comparison, a UK-wide living wage was determined to be £8.45 per hour, and the national minimum wage for 2017 was £7.50 for workers 25 and over, with lower rates for younger workers. The London Living Wage is a voluntary program, but it has been adopted by the GLA and Transport for London, as well as many private businesses. Contracts have been one avenue to adoption of the London Living Wage, since city agencies have made it a condition of participation in the bidding process.

London's high costs affect workers in other ways as well. In 2017, the city's workforce included a lower proportion of working mothers than any other part of the United Kingdom, 61 percent versus 69 percent for the country as a whole. Researchers noted that 80,000 people would be added to London's workforce if the city met the national average, with the potential for 2,200 households to escape poverty because of the additional income they would provide (McNeil and Cory 2017). There are several reasons for London's low rate of maternal employment—for example, in some immigrant communities, particularly those from South Asia and the Middle East, women participate in the paid labor force at rates much lower than average—but lack of access to child care is commonly cited as an obstacle. Average child-care costs are a third higher in London than for the UK as a whole, making it difficult for lower-income workers to afford good-quality care. In 2017 there was also an undersupply of childcare in 70 percent of the city's boroughs (local government districts). Overall, only 32 spots were available for every 100 children under five in the city, potentially limiting access or driving parents into lower-quality, informal care arrangements. This is a difficult problem to resolve, as it involves multiple challenges including the high cost of real-estate and the low wages and transiency of child-care work as a profession; however, it has been suggested that the GLA and borough-level authorities should cooperate to find unused buildings that could serve as child-care facilities, and that increased subsidies should be directed toward child-care costs.

High housing and transportation costs are another challenge facing many workers and some employers. During London's industrial era, most workers found accommodation near their jobs. London's employment patterns changed more quickly than housing patterns, however, leading to the expense in time and money of longer commutes. The city's housing market is also notoriously expensive. In March 2017, the ratio of a median London house price to median annual earnings was 12 to 1 (Nelson 2017), and many businesses were concerned about the impact of high housing costs on their ability to attract and retain workers. For some fields, the lack of affordable housing near places of work could potentially have additional consequences. Advocates for emergency service workers, including firefighters, paramedics, and police officers, noted that as of 2016, 54 percent of such workers lived outside the city, raising the question of how this spatial mismatch could affect responses in the case of a large-scale emergency in London.

In 2015, a group of business and nonprofit leaders, along with the GLA, launched a campaign called "Fifty Thousand Homes," working toward the goal of 50,000 new homes annually by 2020. Its elements include encouraging employers to assist workers with housing by providing loans to cover rental deposits and paying the London Living Wage, and providing support and assistance to employees who are having difficulty procuring or affording housing.

POTENTIAL IMPACTS OF BREXIT

In a 2016 referendum, UK voters chose to leave the European Union. On March 29, 2017, the country began the formal process of withdrawal. The United Kingdom had belonged to the EU and its predecessor institutions since 1973, and London's economy and workforce were deeply enmeshed with the rest of Europe. Between March 2017 and March 2019, the UK and the EU negotiated the terms of Britain's departure from the union. The Brexit process challenged London's jobs and employment outlook in two important ways: freedom of movement for EU citizens, which affected the composition of London's workforce, and its ability to do business with the EU, which affected the availability of jobs.

As of this writing, negotiations are ongoing with outcomes yet to be determined. However, early estimates suggested that Brexit could have a significant impact on London's economy because industries that provide internationally oriented services, such as financial services, travel services, real estate, and other professional, scientific and technical sectors, contributed significantly to the city's economic output. In 2016, such service exports totaled £92.1 billion, almost 40 percent of which went to the EU (Greater London Authority 2016, 14).

The financial services industry, one of the key sectors of London's economy, faced significant changes due to Brexit. British banks and financial services firms could make deals and provide services to customers in other EU member states because of passporting, the ability to sell goods and services across national lines without obstacles. It was immediately clear that British firms would likely lose passporting rights due to Brexit, and by the beginning of 2017, major banks and financial services firms had begun to prepare for this shift by increasing their presence or establishing new branches in EU countries. In some cases, they also began to reduce their presence in London. One worst-case scenario from early 2017 suggested that London could lose as many as 70,000 jobs in financial services due to Brexit (Head 2017).

EU rules and the ability to export products and services also posed challenges to other industries with a presence in London. Creative professions, including advertising and marketing, have been a growth industry in London and the UK as a whole. Although the service exports generated by creative professions are a lower percentage of their output than is the case for financial services, both sectors are much more export oriented than service industries in general. In the case of the airline industry, EU rules could require a decreased presence in London and the UK. In order to operate on internal EU routes, airlines are required to maintain a major base of operations in EU territory and to ensure that at least half of their shares are EU owned. British companies built around EU services—including, ironically, the parent of British Airways, which also operates other airlines—could be required to shift jobs and infrastructure to comply with these requirements.

Reductions or relocations also affected the providers of goods and services that support the directly-affected enterprises. For example, in 2017, two EU agencies located in London, the European Banking Authority and the European Medicines Agency, announced plans to relocate to sites within the EU, leading to a direct loss of about 1,000 jobs between them. However, the European Medicines Agency attracted about 40,000 visitors each year, the equivalent of filling 350 hotel rooms every weeknight; its departure thus raised the potential of job losses in hospitality industries as well.

In sectors that are not EU based or focused on service exports, the major change resulting from Brexit was the availability of workers from EU countries. By early 2017, some employers were beginning to face shortages of workers because EU nationals were choosing not to pursue jobs in the UK or to leave British positions for work in other countries that promised more long-term security. The Royal Council of Nursing reported an early negative impact on the medical professions. As of March 2017, around 57,000 EU nationals worked for Britain's National Health Service, including 10,000 doctors and 20,000 nurses, but since the Brexit referendum in June 2016 the number of nurses from EU countries registering to work in the UK had declined by 92 percent (Boffey 2017). Higher education expected to experience a negative impact. University College London, the British university with the largest number of enrolled students from EU countries, expressed fear that these 4,000 students would leave if they had to pay the much higher tuition rate charged to students from outside the EU. The university, like others, also employed large numbers of faculty from EU countries, raising the issue of how to retain them or replace them if they left. Creative industries similarly expressed concern about the ability to recruit individual workers with very specific skill sets.

Employers in medium- and lower-skilled occupations also faced challenges from Brexit. Small businesses throughout the UK reported difficulty in filling positions. In February 2017, London Mayor Sadiq Khan released a report stating that more than one-fourth of the workers engaged in construction of new housing, about 95,000 out of 350,000, came from the EU. In order to meet this potential gap, he predicted that the city would need to acquire an extra 13,000 workers every year until 2021 (Crerar 2017). The British Hospitality Association reported that it might need a decade to recover from Brexit because its members depended heavily on low-skilled staff from other EU countries. It predicted that some hotel and restaurant chains could go bankrupt. However, this industry also hoped that it could fill some of its projected vacancies by turning to part-time employment of young people and senior citizens.

London is a city of immigrants; in 2015, it was home to 36.8 percent of the UK's total immigrant population, about 3,197,000 people (Vargas-Silva and Rienzo 2017). More than 960,000 workers, many with dependents, came from EU member states (O'Sullivan 2016). As of this writing, the contours of a post-Brexit immigration policy for EU citizens or other potential migrants is not yet clear. However, any final decision by the UK government on freedom of movement will have a significant impact on London's jobs and employment.

Sara C. Jorgensen

See also: Energy and Sustainability: London, United Kingdom: Improving Mobility Can Save Energy; *Migration and Demographic Changes:* London, United Kingdom: Facing the Challenges of Population Growth

Further Reading

Anastassova-Churmiciu, Lubomira. 2008. "The Evolution of UK and London Employment Rates." *GLA Economics Working Paper 33*. London: Greater London Authority.

Boffey, Daniel. 2017. "Record Numbers of EU Nurses Quit NHS." *Guardian*, March 18. https://www.theguardian.com/society/2017/mar/18/nhs-eu-nurses-quit-record-numbers.

Crerar, Pippa. 2017. "Hard Brexit 'Would Cause Crisis for London House Building.'" *Evening Standard*, February 27. http://www.standard.co.uk/news/london/london-house-building-crisis-looming-because-of-brexit-a3476681.html.

Demertzis, Maria, and Fabio Matera. 2017. "Brexit and the UK Creative Industry." *Bruegel*, January 18. http://bruegel.org/2017/01/brexit-and-the-uk-creative-industry/.

Greater London Authority. 2016. *Economic Evidence Base for London 2016*. https://www.london.gov.uk/what-we-do/research-and-analysis/economy-and-employment/economic-evidence-base-london-2016#acc-i-44543.

Head, Simon. 2017. "Britain: An Economy on the Brink." *NYR Daily*, April 4. http://www.nybooks.com/daily/2017/04/04/britain-an-economy-on-the-brink/.

London's Poverty Profile. 2015. "Work and Worklessness." Trust for London/New Policy Institute. http://www.londonspovertyprofile.org.uk/indicators/topics/work-and-worklessness/.

Marsden, Joel, and Hadyn Hitchens. 2016. "Trends in the Demand for Labour and Skills across London as a Whole." *GLA Economics Working Paper 75*. London: Greater London Authority.

McNeil, Clare, and Giselle Cory. 2017. "The Future of Childcare in London: Devolving Funding for Greater Affordability, Access and Equality." *Institute for Public Policy Research*, April 10. http://www.ippr.org/publications/the-future-of-childcare-in-london.

Nelson, Eshe. 2017. "Look upon These Charts of Housing Prices, Ye Londoners, and Despair!" *Quartz*, March 17. https://qz.com/935387/london-houses-prices-are-so-unaffordable-it-now-takes-12-times-the-annual-wage-to-buy-a-home/.

O'Sullivan, Feargus. 2016. "For London, 2017 Could Be the Year That Makes or Breaks the City's Future" *CityLab*, December 29. http://www.citylab.com/politics/2016/12/brexit-effects-on-london-jobs-housing-politics-mayor/511778/.

Thompson, Spencer, Catherine Colebrook, and Izzy Thompson. 2016. "Jobs and Skills in London: Building a More Responsive Skills System in the Capital." *New Skills at Work*. London: Institute for Public Policy Research/JPMorgan Chase & Co.

Vargas-Silva, Carlos, and Cinzia Rienzo. 2017. "Migrants in the UK: An Overview." *Migration Observatory at the University of Oxford*, February 21. http://www.migrationobservatory.ox.ac.uk/resources/briefings/migrants-in-the-uk-an-overview/.

Mumbai, India: Exploring Employment Solutions in Temporary Jobs

Mumbai (formerly Bombay) is the largest city, and the political and administrative center of the Indian state of Maharashtra. Located in India's western region, Maharashtra is the country's most developed and its wealthiest state. In 2010–11, the state contributed almost 23.2 percent of India's GDP. The Labor Bureau of the Indian government's Ministry of Labor and Employment (Labor Bureau) in its 2013–14 survey, found Maharashtra to be India's most industrialized state.

The services sector dominates the economy of Maharashtra. Manufacturing, textiles, chemical, and petroleum are some of Maharashtra's other significant industries. Maharashtra also leads the country in international trade and mass media. Approximately 25 percent of the top 500 companies in the IT sector are situated in Maharashtra. The state accounts for 28 percent of the software exports of India. About 19.4 percent of the its urban population is employed in manufacturing, while 60 percent of the urban population is employed in hospitality, financial services, or other professional and scientific activities.

Mumbai is Maharashtra's most urbanized city. With a population of 20.7 million (2016 estimate), it is also the most populated city in India. A majority of Maharashtra's urban population lives and works in Mumbai. Much of the state's industrial activity is also concentrated in the city of Mumbai and its suburbs. The city generates almost 22 percent of the state's domestic product (state income).

Once known for its textile industry, Mumbai is now India's most important commercial and financial hub. Its two ports handle more than a third of the country's foreign trade. Mumbai is also home to several manufacturing industries, financial institutions, an extensive services sector, and several state government offices. Mumbai houses the headquarters of most of the major corporate and financial institutions. India's main stock exchanges, capital market, and commodity exchanges are located in Mumbai. The country's film and entertainment industry, including Bollywood (Hindi cinema), is also based in Mumbai. According to a 2014 report (McCarthy, 2014), Bollywood is at least a $138 billion industry.

The city of Mumbai attracts migrants from all over India, who come in search of employment opportunities. Migration has largely been responsible for doubling the city's population in the last 20 years. Spread over an area of only 170 square miles, Mumbai has a very high population density, and some of the highest property rates in the world. A large portion of its population lives in small, crammed spaces, including slums, which offer affordable living options to the migrants. According to some estimates, almost 60 percent of the city's population lives in slums. Dharavi, Asia's largest slum with over 1 million inhabitants is located in Mumbai. Congestion, traffic, pollution, and inadequate public transportation are some of the major concerns for the bustling metropolis of Mumbai.

JOBS AND EMPLOYMENT

Beginning in 1975, Mumbai's government started imposing restrictions on the setting up of new industries and commercial establishments in the city, and on the expansion of existing industries. This caused the number of manufacturing industrial workers to decline significantly. In addition, the economic reforms initiated in India in 1991, and the consequent influx of cheap imported goods, further reduced manufacturing activity in the city, and reduced the workforce employed in manufacturing. By 2005, the number of small- and large-scale manufacturing units had significantly decreased. The city has since made a rapid economic transition from trade to services. The share of the manufacturing sector in employment has decreased, while that of the services sector has increased. In 2016, Mumbai had an unemployment rate of 5.1 percent, down from 5.7 percent in 2015. The overall unemployment rate for India during the same period was about 4.9 percent.

Informal sector employment is steadily growing. There is also an increased participation of females in both formal and informal sectors. Almost 68 percent of Mumbai's workforce is employed in the informal sector. Informal sector employment is characterized by low wages and a lack of social benefits or legal protection. These workers are considered the urban poor, who are excluded from formal sector housing and live in slums and other informal settlements across the city. In Dharavi alone, there are more than a thousand small businesses that create an informal economy with a turnover of almost $1 billion. Workers labor as potters, leather tanners, weavers, soap makers, and recyclers. The informal economy provides crucial ancillary support to the formal sector. The state government has been trying to redevelop the slum area to create more residential and commercial spaces in a city where the real estate crunch can impede economic growth. Critics argue that the policy does not take into account the interests of the informal sector, and that the government's move might render thousands of slum workers unemployed.

MUMBAI VERSUS OTHER INDIAN CITIES

Delhi is the capital of the republic of India and also a state for administrative purposes. Tourism, banking and financial services, real estate, agriculture and food processing, and insurance are some of the city's key industries. Under its most recent industrial policy, the government in Delhi is trying to increase the presence of knowledge-based and high-tech IT industries in the state. In its proposed budget, the Delhi government has also proposed an outlay of US$1.06 million for the development of agriculture and allied services.

Bengaluru (formerly Bangalore) is considered to be the "Silicon Valley" of India. A large number of IT companies are located in Bengaluru. Several multinational corporations, particularly computer software and hardware companies, also have operations in India. Bengaluru also accounts for 97 percent of all biotechnology companies in the country. Once recognized for its textiles, and public-sector undertakings (PSUs), Bengaluru is now recognized for its high-technology service industries. The United Nations Human Development Report (2001) ranked the city fourth along with Austin (USA), San Francisco (USA), and Taipei (Taiwan) as the top "technology hubs of the world."

Compared to these large Indian cities, the economy of Mumbai is very diverse, and the workforce is employed across a wide range of industries.

MUMBAI VERSUS SHANGHAI

Like Mumbai, Shanghai serves as the economic and financial center for Mainland China. It is home to major capital markets including the Shanghai Stock Exchange (SSE), the Shanghai Futures Exchange (SHFE), and the Shanghai Gold Exchange (SGE). Shanghai is also an important port, and crucial for China's extensive trade with the rest of the world. The services sector accounts for more than 60 percent of Shanghai's GDP. Other important industries include high-end manufacturing, iron and steel, and petrochemicals. In 2016, Shanghai grew at the rate of 6.9 percent, with unemployment down by 8,200 compared to 2015. Like Mumbai, the city has also experienced a surge in real estate prices. Traffic congestion, population, pollution, and affordable housing are some of the biggest concerns for the city. In the *Global Cities Index*, published by A. T. Kearney (Sunder 2018), Shanghai was ranked at 19, while Mumbai was ranked 52. The index measures city performance largely based on business activity, human capital, and access to information. Even though Mumbai is ranked below Shanghai, it is among the top-rated Indian cities on the list.

CHALLENGES FOR MUMBAI

Reports indicate that hiring in Mumbai is predicted to increase in the near future (SIA 2018). Several employers have, however, reported difficulty in hiring skilled workers who are well suited for the available positions. According to a recent report published in the *Economic Times* (Savlani, 2017), First Advantage, a risk mitigation and business solutions provider, has found that there is an increase in workers fabricating their documents and educational qualifications to get jobs in Mumbai's formal sector. Moving forward, it is important that the city creates opportunities to appropriately and adequately train its workforce, to attract and retain firms in the services sector. The city also needs to provide better and affordable housing to attract more skilled labor from India and abroad.

Another interesting trend in Mumbai is the rise in flexi-jobs. According to data published by the Indian Staffing Federation, transport and communications, and the banking and financial services sector will create 55 percent more "flexi jobs" in the state of Maharashtra between 2015 and 2018 (Kakodkarl 2017). Flexi-jobs are temporary contracts in the formal sector that help meet short-term needs of the economy. The report also suggests that the flexi-jobs are not replacing permanent jobs, but rather creating additional employment opportunities for workers to migrate from the informal to the formal sector. The Indian Staffing Federation warns that the flexi-employees may be subject to exploitation, and that labor reforms are necessary to ensure that the interests of these contract workers are safeguarded.

ROLE OF THE STATE GOVERNMENT

The government in Maharashtra has implemented several initiatives to reduce the level of unemployment in the state. Prominent among them is the Maharashtra Self-Employment Training Board (MSTB). The board provides professional, agricultural, and technical training to the educated unemployed; and also to farmers and women from remote areas to help them with self-employment, albeit on a small-scale, and to make them more competitive in the labor market. As a program of the State Government of Maharashtra, the MSTB has been in existence for over 15 years.

The Directorate of Skill Development, Employment and Entrepreneurship functions as an employment agency that brings together employers and job seekers through an online registration portal and through regular job fairs. In addition, they facilitate skill development through the Maharashtra State Skill Development Society, and also provide assistance and guidance for self-employment.

Dharavi

Located in the heart of Mumbai (Bombay), India's financial capital, Dharavi is Asia's largest slum. Spread over just 535 acres with a population of approximately 1 million (World Population Review 2019), Dharavi is one of the most densely populated neighborhoods in Mumbai. The slum is characterized by long stretches of tiny huts located along dirty, narrow lanes and open sewers. The slum offers affordable housing for migrants in a city that has some of the highest rents in the world. In spite of the lack of proper infrastructure, and issues with sanitation, traffic congestion, and waste management, Dharavi is considered an informal economic powerhouse. The slum is home to several small-scale industries and tiny manufacturing units including those for embroidered garments, leather goods, pottery, and jewelry. These goods have extensive domestic and international markets. According to the most recent available estimates, the annual turnover of the informal sector is more than $650 million a year. The state government has had plans to redevelop the slum area into a modern township with better infrastructure, schools, and hospitals since 1997. There is strong opposition, however, particularly from the residents engaged in the informal sector, who fear that their livelihoods might be ignored in the redevelopment plan.

In addition, the National Skill Development Corporation (NSDC) has helped set up over 80 vocational training institutes in Mumbai. The NSDC is a unique public-private partnership under the leadership of the Ministry of Skill Development and Entrepreneurship, Government of India, that promotes skill development through support for the creation of for-profit vocational training institutes across India. The NSDC targets skill development in 21 sectors, including IT, health care, and government.

Nakul Kumar

See also: Employment and Jobs: Riyadh, Saudi Arabia: Creating Jobs in the Post–Oil-Boom Era; Shenzhen, China: Struggle to Leave Shanzhai Behind; *Energy and Sustainability:* Mumbai, India: Providing Energy for a City of 21 Million

Further Reading

Clark, Greg, and Tim Moonen. 2014. *Mumbai: India's Global City*. Global Cities Initiative, JPMorgan Chase.

Government of Maharashtra, Directorate of Skill Development, Employment and Entrepreneurship. https://www.maharashtra.gov.in/1125/Home.

Government of Maharashtra, Maharashtra Self-Employment Training Board. http://www.mstb.in.

India Brand Equity Foundation. 2017. Delhi State Report. https://www.ibef.org/states/delhi.aspx.

Kakodkarl, Priyanka. 2017. "Flexi Jobs in Maharashtra to Rise by 55% in 3 Years: Study." *Times of India*, March 20. http://timesofindia.indiatimes.com/city/mumbai/flexi-jobs-in-maharashtra-to-rise-by-55-in-3-years-study/articleshow/57724441.cms.

Kingsley, Thomas G. 2007. *Economic Growth and Workforce Development in the Mumbai Metropolitan Region*. Washington, DC: India Urban Initiatives, USAID. http://pdf.usaid.gov/pdf_docs/Pnadn715.pdf.

Labor Bureau of India, Ministry of Labor & Employment, Government of India. http://labourbureau.nic.in.

McCarthy, Niall. 2014. "Bollywood: India's Film Industry by the Numbers." *Forbes*, September 3. https://www.forbes.com/sites/niallmccarthy/2014/09/03/bollywood-indias-film-industry-by-the-numbers-infographic/#1deba9052488.

National Skill Development Corporation. www.nsdcindia.org.

Press Trust of India. 2016. "India's Unemployment Rate Highest in 5 Years in 2015–2016." *Indian Express*, September 29. http://indianexpress.com/article/india/india-news-india/unemployment-india-paints-grim-picture-highest-in-5-years-in-2015-16-3056290/.

Reuters. 2016. "Dharavi Slum's Decades-Old Informal Economy Turnover of $1bn Plus Now Threatened by Development." *Economic Times*, October 11.

Risbud, Neelima. 2003. *Urban Slums Report: The Case of Mumbai, India*. http://www.ucl.ac.uk/dpu-projects/Global_Report/pdfs/Mumbai_bw.pdf.

Savlani, Purushotam. 2017. "Fudging of Documents and Educational Qualifications to Chase Job on Rise." *Economic Times*, April 2. http://economictimes.indiatimes.com/jobs/fudging-of-documents-and-educational-qualifications-to-chase-job-on-rise-report/articleshow/57972640.cms.

Staffing Industry Analysts (SIA). 2018. "India—Jobs Market to See Boost in Next Six Months as Net Employment Outlook Rises." *Daily News*. July 3. https://www2.staffingindustry.com/row/Editorial/Daily-News/India-Jobs-market-to-see-boost-in-next-six-months-as-net-employment-outlook-rises-46595.

Sunder, Sushruth. 2018. Global Cities Index 2018: New York Is World's Most Influential City; Where Delhi, Mumbai Stand. *Financial Express.* June 11. https://www.financialexpress.com/economy/global-cities-index-2018-new-york-tops-global-cities-as-most-influential-where-delhi-mumbai-stand/1201175/.

World Population Review. 2019. "Mumbai Population 2019." http://worldpopulationreview.com/world-cities/mumbai-population/.

Yanlin, Wang. 2016. "Shanghai's Economic Growth Accelerates." *Shanghai Daily*, January 21. http://www.shanghaidaily.com/business/economy/Shanghais-economic-growth-accelerates/shdaily.shtml.

Yardley, Jim. 2011. "In One Slum, Misery, Work, Politics and Hope." *New York Times*, December 28. http://www.nytimes.com/2011/12/29/world/asia/in-indian-slum-misery-work-politics-and-hope.html.

New York City, United States: Economically and Environmentally Friendly

New York is the most populous city in the United States. Its population and economy are unique. New York's development and population density have also resulted in a surprisingly environmentally friendly city.

NEW YORK CITY DEVELOPMENT

New York City was settled by European colonists in the 17th century by the Dutch West India Company. In 1624, Peter Minuit, the third governor, purchased the island of Manhattan from the native Indians for goods and jewelry worth 60 Dutch guilders or about $24. He then named the colony New Amsterdam. The British took over the colony in 1664 and renamed it New York.

George Washington was inaugurated the first President of the United States in New York in 1789 (though the nation's capital was moved to Philadelphia the next year). By then, New York was the largest city in the country with a population of 33,131. A century later, with the annexation of Brooklyn, New York City grew to approximately 3.5 million, making it the second most populous city in the world after London.

A decade later, in 1910, New York's population had grown to almost 4.8 million, almost 2 million of whom were foreign born. The city's foreign-born population has remained high ever since and currently account for about 3 million of the city's 8 million residents (37 percent).

NEW YORK CITY DEMOGRAPHY

New York's population is much more diverse than the rest of the country. While whites comprise 73.6 percent of the United States, they account for only 43.3 percent of New York City. By contrast, the black population is about twice the national average (24.5 vs. 12.6).

The city's Asian population is about two and a half times the national average (13.5 vs. 5.1). Among the Asian population, the Chinese share of New York City's

Table 1 New York City vs. U.S. Demographics

	USA	NYC
White (non-Hispanic)	62.3%	32.5%
Black or African American	12.3%	22.4%
American Indian and Alaska Native	0.7%	0.2%
Asian	5.1%	13.5%
Asian Indian	1.0%	2.6%
Chinese	1.2%	6.5%
Other Asian	2.9%	4.4%
Native Hawaiian and Other Pacific Islander	0.2%	0.0%
Hispanic or Latino (of any race)	17.1%	28.9%
Mexican	10.9%	4.0%
Puerto Rican	1.6%	8.7%
Other Hispanic or Latino	4.5%	16.3%

Source: U.S. Census Bureau (2015). https://factfinder.census.gov/faces/tableservices/jsf/pages/productview.xhtml?pid=ACS_15_5YR_DP05&src=pt; https://www.census.gov/quickfacts/table/PST045215/36.

population is more than five times their national representation, and the city has the largest Chinese population of any city in the world outside China.

Similarly, New York's Hispanic (Latino) population accounts for two-thirds more than their share of the U.S. population. However, whereas those of Mexican descent account for the overwhelming majority of the Hispanic population nationwide, New York's Hispanic population is more diverse, with Puerto Ricans representing the largest group.

While foreign-born residents comprise slightly less than half the city's workforce, they account for a majority of city workers between ages 35 and 64 (Lobo and Salvo 2013, 18). With more than 200 languages spoken in the city, about half of all New York residents speak a language other than English at home. New York's diverse population contributes to its thriving culture and innovative workforce.

GEOGRAPHY

New York is the most densely populated city in the country, with about 28,000 people per square mile (11,000 per square km). New York City comprises five sections, known as boroughs: Manhattan, Brooklyn, Queens, Bronx, and Staten Island. Although Brooklyn has the largest population, Manhattan is by far the most densely populated, with approximately 72,000 people per square mile (28,000 per square km).

Manhattan is the main commercial center, both of New York and of the United States. It is home to the Wall Street Stock Exchange, as well as the headquarters of national and international financial and communications firms. Consequently, Manhattan's real estate is among the highest priced in the world. Manhattan is also the city's cultural hub, with the majority of the city's approximately 100 museums and internationally renowned performing arts centers, which contribute to New York's position as a leading world cultural center.

ECONOMIC DEVELOPMENT

New York developed as a port city. The central location of its natural deepwater port at the time of the country's founding—a midpoint between Boston and Washington, D.C.—and its access by canal—and later rail—to the middle of the country made it one of the country's most important access and commerce points. This helped draw financial interests and population, which further increased its economic importance. By the early 20th century, New York ports still accounted for about 40 percent of the value of all U.S. foreign trade (Harris 1993, 173).

New York's large immigrant population also provided a large pool of labor. One sector that grew from this, along with access to ports to foreign markets and rails to the rest of the country, was the garment industry. In 1860, almost 30 percent of manufacturing employment in New York was in the garment industry. A century later, in 1967, that sector still employed 27 percent of manufacturing employees (Glaeser 2005, 15). This, along with the city's large number of wealthy citizens, helped make New York an international fashion center.

HOW DOES NEW YORK CITY EMPLOYMENT DIFFER FROM THE REST OF THE COUNTRY?

The ways in which New York City residents are employed differs from the rest of the country (see Table 2). New Yorkers are about two-thirds less likely to be employed in goods producing and more than three-fourths less likely to work in manufacturing than the national average. However, New York, as fashion capital of the country, has about four times the rate of employment in apparel manufacturing than the national average.

By contrast, New Yorkers are more likely to work in private service-providing fields. Among these is the information field, which includes publishing, broadcasting, and the motion picture and sound industries, which employ city residents at two to four times the national average.

Not surprisingly, New York, which is home to Wall Street, has employment in financial activities at almost twice the U.S. rate. Within this category, the greatest discrepancy is in the field of credit intermediation and related activities, which accounts for only 0.01 percent of national employment but 2.13 percent of New York jobs, more than 200 times more. Similarly, securities, commodities, and other financial investment-related activities employ more than six times the share of people in New York City than in the country as a whole. With an economy heavily weighted toward financial activity, New York City's residents have a mean annual wage that is about 20 percent higher than the nation as a whole—$48,320 versus $59,990 (BLS).

Table 2 New York City vs. U.S. Employment

Employment Type	USA	NYC	Difference
Total private	84.50%	87.16%	3.1%
Goods-producing	13.50%	5.14%	−62.0%
Manufacturing	8.38%	1.81%	−78.4%
Apparel Manufacturing	0.09%	0.33%	265.5%
Private Service-providing	70.99%	82.03%	15.5%
Trade, Transportation, and Utilities	19.10%	14.79%	−22.6%
Retail Trade	11.21%	8.16%	−27.2%
Information	1.90%	4.48%	135.9%
Publishing Industries (except Internet)	0.50%	1.05%	110.6%
Motion Picture and Sound Recording	0.29%	1.26%	334.8%
Broadcasting (except Internet)	0.19%	0.62%	225.8%
Financial Activities	5.69%	10.48%	84.2%
Finance and Insurance	4.23%	7.53%	78.1%
Credit Intermediation and Related	0.01%	2.13%	21168.8%
Investment-related Activities	0.64%	3.94%	515.7%
Real Estate and Rental and Leasing	1.46%	2.95%	101.9%
Professional and Business Services	14.12%	16.59%	17.5%
Professional, Scientific, and Technical Svs.	6.17%	9.35%	51.6%
Legal Services	0.77%	1.76%	129.0%
Accounting, Tax Prep., and Payroll Svs.	0.69%	1.26%	82.4%
Education and Health Services	15.81%	21.05%	33.1%
Educational Services	2.57%	5.34%	107.9%
Government	15.50%	12.84%	−17.2%

Sources: U.S. Bureau of Labor Statistics. https://www.bls.gov/news.release/empsit.t17.htm; New York State Department of Labor. https://www.labor.ny.gov/stats/cesemp.asp.

ECONOMIC INNOVATION

Beyond the raw numbers for employment, New York's diverse population and access to capital have proved to be a source for innovation over its long history. The Center for an Urban Future (CUF) reports that while manufacturing employment has declined by about 50 percent in the past two decades, new types of manufacturing are developing. The CUF study reveals that New York has become a world leader in 3D printing—also known as "additive manufacturing."

According to the CUF report, "the 3D printing industry is expected to grow from $4.98 billion in 2015 to $30.19 billion by 2022" (Euchner 2016, 4). This type of manufacturing enables small businesses to produce niche products without the cost of larger, expensive machinery. It can allow for the production of custom-made objects from dental work and body organs to car parts.

This type of manufacturing is ideally suited to a city like New York for several reasons. First, unlike traditional manufacturing it does not require large tracts of land, which are very costly in a city like New York. Second, it requires an educated and innovative workforce, something that is readily available within the city's large population. Third, unlike traditional manufacturing, 3D printing is flexible and evolving with new technological developments. This requires both investment money and a dynamic and innovative population that can take advantage of this new production method. New York City has an abundance of both.

Another of the city's niche areas that has seen a growth in employment, according to the CUF, is the food industry. This is the only manufacturing sector to register an increase in jobs over the past decade, and has seen a 27 percent growth in the number employed. Thus, despite the below-average share of manufacturing among New York City employment, the city ranks third in the country for food manufacturing. Here too the city's dynamic population contributes to this particular economic growth. From designer baked goods and ice cream to Middle Eastern and other ethnic foods, the city's diverse tapestry of residents provides fertile ground for innovation in this industry.

ECONOMICS AND THE ENVIRONMENT IN NEW YORK CITY

New York City does not elicit images of an environmentally friendly atmosphere. Densely populated, with residents cramped in small apartments, no backyards, and far from forests, it seems the antithesis of what the term environment calls to mind. However, New York City is, in many ways, one of the most environmentally friendly places in the United States.

New York's 8.5 million people are packed into 305 square miles (790 square km), for an average density of about 28,000 people per square mile (11,000 per square km). That is more than 300 times the average density of the United States. If New York City's population were distributed at the same density as the rest of the country, it would occupy an area twice the size of England. Put another way, eight of the country's least populated states (Nebraska, Idaho, Montana, Vermont, South Dakota, North Dakota, Alaska, and Wyoming) have a combined population equal to that of New York City, but occupy 4,000 times as much land. Hence, the city's density makes for efficient land use and preserves open space.

High population density has also enabled the development of efficient public transportation, which means fewer private cars on the road. New York has one of the most extensive public transit systems in the world. Most trips on public transportation take place on the city's subway system, which has more than 660 miles (1,062 km) of track and 469 stations.

New York's public transportation carries more than 2.5 billion rides per year (MTA). This is more than that of the next 16 largest American public transit systems combined and six times that of the Los Angeles public transit system, the country's second largest (Fischer-Baum 2014). This means that New Yorkers burn less petroleum, on average, in order to reach their destinations than anyone in the country. Since transportation exhaust is one of the leading contributors to climate change, this is another environmentally friendly aspect of New York. Additionally, fewer cars means less land is wasted on parking spaces.

In recent years, New York City has embraced another environmentally friendly form of transportation: bicycles. From 2007 to 2016 the city converted 220 acres (90 hectares) of space from roadway for cars to bicycle, pedestrian, and other transit, giving the city more than 400 miles (644 km) of bicycle paths. In order to encourage bicycle use, the city developed a bike share program called Citibike. This program has grown rapidly since its launch in 2013, and in 2016 it provided 14 million trips, reaching 60,000 to 70,000 trips per day on several occasions. This made it the biggest bike share in the Western hemisphere and one of largest in the world.

New York City's density, through residence in small apartments, also results in city residents using less electricity and water per household than any other place in the country. Since apartment buildings require less energy for heating, cleaning, and maintenance than single-family homes, New York City's carbon footprint is less than one-third the national average (Pasion, Amar, and Zhou 2016).

New York City's special economy also contributes to the city's lower carbon footprint. Since manufacturing comprises a lower share than the national average, there is less resulting pollution per worker. Additionally, the high share of educated and affluent workers in financial services and high-tech industries mean a greater awareness and demand for clean water and air. Furthermore, since the city receives billions of dollars from the 60 million tourists who visit annually (McGeehan 2016), there is added incentive to provide a clean environment.

Although New York City usually conjures images of tall buildings, it also contains 30,000 acres (12,000 hectares) of parkland, comprising 14 percent of city land. The most famous of these is the 843-acre (341 hectares) Central Park, located in Manhattan's geographic center, whose woodlands, lakes, and playing fields provide green space for millions of people.

CONCLUSION: ECONOMICALLY DYNAMIC AND ENVIRONMENTALLY FRIENDLY

Thus, New York City's unique population and economic characteristics have made it both a world leader in finance and a model for environmentally sustainable development. Contrary to the sprawling, car-dependent suburbs and towns that characterize much of the United States, New York's dense urban development has proven environmentally friendly in terms of land use and transportation. This has resulted in a city that is a national and world leader in efficient use of resources and low per capita carbon footprint.

Matt Evans

See also: Energy and Sustainability: London, United Kingdom: Improving Mobility Can Save Energy; *Migration and Demographic Changes:* London, United Kingdom: Facing the Challenges of Population Growth

Further Reading

Brown, Marilyn, Frank Southworth, and Andrea Sarzynski. 2008. "Shrinking the Carbon Footprint of Metropolitan America." *Brookings Institution*, May. https://www.brookings.edu/wp-content/uploads/2016/07/carbonfootprint_brief.pdf.

City of New York. 2015. "Mayor de Blasio and Citi Bike Announce Record-Breaking 10 Million Trips in 2015." December 31. http://www1.nyc.gov/office-of-the-mayor/news/986-15/mayor-de-blasio-citi-bike-record-breaking-10-million-trips-2015.

Euchner, Charles. 2016. "Making It Here: The Future of Manufacturing in New York City." *Center for an Urban Future (CUF)*, July. https://nycfuture.org/pdf/Making_It_Here_Report.pdf.

Fischer-Baum, Reuben. 2014. "How Your City's Public Transit Stacks Up." FiveThirtyEight, July 31. https://fivethirtyeight.com/datalab/how-your-citys-public-transit-stacks-up/.

Florida, Richard. 2012. "What Is the World's Most Economically Powerful City?" *Atlantic*, May 8. https://www.theatlantic.com/business/archive/2012/05/what-is-the-worlds-most-economically-powerful-city/256841/.

Gibson, Campbell. 1998. "Population of the 100 Largest Cities and Other Urban Places in the United States: 1790 to 1990." *U.S. Bureau of the Census*, June. https://www.census.gov/population/www/documentation/twps0027/twps0027.html.

Glaeser, Edward. 2005. "Urban Colossus: Why Is New York America's Largest City?" *Harvard Institute of Economic Research*, June. http://scholar.harvard.edu/files/glaeser/files/hier2073.pdf.

Hamaji, Kate, and Christian González-Rivera. 2016. "A City of Immigrant Workers: Building a Workforce Strategy to Support All New Yorkers." *Center for Popular Democracy (CPD)* and *Center for an Urban Future (CUF)*, April. https://nycfuture.org/pdf/A-City-of-Immigrants.pdf.

Harris, Richard. 1993. "Industry and Residence: The Decentralization of New York City, 1900–1940." *Journal of Historical Geography* 19, 2: 169–90. http://dx.doi.org/10.1006/jhge.1993.1012.

Lobo, Arun Peter, and Joseph Salvo. 2013. "The Newest New Yorkers: Characteristics of the City's Foreign-Born Population." *New York City Department of City Planning*, December. https://www1.nyc.gov/assets/planning/download/pdf/data-maps/nyc-population/nny2013/nny_2013.pdf.

McGeehan, Patrick. 2016. "Record Number of Tourists Visited New York City in 2015, and More Are Expected This Year." *New York Times*, March 8. https://www.nytimes.com/2016/03/09/nyregion/record-number-of-tourists-visited-new-york-city-in-2015-and-more-are-expected-this-year.html.

New York City Department of Parks & Recreation. 2017. "About the New York City Department of Parks & Recreation." https://www.nycgovparks.org/about.

New York City Department of Planning. 2017. "New York City Population." https://www1.nyc.gov/site/planning/data-maps/nyc-population/population-facts.page.

Owen, David. 2009. "The Greenest Place in the U.S. May Not Be Where You Think." *YaleEnvironment360*, Yale School of Forestry & Environmental Studies, October 26. http://e360.yale.edu/features/greenest_place_in_the_us_its_not_where_you_think.

Pasion, Cathy, Mikael Amar, and Yun Zhou. 2016. "Inventory of New York City Greenhouse Gas Emissions." Mayor's Office of Sustainability, New York. http://www1.nyc.gov/assets/sustainability/downloads/pdf/publications/NYC_GHG_Inventory_2014.pdf.

Sreenivasan, Hari. 2016. "How NYC's Streets Became More Pedestrian-Friendly." *PBS*, Transcript of Interview with Janette Sadik-Khan, June 11. http://www.pbs.org/newshour/bb/how-nycs-streets-became-more-pedestrian-friendly/.

U.S. Bureau of Labor Statistics (BLS). 2017. "New York City Economic Summary." https://www.bls.gov/regions/new-york-new-jersey/summary/blssummary_newyorkcity.pdf.

Walder, Jay. 2016. "City Council Transportation Committee Hearing on the Present & Future of Citi Bike." *Testimony before City Council Transportation Committee Hearing on the Present & Future of Citi Bike,* November 28. http://citibikeblog.tumblr.com/post/153782541317/city-council-transportation-committee-hearing-on.

Paris, France: A Locomotive of Job Creation

To many people, Paris is first and foremost a dream destination of tourism and stylish living. What is less known is that Paris is the most powerful engine of economic growth and job creation in France.

In an economic sense, Paris is at the dragon's head of an industrial belt that stretches from Paris westward to the department of Manche, known as the Seine Valley. This industrial zone is home to 11 million inhabitants and 5.5 million jobs. The fact that 61 percent of these jobs are located in the Metropolis of Greater Paris (MGP) indicates the powerful economic role the capital city plays.

SEINE VALLEY AND METROPOLIS OF GREATER PARIS

Geographically, the Seine Valley is composed of nine departments: Metropolis of Greater Paris, Hauts-de Seine, Seine-Sant-Denis, Yvelines, Val-d'Oise, Calvados, Eure, Manche, and Seine-Maritime. These regions share a master development plan—the 2012–20 Inter-regional Planning Agreement, known as CPIER in French. The goal of the agreement is to coordinate regional growth to achieve an overall economic growth, environmental balance of the valley, and higher educational resources. Most of the industries in the Seine Valley concentrate on manufacturing and transportation. More than 1 out of 10 jobs are offered by these sectors in the Seine Valley; and more than 60 percent of transportation and manufacturing jobs concentrate in areas surrounding Paris. During the 2008 economic crisis, the Seine Valley suffered a broad slump in manufacturing and transportation. Areas such as Cherbourg, Evreux, Rouen, Saint-lô, and le Havre lost 8 to 15 percent of jobs. Unemployment hit broadly, from temporary workers to engineers and administrators. As such, a major characteristic of the Seine Valley is its high job displacement rate—approximately 14 percent of the workforce travel to work outside their residential area.

The MGP is located at the eastern end of the Seine Valley, constituted by four departments, including Paris, les Hauts-de-Seine, la Seine-Saint-Denis, and the Commune of Argenteuil. Nearly 8 out of 10 people who work in the Seine Valley reside in MGP. After the economic crisis of 2008, MGP recovered lost jobs at a rate that was about one-third faster than the rest of the valley. One factor in MGP's favor is the capital city's wealth of resources, which allowed its enterprises to open broad economic ties with areas both within and beyond the Seine Valley. In 2014, for example, 9 out of 10 salary-earning jobs offered in the valley were related to businesses in MGP. For example, over 10 percent of the jobs in Auvergne-Rhone-Apes (to the south of Paris) and in Hauts-de-France (to the north of Paris) had ties with enterprises in MGP. The dynamic of MGP's job creation is believed to derive from the main urban functions. These functions are particularly strong in the areas of management, culture and entertainment, consulting, and retail. Management-type jobs, for example, represent 18 percent of MGP's jobs. They represent the leadership strength of MGP (Lebeaupin 2017).

JOB ENGINE—THE ZTIS

The city of Paris is divided into 20 urban districts (*arrondissement*). The urban population is approximately 2.22 million, with a density of 25,600 per square kilometer, according to a recent survey by Institut national des études economiques (Insee) (Fauret et al. 2017). Cultural and historical sites constitute 12 international touristic zones or ZTIs (short for Zones touristiques internationales in French). They occupy 575 hectares or 7 percent of Paris's surface space, and encompass most of the jobs in the city. Population in these areas is 123,000, or 6 percent of the Parisian population. One in five jobs in Paris is located in a ZTI; most jobs are in retail sales, which is the largest business sector in Paris. Population density in these touristic zones is lower than elsewhere in Paris, about 21,500 residents per square kilometer vs. 25,600, respectively (Fauret et al. 2017). ZTIs are also home to hundreds

Rue de la Paix is a fashionable shopping district in Paris. It is one of the largest *zones touristiques internationales* (international tourist zones, or ZTIs) in the city. (Scott Jones/Dreamstime.com)

of government offices; however, the jobs in retail sales and restaurant business are far more prevalent.

The three largest ZTIs, Saint-Honoré-Vendôme, Haussmann, and Champs-Elysées Montaigne, house more than half of the jobs in ZTIs combined. According to Insee, more than 40 percent of salaried retail jobs in Paris are located in ZTIs. For retail business, there is no better location than ZTIs. They attract millions of visitors worldwide and all year round, which translates nicely into business profits. Les Halles, Beaugrenelle, and Rennes Saint-Sulpice, for example, are located in the very center of Paris, in close proximity to the Louvre Museum, the Pompidou Center, and the bank of the Seine River. These areas are also home to most of Paris's department stores. Clothing and shoe stores here, for example, represent 63 percent of employment of Paris's clothing and shoe sales sector. Tourist items are among the top retail sales in Paris. Seventy-six percent of employment in sales of leather craft, including clothing, shoes, bags, and travel items, are concentrated in ZTIs. Stores specializing in these items are abundant in Champs-Elysées Montaigne. The ZTI of Saint-Honoré-Vendôme is the center of jewelry and timepiece stores; 68 percent of Paris' employment in these sectors is located here. For students and those looking for short-term jobs, their best bet may be in the retail sector in ZTIs. Insee data shows that employees working in tourism-oriented retail stores tend to be younger, with a median age of 33, than those in other sectors, where the median age is 39. Employees of clothing and shoe stores have a median age of 29, whereas employees working in department stores, typically outside the ZTIs, have a median age of 41. Moreover, 62 percent of the employees working in retail businesses in ZTIs, especially those in clothing and shoe stores, are female. On the other hand, a higher percentage of male employees are employed in information and communication sectors (Fauret et al. 2017).

However, ZTIs have a lower representation of supermarkets, pharmacies, bakeries, and convenience stores for daily living, due to the fact that residential neighborhoods are typically not located in touristic centers. Jobs in convenience stores are 20 percent fewer in ZTIs than in residential districts, according to Insee data. However, this doesn't mean a shortage of brand-name foods. On the contrary, tourists can find a great variety of chocolate, pastry, and coffee stores in ZTIs where they can stock up on gift-wrapped foods that represent the French palate. Additionally, restaurants and hotels are well-established businesses in ZTIs. According to Insee's data, approximately one-third of the restaurants and a quarter of the hotels in Paris are located in the 12 ZTIs. For example, Montmartre, Le Marais, Les Halles, and Saint-Germain are best known for restaurants, while Maillot Ternes is noted for the most hotels in Paris. These businesses provide one-fourth and one-third of these sectors' jobs in Paris respectively.

In addition to their touristic functions, the ZTIs are also home to government offices, educational institutions, banks, wholesale distributors, and information services including newspapers and publication houses. Table 1 reflects employment capacity of some of these operations during the period of 2013–14.

It should be noted that the train services in Paris are among the most prolific job creators. According to Insee, the six train stations in Paris—Austerlitz, East, Lyon, North, Montparnasse, and Saint-Lazare—offered 3,200 jobs in 2013, of which

Table 1 Employment Capacity of Paris ZTIs

	Jobs in 12 ZTIs	Total Jobs in Paris	% in ZTIs
Public administration	16,400	154,100	11
Banks	29,300	86,700	34
Wholesale	11,400	48,600	23
Information services	13,200	44,800	29
Education	9,200	114,900	8
Social and management	20,000	77,800	26

Source: Insee (Fauret et al. 2017).

approximately 40 percent were in food services and 30 percent in commercial and retail services.

WHERE THE RICH LIVE NEXT TO THE POOR

While one in five salary-paying jobs is in ZTIs, the majority of economic activities take place outside touristic zones. It is in the rest of Paris that one finds foods and goods with local flavors and most of the regular jobs. However, not all districts fare equally, the employment situation varying according to economic conditions. According to the 2012 Insee survey, the median annual income of Paris was 25,700 euros, higher than most urban areas of France. However, the Parisian income gap was wide: the top 10 percent of the affluent group earned 6.7 times more than the lowest 10 percent of the modest-living group (Caenen et al. 2017).

Geographically, the lower-income population mostly live in the northeastern districts, such as the 18th, 19th, and 20th districts.

Insee data shows that unemployment rates in these districts were 10.9 percent, 16.6 percent, and 15.2 percent respectively in 2014. Higher-income population mostly reside in central, central-west, and southern districts, such as the 7th, 13th, 14th, and 15th districts. Unemployment rates in those districts were 9.5, 12.6, 11.5, and 9.9 percent respectively. Behind these numbers lies an interesting characteristic of Paris—the higher- and lower-income neighborhoods share the same districts and are located close to one another. Some believe that tightly knit socioeconomically different communities are a unique aspect of Paris. Certain contributing factors are believed to be: the low-income population includes a great number of students who tend to reside in the center of the city. Younger immigrants who arrived in the 1980s were better educated and worked in government offices or as liberal professionals. They joined relatives on arrival, but gradually rose to affluence while their residence remained in the same enclaves.

IMMIGRATION AND JOBS

Discussions about employment tend to quickly branch out to immigration issues, which is particularly true in France. Immigrants constitute a large proportion of the French population. In 2012, the French population was 65.2 million, of which 5.7 million were immigrants (Brutel 2016). A tier of the French population live in areas where 10 percent are immigrants; another tier live where 5 percent are immigrants. Immigrants are concentrated in urban centers. This situation dates back to the late 1960s when a large wave of Spanish, Algerian, Portuguese, and African immigrants arrived to work in post-WWII reconstruction projects. Fifty percent of the immigrants were attracted to the Department of Ile-de-France, also known as the Parisian Region. The Parisian Region, in particular, and a few frontier regions nearby, concentrated 40 percent of industry-related and salary-paying jobs. Between the 1980s and late 1990s, Turkish and Asian immigrants constituted a second wave of immigration to the same areas. Despite the economic slowdown after the 1970s, the Parisian Region and vicinity continued to create employment opportunities at an impressive rate. The region offers 32 percent of industrial jobs in France in 2012. Between 2009 and 2013, nearly 1.1 million new immigrants arrived in France, of which approximately 38 percent reside in Paris. Immigrant groups tend to reside in the same urban locations for generations. For example, 56 percent of African immigrants and 65 percent of Chinese immigrants who arrived since the late 1960s still live in Paris today.

An increasingly frequently asked question in France in recent years is whether immigrants take away jobs from the locals. A study published in 2014 funded by the European Union in collaboration with the International Labor Office shows that the immigrants who arrived after 2000 had an employment rate over 10 percent lower than native workers. Two causes were indicated: 1) restrictions are stringent on foreign nationals who intend to work in the public sectors; 2) the large proportion of family-driven migration means that many immigrants are not selected by virtue of educational attainment and skills; neither did most immigrants arrive to fill available job openings. The report indicates that new immigrants from North Africa and sub-Saharan Africa tend to cluster in low-skilled activities across most sectors of employment. On the other hand, many are found to be overqualified for their jobs. Overall, 50 percent of new immigrants were active in the labor market one year after their arrival. Their activity rates nearly equaled those of native workers after nine years in France (Simon et al. 2014). This scenario suggests that Paris has much to do in providing job training to immigrants.

Jing Luo

See also: Green Spaces: Paris, France: Returning to Nature; *Traffic and Transportation:* New York City, United States: The New York Subway

Further Reading

Bidoux, Pierre-Emile, Yann Caenen, and Lauren Trigano. 2017. "Domestic Displacement due to Jobs—In Paris, the Metro Has More Advantage Than the Bicycle" (in French). National Institute of Statistics and Economic Studies. https://www.insee.fr/fr/statistiques/2555642.

Brutel, Chantal. 2016. "Geographical Localization of Immigrants" (in French). National Institute of Statistics and Economic Studies. https://www.insee.fr/fr/statistiques/2121524.

Caenen, Yann, Claire Decondé, Danielle Jabot, and Corinne Martinez, Statistics Bureau of Ile-de-France, Samira Ouardi, Pierre Eloy, Lucas Jouny, Bureau of Social Action, and Children's Health of Paris Municipality. 2017. "A Social Mosaic Unique of Paris" (in French). National Institute of Statistics and Economic Studies. https://www.insee.fr/fr/statistiques/2572750.

Fauret, Camille, Philippe Pottier, Insee île-de-France, Bruno Bouvier, and François Mohrt, Apur. 2017. "In Paris, One in Five Jobs Is in International Tourist Zones" (in French). National Institute of Statistics and Economic Studies. https://www.apur.org/sites/default/files/documents/note_112_zones_internationales_touristiques_paris.pdf.

Lamarche, Pierre, and Maud Romani. 2015. *The Assets of Self-Employed Workers.* National Institute of Statistics and Economic Studies. https://www.insee.fr/en/statistiques/1908049?sommaire=1908062&q=paris%2C%20emploi.

Lebeaupin, François. 2017. "The Seine Valley—Paris, Motor of Economy and Employment" (in French). National Institute of Statistics and Economic Studies. https://www.insee.fr/fr/statistiques/2590417.

Simon, Patrick, and Elsa Steichen. 2014. "Slow Motion: The Labor Market Integration of New Immigrants in France." Migration Policy Institute. https://www.migrationpolicy.org/research/slow-motion-labor-market-integration-new-immigrants-france.

Riyadh, Saudi Arabia: Creating Jobs in the Post–Oil-Boom Era

The Kingdom of Saudi Arabia is the largest Arab economy and the twentieth largest in the world with a 2016 gross domestic product (GDP) of approximately $646 billion. It is also the world's biggest exporter of oil. Saudi Arabia controls the world's second-largest oil reserve and the sixth-largest gas reserve. The World Bank has categorized Saudi Arabia as a high-income economy. The country also ranks very high on the Human Development Index (HDI). It is also the only Arab country to be included in the list of G20 major economies. The Saudi economy lacks any significant services or production sectors (other than natural resource extraction), and is thus considered an economy with limited diversification.

In 2015, the petroleum sector accounted for almost 43 percent of the nation's real GDP, while the private sector, outside of the oil business, contributed 39.5 percent to the real GDP. According to the United Nations Statistics Division, industry (including petroleum) and the services sector contribute almost 90 percent of the nation's gross value added (GVA). GVA provides the value of all goods and services produced in an economy after deducting the cost of raw materials and inputs directly attributable to the production. The share of government in real GDP has remained constant at around 17 percent since 2013. Saudi Arabia is also referred to as the land of the two holy mosques, Al-Masjid al-Haram (in Mecca), and Al-Masjid an-Nabawi (in Medina) in reference to the two holiest places in Islam.

Riyadh is Saudi Arabia's most populous city, and the kingdom's political, administrative, and financial capital. It is also considered one of the wealthiest cities in the world. Riyadh also serves as the capital of the Riyadh province, and belongs to the historical regions of Najd and Al-Yamama. The city is divided into 15 districts, managed by the Municipality of Riyadh and the Development Authority of Riyadh. Riyadh ranks fourth in the list of global cities of the future, in a report prepared by the global management consulting firm A. T. Kearney. According to a KPMG (2016) report, the city had a population of 6.15 million in 2015, of which 58 percent were Saudi nationals. The population is expected to grow to 6.82 million by 2020.

Riyadh is home to numerous government ministries and public-sector headquarters, making the public sector the city's largest employer. A number of banks are headquartered in the city, including Saudi Arabia's central bank, the Saudi Arabian Monetary Authority (SAMA). The city also houses several private-sector companies. Every publicly quoted company is required by law to have an office in the city. Migration of Saudi nationals into Riyadh, particularly from the kingdom's rural areas, is very high. The non-Saudi population of the city largely constitutes expatriate workers from Asia (particularly India and Pakistan), Africa, and a smaller number from Europe and America. Several of these expatriates are employed in the construction sector. Construction-sector jobs are considered exhausting, dangerous, and underpaid, and therefore tend to be shunned by the Saudis.

Jeddah, the second-largest city in Saudi Arabia, is a trading hub primarily due to its proximity to the Red Sea. Jeddah is also a popular resort city, and serves as the gateway to the two holy mosques in Saudi Arabia. Trade and tourism are two major industries in the city. Thus, the economies of both Riyadh and Jeddah are largely dependent on non-oil-based industries.

JOBS AND EMPLOYMENT IN SAUDI ARABIA AND RIYADH

According to the Government of Saudi Arabia's Ministry of Labor and Social Development (2016), agriculture, forestry, fishing, wholesale and retail trade, repair of motor vehicles, construction, mining, and transportation and storage are some of the most important private-sector industries in Saudi Arabia. Education, public administration, and defense are the prominent government sectors.

Despite the growth in the private sector, the public sector is the largest employer of the local Saudi population. According to the Ministry of Labor and Social Development (2016), the skilled local population views public sector jobs as being more prestigious than the private sector. According to James Reeve, deputy chief economist at the Samba Financial Group in London, the average public-sector salaries in Saudi Arabia are about 70 percent higher than the private-sector average (Reuters/Jeddah 2016), which makes public-sector jobs more lucrative for the Saudis. Jamal Khashoggi, a former prominent Saudi journalist, has also argued that Saudis are often hesitant in taking on jobs that are considered "lower class," such as taxi drivers or auto mechanics (Murdock 2016). The Saudi economy is overdependent on expatriate workers for jobs in the private sector. The Saudis have little to no incentive to acquire skills that make them competitive in the private sector.

Riyadh closely mirrors the labor characteristics of Saudi Arabia. The government is the largest employer in the city of Riyadh, and accounts for approximately half of all goods and services produced in the city. More than 90 percent of the government employees are Saudi nationals. The private sector is predominantly staffed by expatriate labor. Services, construction, and trade are the city's significant private-sector employers. Migrants, particularly from Asia and Africa, work primarily in the construction sector. Others work in the hospitality industry or as taxi drivers. The more qualified expats work in Riyadh's diplomatic mission, either at a foreign embassy or a cultural institution. Several multinational corporations such as J.P. Morgan, IBM, Pepsi Cola, and Holiday Inn also have international staff working in Riyadh.

CURRENT PROBLEMS

The growing private sector has attracted large numbers of expatriates to Saudi Arabia. In 2013, for example, there were 7.5 million foreign workers legally working in the nation's oil and services sector. The average population growth rate of expatriates now exceeds that of the local Saudi population. According to the Ministry of Labor and Social Development (2016), the total population in Saudi Arabia has grown at an average rate of 3 percent since 2000. In 2015, the population of Saudi Arabia was just over 31 million. Almost half of the population is under the age of 44. The country thus has an excellent window of demographic opportunity. Unfortunately, the unemployment rate for young people in Saudi Arabia is high at 39 percent (Ministry of Labor and Social Development). The overall unemployment rate for Saudi Arabia (including expatriates) is 5.6 percent, while that for the local Saudis is 11.5 percent. The Saudi economy has created 433,000 jobs on average every year in the last 10 years, but non-Saudis have taken most of these jobs. Based on the current trends, the public sector will need to expand rapidly to reduce the level of unemployment among the Saudi youth.

There are limits on the growth of the public sector, however. The Saudi government relies extensively on oil revenue, and the global crude-oil prices have been falling since 2014. In 2015, the Saudi government had a budget deficit of US$98 billion, and US$79 billion in 2016. The falling oil prices and the budget deficits have prompted the government to revisit the country's economic model, which involves low taxes, heavy subsidies, and an extensive public sector. The government is now looking for ways to actively engage the Saudi population with the private sector, while also trying to diversify and reduce their dependence on oil revenue.

Saudi Arabia also has a very small labor force participation rate for women, despite the women being highly educated. In 2015, 9.1 million of the 13.5 million women in Saudi Arabia were of working age, but their labor force participation rate was only 20.2 percent. The unemployment rate among women also tends to be higher than the unemployment rate for men. According to the Ministry of Labor and Social Development, Saudi women tend to focus on skills that are not in high demand in the private sector. In addition, several traditional workplaces are not designed to accommodate women (e.g., the women in Saudi Arabia are not allowed to have direct contact with men in the workplace), which discourages women from applying for these jobs.

In Riyadh, too, the unemployment rate is high for the Saudi population, particularly among the youth and women. The decrease in oil revenue has caused the Saudi government to shrink the size of the public sector, and also cut back on several large infrastructure projects in the city that had created employment in the construction sector. The government stopped payment to contractors on several such projects, including Riyadh's new metro lines in the last quarter of 2015. The construction projects picked up the momentum again in 2017, as the government starts to clear pending payment to contractors.

PROMINENT POLICY CHANGES

Saudization, the government's *Nitaqat* program, was initiated in 2011 to promote and increase the number of Saudi nationals working in the country's private sector. Under this scheme, firms hiring a larger proportion of Saudi workers are given preferential treatment by the Ministry of Labor in processing work permits for expatriate workers. The scheme has only had limited success. The government now intends to refine the Nitaqat program by considering not just the number of Saudi workers hired by firms, but also other factors, such as women's employment and average pay for Saudis.

The government is expected to spend millions of riyals on technical training and other initiatives to boost the number of its citizens in private-sector jobs. In April 2017, the kingdom announced that foreigners would no longer be allowed to work in malls. The policy is meant to encourage the employment of more Saudis in the retail sector. In May 2017, Riyadh announced that the expats working in the public sector would be replaced with Saudi nationals over the next three years.

According to the Ministry of Labor and Social Development (2016), as part of the country's vision for 2030 for increased economic diversification, the government is taking steps to increase religious tourism—the annual hajj pilgrimage—to the Saudi Arabian city of Mecca. According to Mecca's Chamber of Commerce and Industry, the pilgrims are expected to spend anywhere between US$5.3 and 6.7 billion this year.

The G20 Economies

The "Group of Twenty (G20)" refers to the world's 20 leading industrialized and emerging economies. As a whole, the group represents 85 percent of the global GDP and two-thirds of the world's population. G20 was founded in 1999 in Berlin, Germany, aiming to "strengthen the resilience of the global financial system." Member countries include Argentina, Australia, Brazil, Canada, China, France, Germany, India, Indonesia, Italy, Japan, Mexico, Russia, Saudi Arabia, South Korea, Turkey, United Kingdom, United States of America, South Africa, and the European Union represented by the European Commission. G20 summits are held once a year. However, leaders may meet more frequently under the circumstances of global crisis. G20 summits are chaired by representatives of member countries on an annual rotation basis. China hosted the 2016 summit; Germany and Argentina held the presidency in 2017 and 2018 respectively. The hosting party has the opportunity to set the agenda and lead the discussions. The G20 summit of 2017 was held in Hamburg, Germany. The forum was dominated by North Korea's nuclear weapons test, the withdrawal of the United States from the Paris climate agreement, and the meeting between Mr. Trump and Mr. Putin. G20 summits tend to attract massive protests and, as a result, typically incur large bills on security spending.

Following the Chinese model, where "special economic zones" (SEZ) have made significant contributions to China's economic success, the Saudi government is looking at converting the King Abdullah financial district in Riyadh to a special zone with competitive regulations and procedures, visa exemptions, and better access to the King Khalid International Airport.

CHALLENGES FOR THE FUTURE

Creating jobs is considered one of the toughest challenges for Saud Arabia. Declining oil prices have caused the economy to slow down and for the government to shrink its payroll. According to a 2015 report by the McKinsey Global Institute, the working-age population in Saudi Arabia is expected to increase significantly by 2030, and the government will need to create three times as many opportunities (either through the public sector or through an expansion of the private sector), as it has in the past; otherwise the unemployment numbers for the Saudis could go as high as 22 percent by 2030.

Nakul Kumar

See also: Employment and Jobs: Mumbai, India: Exploring Employment Solutions in Temporary Jobs

Further Reading

Agence France-Presse. 2017. "As Oil Prices Fall, Saudi Arabia Taps Its White Gold—Religious Tourism." http://www.ndtv.com/world-news/as-oil-prices-fall-saudi-arabia-taps-its-white-gold-religious-tourism-1745308.

Al-Kibsi, Gassan. 2015. "Moving Saudi Arabia's Economy beyond Oil." McKinsey Global Institute, December. http://www.mckinsey.com/global-themes/employment-and-growth/moving-saudi-arabias-economy-beyond-oil.

Business Times. 2017. "Saudi Unemployment Rate Climbs to 12.7%." July 31. http://www.businesstimes.com.sg/government-economy/saudi-unemployment-rate-climbs-to-127.

Dudley, Dominic. 2016. "Rising Unemployment Suggests That Saudi Government Reforms Are Failing." *Forbes*, December 8. https://www.forbes.com/sites/dominicdudley/2016/12/08/saudi-unemployment/#319273982022.

Ernst & Young. 2016. "Saudi Arabia Delays Implementation of Third Phase of Nitaqat 'Saudization' Program." *HR and Tax Alert*, July. https://www.ey.com/gl/en/services/people-advisory-services/hc-alert--saudi-arabia-delays-implementation-of-third-phase-of-nitaqat--saudization--program.

Feteha, Ahmed, and Zainab Fattah. 2016. "Main Features of Saudi Arabia 2017 Budget, 2016 Performance." Bloomberg, December 23. https://www.bloomberg.com/news/articles/2016-12-22/main-features-of-saudi-arabia-s-2017-budget-2016-performance.

G20 Official Website. https://g20.org/en/.

KPMG Real Estate Services. 2016. *Riyadh Real Estate Market Overview*. KPMG International, June. https://home.kpmg.com/content/dam/kpmg/sa/pdf/2016/08/Riyadh%20Market%20Study%20Report%202015.pdf.

McDowall, Angus. 2016. "Focus on Jobs at Heart of Saudi Reforms." Reuters, June 7. http://www.reuters.com/article/us-saudi-plan-employment/focus-on-jobs-at-heart-of-saudi-reforms-idUSKCN0YT1B5.

Murdock, Heather. 2016. "Saudi Arabia Seeks to Shed Dependence on Foreign Labor." *VOA News*, January 25. https://www.voanews.com/a/saudi-arabia-seeks-to-shed-dependency-on-foreign-labor/3162055.html.

Nereim, Vivian. 2016. "Saudi Arabia's Vision for Future Looks Dim to Jobless Growth." Bloomberg, November 22. https://www.bloomberg.com/news/articles/2016-11-22/saudi-arabia-s-vision-for-the-future-looks-dim-to-jobless-youth.

Paul, Katie, and Andrew Torchia. 2017. "Riyadh's New Financial Hub Struggles with Ownership Uncertainty." Reuters, April 25. http://www.reuters.com/article/us-saudi-economy-finance/riyadhs-new-financial-hub-struggles-with-ownership-uncertainty-idUSKBN17R1OV.

Reuters/Jeddah. 2016. "Focus on Jobs at Heart of Reform Plan in Saudi." *Gulf Times.* June 7. https://www.gulf-times.com/story/497229/Focus-on-jobs-at-heart-of-reform-plan-in-Saudi.

Saudi Arabia Labor Market Report. 2016. Ministry of Labor and Social Development, Kingdom of Saudi Arabia, July.

San Juan, Puerto Rico, United States: A Stronger Local Government Is Key to Job Creation

San Juan, the capital of Puerto Rico, is situated on the Caribbean island's Atlantic coast. The island has been a U.S. territory since 1898, and a U.S. Commonwealth since 1952. Puerto Rico has been torn by deep ideological rifts, stemming from three distinct future political scenarios: the status quo (commonwealth), statehood in the United States, or independent state. These antecedents shape the current economic crisis in Puerto Rico, which has led to mass unemployment and a poverty rate twice that of the U.S. mainland's poorest state, Mississippi (Robles 2017b). As of 2015, Puerto Rico is $72 billion in debt after a 10-year recession. As a result, it increased taxes from 7 percent in 2010 to 11.5 percent in 2016 to repay debt (Walsh and Moyer, 2016; Beyer, 2015). Due to this economic crisis, Puerto Rico is currently experiencing an exodus, with approximately 230 islanders emigrating to the U.S. mainland daily (Krogstad, 2015). The following paragraphs provide a synthesis of the historical and political context that explains how and why Puerto Rico's economy and employment are at an all-time low.

Puerto Rico is a key landmark for the colonization of the Americas. In his second voyage, Christopher Columbus (1451–1506) arrived in Puerto Rico, naming the island San Juan Bautista, after John the Baptist. The island quickly became known as Puerto Rico, or "rich port," due to its rich resources in gold, and the capital city became known as San Juan. In 1897, Spain granted Puerto Rico autonomy after 400 years of colonial rule, which became one of the concessions that led to the end of the Spanish-American War (1898). Subsequently, in March 1898, Puerto Rico held elections, and began to function as an independent nation on July 17, 1898. Eight days later, on July 25, U.S. Commanding Army General Nelson A. Miles (1839–1925) led 16,000 troops to invade Puerto Rico, ending its brief independence. As a result, it became a U.S. territory, substituting Spanish colonial rule with U.S. oversight, which was not intended as permanent. These events created three different possibilities for Puerto Rico's governance: 1) remain a U.S. commonwealth, 2) obtain U.S. statehood (i.e., as the 51st state), 3) become an independent nation.

First, as a U.S. commonwealth, Puerto Rico is an organized yet unincorporated and dependent territory. Today there are two islands with commonwealth status, Puerto Rico and the Northern Mariana Islands. Under commonwealth status, Puerto Rico has its own elected state and local government (i.e., governor of Puerto Rico, mayor of San Juan), but depends on U.S. government oversight in policy creation, implementation, federal fund distribution, spending, and trade.

Second, if Puerto Rico gains statehood in the United States, it will have the same state governance liberties as all 50 states, such as direct decision-making in the use of federal and state funds. Statehood would grant Puerto Ricans full citizenship, including the right to vote in U.S. presidential elections and obtain representation with voting participation in the U.S. Congress, which they currently lack. In the last Puerto Rican election (2017), the people held a vote for U.S. statehood. Although the majority voted in favor of it, only 20 percent of the population showed up to the polls due to a mass voting boycott, demonstrating no allegiance to current governance and U.S. oversight (France-Presse 2017). As a result, Puerto Ricans view the U.S. statehood vote as merely symbolic, since U.S. statehood must be initiated and facilitated by the U.S. Congress (Newkirk 2017).

Third, the independence movement advocates for Puerto Rico's independence as a nation free from colonization and oversight from colonists, as it was in 1898 (Hinojosa and Bishop 2017; Fernandez 2012). The independence movement is experiencing a reemergence as a result of student and professor-led strikes, which extend beyond university funding to include basic public services for all (Morales 2017). Moreover, President Obama's executive pardon for Oscar Lopez Rivera (1943–), the world's longest-held political prisoner, activist, and advocate for Puerto Rican independence, has renewed interest in the movement. From 1974 to 1983, Lopez Rivera was part of a militant group that fought for independence, known as FALN (Fuerzas Armadas de Liberación Nacional; English translation: "Armed Forces of National Liberation") (Kennedy 2017; Abad 2012). The group claimed responsibility for 70 bombings in Washington, D.C., New York, and Chicago, resulting in property damage, injuries, and five deaths (Hinojosa and Bishop 2017). Although Lopez Rivera was not charged in connection with the bombings, and the FBI had no physical evidence to prove he participated in these acts, he was convicted of conspiracy against the United States due to his role in FALN (Hinojosa and Bishop 2017; Abad 2012). Independence sympathizers claim Lopez Rivera's sentence was unjust, arguing he was imprisoned for "simply for opposing the United States government" (Hinojosa and Bishop 2017). In contrast, Lopez Rivera's opponents label him "an unrepentant terrorist" (Hinojosa and Bishop 2017).

U.S. federal policies have shaped Puerto Rico's economy and employment, essentially weakening its governance and creating a dependent relationship between the island and the U.S. government. For example, the Jones Act of 1917 requires Puerto Rico to purchase goods from American-made cargo ships with an American crew, which limits business choices (Bury 2015). In an interview with the U.S. Public Broadcasting Service, a Puerto Rican resident described the impact of the Jones Act as

> limiting. I try buying from different counties, but things are so expensive that I then actually have to go through U.S. distributors to be able to get products that are

affordable for the economy here. So it is very difficult. I don't know enough of the politics to know why it hasn't changed, since it's such an old law. And most of the states that are affected by that law are against it. But for us, being an island, it's even worse, because everything has to go through the United States, even the things that we produce here for U.S.-owned businesses or industries. Usually they're made here and bottled in the United States, and we have to ship them back and actually buy them from the states, not from us. (Bury 2015)

Second, Operation Bootstrap, a federal campaign to modernize Puerto Rico, led to a series of economic and development projects during the 1950s. In general, Operation Bootstrap had two main goals: to alleviate the island's unemployment and control overpopulation (Fernandez 2012). As a result, the campaign drove the transition of Puerto Rico's economy from agricultural to industrial. Operation Bootstrap became an economic model for developing countries as it succeeded in bringing foreign investment to the island through the establishment of manufacturing companies, offering tax cuts and duty-free export to the U.S. mainland. Consequently, Operation Bootstrap affected farmers as agricultural labor declined, forcing many to work in industrial labor or migrate to work in the United States (Fernandez 2012). As a result, Puerto Rico's farmers, most of whom were closely aligned with the independence movement, were dispersed, which critics view as a U.S. government tactic to stifle the growth of the movement (Denis 2015). Since Puerto Ricans are U.S. citizens, they have the freedom to travel to the United States. However, like immigrants from foreign countries, Puerto Ricans face challenges adapting to American society as they encounter racial, ethnic, and linguistic discrimination because most speak Spanish. Moreover, Puerto Rico's land and population have served as a U.S. military and pharmaceutical testing ground. For example, the U.S. military tested bombs in Puerto Rico for over 60 years (Denis 2015).

During this modernization period, the American pharmaceutical industry conducted birth control experiments on Puerto Rican women, forcibly sterilizing approximately a third of the women between 1950 and the 1970s (Davis 2003). This was institutionalized through the implementation of Law 116: Sterilization Law from 1937 to 1960, also known as "La Operacion." Law 116 targeted poor and unemployed Puerto Rican women through coercive strategies such as door-to-door visits by health workers, misinformation, and providing no alternative methods of birth control. In 1976, the U.S. Department of Health, Education, and Welfare reported that over 37 percent of women of childbearing age in Puerto Rico had been sterilized. The majority were in their twenties. Critics of Law 116 argue that the purpose of the sterilization program was not only for pharmaceutical experimentation, but also to test the use of an institutionalized program to address overpopulation, and in turn, mitigate predicted unemployment trends. Latin American and gender studies scholars critique this institutional approach to population health due to the coercive strategies targeting poor women on the island (Briggs 1998; Presser 1969). While the 1960s technological boom paved the way for women's sexual liberation, reproductive freedom was dealt with as an issue for white women. By contrast, women of color—in this case, poor Puerto Rican women—had their reproductive freedom obstructed to reduce overpopulation. Similarly, poor Mexican women in Los Angeles, California, underwent federally funded forced sterilization and its coercive strategies in the 1970s, a period of large poor and working-class Mexican migration to the U.S. West region (Stern 2005).

Today, Puerto Rico's economy is mainly driven by manufacturing (such as pharmaceuticals, petrochemicals, and electronics), followed by the service industry (finance, real estate, tourism). In recent years, the island has become a prime destination for conferences, with a modern convention center district overlooking the Port of San Juan. As of April 2017, Puerto Rico's unemployment rate was 11.5 percent and 7.2 percent in San Juan compared to 4.4 percent in the U.S. mainland (Bureau of Labor Statistics 2017). Due to high unemployment rates and a lack of economic opportunities for the working class and middle class, a Puerto Rican exodus to the United States has emerged since the recession in 2008. Simultaneously, foreign investors are acquiring land in urban centers—particularly, San Juan—as the city elevates its status as a trending convention destination. Although San Juan's real estate industry is currently booming, its tourism has declined in the wake of renewed U.S. economic interests in Cuba and relaxing certain travel restrictions, which allow more U.S. citizens to travel to the previously restricted nation. In an interesting historical twist, San Juan experienced high levels of tourism in the years after the Cuban Revolution in 1959 as hostility developed between Cuba and the United States (Francis 2015).

In recent decades, the employment crisis in San Juan has become so dire that it has escalated into violent conflict among Puerto Ricans. Today, this crisis is reflected

Teachers in San Juan, Puerto Rico, strike against the government's plan to privatize public education, March 19, 2018. Also motivating the strike is anxiety over the shortage of job opportunities and cuts to education funding. (Ricardo Arduengo/AFP/Getty Images)

in everyday life in San Juan among taxi drivers and on-demand transportation services, such as Uber. On-demand drivers report aggravated assault and battery, and damage to vehicle property by taxi drivers, who attack them for encroaching on their "turf." While the conflict between on-demand ride services and taxis exists in many cities across the world, Puerto Rico's employment crisis has prompted escalation to violence (Victorian 2016; Telesurtv 2016).

As a result of the island's employment crisis, the trend in Puerto Rican emigration shifted from the U.S. mainland to nearby Caribbean islands, mainly the Dominican Republic. In particular, Puerto Rican middle-aged men seek business visas in the Dominican Republic requesting permission to work in the tourism industry (Associated Press 2016). Concurrently, Dominican Republic's poorest are immigrating to Puerto Rico, creating an immigrant working class competing for labor with its unemployed citizens. Like Puerto Rico, the Dominican Republic is situated in the Caribbean. Approximately 80 miles east of Puerto Rico, Santo Domingo, the capital of the Dominican Republic, has also become a popular tourist destination for Americans, emerging as a tourist economy powerhouse in the Latin American and Caribbean region (Reichard 2016).

The Puerto Rican government recently implemented policies to mitigate the economic and employment crisis. On June 29, 2016, the Puerto Rico Oversight, Management, and Economic Stability Act (PROMESA, an acronym that translates to "promise") was approved by the U.S. Senate and signed into law by President Obama a day before the island defaulted on its payments. PROMESA provides more U.S. federal oversight of the island, establishing a management committee that supervises fiscal spending in Puerto Rico with the goal of providing cost-effective public services to pay debts. However, the effects of PROMESA are negatively impacting the working class and students on the island. For example, under PROMESA, the management committee has imposed austerity measures, cutting pensions, minimum wage, university funding, and closing down schools and hospitals (Martin, 2016; Reuters, 2016; Rosario, 2017). As a result, vital public services have been reduced, adding to the factors pushing Puerto Ricans to leave the island at an exponential rate. College students and activists reacted to PROMESA and the management committee's austerity measures with mass protests and civil disobedience in San Juan. This resulted in a resistance movement led by students and professors at the island's largest public educational institution, the University of Puerto Rico, effectively shutting down the university for several months (Robles 2017; Martin 2017; Morales 2017).

As Puerto Rico's financial and employment crisis continues, the future of its population on the island is uncertain, especially under the accelerated condominium and hotel development in San Juan. Puerto Rico is experiencing population loss as a result of the largest outmigration in more than 50 years. Between 2010 and 2015, San Juan's population declined by 40,000 people (–10 percent) (Krogstad 2016). The island's population declined by 9 percent between 2000 and 2015. The decline rate was 2 percent in 2000–2010, but accelerated to 7 percent between 2010 and 2015.

Today, Puerto Rico's future remains uncertain as the status quo commonwealth ideology has demonstrated that the island needs significant reform. For example, job opportunities are increasingly only available to Puerto Ricans with high proficiency in English, whereas only 20 percent of the island has proficiency (Johnson 2012). English-language proficiency is often linked to high socioeconomic status and access to private American schools on the island, as well as access to cable TV, Internet, and other educational resources. As schools shut down and university budgets are cut, Puerto Rico's youth are most impacted as these measures impede their social and economic mobility on the island. However, they have recently demonstrated their collective political power as they've led the resistance against U.S. oversight and austerity measures. The future of Puerto Rico will be decided by today's youth, who are socially and politically engaged.

Marisol Becerra, Ashlee L. Dauphinais Civitello, and Kerry Ard

See also: Employment and Jobs: Lagos, Nigeria: Government Reform Is Key to Job Creation; Mumbai, India: Exploring Employment Solutions in Temporary Jobs

Further Reading

Abad, E. G. 2012. *Is There Potential for Eden on Division Street: Anti-Colonial Discourse, Migration, and the God of Nationalism.* Dissertation, Washington State University.

Agence France-Presse. 2017. "Puerto Ricans Voted for Statehood. But Only about 20 Percent Showed Up." *Public Radio International*, June 12. https://www.pri.org/stories/2017-06-12/puerto-ricans-voted-statehood-only-about-20-percent-showed.

Associated Press. 2016. "Dominican Economy Lures Puerto Ricans in Crisis." *Daily Mail.* January 25. https://www.dailymail.co.uk/wires/ap/article-3415856/Dominican-economy-lures-Puerto-Ricans-crisis.html.

Beyer, Scott. 2015. "Puerto Rico, at 11.5%, Has America's Highest Sales Tax." *Forbes*, August 17. https://www.forbes.com/sites/scottbeyer/2015/08/17/puerto-rico-at-11-5-has-americas-highest-sales-tax/#2bb51e9a308f.

Briggs, L. 1998. "Discourses of 'Forced Sterilization' in Puerto Rico: The Problem with the Speaking Subaltern." *Differences: A Journal of Feminist Cultural Studies* 10, 2: 30–33.

Bureau of Labor Statistics. 2017. *Economy at a Glance: Puerto Rico.* Washington, DC: Bureau of Labor Statistics. https://www.bls.gov/eag/eag.pr.htm.

Bury, Chris. 2015. "Is This 1917 Law Suffocating Puerto Rico's Economy?" Making Sen$e. *PBS News Hour*, August 13. http://www.pbs.org/newshour/making-sense/jones-act-holding-puerto-rico-back-debt-crisis/.

Davis, A. 2003. "Racism, Birth Control and Reproductive Rights." In Reina Lewis and Sara Mills, eds. *Feminist Postcolonial Theory—A Reader.* New York: Routledge, 353–67.

Denis, N. 2015. *War against All Puerto Ricans: Revolution and Terror in America's Colony.* Reprint ed. New York: Nation Books.

"Dominican Economy Lures Puerto Ricans in Crisis." 2016. *Daily Mail*, January 25. http://www.dailymail.co.uk/wires/ap/article-3415856/Dominican-economy-lures-Puerto-Ricans-crisis.html.

Fernandez, L. 2012. *Brown in the Windy City: Mexicans and Puerto Ricans in Postwar Chicago.* Chicago: University of Chicago Press.

Francis, David. 2015. "Cuba's New Tourism Industry Is Potentially Bad News for the Rest of the Caribbean." *Foreign Policy.* July 7. http://foreignpolicy.com/2015/07/07/cubas-new-tourism-industry-is-potentially-bad-news-for-the-rest-of-the-caribbean/.

Gonzalez, Juan. 2000. *Harvest of Empire: A History of Latinos in America.* New York: Penguin Group.

Hinojosa, Maria, and Marlon Bishop. 2017. "Pardon Sought for Prisoner Who Fought for Puerto Rican Independence." *National Public Radio*, January 15. http://www.npr.org/2017/01/15/509914267/pardon-sought-for-prisoner-who-fought-for-puerto-rican-independence.

Johnson. 2012. "Hablen ingles . . . por favor? Language in Puerto Rico." *Economist*, November 12. https://www.economist.com/blogs/johnson/2012/11/language-puerto-rico.

Kennedy, Merrit. 2017. "Puerto Rican Nationalist Oscar Lopez Rivera Is Released." *National Public Radio*, May 17. http://www.npr.org/sections/thetwo-way/2017/05/17/528787071/puerto-rican-nationalist-oscar-l-pez-rivera-is-released.

Krogstad, Jens Manuel. 2015. "Puerto Ricans Leave in Record Numbers from U.S. Mainland." Fact Tank: News in the Numbers. *Pew Research Center,* October 14. http://www.pewresearch.org/fact-tank/2015/10/14/puerto-ricans-leave-in-record-numbers-for-mainland-u-s/.

Krogstad, Jens Manuel. 2016. "Historic Population Losses Continue across Puerto Rico." *Pew Research Center*, March 24. http://www.pewresearch.org/fact-tank/2016/03/24/historic-population-losses-continue-across-puerto-rico/.

Martin, Michel. 2016. "Severe Budget Cuts Loom as Puerto Rico's Debt Crisis Continues." *National Public Radio,* December 17. http://www.npr.org/2016/12/17/505996778/severe-budget-cuts-loom-as-puerto-ricos-debt-crisis-continues.

Martin, Michel. 2017. "Students at Puerto Rico's Largest University Continue Strike Amid Shutdown." *National Public Radio*, May 20. http://www.npr.org/2017/05/20/529309138/students-at-puerto-ricos-largest-university-continue-strike-amid-shutdown.

Morales, Ed. 2017. "Students Are Now Leading the Resistance to Austerity in Puerto Rico." *Nation*, April 27. https://www.thenation.com/article/students-are-now-leading-the-resistance-to-austerity-in-puerto-rico/.

Newkirk, Vann R., II. 2017. "Puerto Rico's Plebiscite to Nowhere: The Territory's Recent Vote in Favor of Statehood Faces Long Odds in Congress." *Atlantic*, June 13. https://www.theatlantic.com/politics/archive/2017/06/puerto-rico-statehood-plebiscite-congress/530136/.

Presser, H. 1969. "The Role of Sterilization in Controlling Puerto Rican Fertility." *Population Studies* 23, 3: 343–61. doi:10.2307/2172875.

Reichard, Raquel. 2016. "Puerto Ricans Flee to the Dominican Republic to Escape Island's Economic Crisis." *Fox News*. January 26. https://www.foxnews.com/world/puerto-ricans-flee-to-dominican-republic-to-escape-u-s-territorys-economic-crisis.

Reuters. 2016. "The U.S. House Just Passed a Puerto Rico Debt Relief Bill." *Fortune,* June 10. http://fortune.com/2016/06/10/house-puerto-rico-debt-relief-bill/.

Robles, Frances. 2017a. "23% of Puerto Ricans Vote in Referendum, 97% of Them for Statehood." *New York Times,* June 11. https://www.nytimes.com/2017/06/11/us/puerto-ricans-vote-on-the-question-of-statehood.html.

Robles, Frances. 2017b. "Puerto Rico's University Is Paralyzed by Protests and Facing Huge Cuts." *New York Times*, May 25. https://www.nytimes.com/2017/05/25/us/puerto-ricos-university-is-paralyzed-by-protests-and-facing-huge-cuts.html.

Rosario, Richy. 2017. "Puerto Rico's Economic Crisis Forces School Closings on the Island." *VIBE*, May 10. https://www.vibe.com/2017/05/puerto-rico-economic-crisis-schools-shut-down/.

Stern, A. M. 2005. "Sterilized in the Name of Public Health: Race, Immigration, and Reproductive Control in Modern California." *American Journal of Public Health* 95, 7: 1128–38. doi:10.2105/AJPH.2004.041608.

Telesurtv. 2016. "Uber's Arrival in Puerto Rico Met with Protests." Telesurtv, July 13. http://www.telesurtv.net/english/news/Ubers-Arrival-in-Puerto-Rico-Met-With-Protests-20160713-0035.html.

Victorian, Brande. 2016. "6 Taxi Drivers Barricaded My Uber in Puerto Rico and Refused to Let Me Use the Cab Service." *Madame Noire*, August 29. http://madamenoire.com/714835/uber-in-puerto-rico/.

Walsh, Mary Williams, and Liz Moyer. 2016. "How Puerto Rico Debt Is Grappling with a Debt Crisis." *New York Times,* July 1. https://www.nytimes.com/interactive/2016/business/dealbook/puerto-rico-debt-crisis-explained.html.

Seattle, United States: Have Job, Going Homeless

Can a city have too many good jobs? The answer may be yes when the urban area (Seattle and several other Puget Sound-area communities) has become a high-tech mecca with the explosive development of Amazon.com, Microsoft, and many other lesser-known names, and the price of an average home has surpassed $1 million in some areas of the city. The result has been a boom not only in employment, but in homelessness. The number of people living outdoors (in tents, under bridges, and even in sewers) has been rising 10 percent a year. Thus, the flip side of this employment boom with its three-figure salaries and stock options has been ranks of homeless tents, people living in cars, and a few children having their eyes gouged out by rats. This is not a good time to be without a job (and a well-paying one at that) in Seattle. Many people who work for minimum wage (even at $15 an hour, the new Seattle-area standard) can't afford anything but the most basic shelter.

How much does one need to get paid these days to afford an average house in Seattle and its suburbs? Assuming a 4 percent mortgage rate for 30 years, the average as of this writing, and a requirement that the payment consume no more than a third of income, a $1 million loan would require $40,000 in interest per year on the first payment, slowly falling as it was paid off. This figure would require an annual salary of about $120,000. The average household income in Seattle in 2016 was a bit more than half of that (about $67,000). What this means is that perhaps two-thirds of people can't afford an average house in a decent neighborhood. This situation is similar in Vancouver, British Columbia, and in California's largest urban areas.

In 2014, Seattle became the fastest-growing city in the United States, in terms of population. Tim Egan, a native of the city (and a *New York Times* columnist), observed in 2016:

> Job growth [in Seattle] is steroidal. The big urban carnivore is Amazon.com, with its global headquarters now gobbling up enough office space in the formerly funky South Lake Union district to fill almost two skyscrapers the size of the city's tallest building, the 76-story Columbia Center. Twice that amount is in the pipeline, as Amazon seeks to become the world's largest retailer. Google just announced grand plans for the same neighborhood. A metro area of 3.5 million is adding 60,000 people a year . . . a forest of construction cranes blocks views of the snowcapped Olympic mountains to the west of the clangorous technopolis. (Egan 2016)

SPRAWLING HOMELESS CAMPS

Income inequity has risen sharply as well, along with homelessness. As the price of an average single-family house on Beacon Hill, once an inner-city neighborhood southeast of downtown Seattle, rose 45 percent during 2015, a rambling, three-mile-long homeless camp that came to be called The Jungle developed under the overpasses of Interstate 5 between Beacon Hill and downtown.

The Jungle became home to several hundred people by 2016, with two people killed there in a shooting during January of that year. The Jungle sprawled over 150 acres (about the area of a golf course), and housed as many as 400 people at a time, many of whom had problems with mental health, addiction, poverty, and criminal backgrounds. "Despite their scars and lookouts they now post," wrote Bob Young and Vernal Coleman in the *Seattle Times* (2016), many who lived in the Jungle "described it as the place they feel most comfortable. . . . Inside the grim world of The Jungle, we spent a few days . . . talking with its residents and those working to clear them out. We found a subsection of the camp called The Caves. We met the survivors of a fatal shooting there earlier this year. And we heard a tale of a man who lost an eye—to an eyeball-eating rat."

During October 2016, the city of Seattle closed The Jungle, describing it as a humanitarian disaster in the midst of one of the United States' most affluent cities. Its 357 remaining residents were moved to homeless shelters.

In the meantime, utility workers in Federal Way, a suburb south of Seattle, found evidence of children living in city sewers. The *Washington Post* reported:

> Meter readers with Lakehaven Utility District first noticed [a] sewer cover left ajar. They pushed it shut. . . . It proved to be a stubborn grate. Later in the day—twice—workers found the manhole open again. . . . At the bottom of the 14-foot descent was a cache of kids' items, miscellany that belonged in a treehouse or rec room: a pair of binoculars, snacks and toys, including a pistol for shooting foam darts. They discovered clothes, too, as well as a makeshift bed made out of plywood. (Guarino 2016)

This is not Seattle's first experience with urban homelessness. Seattle was home to the first Skid Row—then Skid Road, because logs had been slid to the waterfront from nearby hills (one of which was Beacon Hill), not because people in the camp had "hit the skids." The same area later became the United States' first and most notable "Hooverville," a homeless encampment (near the trendy tourist district that is now Pioneer Square) during the Great Depression.

HOUSING, DEVELOPMENT, AND ECONOMIC JUSTICE

Ed Murray, who was Seattle's mayor in 2016, called homelessness a human tragedy seldom seen in the history of the city. At the same time, median incomes in Seattle jumped $10,000 a year in 2016. The high-tech boom "has driven up rents and home prices, fueling a homeless crisis so severe that last fall [2015], the mayor declared a state of emergency," according to a report in the *New York Times* (Johnson 2016, A-14).

All over the city, solutions were being sought to bridge the gap between average incomes and soaring housing costs. Amazon has added 20,000 new jobs in Seattle over a few years, and Google is planning to add 4,000 along with other business growth. Amazon.com by 2017 occupied a large corporate campus south of downtown, from which the *Seattle Times* said that the company "cuts an astoundingly low profile in the civic life of its hometown" (Wamsley 2017). At first Amazon.com responded to criticism of its role in high housing prices by converting an old 200-bed motel near its South Lake Union campus, once a Travelodge, to a homeless shelter. In 2017, the company put several million dollars into a six-floor shelter for families lacking housing.

Amazon's new building mixed high-tech office space with housing for 65 previously homeless families (about 200 people), whose quarters (named "Mary's Place") occupy about 47,000 square feet, half of the structure. "Doing things like [the homeless shelter] may be in its enlightened self-interest, right on site for the world to see," Alan Durning, executive director of Sightline Institute, a nonprofit public policy research organization focused on the Pacific Northwest, told National Public Radio (Wamsley 2017).

EL CENTRO DE LA RAZA'S PLAZA ROBERTO MAESTAS

El Centro de la Raza, a Seattle social service center, built Plaza Roberto Maestas, a $43 million Latin American-style living area with 112 low- and moderate-income residential units, housing 350 people, as well as retail and park spaces at the south end of the building, adjacent to a new light-rail transit station. (Maestas, El Centro's principal founder in 1972, died in 2010.) The apartments were built to house families, whereas much of Seattle's new housing was single-person studio units. In addition to affordable housing, the plaza includes open space for a farmer's market and other public gatherings, to coordinate housing and retail activity with El Centro de la Raza's many social programs.

"So many of our people are being pushed out into the county because rents are more affordable there, so this is a wonderful opportunity with this project," El Centro de la Raza Executive Director Estela Ortega said. "A lot of the units that were developed in the city were studio and one bedroom apartments, and they were not family units" (Rozier 2016). Ortega said that demand was overwhelming when applications were sought for the apartments: "We had anywhere between 900 and 1,000 people who were in the hallway waiting for a chance to turn their applications in" (Rozier 2016).

The apartments are meant for families making $24,000 to $49,000 per year, which are 30 and 60 percent Seattle's average median income for a year. The apartments are located within easy access of El Centro de la Raza and the 44 social service programs it provides. They are also across the street from a major light-rail station that gives people without cars access to metropolitan services. They also offer shops and a 12,900-square-foot gathering space.

When El Centro de la Raza was established in 1972, it was surrounded by a modest neighborhood of wood-frame homes occupied by middle-class families, a mixture mainly of several Asian, Latino, and European American nationalities, bordered on the north by the Central Area, with its family-occupied frame homes, occupied

> ### *Displaced by the Technology Boom*
>
> Housing prices in the Seattle area have risen so quickly that most people without three-figure annual salaries cannot afford them. The city has become an astoundingly expensive place in which to live, with the cost of the average single-family house hitting $800,000 in 2018, up $60,000 in one year, having doubled in five. The trend is similar along the West Coast, in Vancouver, B.C., Portland, Oregon, the San Francisco Bay Area (including Silicon Valley), Los Angeles, and San Diego, all places where a surge of prosperity related to new technology has caused housing prices to rise.
>
> Seattle has been debating a "head tax" that will assess high-technology companies a tax for each employee, with proceeds going to provide services for the homeless. As many people have prospered, the number of people living in their cars also has been increasing to the point where some parking lots in Seattle have become informal homeless shelters. School bus drivers in the Puget Sound urban area reported dropping children at tents and cars with no fixed addresses. The University of Washington opened a homeless encampment on campus in 2016, and the city created a 24-hour service center for homeless people modeled on San Francisco's Navigation Center, with showers, restrooms, laundry machines, lockers, and dining facilities.

mainly by African Americans. Both areas are adjacent to downtown Seattle, and were known as inner-city neighborhoods. At that time, these two neighborhoods offered some of the least expensive housing in the city.

Forty-five years later, the city had become a vibrant high-tech boomtown, with Microsoft, Amazon.com, and many other affiliated businesses attracting well-paid talent. The city has become one of the fastest-growing urban areas in the United States, and inner-city living has become chic, with residential spires rising downtown and ranks of condominiums marching along the hills in and near the Central Area and Beacon Hill.

One City of Seattle projection forecast that by 2020, the Central Area, once the heart of Seattle's black community, would be less than 10 percent black. The high-tech boom was accelerating month by month, pricing many inner-city residents out of their own homes. In one graphic illustration of the boom, a crumbling house was sold for about $400,000, torn down, and replaced by a new one for $1.2 million.

By the end of 2017, housing prices were rising more quickly than ever in Seattle and surrounding King County, with the average single-family house nearing $1 million in several areas, an increase of about 13 to 15 percent in one year—or as much (about $140,000) as an entire house in many Midwestern cities, such as Omaha. An annual salary of about $150,000 was required to close a mortgage on a modest home. One-bedroom condos in King County were averaging $400,000 to $500,000. At the same time, the number of homeless people in Seattle, according to the U.S. Department of Housing and Urban Development, had surpassed all other U.S. cities except New York and Los Angeles. The price of a share of Amazon.com stock had surpassed $1,160, up from about $20 in two decades.

Bruce E. Johansen

See also: Employment and Jobs: Mumbai, India: Exploring Employment Solutions in Temporary Jobs

Further Reading

Egan, Tim. 2016. "Dude, Where's My City." *New York Times*, April 1. http://www.nytimes.com/2016/04/01/opinion/dude-wheres-my-city.html.

Guarino, Ben. 2016. "'This Could Have Been Life and Death': Utility Workers Find Signs Children Lived in Sewers Near Seattle." *Washington Post*, August 30. https://www.washingtonpost.com/news/morning-mix/wp/2016/08/30/this-could-have-been-life-and-death-utility-workers-find-signs-children-lived-in-sewers-near-seattle/.

Johnson, Kirk. 2016. "In Seattle, Amazon Delivers Something New." *New York Times*, April 22, pA-14.

Ortega, Estela, and Alejandro Bautista. 2011. Audio Interview. StoryCorps. Tacoma, WA. September 8. Copy in El Centro de la Raza files.

Rozier, Alex. 2016. "Seattle Affordable Housing Project Focuses on Families." KING TV News Seattle, March 30. http://www.king5.com/news/local/seattle/new-affordable-housing-project-focused-on-families/109926001.

Wamsley, Laurel. 2017. "New Amazon Building in Seattle Will Include a Homeless Shelter." National Public Radio, May 10. http://www.npr.org/sections/thetwo-way/2017/05/10/527801805/new-amazon-building-in-seattle-will-include-a-homeless-shelter.

Young, Bob, and Vernal Coleman. 2016. "Inside the Grim World of The Jungle: The Caves, Sleeping in Shifts and Eyeball-Eating Rats." *Seattle Times*, June 17, A-1. http://www.seattletimes.com/seattle-news/inside-the-grim-world-of-the-jungle-the-caves-sleeping-in-shifts-and-eyeball-eating-rats.

Shenzhen, China: Struggle to Leave Shanzhai Behind

Shenzhen is a port city of the Guangdong Province. It is located next to Hong Kong. One can conveniently travel between Hong Kong and Shenzhen via ferries and bridges. Witnessing the tens of thousands of white- and blue-collar workers going between the two cities at a very fast pace during rush hours is an experience that no tourist wants to skip. Shenzhen's climate is subtropical, with a high level of humidity and temperature throughout summertime and most times of the year.

Shenzhen is one of the nine cities in the Pearl River Delta region (PRD). This fastest-growing development zone of China includes Guangzhou, Shenzhen, Zhuhai, Dongguan, Zhongshan, Foshan, Huizhou, Jiangmen, and Zhaoqing, all belonging to the Guangdong Province.

In terms of total area, Shenzhen covers 1,997 square kilometers (approximately 771 square miles), twice the size of New York City. Its population is larger than New York City's 8.5 million—by the end of 2015, the total number of permanent residents was 11.37 million, which includes a million migrants who arrived just in the previous five-year period.

The demographic characteristics reflect a dynamic gentrification of an emerging city. One noticeable characteristic would be the male-to-female ratio of 53.61 percent versus 46.38 percent, reflecting that a great number of migrant workers are unaccompanied by family members. The 2015 census shows that 78 percent of the population are first-generation Shenzheners. Likewise, family size is typically small—the average household has 2.49 people. Age structure shows a very high concentration of the working-age group—83 percent are between ages 15 and 64, while only 3.37 percent are above age 65 (Shenzhen Statistics Bureau 2016).

Founded in 1979, Shenzhen was designated one of the first special economic zones (SEZs) in 1980 to experiment with Western-style management. In the early 1980s, people in Shenzhen still made a living by growing rice and fishing. The community was known as a "small sleeping fishing village." Back then, the total population was only 300,000, and most of the working-age people were employed by state-owned enterprises (SOEs). Workers received a fixed salary, plus ration coupons for food and utilities, like everywhere else in the country. After becoming an SEZ, Shenzhen turned itself into a metropolis within a decade. Rice paddies disappeared and the traditional villages evolved into "villages in the city" providing rental housing and office spaces to businesses. Today, labor-intensive factories have been mostly replaced by technology firms, among which Huawei Technologies and ZTE Corp are world-class companies. High-tech industrial parks are becoming the new business engine. The city's Nanshan district, for example, was built around the Shenzhen Hi-Tech Industrial Park (SHIP), hosting more than 8,000 tech firms. The city has become a cradle of tens of thousands of China's millionaires (Desjardins 2018). Innovation is the slogan here. As of 2016, Shenzhen's GDP ranks number 4 in China, after Shanghai, Beijing, and Guangzhou, and is bigger than even some of the provinces (Xinhua 2017). If you arrive here smart and willing to work hard, locals will tell you, you can find a place for yourself.

Shenzhen's fast rise is attributable to its connection with Hong Kong. In 1997, Hong Kong's GDP was $177 billion versus Shenzhen's $14 billion. By 2016, the gap had almost disappeared with Shenzhen's GDP of $281 billion versus Hong Kong's $321 billion (Khan et al. 2017). Shenzhen's cheaper manufacturing and fast turnaround process have been a key attraction to Hong Kong's investment community. On the other hand, Hong Kong, with its aging population and anemic growth since the global recession of 2008, relies on Shenzhen and the broader PRD region for growth. The Chinese government's plan is to merge Hong Kong and Macau with cities of the Guangdong Province, to form a megapolis with a population of 60 million (Khan et al. 2017). When Deng Xiaoping declared "one country two systems" (a communist China with capitalist-run territories) in the 1980s, who could have predicted a combination of such a grand scale?

TECHNOLOGY AND LABOR FORCE

Technology start-ups are the hallmark of Shenzhen's economy. The rise of Shenzhen was due to the tens of thousands of small firms that provided jobs. The low concentration of SOEs has been seen as a favorable condition. Guangdong has only 14 percent of its total industrial revenues generated by SOEs, compared to 31 percent of the Liaoning Province in the northeast and 36 percent in Shanghai (*Economist* 2017b). Businesses love places where state interference is weak. As such, Shenzhen has attracted more than 110,000 foreign-invested firms, compared to Shanghai's 75,000 and the Zhejiang Province's 33,000.

Shenzhen's economy is made up almost entirely of private-sector firms. According to Shenzhen's 2015 survey data, in 2013, out of the 61,480 registered firms, only 29, or 4 percent, are SOEs. Overall, 63 percent of the GDP is generated by service industries and 37 percent by manufacturing. The census of 2015 shows a high population of college-trained workers of 257.93 million, or about 23 percent of the workforce; most work in start-ups and tech firms. The private sector has proven its capability to adapt in a slow-growth economy better than SOEs. Its ability to recover from economic crisis has clearly been proven superior to the state-owned sector. The PRD region alone generates nearly 50 percent of China's high-quality patent filings, the highest in China (*Economist* 2017a).

Shenzhen's main GDP generators, as well as its job engine, are the great number of innovative start-ups. There is a dynamic ecosystem at work at every moment. Engineers typically do research and testing outside the manufacturing arena, not because they want to, but rather because of a lack of convenient access to manufacturing. In Shenzhen, the inventor meets the manufacturer. Inventors can easily have their designs turned into products, and order the products at very low prices. For that reason, Shenzhen has been called "the world's tech incubator," "Silicon Valley for hardware," "mecca for makers," "easy China," "a sprawling electronics ecosystem, and "the digi-Key catalog meets *Blade Runner*" (Branwyn 2015).

In the Huaqiangbei Electronics Market, 800–900 small tech firms work separately to tacitly form an electronic equipment development conglomerate. Designers and solderers may be seen working separately on a piece of motherboard bought for a fraction of the usual price from a recycler who had stripped it out of a used

Huaqiangbei electronics market in Shenzhen, China, April 22, 2015. Electronics manufacturing constitutes a large share of Shenzhen's economy. (Fred Dufour/AFP/Getty Images)

cell phone. The idea of their product may have been inspired by *kickstarter.com* or some other source. The sales specialist, another tech firm, would bring the end product to the market in well-designed packaging. The whole process from start to marketing could be as short as three months, while a typical industrial standard is nine months to a year. Essentially, these start-ups are effective in assembling available technologies into products on demand. Huang, an engineer in the United States, appreciates the support infrastructure of Shenzhen. He shares a story of his own experience: "I'm in my apartment in Huaqiangbei, and I get a call early in the morning. My factory is short of transistors. So, I get up, walk downstairs, buy 3,000 transistors on the street, walk over to the factory, thread it into the reel on the line, and two hours later, the line's up and running again" (Branwyn 2015). Huang believes that a similar process could take a day or two elsewhere.

It is not rare for products that are not yet officially introduced to have been produced here and put on the market, and the products work just as well as the original version (Wired UK 2016). However, a city once known as a main base of "shanzhai industry" (copycat manufacturing) is increasingly known for world-class technologies. For most start-ups today, however, the goal is not to build something brand new, but to take something available and make it better. There are niche products in hardware, such as accessories, and this is where Shenzhen's start-ups find their strengths. On the other hand, more and more shanzhai firms are now looking into developing proprietary products. Copycat manufacturing is understood in

---

Shanzhai

The word is said to have come from Shenzhen's lexicon. Its original meaning, "rural village," has expanded to imply "imitated, duplicated, and plagiarized fake products" (Baidu Baike). The shanzhai industry arose in the 1980s when foreign commodities arrived in the Chinese market, and surplus rural labor started village industries to produce items for daily use. In the IT area, shanzhai products are typically low-priced, attractively designed, mass-produced, and sold without warranty to low-income consumers. Producers sometimes resort to spelling errors in brand names—e.g., SQNY, SAMSING, ADIDOS, IBM, FUMA, HIKE, TOCHIFA—to make products more appealing.

There has been a long-lasting debate in China about shanzhai's legitimacy. Pro opinions argue that shanzhai represents a rebellion against state control and the monopoly of big companies and their abusive pricing. From the perspective of everyday life, shanzhai advocates hold that the products meet a demand that would not otherwise be met. From the employment and jobs perspective, many believe that shanzhai allows a great number of jobless college graduates and laid-off workers to make a living.

Those who oppose it believe that shanzhai is an attack on IP rights. Shanzhai, the argument goes, suppresses creativity and will only lead to the weakening of the economy in the long run. Additionally, shanzhai firms go after profits first and foremost, they avoid paying taxes, and their products are illegal and unsafe for use. Moreover, opponents deny that shanzhai is likely to give rise to a sustainable modern economy, despite the fact that the practice has been sustained for decades.

These opposing views seem to agree that shanzhai is tied to a historical time, and will eventually phase out as living standards rise. "Copycats out, innovators in" will characterize Shenzhen's economic future (*Economist* 2017a).

Shenzhen as a transient phase. Richard Chiai, VP, Global Channel Sales, 3NOD Group China, believes that Shenzhen has a lot of smart people and they should create new technology made in China (Wired UK 2016).

OPEN SOURCE PHILOSOPHY

Despite the widespread existence of crude copying, many firms are transforming technology to serve China's reality. Baidu and Alibaba are two successful companies that actively engage in R&D and obtain proprietary technologies through acquisitions. At the core of Shenzhen's start-up culture is an open source philosophy, better known as "let's trade" and "let's share." Shenzhen's start-up firms are typically small and low in funding. Because banks are state-owned, they serve SOEs first and foremost. Start-up operators believe it is more beneficial for software and hardware makers to share source codes, in order to focus on developing the product, rather than spend time and money litigating one another. Their strategy is to break away from the traditional practice whereby a contract must be signed, and a down payment made, before giving access to the source. Start-ups are generally uncomfortable with the concept that big companies can own large numbers of patents just because they were the first ones to file. Instead, they believe in making source information freely available so everyone can modify it to suit their needs. As such, "makers," or inventors, who create out of passion can form a continuum with start-ups, according to Li, the leader of a software firm. "You should forget having to choose between open and proprietary source, just focus on what you want to do," he says (Wired UK, 2016).

The open source philosophy has generated an ecosystem that is spontaneous and efficient in getting design ideas realized. This approach has been the subject of much debate and reflections. HAX Managing Director Duncan Turner believes that while everyone should properly file IP for their product, when they come to Shenzhen, they should focus on building better products and constantly improve the quality. The way to stop people from copying, in his opinion, is to come up with the next better product ahead of others (Wired UK, 2016). Opponents of such views are concerned that violation of intellectual property rights may result in loss of jobs in the developed economies (Branwyn 2015).

"MODEL FOR ALL OF CHINA?"

As a new city with fewer SOEs and more tech start-ups, Shenzhen has been outperforming China's first-tier cities. It offers a trove of experience other Chinese cities can learn. However, to become the world's tech industry innovation center, as its municipal leadership intends, Shenzhen has a way to go. There are multiple challenges in its path. First, in an environment where banks continue to favor SOEs, there are few opportunities for start-ups. There are strong headwinds for small firms to be innovative and to grow above the shanzhai level. Second, how deeply the Chinese government will reform the state-owned sector is anybody's guess (Sender

2016). In the situation of stagnation, SOEs will continue to consume the lion's share of available funding, leaving crumbs to small and medium-size companies. Such a scenario may be a drag on the development of intellectual property. Additionally, there is concern, as has been pointed out, about the private sector's predominant mentality of "getting rich fast." The money-mindset can hinder long-term and in-depth research, and will likely lead to too much focus on consumer products (Roeding 2016). These challenges may continue to mark China's economic struggle as a whole for quite some time.

Jing Luo

See also: Employment and Jobs: Mumbai, India: Exploring Employment Solutions in Temporary Jobs; *Housing and Infrastructure:* Dandong, China: One Bridge, Two Islands; *Migration and Demographic Changes:* Guangzhou, China: Foreign Communities Facing Challenges of Adaptation

Further Reading

Branwyn, Gareth. 2015. "An Insider's Guide to Shenzhen Manufacturing." *Makezine.com*, June 15. http://makezine.com/2015/06/15/making-in-shenzhen/.

Desjardins, Jeff. 2018. "Visualizing the Global Millionaire Population." *Visual Capitalist.* https://www.visualcapitalist.com/global-millionaire-population/.

Hernandez, Javier C. 2016. "Labor Protests Multiply in China as Economy Slows, Worrying Leaders." *New York Times*, March 15. https://www.nytimes.com/2016/03/15/world/asia/china-labor-strike-protest.html.

Horwitz, Josh. 2016. "Your Brilliant Kickstarter Idea Could Be on Sale in China before You've Even Finished Funding It." *Quartz Media*, October 17. https://qz.com/771727/chinas-factories-in-shenzhen-can-copy-products-at-breakneck-speed-and-its-time-for-the-rest-of-the-world-to-get-over-it/.

Khan, Natasha, and Enda Curran. 2017. "Hong Kong Cozies Up to Shenzhen to Create Future Tech Giants." *Bloomberg Businessweek*, June 11. https://www.bloomberg.com/news/articles/2017-06-11/hong-kong-cozies-up-to-shenzhen-in-border-swamp-to-lure-startups.

Qin, Pekjing, Chen Letian, Yang Lingxiu, Lin Sha, Liu Fang, and CITICS Research Team. 2015. "Group Study—Consumerism of People Born after 1990" (in Chinese). *199IT.* November 3. http://www.199it.com/archives/400341.html.

Roeding, Cyriac. 2016. "After Three Weeks in China, It's Clear Beijing Is Silicon Valley's Only True Competitor." *Recode.net,* May 13. https://www.recode.net/2016/5/13/11592570/china-startup-tech-economy-silicon-valley.

Sender, Henny. 2016. "Bright Hopes for China's Private Sector Have Dimmed." *Financial Times.* https://www.ft.com/content/9ed86960-b549-11e6-ba85-95d1533d9a62.

"Shanzhai" (in Chinese). 2017. *Baidu Baike*, June 15. http://baike.baidu.com/item/%E5%B1%B1%E5%AF%A8/7401?fr=ala0_1_1.

Shenzhen Government Online. http://english.sz.gov.cn/.

Staff Writer. 2017a. "Shenzhen Is a Hothouse of Innovation." *Economist*, April 8. http://www.economist.com/news/special-report/21720076-copycats-are-out-innovators-are-shenzhen-hothouse-innovation.

Staff Writer. 2017b. "What the Country Can Learn from the Pearl River Delta." *Economist*, April 8. http://www.economist.com/news/special-report/21720074-prd-shows-what-china-could-achieve-setting-entrepreneurs-free-what-country-can.

Statistics Bureau of Shenzhen City. 2016. "Statistical Communique—Shenzhen 2015 Census Based on 1 Percent Sampling" (in Chinese). http://www.sztj.gov.cn/xxgk/zfxxgkml/tjsj/tjgb/201606/t20160614_3697000.htm..

Whitwell, Tom. 2014. "Inside Shenzhen: China's Silicon Valley." *Guardian*, June 13. https://www.theguardian.com/cities/2014/jun/13/inside-shenzen-china-silicon-valley-tech-nirvana-pearl-river.

Wired UK. 2016. "Shenzhen: The Silicon Valley of Hardware." *Youtube.com*. https://www.youtube.com/watch?v=SGJ5cZnoodY&t=8s.

Xinhua. 2017. "Shenzhen GDP Up 9 Percent, Ranks Fourth in Mainland Cities." *China Daily,* January 24. http://www.chinadaily.com.cn/business/2017-01/24/content_28041580.htm.

Zhang Yangpeng. 2016. "Overcapacity May Lead to 3m Layoffs." *China Daily*, June 13. http://usa.chinadaily.com.cn/china/2016-01/13/content_23060620.htm.

Stockholm, Sweden: Employers Stress Educational Credentials

The largest Scandinavian city, Stockholm is the capital of Sweden. At the junction of Lake Malaren and the Baltic Sea, Stockholm has long been the cultural, political, and economic engine of Sweden. The economic fate of Stockholm is inseparable from that of the rest of Sweden. Jobs and employment in Stockholm do not cluster in the energy and industrial sectors because these sectors are not a primary feature of Sweden's economy, having a comparative dearth of fossil fuels and a factory system that has never been robust. Accordingly, jobs and employment in Stockholm are oriented toward the provision of services rather than the production of goods. Such a scheme is a feature of an economy in which the service sector dominates. The prominence of the service sector demonstrates that Stockholm has a modern economy.

Baltic Sea

Linked to the North Sea at Skagen, Denmark, the Baltic Sea is part of the Atlantic Ocean. In addition to Sweden and Denmark, the Baltic Sea borders Germany, Poland, Estonia, Latvia, Lithuania, Finland, and Russia. The sea's ecological importance lies in its status as the world's largest aggregate of brackish water. Having more salts than fresh water but less than seawater, brackish water supports microbes, plants, and animals that cannot thrive in either extreme, making the Baltic Sea a sanctuary for endangered species, including the harbor porpoise, sturgeon, and European eel. The Baltic Sea's economic value lies in its cod, herring, and salmon, but overfishing threatens them. Pollution threatens the sea and its life. One type of pollution is eutrophication, the deposition of too many nutrients in water. Fertilizers, which contain plant nutrients, flow into bodies of water, including the Baltic Sea, causing eutrophication. These nutrients spur plants and other photosynthetic organisms to grow. When they die, bacteria decompose them, using oxygen in the process. But oxygen's removal from the water kills fish. Moreover, bacteria emit carbon dioxide into the water, making it more acidic and causing fish and shellfish to grow slowly, thereby limiting their catch in the Baltic Sea. Other pollutants further degrade it.

EMPLOYMENT IN A TEPID ECONOMY

Stockholm shares its employment trends with the rest of Sweden. Sweden's economic growth was robust between roughly 1800 and 1970. Since the 1970s, however, growth has slowed. This sluggishness reveals economic weaknesses. Notably, Sweden is not well endowed with fossil fuels, so the energy sector is not vigorous. Moreover, Sweden has never relied heavily on industry, which accounts for the relative dearth of factory jobs.

These circumstances put in context employment trends. In an economy that is imperfect, Sweden had in January 2017 an unemployment rate of 7.8 percent (Roden 2017). Stockholm fared better than the national average at just 6 percent. The reader should keep in mind that the unemployment rate tends to underestimate the number of unemployed people because it counts only those who are seeking work. It does not count people who have become too discouraged to seek work.

In Stockholm, unemployment tends to be lower among the most educated people. In fact, some sectors with a dearth of workers are hiring in Stockholm, a city that needs teachers at all levels, people with expertise in computers, and construction workers.

Unemployment is also lower for native Swedes. Foreign workers in Stockholm and the rest of Sweden, however, have an unemployment rate roughly three times

Julia Fridell and Rebecka Viberg chat in a Stockholm coffee shop about problems facing Swedish youth, March 13, 2014. Fridell is studying organic chemistry and working in a bakery. Viberg is a part-time nanny and wants to be a social worker. Sweden is a successful welfare state with a high standard of living, but youth unemployment is high. (Melanie Stetson Freeman/The Christian Science Monitor via Getty Images)

higher than Swedes. The problem is likely to worsen as migrants and refugees from other countries enter Sweden.

Furthermore, youths in Stockholm and the rest of Sweden have a harder time finding work than adults. This problem appears to be more severe in Sweden, where youth unemployment approaches 25 percent, than in many other developed countries (UNRC 2012). The United Nations blames this problem on the fact that youths in Stockholm and the rest of Sweden tend to have less education than adults. Moreover, young people tend to have less work experience than adults. In addition, because it tends to be easier for an employer to fire a young worker than an adult, these youths find themselves too often with short stints of work and long periods of unemployment.

Stockholm and the rest of Sweden promote internships as a way of helping youths gain experience necessary to progress to better jobs. Of course, internships do not always pay a wage. Part-time work is another way to gain experience, though the danger is that Stockholm's employers already rely disproportionately on young people to fill part-time, poorly paid jobs. Stockholm's Employer's Union advocates a reduction in the minimum wage as a way of encouraging employers to take a chance on young workers. Trade unions resist this idea, instead calling on local and national authorities to increase government subsidies to employers who create jobs for young people. The reader should bear in mind that youth unemployment is not unique to Stockholm and the rest of Sweden. The problem afflicts other European countries.

THE SERVICE SECTOR

With meager energy and industrial sectors, Stockholm must look elsewhere for jobs. Like the rest of Sweden and many other developed countries, Stockholm is part of a global economy. One effect of this integration is the fact that the residents of Stockholm can purchase cheap imports. This fact is not surprising given that, as a rule, labor costs are lower in emerging economies than in Stockholm. A reduction in labor costs overseas reinforces the trend toward the formation of industries and factory goods overseas and their export to Stockholm. This differential in labor costs also helps explain why industry does not thrive in Stockholm.

It follows that jobs are concentrated in other sectors. A notable feature of Stockholm's economy, and those of many other developed cities and nations, is the proliferation of jobs in the service sector. Such jobs differ from traditional manufacturing jobs in that workers provide a service rather than produce a good. Of course, Stockholm is not alone in being oriented toward the provision of services. Such an orientation is a feature of many developed economies. Accordingly, Stockholm's robust service sector indicates the degree to which Sweden has a modern, mature economy rather than an emerging economy.

The service sector is so important in Stockholm that it accounts for more than four-fifths of all employment in the city. The service sector is, of course, diverse, and this diversity is evident in Stockholm. This diversity does not mean that the service sector is not oriented in a particular direction. In fact, jobs are particularly numerous in banks because Stockholm is Sweden's financial center. In this regard, the large employers, headquartered in Stockholm, are Sweden's chief banks: Nordea, Swedbank, Handelsbanken, and Skandinaviska Enskilda Banken.

Stockholm's financial sector receives an additional boost from the fact that the city is the headquarters of Sweden's stock market. The jobs in this area, as is true of many of Stockholm's jobs, tend to require a university education. The trend, accordingly, is the hiring and retention of mature, established people with experience rather than youths in search of their first job.

Stockholm is also the headquarters of Sweden's primary insurance companies, which are also large employers. These companies include Skandia, Folksam, and Trygg-Hansa. Here again, the best jobs in the insurance industry go to people with a university education and experience.

Technology companies have become increasingly visible in Stockholm in recent decades. In this sector, large employers include International Business Machine (IBM), Ericsson, and Electrolux. IBM will likely be familiar to the reader. Ericsson produces telecommunications equipment. Electrolux manufactures appliances. IBM, Ericsson, and Electrolux provide a diversity of jobs including employment for engineers and laborers. Significantly, these companies account for a portion of factory jobs, which would otherwise be absent from Stockholm. Kista, a neighborhood in northern Stockholm, is a center of employment in information technology. Indeed, Kista contains the largest concentration of high-technology companies outside Silicon Valley, California, and so is an important employer. Employment is conspicuous in various branches of computer and information science including software engineering.

Such technologically intensive jobs offer a variety of options. Some jobs are available for recent university graduates, whereas more senior positions require experience. Full- and part-time work is available. Jobs may be permanent. Alternatively, workers may opt for one or a series of contracts and so operate as an independent contractor.

The trend toward a university education and experience does not mean the absence of jobs at lower grades of pay, training, and experience. In this context, it is important to note that Sweden's largest retailer, the clothier Hennes and Mauritz AB, known in Stockholm simply as H & M, has jobs for clerks, cashiers, and salespeople. These jobs tend not to require a university education and extensive experience.

In recent years, as tourism has become increasingly important in Stockholm, the proliferation of hotels and inns provides another source of employment. As with retail, a university education and experience are not often required in tourism.

FINDING EMPLOYMENT IN STOCKHOLM

Being a cosmopolitan city, Stockholm has jobs for people proficient in languages other than Swedish. Jobs are available, for example, for English-language speakers, though some proficiency in Swedish is often desirable. Stockholm's multinational corporations are the most flexible in offering employment to speakers of languages other than Swedish. As a rule, these jobs require experience and a university education.

Because of the professional nature of such jobs in Stockholm, job seekers, as in other areas of the world, must be proficient in designing a curriculum vitae (CV) and cover letter. The CV tends to have features applicable to job seekers in a variety of competencies. The job seeker should know that the CV is a distinctive document in Stockholm and in other parts of Sweden. Whereas the traditional CV in the United States, often known as a resume, lists accomplishments, Stockholm employers expect a more detailed document, one that lists what the applicant did in the positions included on the CV. The Swedish CV should not be a detached, dry document but rather convey interest and enthusiasm for the job sought. Foreign workers must highlight international experience to demonstrate their capacity to thrive in a new environment. The job seeker must take cues from the employment posting. All employment documents should be crafted in the language of the advertisement. When in doubt the employer may be contacted.

Unless stated otherwise in the advertisement, the job seeker should furnish a cover letter with the CV. As a rule, Stockholm employers expect a cover letter to accompany a CV and may not consider an applicant who neglects to draft a letter in support of the CV. When Stockholm employers have winnowed the list of applications, the cover letter often separates those who receive an interview from other applicants. The letter must be compelling if it is to entice the human resources professional to spend more than the standard 30 seconds skimming it. The 30-second threshold requires the applicant to state forcefully in the letter the connection between his or her experience and the requirements of the job. The letter should be a formal document except for the practice in Stockholm of addressing the recipient by his or her first name, thereby dispensing with the designations "Mr.," "Ms.," and their variants.

Employment listings are available in a variety of formats. The aspirant may start with the jobs listed in Arbetsbormedlingen, known in English as the Swedish Public Employment Service. This service also contains advice on starting a business and other aspects of working in Stockholm and other areas of Sweden.

Because of the importance of education and experience, consideration is given to university graduates. The best options are available for graduates of Swedish universities because these universities have ties to the job market in Stockholm. The university career center may be especially helpful in preparing a candidate for an interview or in helping him or her compile the proper documents for an application for employment. Swedish university career centers are often proficient in helping an applicant prepare documents in English in addition to Swedish.

Employers, especially the larger ones, often host career fairs, which the prospective applicant should attend to form networks as well as to seek work. Such career fairs may feature seminars in addition to intensive interview sessions. The Stockholm School of Economics hosts the Handelsdagarna, one of Sweden's most well-attended career fairs. The city of Stockholm also hosts a series of career fairs that are not tied to a particular university. These venues are open to aspirants irrespective of education.

As with education, experience is important. Aspirants should apply for internships, even if unpaid, and part-time work while in school to gain experience that may translate into a job upon graduation. Academicwork.se is a website with a comprehensive list of part-time jobs in Stockholm and other regions of Sweden. Competition for these jobs is often intense.

Swedish universities require a thesis from all students. If this document is to be impactful, it is best researched and written at a company in Stockholm. The experience will cement ties with management and bring a student to the attention of the company. Swedish universities often have close connections to a variety of companies and can help a student arrange a thesis at a suitable venue.

Christopher Cumo

See also: Employment and Jobs: Paris, France: A Locomotive of Job Creation; *Schools:* Berlin, Germany: Making the City a Center of Learning

Further Reading

Griffiths, Tony. 2009. *Stockholm: A Cultural History.* Oxford and New York: Oxford University Press.

"Introducing . . . Finding a Job in Stockholm." 2014. *Local,* October 10. https://www.thelocal.se/20141010/introducing-finding-a-job-in-stockholm-tlccu.

Roden, Lee. 2017. "This Map Shows Where You're Most Likely to Be Unemployed in Sweden." *Local,* February 13. https://www.thelocal.se/20170213/this-map-shows-where-youre-most-likely-to-be-unemployed-in-sweden.

"Study in Sweden: 10 Tips for Finding Work in Sweden." Studyinsweden.se/life-in-sweden/10-tips-for-finding-work-in-sweden.

UNRC. 2012. "Sweden: Highest Ratio of Youth Unemployment." United Nations Regional Information Centre for Europe. March 12. https://www.unric.org/en/youth-unemployment/27411-sweden-highest-ratio-of-youth-unemployment.

Energy and Sustainability

OVERVIEW

Sustainability is the key challenge for cities of the 21st century. According to a 2017 report by the International Energy Agency (IEA), global energy demand reached an all-time high and fossil fuels were responsible for over 70 percent of the growth in energy demand around the world. The fossil fuel burning contributed over 60 percent of the greenhouse gas (GHG) responsible for climate change, according to a 2017 emissions report by the Environment Program of the UN. The consequence is astounding—the continents are battered by more prolonged and more damaging natural disasters. More people are living constantly under air pollution, and more lives are lost in wars and famine caused by climate change–related disasters. Yet, not all world leaders are convinced of the anthropogenic effects. However, these articles show that cities around the world are taking a risk by leaving the matter to politicians. These cities are seeking every way to cut down fossil fuel consumption. Many are taking the lead in exploring renewable energy and energy conservation. Articles in this section demonstrate what is being done to rein in excessive consumption and keep cities sustainable.

War on Water Shortage

A direct impact of urbanization on natural resources is that it quickly exhausts water supply. Shortage of water is one of Beijing's most serious concerns and has been raised by the government as an urgent issue. Beijing was aware of an upcoming water shortage back in the early 1950s when the city was designated as the nation's capital. More than a dozen reservoirs have been built since that time; the two that are directly related to people's daily lives are the Guanting and the Miyun reservoirs. However, what Beijing failed to anticipate was the city's explosive rate of growth during the past three decades. The population grew by seven times from 2.8 million in 1953 to 22 million in 2016; the city's GDP rose by 10,000 times, from $19 million in 1953 to $206.5 billion in 2010. Moreover, Beijing failed to anticipate that surface water can be so badly polluted that it is not suitable for human consumption without treatment. As a result, the city has grown increasingly dependent on underground water. However, this solution fell short due to drought and the runaway urban sprawl. As a result, Beijing has launched several large-scale projects to increase supply. In 2016, the Huaifang Underground Water Recycling Plant, reputed to be Asia's largest water recycling facility, was built in Beijing. In the meantime, the city has announced its plan to build, by the end of 2019, 27 new sewage treatment plants and upgrade the existing ones. An even larger project inaugurated in 2014 was the Coordinated Development for the Beijing-Tianjin-Hebei Region. This plan was to construct a complex system of canals to divert waters from southern China to north-bound streams. The construction goes on despite concerns raised over financial and environmental costs. Beijing is also making efforts to curb the demand. In addition to urging citizens to save water, the city takes more aggressive measures, one of which is to limit its urban population to below 23 million by 2030.

Struggle for Greener Energy

Reducing CO_2 emissions is an important part of sustainability. Citizens of Melbourne, Australia, take emission control to heart, since Melbourne is the second-largest city and generates more greenhouse gases than most cities in Australia. Countless examples of cities living under heavy smog have shown that air pollution can cause significant damage to people's health. In Melbourne, the goal is to curb emissions and be carbon-neutral by 2020. A major strategy for achieving this goal is to substitute renewable energy for coal in power generation. Australia's current reliance on coal is 63 percent (as of 2016). Melbourne's solution is to replace coal with bagasse from sugarcane and algae-generated biodiesel. Both bio materials are abundantly available in Australia's natural environment. Using bagasse as a renewable biofuel, in itself, has an additional benefit: it serves to control methane, a polluting ozone gas that can be generated by decaying bagasse. Additionally, bagasse can be used to make ethanol, which can be mixed with gasoline as a fuel source. On the consumption side, Melbourne promotes efficiency in energy use. A few examples are replacing streetlights with LEDs, remodeling existing buildings for improved energy efficiency, reducing loss of power in the transmission process, and encouraging residents to grow "green roofs" or installing "wet roofs" for better energy conservation. Furthermore, as Cumo notes, Melbourne is making great strides in improving the use of energy in transportation. The city aims to raise the percentage of travel in low-emission vehicles to 60 percent by 2018, a great leap forward from the 50 percent level in 2009.

With a population of approximately 1.3 million, Copenhagen is one of the most populous cities in Europe, and has a rich cultural tradition dating back to the time of the Vikings. As a coastal city, Copenhagen faces the consequences of the rising sea level and increasingly severe climate changes. The Copenhageners are doing everything they can to improve the climate conditions. Copenhagen has the reputation of proactively promoting sustainable urban living. In 2009, the city adopted the Copenhagen 2025 Climate Plan (CPH 2025), which offers a roadmap to reaching the goal of being carbon-neutral by 2025. In addition to substituting fossil fuel with renewable energy, Copenhagen showcases a number of unique approaches combining environmental conditions, cultural tradition, and scientific solutions. One solution is to install centralized cooling and heating systems in urban districts powered by seawater and geothermal energy. The use of biking as a mainstream transportation means in daily life and work is an eye-catching initiative. Biking is both an emission-free way of travel and a national hobby in Denmark. To facilitate biking, the city is willing to invest in building bike lanes and make traffic information more accessible to bikers. Another initiative is to make cars run on windmill-generated energy, seen as an expansion of Denmark's cultural tradition.

With a population of 21 million and a projected growth to 27.8 million by 2030, Mumbai is the second most populated city in India (after New Delhi). In the world economy, Mumbai is one of the alpha urban centers in almost every economic aspect. The headwinds for the city to maintain a sustainable living environment for its citizens, as Roy shows, are also strong: India's power generation is 67 percent reliant on coal, compared to less than 40 percent among OECD countries. Coal has been a primary source of air pollution, causing tens of thousands of premature deaths and rising respiratory diseases in India. The situation is worsened as a result of a quarter of the power produced being lost in transmission. Power generation using coal in India is expected to triple between 2013 and 2030. A disadvantage for India is the lack of land to grow fuel crops, the farmlands being barely sufficient to produce food crops. To tackle the energy shortage and the need to expand the supply of clean and renewable energy, Mumbai invests in harvesting ethanol from marine algae and from municipal solid waste, of which Mumbai generates 9,000 tons per day. A project that is already producing positive economic results is the use of the jatropha plant growing along the Mumbai-New Delhi Railway to produce electricity that powers the train. India's goal is to increase the proportion of renewable energy 40 percent of the total by 2030. To that end, citizens are participating proactively. The Siddhivinayak Gnapati Temple, for example, is using rooftop solar panels, reducing their utility bill by about a third. Rooftop solar panels are expected to transform Mumbai's power use significantly.

Toward Better Energy Conservation

London's population stands at 8.6 million, giving London the reputation of the most populous city in Europe. More people means more energy consumption. Londoners take sustainability to heart. As Evans shows, the city has made tremendous efforts in recent years to reduce its carbon footprint through increasing its public transportation and promoting alternative energy. The city provides efficient public transits ranging from buses to crossrails. Approximately half of Londoners use public transportation, far exceeding the 35 percent who use private cars. The city imposes rules to further curb private car usage. These rules either designate congestion charging zones (CCZ) or impose toxicity charges on cars that fail to meet the Euro IV standard. Additionally, London implements environmental practices that many other European countries adopt, such as upgrading buildings to assure energy efficiency, expanding use of renewable energy, and reducing the use of fossil fuel. These measures will keep London's environment sustainable, despite the fact that the city already has one of the lowest levels of manufacturing industry in Europe.

With a population of 750,000, Frankfurt is a populous city in Germany and popularly known as Europe's financial center. It is a touristic city and one of the busiest transportation crossings in Europe. Yet Frankfurt is praised as the most sustainable city in the world. Its goal is to satisfy its entire power needs through renewable energy by 2050, and reduce carbon emission by 95 percent by that time. In Frankfurt, energy saving, sustainability monitoring, and climate protection are integral to people's way of living. Frankfurt conceives energy sustainability as the outcome of three elements: conservation, efficient usage, and renewable sources. The city invests in cogeneration (capture and reuse of exhaust heat), improvement of energy efficiency of buildings, and upgrade of transportation efficiency. In power generation, cogeneration is able to make use of 90 percent of the available energy, whereas in the conventional power generation process, 60 to 70 percent of available energy is lost. Applying the same technology, Frankfurt is able to upgrade hospitals, public office buildings, and dwellings. The concept of "passive house" refers to a housing design that utilizes maximum solar energy and minimum mechanical cooling, such as fans and pumps, to balance energy use. In Frankfurt, this technology has been applied to dwellings and large edifices such as hospitals. To expand the capacity of renewable power, Frankfurt invests in photovoltaic systems that allow solar panel users to contribute to the solar grid and receive a stream of income. The city is also a model in green space conservation—52 percent of its area is dedicated for green spaces.

Located in the tropical zone, Rio de Janeiro is a large city in Brazil that consumes a great amount of energy for cooling and water-heating purposes. The electricity used for cooling accounts for one-fifth of the city's consumption. Not being endowed with rich oil reserves, the city strives to utilize natural conditions for cooling and heating purposes. Cumo explains in detail Rio's exquisite designs in this regard, such as windows shaped in different sizes according to their directions; vents in buildings functioning as natural AC; and roof water collectors with built-in solar heating and temperature preservation functions. Some of the water collector/heaters cost up to thousands of dollars to install. Yet these costs are quickly recuperated because as much as 20 percent of the city's electricity consumption is used in bathing. Brazil's government encourages the use of solar energy by subsidizing investments. Additionally, Rio takes advantage of the abundantly available bagasse as a renewable energy source. Wind energy is also harvested for power generation, though there are reservations due to aesthetic concerns about wind turbines in the pristine coastal environment.

Being the largest city in Canada, Toronto manages its energy consumption with great care. The city fosters good habits in energy consumption and conservation. In conservation, the city implements three policies: The Toronto Green Standard, Community Energy Planning, and Home Energy Loan Program. These policies combine requirements with financial rewards, so that energy savers benefit when they consume less than the standard. Additionally, these policies enhance urban planning and financial programs that provide loans for house energy efficiency upgrades. On the consumption side, the microFIT program encourages residents to install rooftop solar panels with options to sell back extra electricity. Meanwhile, Green Commute, Green Taxis, Congestion Management Plan 2014–2018, and Zero Waste Building programs mandate maximum use of clean energy in transportation and maximum reduction of landfill materials. The city promotes biking to work and invests in bicycle lanes, much like the practice in Copenhagen. Residents are also encouraged to use public transit and carpooling. Environment-minded taxi riders will find a taxi fleet running Toyota Priuses in Toronto. Under the zero-waste building program, residents are required to separate recyclables and organic materials and cut down the amount of landfill waste. Thanks to these measures, Toronto is one of the greenest cities in the world.

Singapore is reputed to be one of the cleanest cities in Asia. However, dense population and limited space pose challenges for the city's energy usage. The solution is to use natural gas more than oil and coal wherever possible. Ninety percent of the city's electricity is generated with natural gas. However, Singapore must reduce natural gas import from Malaysia and Indonesia due to a national security mandate. As a result, the city pursues solutions in conservation and renewable energy. In conservation, the government calls on residents to travel by public transit. The goal is to reach 75 percent usage level by 2030. Meanwhile, the city encourages greener cars through imposing taxes on less energy-efficient ones. In homes, the city mandates the use of energy-efficient refrigerators and other kitchen appliances. On the energy production side, the government encourages residents to install rooftop solar panels and allow households to resell extra electricity to utility companies.

Environmental Justice

Pittsburgh, Pennsylvania, was once known for being one of the most advanced metalworking and iron and steel production centers in the world. The perpetual fog, however, was also part of that reputation. The production of coke emitted tons of soot into the air daily in the 1950s. Today, Pittsburgh's sky is blue and its air is fresh. However, Johansen asks, when cities like Pittsburgh get an environmental upgrade, who takes over environment-damaging production, and where do pollutants go. Johansen is concerned about an "unfair relay," and calls for attention to the issue of "environmental racism and justice." He argues that when Pittsburgh's CO_2-infused smog was gone, it didn't vanish, but rather it shows up today in the air of Beijing, Shanghai, New Delhi, and Mexico City. He indicates, for example, that by 2007, China had surpassed the United States as the world's largest emitter of greenhouse gases from manufacturing, vehicle exhaust, and coal-fired power plants, and had become the world's largest steel producer. Consequently, Beijing's air quality has been fast deteriorating—smog attacks are color-coded for severity levels, the top levels shutting down schools and businesses. What the world has witnessed in the last century, Johansen argues, has been a shift of the worst air quality from cities like New York, London, and Pittsburgh, to cities in emerging economies; and that shift took advantage of the economic conditions of needy cities and population groups. Even in the United States, as Johansen shows, low-income people are found to be more tolerant of pollution by industry, because they need to hold on to the jobs. Johansen frames the issue in terms of moral justice.

Further Reading
International Energy Agency (IEA). 2017. "Global Energy and CO2 Status Report." http://www.iea.org/geco/.
The United Nations Environmental Programme (UNEP). 2017. *The Emissions Gap Report 2017.* https://wedocs.unep.org/bitstream/handle/20.500.11822/22070/EGR_2017.pdf.

Beijing, China: Battling Water Shortage

Water shortage is one of the most serious challenges to the sustainability of modern cities, especially metropolises such as Beijing. Rapid urbanization and increase in population, fast economic growth, precipitation decrease due to deforestation and climate change, adoption of modern lifestyle, irrational use of water, and pollution are the key factors that have put great pressure on the already scarce surface and underground water resources in Beijing. Coordinated efforts at both the municipal and the national level have been made in the past decades, including the launch of several mega projects, one of which was the South-North Water Diversion Project, to mitigate the chronic water shortage problem. These efforts also include the implementation of better water management and audits, policies to promote water conservation, exploiting water resources from rains and floods, readjusting industrial and agriculture structures, and wastewater treatment and reuse.

HISTORICAL BACKGROUND

Beijing is the capital city of China and the world's third most populous city. The metropolitan area has six districts with a total population around 13 million. The greater Beijing area, however, has a much larger population of 22 million (estimated based on the figure of 21.7 million at the end of 2015). Beijing is a city both ancient and modern. Its history stretches across three millennia. Beijing is the last of China's Four Great Ancient Capitals (Xi'an, Nanjing, Luoyang, and Beijing), and has served as the political heart of the country for about 800 years. As such, the city inherits an efficient water supply system. The canals surrounding the outer city walls, for example, were built for both defense and water supply. The outskirts of Beijing also have a long history of agriculture utilizing an efficient irrigation system.

Beijing is located in the cold North Temperate Climate Zone, which has little precipitation in winter, most of the precipitation being concentrated in summer. The city's annual average precipitation measures only 580 mm, or 22.8 inches; by comparison, New York, which is located at about the same latitude, records 1,090 mm, or 42.9 inches, per year. Since the Yuan dynasty (1271–1368), Beijing's water supply has come mainly through canals from rivers north and west of the city. The most important water-supplying river, historically, was the Yongding River, also known as the mother river of Beijing. It is the largest river in the region and now is dry, exposing the riverbed. The water from the canals feeds into a system of lakes designed by Guo Shoujing (1231–1316), a well-known Chinese astronomer, engineer, and mathematician. With such a complete water system, the urban area of Beijing thrived during the Yuan, Ming, and Qing dynasties (1271–1911), and sustained a population well above 1 million at its peak (in 1825, Beijing's population reached 1.35 million during the Qing dynasty, the highest level during this period).

Urbanization has tipped the balance. Water levels in these rivers have declined gradually because of deforestation and drought, and could no longer supply Beijing with enough water. The city's water supply was gradually replaced by underground water. As the population has steadily grown, especially after 1949 when the new People's Republic of China was founded, Beijing has been facing a chronic water shortage.

FACING THE CHALLENGE

In 1949, the first conference of the Chinese People's Political Consultative Conference (CPPCC) approved Beijing, among other candidate cities such as Nanjing, Xi'an, and Kaifeng, as the capital city of new China. The founders of the People's Republic were fully aware of the water shortage problem in Beijing, and decided to face the challenge.

Since 1950, the central government mobilized all resources and manpower to construct reservoirs and dams in the areas surrounding Beijing as the major sources of water supply for the city. More than a dozen reservoirs and other water projects have been constructed since then. Among these projects, the most important are Guanting Reservoir on Yongding River, and Miyun Reservoir bringing water to Beijing from Chaobai River, designated a class-I protected water resource in 1985 and now the city's largest single source of water.

Over the decades, the reservoirs constructed in the 1950s dried up. By the early 2000s, Miyun and Guanting reservoirs received less than 10 percent of the water from the feeding rivers than they used to in the 1950s. Urbanization in upstream cities and provinces had diverted most of the water from these rivers. As a result, water levels were lower in ponds and lakes in Beijing, and water shortage gradually became a crisis.

In the meantime, the city's population has grown from 2.8 million in 1953, to a staggering 22 million in 2016, and the city's gross domestic product (GDP) has grown from a mere $19 million in 1953 to $206.5 million. During this period, the population has grown by seven times, while the GDP has increased by more than 10,000 times! (See Table 1 for detailed information about the population and GDP growth.)

Due to the rapid population increase and unprecedented economic growth, especially since the 1980s when China adopted reforms and an open-door policy, the

Table 1 Beijing Population and GDP

Census Year	1953	1964	1982	1990	2000	2010
Population (million)	2.768	7.568	9.231	10.819	13.569	19.612
GDP (million USD)	19.28	35.99	8,185	10,470	38,192	208,488

Source: China Bureau of Statistics.

demand for water has grown dramatically. The situation was further exacerbated due to a decade-long drought (1999–2011), mismanagement of water, and water pollution.

Pollution of surface water is a general problem in China and adds challenges to the water shortage. Most of China's surface water resources are polluted with industrial discharge released by small factories. Beijing's reservoirs are no exception. This made the supply of drinking water to Beijing a staggering problem by the late 1990s. To ease the situation, the State Council implemented projects to divert streams and rivers from Shangxi and Hebei provinces toward Beijing.

CURRENT IMPROVEMENT AND FUTURE PERSPECTIVES

Beijing's water consumption levels are proportional to the city's expansion. According to the *Beijing Water Resources Bulletin*, a publication of the Beijing Water Authority, the 2015 data showed that the average water resource per capita of Beijing was much lower than elsewhere in China and shrinking. For a population of nearly 22 million in the capital city, the total water resource was only 123 cubic meters per capita, compared to a per capita resource of 2,100 cubic meters elsewhere in China. A direct cause of this situation is overuse. Overexploitation and overdependence raised the ground water supply to two-thirds of the city's water consumption. The *Bulletin* indicates Beijing's groundwater level in 1999 was 12 meters; this depth had gone down to 24.5 meters by 2013, and to 40 meters in some areas.

The water shortage prompted the city to invest in water recycling. Beijing's first water treatment plant was constructed in 1986 for the Miyun Reservoir. Over the years, its capacity was expanded, making it Asia's largest water treatment facility. By 2009, the plant was capable of treating 1.5 million cubic meters of water daily, and processed both surface and ground water.

Effort has also been made to improve the water quality in the Guanting Reservoir. The government aims to improve the water quality to class III (of five water quality categories, I being the best and V being the worst). The quality of the reservoir's water has improved to some extent since 2000, but failed to reach the quality standard as a drinking water supply source.

Wastewater treatment and reuse has also been on the city's agenda. Since 2000, one sewage plant has been built every year in Beijing. Sewage treatment capacity increased from 0.32 billion cubic meters in 2001 to 1.5 billion cubic meters (4 million cubic meters per day) in 2016, achieving 90 percent of the wastewater treatment rate, and the city utilized about 1.0 billion cubic meters of recycled water.

According to the Beijing Water Authority, the city government has announced the next three-year (from July 2016 to June 2019) action plan to construct 27 new sewage plants and upgrade 14 existing ones. The goal is to reach 94 percent wastewater treatment rate for the whole region under the administration of the municipality by the end of 2019, and 100 percent in the metropolitan area.

In June 2016, the largest underground water recycling plant in Asia was completed in Beijing. The Huaifang Underground Water Recycling Plant, one of China's mega projects with a budget of 40 billion RMB (approximately $5.9 billion), is capable of recycling 200 million cubic meters of sewage a year and can treat most of the wastewater from Beijing's western urban area. The project will contribute greatly to the city's environmental protection by supplying recycled water to the artificial wetland above the plant. The facility, built underground to save valuable land, consists of three layers, occupies an area of more than 40 acres, and is equipped with cutting-edge technology, featuring an ultrafiltration-membrane bioreactor and an ozone system, according to the Beijing Drainage Group, a large public-service enterprise and the operator of the plant.

The water shortage in north China is an age-old problem. To expand the water supply, the State Council approved the strategic South-North Water Diversion Project in 2002, in order to fundamentally mitigate the water shortage problem facing the region in North China Plain. This is a grand infrastructure project with a capacity of moving 44.8 billion cubic meters of water annually from the south to the north by constructing bypasses over the Yangtze River. These bypasses utilize what's known as a "three dyke-tunnel-canal system." The design was not without controversy and aroused debate and dissent with respect to environmental and ecological consequences. Additionally, the high cost of 500 billion RMB or $73 billion at the current exchange rate was blamed as a steep cut into the economy. Nevertheless, the South-to-North Water Diversion, a project unprecedented in terms of engineering challenges and cost, was inaugurated on December 12, 2014. The government considers the 2,400-kilometer project a bloodline to save China's development, according to a *Guardian* report (2014); and so it happened.

With all the efforts described above to stabilize water resources and expand supply, Beijing has reached a critical balance in water resources and demand, although the situation is still vulnerable. The coordinated efforts now focus on reducing the demand side, which includes limiting population growth in Beijing, moving water-intensive industries out of the region, modernizing the irrigation system to adopt water-saving agriculture, and moving the municipal government functional departments to a different location. According to the National Development and Reform Commission (NDRC) policy paper titled "Coordinated Development for the Beijing-Tianjin-Hebei Region," the central government calls on an integrated and sustainable development in the region, with a particular emphasis on environment and resources protection. Beijing has placed a population cap at 23 million by 2030, and the government encourages the reduction of the population in the urban area, known as the six district of Beijing metropolis.

On the water conservation side, Beijing could do much better. The media calls on residents to conserve water by lowering the average consumption of 160 liters per capita per day to between 115 and 150, or the levels of Germany and France respectively. Citizens of Beijing should and could adopt a more sustainable lifestyle to conserve water and ease the water shortage, as the media says.

Ju Xin

See also: *Traffic and Transportation:* Beijing, China: Beijing's War on Traffic Congestion

Further Reading
Beijing Municipal Environmental Bureau. 2014. "2014 Beijing Environment Report" (in Chinese). http://www.bjepb.gov.cn/bjhrb/xxgk/jgzn/jgsz/jjgjgszjzz/xcjyc/xwfb/607548/index.html.
Beijing Water Authority. 2015. "Beijing Water Resources Bulletin." http://www.bjwater.gov.cn.
"Beijing's Water Crisis 1949–2008 Olympics." 2008. Probe International Beijing Group, June. http://www.chinaheritagequarterly.org/016/_docs/BeijingWaterCrisis1949-2008.pdf.
Cai Qi. 2017. "Coordinated Development for the Beijing-Tianjin-Hebei Region" (in Chinese). Top News, November 11. http://paper.people.com.cn/rmrb/page/2017-11/20/06/rmrb2017112006.pdf.
Chen Te-Ping. 2015. "China's Water Problems Are Even Worse Than You Think: Report." *Wall Street Journal*, January 13. https://blogs.wsj.com/chinarealtime/2015/01/13/chinas-water-problems-are-even-worse-than-you-think-report.
China Statistical Year Book 2008 and *China National Economic and Social Development Statistical Report 2004*. "GDP Data and Exchange Rate." China Bureau of Statistics. https://www.ceicdata.com/search_campaign.html?ui_lang=EN&how_hear=110&spage=11618&gclid=EAIaIQobChMI9Z3zwp6o2AIVkIizCh3fvActEAAYASAAEgJMKfD_BwE#page=page-1.

Copenhagen, Denmark: Striving to Be Carbon-Neutral by 2025

If Charles Chaplin's 1936 film *Modern Times* was an exaggeration of the crazy industrial era, it doesn't get even close to the chaos that modern urbanization has brought to people's lives today. High traffic congestion, high consumption of energy, high waste, increasing urban warming, diminishing resources, contamination of water resources, high population density in urban neighborhoods, food shortages, rising violence and crime rates, and worsening overall health conditions—these are just some of the problems that are making urban life unsustainable. To reverse this negative trend, world cities have risen to the challenge, but Copenhagen seems to take it more aggressively than most. Wind energy is already supplying 25 percent of the electricity consumed in Denmark, according to the national website, and Copenhagen has 390 kilometers of designated bike lanes, making it the most bike-friendly city in the world.

In 2009, the Copenhagen City Council unanimously adopted the Copenhagen 2025 Climate Plan (CPH 2025), the goal of which is to make Copenhagen a carbon-neutral city by 2025. If it succeeds, it will be the first carbon-neutral city in the world. This article will introduce some of CPH 2025's features.

PRESERVATION OF GREEN SPACE

Copenhagen is the most populous city in Denmark. In 2016, its population was approximately 60,000 in the central city, while 1.3 million live in what's known as the Greater Copenhagen Region (Statistical Yearbook 2016). Originally a Viking village, Copenhagen became the capital of Denmark in the 15th century. Historically, Copenhagen was a fishing and port town, with marine transportation its main business. The city's expansion and lifestyle today appear to have optimally preserved this tradition. The streets between the Sjaelland Island and Kongens Nytorv, Copenhagen's main square, preserve the old town's original layout. Kongens Nytorv, however, has been transformed into a fashionable space, with a mixture of royal palaces and office buildings. Copenhagen is known as a garden city due to its shaded boulevards constructed in the 19th century. Pedestrian lanes are typically paved with a gravel surface, with benches on the side. Trees that were planted later were selected to bud, bloom, and shed leaves in different seasons. This arrangement gives the roads a changing appearance all year round.

In Copenhagen, green spaces have more practical functions. The city's geographical location makes it vulnerable to increasingly higher levels of precipitation. Intensive rain events are happening more frequently in summers and winters are wetter. With surges of storms, floods will be more frequent. A rise in precipitation by 30 to 40 percent is expected by 2100, and a rise of water levels around Copenhagen to between 33 and 61 cm (about 12 to 24 inches) in the period 2000–2100. Most changes are expected to happen after 2500. Increased volumes of rainwater must be properly managed. In view of these changes, Copenhagen will implement measures to prevent droughts and downpours. The city will build additional draining systems, more green spaces including green roofs to slow rainfall runoff, and develop plans to deal with sea-level changes. Pocket parks will be built all over the city between buildings and as road dividers both as green spaces and a mechanism to absorb rainwater.

"IT'S ALL ABOUT LIVABILITY"

Achieving a sustainable urban environment is Copenhagen's goal. "Our focus as a city, as citizens, is all about livability," says Mayor Frank Jensen (Gerdes 2013). According to CPH 2025, Copenhagen's renovation projects will be organized around four concepts: energy consumption, energy, mobility, and city administration. The city council has a master plan to reduce CO_2 consumption from the current 2.5 million tons to under 1.2 million tons in less than two decades. This will be done by improving building emission, since most buildings were constructed in the 1960s–1970s and thus do not meet modern efficiency standards. The city will build district cooling systems to provide air conditioning to public buildings. These AC systems are energy efficient because they make use of seawater to lower the temperature. Street lighting will be more efficient due to the use of energy-friendly lighting mechanisms; renewable energy will be integrated into the energy supply to reduce carbon emissions; greener transport will be increasingly popular; and buildings will be renovated to enhance energy efficiency.

Because currently 73 percent of Copenhagen's electricity is generated by burning coal, a top goal of the city is to gradually replace coal with renewable energy. To implement this goal, the city has creatively established a windmill plan to harvest energy from wind. The project will also contribute to a desirable aesthetic purpose—making the city more attractive. Wind turbines supplied 30 percent of Denmark's electricity by 2012; that will rise to 50 percent by 2020 (Gerdes 2013).

Converting coal to renewable energy means increasing the number of biomass stations. To reduce the pressure of building more treatment plants, Copenhagen is exploring the economical usage of traditional wind turbines that are seen in windmill parks. On the other hand, energy conservation will be critical. To raise energy efficiency, Copenhagen will connect 98 percent of all homes to a district heating system that is powered by combined heat from power plants and incineration of solid waste. The city's goal is to reduce combined CO_2 by 75 percent through these efforts, saving 375k tons of CO_2 per year. One of the initiatives included in GPH 2025 is to improve the Amager power station so that it will use biomass wood chips to replace 50 percent of coal-derived fuel. Another initiative is to raise geothermal energy for heating purposes by sixfold at Margretheholm, a historical Danish naval base that was later transformed into living communities. A third initiative is to build a fuel gas condensation system that converts waste incineration to a heat-generating source. Meanwhile, the city will implement procedures to reduce heat loss from pipelines.

Energy distribution is a critical issue, allowing the city to budget energy according to usages in different seasons. If managed poorly, a leaking system results in losses in the supply chain. Thus, Copenhagen will revamp its energy storing systems. The city conducts ongoing research, for example, in developing systems that store surplus electricity in car batteries, or deliver unused electricity to heating plants.

Effective electrical power conservation is essential to greener transport. One of the Lighthouse Projects (projects that are given high attention) is to let cars run on wind energy. The city encourages individual drivers and businesses to drive electrical vehicles and hydrogen-powered cars. These types of vehicles contribute to reduction of carbon emission as well as urban noise.

BIKING FOR FUN, GOOD HEALTH, AND WORK

Copenhagen makes a continuing effort to promote biking, a national hobby, as a mainstream strategy for people to go to work and take care of daily routines. The city has created a biking-friendly environment, through integrating biking routes into public transportation systems, including convenient parking facilities. For Copenhageners, biking is an important part of life. Not just a weekend exercise, it performs serious functions during the workday.

There are about 400 kilometers (249 miles) of bike lanes specifically designed for cyclists, and 40,000 cyclists ride on these lanes daily. Forty percent of Copenhagen's population commutes via bike. The rush hour in Copenhagen is not the same as the ones in Beijing and Mexico City, with bumper to bumper lines of cars and frustrated drivers. The scene in Copenhagen is one of crowds of bike riders (Tan 2015). One writer describes the scene as follows:

Energy and Sustainability

A bicyclist rides in the designated bike lane in Copenhagen, Denmark. The city promotes biking—a national hobby and energy-efficient means of travel—as a mainstream form of transportation. (Dean Pictures/Dreamstime.com)

> Everywhere, visitors are greeted by streams of bicyclists; 36 percent of trips to work or school in the Danish capital are made by bike, and more than 20,000 cyclists enter the city center at peak hours, filling Copenhagen's 249 miles of cycle tracks. Less visible are state-of-the-art facilities where waste heat from power plants is used to keep buildings warm via the world's largest district heating network, or where waters from the city harbor are deployed to cool department stores, office buildings, hotels, and data centers. (Gerdes 2013)

Is there evidence supporting biking's health benefits? A study by Lars Bo Andersen et al. published in 2000 examined the relationship of mortality of all causes and the level of physical activity one experienced during work, during leisure time, and when cycling to work and participating in sports. The study collected data continuously for 14.5 years from 13,375 women and 17,265 men from regions of Copenhagen. The study found that those who were moderately or highly active participants had half the mortality of nonparticipants; biking to work cut the mortality risk by about 40 percent. A more recent study by Veisten et al., published in 2011 examined how cycling and walking to work might improve health. The study estimates that regular cyclists could enjoy a 30 percent improvement in health. They further found that the urban infrastructure, when it is friendly to cycling and walking, gives people more motivation to bike. More people would likely consider biking "fast and flexible" when road conditions are favorable (Veisten et al. 2011).

Biking and walking on foot, however, are limited by distance. Urban planners are mindful of this shortfall and strive to make urban space energy-conservation friendly. GPH 2025 involves remodeling urban spaces such that stores, schools, public transit, and green areas are reachable by foot. In a sense, the future carbon-neutral city may appear to revert to the layout of pre-industrial cities where things were close to one another.

MAKING PUBLIC TRANSIT MORE EFFICIENT

To promote greener transport, Copenhagen encourages maximum use of public transportation, such as metro, busses, trains, and car sharing. The city's subway system, constructed in the 1990s and opened in 2002, has been a modest but effective public transit.

To improve traffic efficiency and safety, Copenhagen pays attention to improving traffic signaling and information systems. For example, a GPS-guided information system will be widely deployed for cars and mounted on bicycles as well. Making biking more convenient is an essential part of the project. GPH 2025 envisions a "bicycle superhighway," designed to connect the center city with the suburbs. According to GPH 2025, people will take 75 percent of trips by bike, on foot, or by public transportation. Out of the total trips, one-third will be made by biking. Thanks to improved traffic information systems, riders of Copenhagen's GoBike can plot routes and check travel bookings from an on-board GPS (*Economist* 2015). GPH 2025 targets 50 percent of trips to work or school to be made by bike by 2025.

IMPROVING BUILDING INSULATION

To improve energy conservation, Copenhagen has developed plans to improve building insulation. An energy-efficient building is not only economical due to lower energy bills, it also creates a more comfortable living environment thanks to reduced noise levels. The city has developed a new energy class-coding system to measure CO_2 emissions and gauge ventilation, electricity, and insulation. Each year roughly 400,000 square meters of residential and business space are built in Copenhagen. The city is committed to achieving the lowest emission standard.

Copenhagen has plans to renovate both traditional buildings in the historic Latin Quarter and modern buildings in other sections. The city will renovate its office buildings, which occupy approximately 5 percent of the city's floor space, and improve conditions on 1 million square meters of rented space. In addition to installing proper insulation material in the interior, designers will also utilize gardening technology to transform the buildings' exteriors into green spaces.

EDUCATION IS CRITICAL IN THE MAKING OF A SUSTAINABLE CITY

GPH 2025 views education as a critical component in fostering environmental consciousness. It encourages educational and scientific communities to develop instructional programs. This includes building physical and virtual science centers to educate the youth about climate, nature, and sustainable city life. GPH 2025 requires that each year children from infancy to 18 be given the opportunity to participate in at least one center-sponsored activity. Copenhageners believe that encouraging the youth to turn off the computer and pick up a bike will not only conserve energy, but also form a healthy way of living.

Jing Luo

See also: Energy and Sustainability: Melbourne, Australia: Toward a Greater Reliance on Alternative Energy; *Green Spaces:* Rotterdam, The Netherlands: Building an Edible City

Further Reading

Andersen, L. B., P. Schnohr, M. Schroll, and H. O. Hein. 2000. "All-Cause Mortality Associated with Physical Activity during Leisure Time, Work, Sports, and Cycling to Work." https://www.ncbi.nlm.nih.gov/pubmed/10847255.

City of Copenhagen. *CPH 2025 Climate Plan—Roadmap 2017–2020.* http://kk.sites.itera.dk/apps/kk_pub2/pdf/1586_0kE7bzR28V.pdf.

Copenhagen Municipality. "Copenhagen Climate Plan" (the short version). https://webcache.googleusercontent.com/search?q=cache:qg5Vma95sYYJ:https://www.energycommunity.org/documents/copenhagen.pdf+&cd=1&hl=en&ct=clnk&gl=us.

Copenhagen Municipality. *CPC Climate Plan 2025.* https://www.energycommunity.org/documents/copenhagen.pdf.

den Elzen, Michel G. J., Andries F. Hof, Angelica Mendoza Beltran, Giacomo Grassi, Mark Roelfsema, Bas van Ruijven, Jasper van Vliet, and Detlef P. van Vuuren. 2011. "The Copenhagen Accord: Abatement Costs and Carbon Prices Resulting from the Submissions." https://www.sciencedirect.com/science/article/pii/S1462901110001401.

Gerdes, Justin. 2013. "Copenhagen's Ambitious Push to Be Carbon-Neutral by 2025." *Guardian*, April 12. https://www.theguardian.com/environment/2013/apr/12/copenhagen-push-carbon-neutral-2025.

Ministry of Foreign Affairs. n.d. "The Danish Approach to Innovation and Design." https://denmark.dk/innovation-and-design.

Staff Writer. 2015. "Urban Planning—Streetwise." *Economist.* http://www.economist.com/news/international/21663219-cities-are-starting-put-pedestrians-and-cyclists-motorists-makes-them.

StatBank Denmark. 2013. "FRLD113: Population Projections 2013 by Region/Province, Sex and Age (Discontinued)." http://www.statbank.dk/FRLD113.

Statistics Denmark. 2016. *Statistical Yearbook 2016.* https://www.dst.dk/Site/Dst/Udgivelser/GetPubFile.aspx?id=22256&sid=sy.

Tan, Alicia Marie. 2015. "Copenhagen's Morning Traffic Isn't What You'd Imagine in a Big City." Mashable.com, October 29. http://mashable.com/2015/10/29/copenhagen-bike-traffic/#349xyBSt.Zq2.

Thandi Norman, Rebecca. 2015. "A Brief History of Urban Planning in Copenhagen." http://www.scandinaviastandard.com/a-brief-look-at-urban-planning-in-copenhagen.

Veisten, Knut, et al. 2011. "Cycling and Walking for Transport: Estimating Net Health Effects from Comparison of Different Transport Mode Users' Self-Reported Physical Activity." *Health Economics Review* 1, 3. http://www.healtheconomicsreview.com/content/1/1/3.

Frankfurt, Germany: Protecting the City from Climate Changes

Frankfurt, Germany, a dynamic financial, service, and traffic hub of Europe, was crowned the world's most sustainable city in 2015, according to a ranking by a

Singapore consultancy firm, Arcadis' Sustainable Cities Index, which evaluates the world's most developed cities with respect to sustainability. The top 50 cities are ranked annually, and Frankfurt maintains a high position. The city was among the three finalists for the European Green Capital Award competition in 2014. A prominent goal of the city is to meet its power needs by entirely relying on green energy by 2050. This includes cutting greenhouse gas emissions by as much as 95 percent.

BACKGROUND

Frankfurt is the fifth-largest city in Germany with a population of around 750,000. It is located at the heart of the Frankfurt/Rhine-Main metropolitan region, an area inhabited by 6 million people. Frankfurt is a major financial and service center in Europe. It functions as a key traffic hub for the region. A number of top financial facilities located in Frankfurt include the European Central Bank, German Federal Bank, Deutsche Bank, and the Frankfurt Stock Exchange. The city is host to many global and European headquarters and operates the world's busiest international airport. Additionally, it demonstrates global importance in commerce, culture, education, exhibition, and tourism.

Frankfurt is recognized for continuously investing in improving and maintaining its environment. Since 2008, the city has adopted a number of guidelines in reducing greenhouse gas emissions. This effort can be traced to 1983 when the city council established the Energy Office dedicated to conservation and promotion of responsible environmental behavior. To further its climate protection campaign, the city established the Municipal Energy Agency within Frankfurt's Environmental Department. The goal of these agencies was to reduce urban carbon emissions and contribute to controlling global warming. In addition to the efforts made at the level of the government, citizens established the Climate Alliance of European Cities with Indigenous Rainforest Peoples in 1990 to promote environmental protection.

In 2008, the Energy Agency proposed the Energy and Climate Protection Concept with the support of the city council. The concept included 50 energy-saving and climate protection measures, and elaborated steps for the city to meet its obligations in curbing CO_2 emission. The plan aimed at an emission reduction of 10 percent every five years. Once it has succeeded in satisfying its entire power needs with renewable energy by 2050 and reduced its carbon emission by 95 percent, Frankfurt will become a total carbon-neutral city.

On the other hand, efforts made by Frankfurt are rooted in a broader base of practice, that of the European Community, where two-thirds of the population live in urban areas. Because cities in Europe face the challenges of climate change as a whole (although some are more threatened by natural disasters than others are), there is a general consensus on energy conservation and environmental protection. The leadership of the European Commission thus stresses motivating each member of the community to creatively participate to ensure that genuine progress can be achieved. For this purpose, 15 European cities established the European Green Capital Award (EGCA) in 2006. Their vision was that urban living can't be sustainable without being environment-friendly. In operation, EGCA takes the charge of assessing countries and local authorities in terms of their environmental protection achievements. EGCA has set up awards to recognize top achievers. Since the initiation of the program by the European Commission in 2008, many EGCA awards have been announced, and Frankfurt has been a top winner.

In addition to EGCA, there are many environmental action plans and policy instruments in place across Europe to support sustainable urban development. Some of the popular ones include the 7th Environment Action Program (EAP) launched in 2013, Reference Framework for Sustainable European Cities (RFSC), Roadmap for a resource-efficient Europe by 2050, Thematic Strategy on Urban Environment, EU Sustainable Development Strategy, Green Thinking and Best Practice Guides and Reports, and Europe 2020 Strategy. These action plans reflect the general spirit and tailor it according to local challenges. They support the shift toward sustainable growth, resource efficiency, low-carbon footprint, and green initiatives. The new EU budget 2014–2020 allocates at least 5 percent of the European Regional Development Fund to supporting sustainable urban development. Thanks to these efforts, some countries have made leaps in progress. For example, Germany has already become a leader in promoting photovoltaics and wind energy. Germany has demonstrated that it is already able to substantially satisfy the country's electricity supply with renewable energy.

Nuclear power has been a debated issue in Germany, many people question its reliability, and some believe that the technology should be phased out. The Fukushima Daiichi nuclear accident in Japan in March 2011 further increased anxiety about nuclear energy. Large antinuclear protests broke out following the event, which led to Chancellor Angela Merkel's government's announcement that it would close all of its nuclear power plants by 2022. As a result, the contribution of nuclear energy has been on the decline—from one-quarter of Germany's electricity supply in 2011 down to the current 14 percent generated by eight reactors. Forty-three percent of electricity still comes from coal of which lignite (brown coal) is preponderant. However, the government has implemented a two-pronged approach—combining the phase-out of nuclear energy with the exploration of renewable energy. In the meantime, industries strive to increase the efficiency of fossil fuel production in an effort to reduce the reliance on coal. According to the former German Minister for the Environment Jürgen Trittin, by 2020, these efforts will cut carbon dioxide emissions by 40 percent from the 1990 levels.

Today, Germany has become a leader in the efforts to fulfill the commitments of the Kyoto Protocol. The Kyoto Protocol is an international agreement adopted in Kyoto, Japan, in 1997. In conjunction with the United Nations Framework Convention on Climate Change (UNFCCC), and with over 190 participating member states, the Kyoto Protocol commits to setting internationally binding emission reduction targets.

TOWARD A GREEN FUTURE

Frankfurt is a founding member of the Climate Alliance of European Cities. It pledges to continuously reduce its carbon emissions by 10 percent every five years, leading to a 50 percent reduction by 2030, and realizing carbon-neutral by 2050.

In the meantime, however, Frankfurt, as a fast-growing city, has the obligation of creating new living spaces and jobs. How does it achieve its goal? The city proceeds with a comprehensive approach.

First, at the end of September 2015, the city council commissioned the Fraunhofer Institute for Building Physics (IBP) Master Plan for 100% Climate Protection to conduct a feasibility study. The project was sponsored by Frankfurt's Department of Environment and Health and serves as the basis for the Frankfurt to progress in its energy and climate protection plan.

Second, the environmental plans enjoy top-down support. The Master Plan for 100% Climate Protection is backed by the Federal Ministry for the Environment, Nature Conservation, Construction and Nuclear Safety (BMUB). The latter integrates the master plan as part of the National Climate Protection Initiative (NKI) subsidy program. In addition to Frankfurt, 18 other cities, regions, and districts joined in as "master plan communities." On the implementation side, the Frankfurt Energy Department is responsible for executing the plan.

Third, the city council views environmental protection as a concerted social effort. The administration adopted an Integrated Urban Development strategy to encourage growth and jobs and promote a more cohesive society and better environment at the same time. Components include sustainable urban planning, mitigation, and adaptation to climate change, innovative mobility, and management of urban services to provide the best municipal service for its citizens. The latter involves a wide range of involvement and broad-based collaboration.

Finally, the implementation touches on a wide range of operations, from technical measures such as expanding heat and power cogeneration facilities to indirect measures such as information distribution. job training, and the setup of climate protection networks. On the other hand, the city authority recognizes that a sustainable green city is primarily a function of lifestyle change, despite technology or policies. New urban lifestyles that encourage citizens to join hands in making Frankfurt a greener, climate-friendlier, and more equitable place to live are more fundamental than anything else.

Roughly half of Frankfurt's space is "green," according to the city's Environmental Department, most of the city area having been set aside for recreation and to offset the climate impact. The green spaces are in the forms of parks, woodland, farmland, orchard meadows, grassland, allotments and hobby gardens, cemeteries, roadside grass verges, and bodies of water.

The Master Plan for 100% Climate Protection is an extension of the Frankfurt energy and climate protection concept of 2008. The original plan aimed to convert the city to rely 100 percent on renewable energy as well as reducing greenhouse gas emissions by 95 percent by 2050. Economically viable measures were envisioned to realize energy conservation and emissions reduction. Initial stages aimed at reducing energy consumption in Frankfurt to 50 percent of the 2010 levels. The next stage is to be dependent on purely renewable energy sources. Half of the energy demand can then be generated from renewable sources within Frankfurt and surrounding regions.

Energy Conservation is the broad foundation of the energy pyramid. How important is conservation in a transition to clean energy? The illustration of "energy pyramid" answers this question well. Renewable energy, energy efficiency, and energy conservation form the energy pyramid; and conservation is the most important part of the three. Conservation is essential to energy efficiency.

In Frankfurt, the energy conservation campaign starts from electricity-saving households. Modification for energy-saving purposes of residential buildings, energy efficiency in nonresidential buildings and commercial premises to reduce the demand for heat and electricity—these are an important part of construction and remodeling projects. To encourage energy saving, Frankfurt rewards electricity saving with a cash bonus. It is the first city to adopt the reward system in Germany. According to the plan, households that reduce their electricity consumption by at least 10 percent within a year receive a bonus of €20 from the city plus 10 cents for every additional kilowatt hour (kWh) saved. Participants are thus rewarded for their efforts in environmental protection. Electricity measuring devices are provided free of charge by the municipal Energy Agency. The same office also represents a network of consultants for all aspects of energy efficiency: cogeneration, solar heat, photovoltaics, passive houses, renovation, and electricity saving.

In Frankfurt, improvement of efficiency at the city level focuses on three areas: constructing decentralized cogeneration facilities, improving power usage of residential and office buildings, and upgrading mobility technology. Cogeneration captures the exhaust heat from power generation units and turns it into heat-supplying sources. Cogeneration systems are particularly efficient in generating electricity, as heat is produced simultaneously. Heat and power cogeneration thus uses 90 percent of the available energy. A conventional power plant, however, loses typically 60 to 70 percent of energy as exhaust heat. Cogeneration in Frankfurt has a long tradition. The first cogeneration plant was built in 1926.

Installing decentralized home power stations (block-type thermal power stations) is one of the most effective measures to improve energy efficiency for the community neighborhood. It is also a good way to reduce CO_2 emissions. In Frankfurt, the Energy Agency together with local utility companies have engaged in innovations to reduce cogeneration units to a smaller scale, from a few kW to 200 kW. A unit such as the fuel-cell cogeneration unit (ONSI PC25; 200 kW 1998) may be used to provide heat and electricity for a public swimming pool. Another example is a pilot power generation unit equipped with an additional heat exchanger to utilize the sensible heat in the flue-gases for preheating hot water for the building. Some of the experiments have been successful at highly efficient levels.

"Passive houses" refers to buildings equipped with better insulation, and need only 10 percent of the energy used in average German houses. These houses tap solar energy for heating and cooling using what's known as "passive design." Essentially, these buildings are able to balance energy supply without additional mechanical equipment. For example, solar energy is channeled through windows and natural convection. As a result, pumps and fans are used minimally. Apart from low energy bills, passive houses offer the advantages of a comfortable ambient temperature and good air quality. Frankfurt's administration takes the lead in adopting passive design. Administrative buildings are now being built to maximally utilize natural conditions. Furthermore, buildings constructed on land purchased from the city of Frankfurt are required to comply with passive house standards.

To promote the design, the city authority has set up a Green Building Frankfurt" architectural award to encourage innovative, exceptionally well-designed and sustainable passive houses. It serves as a call for the broad public to appreciate "green" buildings and to inspire others to follow. As an example, Frankfurt built the world's first passive hospital to the standard of the passive house, in the Höchst district of Frankfurt with 666 beds and 10 operating theatres planned over six floors, as reported by the Passive House Institute in August 2016.

E-mobility is an important way of energy saving. As part of the Frankfurt E-mobility 2025 strategy, Frankfurt will promote the use of electric cars and build a charging infrastructure. The project aims at integrating it into travel chains with linking transportation means other than electrically powered vehicles by 2025. A recent ruling by a top German court banned old diesel cars that fail to meet the "Euro 5" standard in Frankfurt effective February 2019, taking 74,000 diesel cars off the city's roads (Clugston 2018). The court announced its decision just one day after Mercedes showcased a new generation of electrical SUVs (Wiessenbach 2018).

Photovoltaics technology is widely adopted in Frankfurt as a renewable source. The city links photovoltaics energy generation to a grid-connected solar power system. The system has reportedly increased power generation in Frankfurt by hundreds of times, and continues to grow. Today, solar panels are seen on the roofs of stadiums, school buildings, city-owned real estate. Energy-sharing deals offer tenants an opportunity to purchase shares of power plants on the basis of rooftop space. Tenants can make a personal contribution to climate-friendly energy production, CO_2 reduction, and make additional income, an exemplary win-win situation.

Frankfurt explores the potential of biomass as a renewable source. On the one hand, the city collects urban biowaste and green waste from parks and gardens. The material is then used by local biomass companies to produce biogas. Power and thermal stations convert the material into electricity and heat.

THE FUTURE OF FRANKFURT

Frankfurt is recognized as successful in implementing an integrated approach to build a sustainable city. Its achievement in involving individual citizens, communities, and urban authorities to work together in the conservation of energy is exemplary. Additionally, appropriate use of technology opened a variety of innovative venues. In comparison with prominent international cities on sustainability and future prospects, Frankfurt is well ahead, and the majority of its citizens see the development as mostly positive. Now the Frankfurt-green-city reporting becomes a continuous reporting on sustainability, which serves as both communication with its citizens and an assessment tool using a set of sustainability indicators.

In conclusion, Frankfurt is on its way toward a sustainable green future. By 2050, the city will reach the target of satisfying its entire power needs with renewable energy and save about 50 percent of energy consumed today, if the current trend continues. The city could realize its great potential in reducing energy consumption and replace the remaining demand with renewable energy. However, the city cannot supply all of its electrical power need from renewable energy sources alone

> ### Return of the Electrical Vehicle
>
> There are mainly three kinds of electrical vehicles (EVs): the hybrid electric vehicles (HEVs), the plug-in hybrid electric vehicles (PHEVs), and the battery electric vehicles (BEVs). Declining battery prices and government influence through the offer of purchase incentives and stricter regulation on emissions are expected to boost EV sales. The growth of EV share is expected to reach nearly 7 percent per year globally by 2020, according to a report by Navigant Research.
>
> In the United States, EVs have a longer history than vehicles with internal combustion engines. In the early 1900s, EVs were the preferred choice for urban residents. With gasoline prices dropping in the 1920s, gasoline-powered cars soon replaced EVs by the 1930s. They allowed urban residents to travel farther and at much cheaper cost.
>
> A number of factors revived the EV market. The gasoline shortages in the early 1970s raised concerns over reliance on foreign oil. However, it was finally environmental concerns arising in the 1990s that drove EVs forward. In 2006, Tesla let the charge by producing a luxury electric sports car able to cover 200 miles on a single charge. Other carmakers followed suit. According to a report published by the Department of Energy, there are more than 3 million hybrids and EVs on the road in the United States today. The report draws an optimistic picture for the EVs market: if all light-duty vehicles in the U.S. are replaced with hybrids or plug-in electric vehicles using our current technology mix, dependence on foreign oil could drop by 30–60 percent. Better yet, carbon pollution from the transportation sector could be lowered by as much as 20 percent.

without the backup of the regional power grid or electrical storage facilities. After all, the sun will not shine at night nor during overcast or raining days; solar energy needs backup sources. The city needs to collaborate with the Rhine-Main metropolis to tap to the regional power grid, and to finance the installation of the electrical storage facility together, to reduce the costs.

Ju Xin

See also: Energy and Sustainability: Melbourne, Australia: Toward a Greater Reliance on Alternative Energy; *Green Spaces:* Tokyo, Japan: Making the City More Livable

Further Reading

Brenscheidt, T., K. Janowitz, H.-J. Salge, H. Wendt, and F. Brammer. 1998. "Performance of ONSI PC25 PAFC Cogeneration Plant." *International Journal of Hydrogen Energy* 23, 1 (January): 53–56 (ScienceDirect).

Climate Alliance of European Cities. http://www.climatealliance.org/home.html.

Clugston, Erika. 2018. "Court Rules Frankfurt Must Implement Diesel Ban." *Clean Technica.* September 11. https://cleantechnica.com/2018/09/11/court-rules-frankfurt-must-implement-diesel-ban/.

European Green Capital Award (EGCA). http://ec.europa.eu/environment/europeangreencapital/about-the-award.

Kyoto Protocol. http://unfccc.int/kyoto_protocol/items/2830.php.

Leipzig Charter on Sustainable European Cities. http://ec.europa.eu/regional_policy/archive/themes/urban/leipzig_charter.pdf.

Nuclear Power in Germany: World Nuclear Association. http://www.world-nuclear.org/information-library/country-profiles/countries-g-n/germany.aspx.

Passive House Institute US (PHIUS). http://www.phius.org/home-page.

Wiessenbach, Ilona. 2018. "German Court Says Frankfurt Must Ban Older Diesel Cars." *Reuters.* September 5. https://www.reuters.com/article/us-volkswagen-emissions-frankfurt/german-court-says-frankfurt-must-ban-older-diesel-cars-idUSKCN1LL2GC.

London, United Kingdom: Improving Mobility Can Save Energy

The city of London has grown considerably since it was founded by the Romans, a little more than two thousand years ago, to become one of the largest and most important cities in the world. London experienced its most dramatic growth during the industrial revolution, expanding from a population of 1 million in 1800 to more than 6 million by the year 1900. Thirty years later, the city's population peaked at a little more than 8 million, and did not rise above this level for almost 80 years (University of Portsmouth 2017).

The rapid population boom during the industrial era caused increased crowding, slums, and disease. This led to many changes in the city's landscape as planners, business leaders, and policymakers sought to address these problems. Some of the measures taken included tearing down impoverished neighborhoods and building new satellite towns. The opening of the London Underground, the first urban underground railway in the world, in 1863 enabled people to move out of the city's crowded center. Following World War II, the British government built more than two dozen new towns that helped reduce London's population by several hundred thousand. In recent decades, however, the city's population has again increased.

Today, the city of London has more than 8.6 million people in its 607-square-mile (1,572-square-kilometer) area. Not including Moscow or Istanbul, which are culturally, politically, and economically distinct from other European cities, London is the most populous city in Europe. However, research by the European Commission marks the Functional Urban Area (FUA) of London as having 12.2 million people, or about one-fifth of the British population (Eurostat 2016). London is also the most densely populated European city. With about 14,000 people per square mile (5,500 per square kilometer), it has approximately twice the population density of Paris or Berlin.

London's population continues to grow as it provides economic and cultural opportunities that attract young migrants from all over Britain. As a result, it has one of the youngest populations among large European cities (Eurostat 2016). Additionally, due to its thriving economic activity, London has drawn many migrants from Europe and other parts of the world. Consequently, London has one of the lowest rates of native-born population among large European cities. In fact, it absorbs most of the immigrants to Britain, and more than one-third of the city's workforce (37 percent or 3 million) was born outside of the country (Clear 2016; Christie and Douglass 2017). Thus, due to its draw to young people and immigrants, London's population has grown at twice the rate of the United Kingdom (UK) since 2011—5.7 percent versus 2.9 percent (Osborne 2016).

ECONOMY

One of the reasons that London attracts so many people from Britain and the rest of the world is its economic significance nationally and internationally. Within the UK, London accounts for 22.7 percent of the country's economy, with a per capita GDP that is almost twice the national average (ONS 2016). There are several sectors of the economy in which London plays an outsized role. The city accounts for 33.7 percent of financial and insurance activities, 31.4 percent of information and communication positions, and 26.2 percent of professional scientific and technical activities in the UK workforce. One of the only major sectors in which London's role has declined, and in which the city does not have a significant share of the national economy, is manufacturing (Christie and Douglass 2017, 5). London's vital role within Britain was apparent in a recent study that found that the city generates almost as much in tax revenue as the next-largest 37 cities combined (Inman 2016).

One indication of London's importance internationally is the fact that (as of 2014) London's Heathrow airport was the busiest in the European Union, with 73 million passengers per year, well ahead of the next most traveled, Paris's Charles de Gaulle airport, with 64 million (Eurostat 2016). One of the reasons for much of the air traffic is the fact that London is home to the largest number of headquarters of the top 250 companies with global or regional headquarters in Europe. With 40 headquarters, London far outpaces second place Paris's 8 (Christie and Douglass 2017, 23).

Various international economic analyses have ranked London very highly among world cities. For example, the *Economist* ranked London second (behind New York) among 120 cities' world financial centers (*Economist* 2013a, 11). In the 2017 *City Momentum Index* London dropped from second to sixth place. However, it was the only European city ranked in the top 10, based on its strong global position in technology, innovation, and education (JLL 2017).

In the *Global Power City Index*, London was ranked first among 42 world cities (Institute for Urban Strategies 2016). This analysis comprised several components. Among them, London was ranked first in accessibility and cultural interaction, second in economy, and third in research and development. However, London only came in 8th for environment and fell to 22nd place in the category of Livability.

ENVIRONMENT

Examination of environmental policies and conditions of a city like London must take into account its context nationally and internationally. London is subject to national policies for energy, waste, water use, and many other issues related to sustainability and the environment. Despite this, there are several aspects of environmental sustainability for which the city can be examined independently and compared with other parts of the country as well as other world cities. For example, despite accounting for a large share of Britain's economy, London's CO_2 emissions are well below the national average (5.4 vs. 7.1 tons per capita) (Centre for Cities 2015, 55).

TRANSPORTATION

One of the areas in which cities' sustainability is often assessed is public transportation. High levels of public transit service reduces the use of private cars, which in turn reduces CO_2 emissions and the need for paving additional roadways and parking areas. The first underground rail system in the world was built in London. Currently, there are approximately 3 million passenger journeys on London's Underground every day. Additionally, the city has one of the largest bus networks in the world, with 7,500 buses and more than 700 bus routes (*Journeys* 2012, 68). In a comparison between London and four cities with similar population sizes—New York, Tokyo, Hong Kong, and Singapore—London was found to have the most length (kilometers) of track per person and the largest public bus fleet (per million). Although London's daily rail ridership per person lagged behind the other four cities, its daily per person bus ridership was the highest. This discrepancy may be explained in part by the fact that while London's rail fares were the highest of the five cities, its bus fares were second lowest. London's high transit use came despite the fact that it has the highest rate of car ownership among the five cities examined (*Journeys* 2012, 68–69).

The number of daily public transit trips in London exceeds 10 million, and the 46 percent of Londoners who use public transportation (together with the 11 percent who walk and the 3.8 percent who use bicycles) far exceeds the 35 percent who use their cars (*Economist* 2013b). Not only does London provide excellent public transportation, in 2009 it began work on the Crossrail project to add new rail lines in Europe's largest construction project. The Crossrail routes are planned to run over 100 kilometers and include 40 stations. It is estimated that Crossrail will increase London's rail capacity by 10 percent, the largest increase since the Second World War. The first service on this addition began in May 2017, and the entire project is scheduled to be completed at the end of 2019 (TfL 2017).

In addition to providing a high level of public transportation, London has adopted additional measures to reduce vehicle-related air pollution. The city's ultra-low-emission zone (ULEZ) will come into force in April 2019. This policy will add a daily charge of £12.50 for any vehicle that does not meet the zone's exhaust emission standards. In addition, London will implement at the same time a congestion charging zone (CCZ), which will further discourage private vehicle traffic. Furthermore, London Mayor Sadiq Khan introduced a "toxicity charge" (T-Charge) for the capital's most polluting vehicles, which was scheduled to come into effect in October 2017. This charge applies to vehicles that do not meet the Euro IV emission standards. While these charges will act as a costly deterrent to private vehicle traffic, the city has also launched the first of 12 low-emission bus zones (LEBZ), which allow only the greenest buses to travel through the zone (Climate Action 2017).

CLIMATE CHANGE AND SUSTAINABILITY

Increased use of public transportation is an important element in providing cleaner air to city residents and in reducing CO_2 emissions that contribute to global climate change. London has an important role to play in this regard since Britain is the world's eighth-largest producer of CO_2 emissions, of which London is responsible for 8.4 percent. Yet, as a result of its high level of public transportation use and low level of manufacturing employment, London has the lowest level of annual domestic carbon dioxide emissions per person in Britain (Mayor of London 2016, 179).

London's Climate Change Plan requires the mayor to "use all of his powers, resources and influence to work with other agencies to raise awareness and promote behavioural change" in order to further reduce CO_2 emissions (Mayor of London 2016, 177). This has included developing strategies for waste management, air quality, water, and biodiversity in the city.

One important way to diminish output of greenhouse gases is by reduction of fossil fuels as a source of electricity. To this end, London's mayor has set a target of reducing CO_2 emissions by 60 percent of their 1990 level by 2025 (Mayor of London 2017). The city has adopted a multifaceted approach to reach these goals, including making buildings more energy efficient, supplying more local low-carbon energy, adopting hydrogen sources to power transport and buildings, and investing in technology to cut energy usage (Mayor of London 2017).

Housing construction is seen as an important component of reaching these goals. Consequently, the city promotes sustainable design and construction to improve buildings' environmental performance and plan for adaptation to the effects of climate change (Mayor of London 2016, 183). One example of planning buildings to meet climate change goals is the city's advocacy of design features such as green roofs. These "can enhance biodiversity, absorb rainfall, improve the performance of the building, reduce the urban heat island effect and improve the appearance of a development" (Mayor of London 2016, 184).

Another aspect of London's climate change policy is the promotion of open green spaces. The mayor's plan "seeks to increase the amount of surface area greened in the Central Activities Zone by at least five percent by 2030, and a further five per cent by 2051" (Mayor of London 2016, 197). One additional element of London's efforts to achieve greater sustainability is encouraging waste recycling. The city has improved recycling rates, from 8 percent in 2001 to 30 percent in 2012. The mayor's plan sets a goal of a 50 percent recycling rate by 2020.

One of the keys to reducing CO_2 emissions is through the use of renewable energy instead of fossil fuels. In assessing this particular aspect of sustainability, it is difficult to distinguish local from national policies. On the one hand, Britain has been rapidly reducing its use of coal (BBC 2017). On the other hand, London was been ranked the worst city in England and Wales for its use of renewable energy in an analysis by the Green Alliance think tank, which found that just 0.05 percent of electricity consumption in the city was met by renewables (Pratt 2016). Despite that, the 175 turbines in London's Thames River estuary currently comprise the largest offshore wind farm in the world, providing enough energy to power 470,000 homes (Shankleman 2012).

LONDON IN A GLOBAL CONTEXT

The individual aspects of environmental policies and planning provide an incomplete picture of where cities stand as far as meeting sustainability goals. Several organizations' research combine different components of sustainability in order to provide a more comprehensive comparative assessment of how successful different cities have been in pursuing environmental goals.

The complexity of comparing cities is evident, for example, in the *Cities of Opportunity* report (PwC 2016). In this assessment, London is ranked first among 30 world cities. However, it is only ranked 13th in the category of *Sustainability and the Natural Environment*. Among the different factors that comprise this category, London fares poorly compared to other cities in terms of public park space, recycled waste, and water risk. In addition, while London does reasonably well in most categories connected with transportation and infrastructure (overall ranked 8th), it is ranked second to last in *Affordability of Public Transport*.

In another comprehensive comparative analysis, London ranked 11th of 30 cities in the *European Green Cities Index* (Shields and Langer 2009). In this report, London remained in the middle of the pack for most categories, with its best ranking in water quality (8th) and its worst in transportation (16th). The more recent *Arcadis Sustainable Cities Index* (2016) ranks London 5th among 100 world cities. The Sustainability index comprises three broad categories: *People, Planet,* and *Profit*. In the *Planet* subcategory, which analyzes environmental risks, air and water pollution, energy, greenhouse gas emissions, green space, and waste management, London is ranked 9th.

The different international comparisons help provide context to the city of London's policies regarding energy, the environment, and sustainability. London is a world economic leader and the engine that drives Britain's economy. In recent years, it has adopted policies to reduce its carbon footprint by increasing its already extensive transportation network and promoting alternative energy. International assessments indicate that these efforts have made the city one of the best in terms of the environment and sustainability, but also show that in several categories there is room for London to keep improving.

Matt Evans

See also: Employment and Jobs: London, United Kingdom: Brexit, the Known Unknown; *Migration and Demographic Changes:* London, United Kingdom: Facing the Challenges of Population Growth

Further Reading

Arcadis. 2016. "Sustainable Cities Index 2016." https://www.arcadis.com/media/0/6/6/%7B06687980-3179-47AD-89FD-F6AFA76EBB73%7DSustainable%20Cities%20Index%202016%20Global%20Web.pdf.

BBC. 2017. "First Coal-Free Day in Britain since 1880s." April 22. http://www.bbc.com/news/uk-39675418.

Centre for Cities. 2015. *Cities Outlook 2015.* http://www.centreforcities.org/wp-content/uploads/2015/01/15-01-09-Cities-Outlook-2015.pdf.

Christie, Emma, and Gordon Douglass. 2017. "London and Europe: Facts and Figures." Greater London Authority, GLA Economics, February. https://www.london.gov.uk/sites/default/files/london-and-europe-cin51.pdf.

Clear, Robert. 2016. "London's International Workforce." City of London's Economic Research Programme, September 13. http://colresearch.typepad.com/colresearch/2016/09/londons-international-workforce.html.

Climate Action. 2017. "London Accelerates Plans for Ultra Low Emission Zone." April 12. http://www.climateactionprogramme.org/news/london-accelerates-plans-for-ultra-low-emission-zone.

Economist. 2013a. "Hot Spots 2025: Benchmarking the Future Competitiveness of Cities." http://www.citigroup.com/citi/citiforcities/pdfs/hotspots2025.pdf.

Economist. 2013b. "Underground, Overground." http://www.economist.com/news/britain/21588072-london-has-built-about-good-transport-network-it-could-given-its-constraints-time.

Eurostat. 2016. "European Statistics on Cities." European Union. http://ec.europa.eu/eurostat/documents/4031688/7672011/KS-04-16-588-EN-N.pdf/418067e1-67a5-4c43-bb3f-b10181194447; http://ec.europa.eu/eurostat/statistics-explained/index.php/Statistics_on_European_cities.

Florida, Richard, and Aria Bendix. 2015. "How London and Berlin's Daily Travel Habits Compare to the U.S." *Atlantic, CityLab*, September 24. https://www.citylab.com/transportation/2015/09/how-london-and-berlins-daily-travel-habits-compare-to-the-us/406840.

Hall, Peter. 1974. *Urban and Regional Planning.* Middlesex, UK: Penguin Books.

Hanley, Chris. 2012. "London 2012 Travel Demand Management." *Journeys* 9: 29–38.

Inman, Phillip. 2016. "London Pays Almost a Third of UK Tax, Report Finds." *Guardian*, July 6. https://www.theguardian.com/money/2016/jul/07/london-top-taxpaying-city-uk-report.

Institute for Urban Strategies. 2018. Global Power City Index 2018. http://mori-m-foundation.or.jp/english/ius2/gpci2/index.shtml.

JLL. 2017. "City Momentum Index 2017: Identifying the World's Most Dynamic Cities." http://www.jll.com/Research/Jll-city-momentum-index-2017.pdf?770e8de8-22f0-4580-9c2b-f449158f0e60.

"Key Transport Statistics of World Cities." 2012. *Journeys* 9: 68–70.

Mayor of London. 2016. The London Plan: The Spatial Development Strategy for London, Greater London Authority. https://www.london.gov.uk/sites/default/files/the_london_plan_malp_final_for_web_0606_0.pdf.

Mayor of London. 2017. https://www.london.gov.uk/what-we-do/environment.

Office for National Statistics (ONS). 2016. Regional Gross Value Added, UK: 1997 to 2015. https://www.ons.gov.uk/economy/grossvalueaddedgva/bulletins/regionalgrossvalueaddedincomeapproach/december2016.

Osborne, Hilary. 2016. "London Population Growth Rate Twice That of UK, Official Figures Show." October 12. https://www.theguardian.com/uk-news/2016/oct/12/london-population-growth-twice-that-of-uk-official-figures-show.

Pratt, David. 2016. "London Ranked Worst of All Cities for Renewable Energy Use." Solar Power Portal, March 2. http://www.solarpowerportal.co.uk/news/london_ranked_worst_of_all_cities_for_renewable_energy_use_7142.

PwC. 2016. "Cities of Opportunity 7." http://www.pwc.com/us/en/cities-of-opportunity/2016/cities-of-opportunity-7-report.pdf.

Roumpani, Flora, and Polly Hudson. 2014. "The Evolution of London: The City's Near-2,000 Year History Mapped." *Guardian*, May 15. https://www.theguardian.com/cities/2014/may/15/the-evolution-of-london-the-citys-near-2000-year-history-mapped.

Semple, Brian. 2015. "London Still Generates More Than Twice the Tax Revenue Than the Entire Northern Powerhouse Region." *New Statesman*, July 16. http://www

.citymetric.com/politics/london-still-generates-more-twice-tax-revenue-entire-northern-powerhouse-region-1235.

Shankleman, Jessica. 2012. "World's Largest Offshore Windfarm Opens in Thames Estuary." *Guardian*, July 4. https://www.theguardian.com/environment/2013/jul/04/offshore-windfarm-opens-thames-estuary.

Shields, Katherine, and Harald Langer. 2009. "European Green City Index." Economist Intelligence Unit, Siemens AG Corporate Communications and Government Affairs, Munich.

Transport for London (TfL). 2017. Crossrail in Numbers. http://www.crossrail.co.uk/news/crossrail-in-numbers.

University of Portsmouth. 2017. A Vision of Britain through Time. http://www.visionofbritain.org.uk/data_cube_page.jsp?data_theme=T_POP&data_cube=N_TOT_POP&u_id=10097836&c_id=10001043&add=N.

Vaughan, Adam. 2016. "UK Hits Clean Energy Milestone: 50% of Electricity from Low Carbon Sources." *Guardian*, December 22. https://www.theguardian.com/environment/2016/dec/22/uk-hits-clean-energy-milestone-50-of-electricity-from-low-carbon-sources.

Melbourne, Australia: Toward a Greater Reliance on Alternative Energy

Not to be confused with a city of the same name in Florida, Melbourne is the second-largest metropolis in the country and continent of Australia. Like other cities, Melbourne consumes energy at a prodigious rate. As elsewhere, fossil fuels supply Melbourne with energy. Well endowed with fossil fuels, Australia is both a producer and consumer. Coal is important in the derivation of electricity, and the country as well as the city of Melbourne have come to rely increasingly on coal in this capacity in recent years. According to the Department of Industry, in 2016, for example, coal met 63 percent of Australia's demand for electricity, whereas renewable sources of energy accounted for just 14 percent of the generation of electricity. Oil is also important, though natural gas plays a smaller role. Because of the reliance on coal, a particularly dirty fuel, and oil, Australia and the city of Melbourne produce more greenhouse gases per person than any other nation. This is unhealthy and unsustainable, and Melbourne is moving toward a greater reliance on alternative sources of energy.

BIOMASS

The use of biomass to generate heat when it decays or electricity when it is burned holds promise in Melbourne. Of the potential sources of biomass, bagasse, the residues of sugarcane plants left after the cane juice is extracted, has a long tradition of being burned to generate electricity throughout Australia. The traditional region of sugarcane cultivation is Queensland. Melbourne, being in the state of Victoria, relies less on bagasse for electricity than Queensland, but the potential for growth is apparent. Current harvesting techniques, however, limit the potential for bagasse to generate electricity because Australian harvesters leave about half the sugarcane plant in or on the ground. Merely by collecting all the sugarcane stalks and the rest of the plant, Australia, and Melbourne in this instance, could double its generation of electricity from bagasse. The potential of bagasse to generate electricity is particularly important given that the harvest coincides with peak demand for electricity. A benefit from the use of bagasse is the fact that its burning produces fewer greenhouse gases than does the burning of fossil fuels. The burning of bagasse, however, is not an entirely green alternative because it produces some greenhouse gases. The burning of bagasse to generate electricity is thus more sustainable than the burning of fossil fuels while being less sustainable than the use of other renewable sources of energy. Bagasse is, however, a renewable source of energy because sugarcane regenerates year after year. Part of the appeal of using bagasse is that sugarcane is a perennial grass and so need not be planted year after year, only after every second or third year when yields diminish. Bagasse also holds promise as a potential source of ethanol. Ethanol is a type of alcohol that may be mixed with gasoline or diesel to power automobiles. Under current technologies, ethanol cannot replace gasoline or diesel, but it can reduce its use in Melbourne and other areas of dense population where the automobile remains an important source of transportation and a polluter. Ethanol is comparatively easy to produce from bagasse, arising naturally during the process of fermentation. Care must be taken, however, to use bagasse soon after the harvest. If left to rot, sugarcane plants produce methane, a light hydrocarbon that is much more potent than carbon dioxide as a greenhouse gas.

The University of Melbourne has taken the interest in biomass in a different direction by producing what is known as biodiesel, a substitute for the distillate of petroleum known as diesel, from algae. Algae are single-celled organisms that can convert sunlight into energy, in this case into biodiesel, in a process known as photosynthesis. The technique of biodiesel generation is appealing because algae generate no greenhouse gases. A byproduct of photosynthesis is oxygen, so that the sustained use of algae for the generation of biofuels holds the potential to increase oxygen concentrations in the atmosphere. Because oxygen does not trap sunlight, its production will not warm the earth and may cool it. Algae may thus be an antidote to the problems of global warming and climate change, reducing Melbourne's carbon footprint. Biofuels have the potential to reduce Melbourne's dependence on gasoline and diesel to power automobiles.

OTHER SOURCES OF RENEWABLE ENERGY

The interest in renewable sources of energy has prompted Melbourne authorities to act in a variety of ways. In an act almost unprecedented at the time, Melbourne in 2002 outlined plans to become the world's first city to be neutral in carbon emissions by 2020. Obviously, such a goal requires a robust transition to renewable sources of energy. As part of a carbon-neutral agenda, Melbourne has spent $ 14.8 million to replace streetlights with light-emitting diodes (LEDs), a practice that has reduced the city's consumption of electricity by $1 million and in the process reduced the emission of greenhouse gases by making Melbourne a less ravenous consumer of electricity, especially given the use of coal in generating it (Kane

2016). Among capital cities in Australia, Melbourne leads with 138 green star–rated buildings. One renowned library in Melbourne touted six green-star ratings in 2014, the most of any public building. As part of its agenda, Melbourne aims to generate one-fourth of its energy from renewable sources by 2018.

In keeping with its principles, Melbourne has issued a series of directives, the first being a zero net emissions strategy in 2003 with updates in 2008 and 2014. These reports promote carbon neutrality in a number of important ways that appear poised to put Melbourne on a path toward sustainability. Among its pronouncements, Melbourne aims to reduce greenhouse gas emissions 10 percent by 2020. Second, it aims to construct buildings and improve existing structures such that the average building in the city will use 40 percent less energy by 2020. This mandate applies not only to public buildings but to structures in the private sector. This plan does not yet apply to homes and apartments, though the zero emissions strategy promises action in the coming years. Third, Melbourne aims to increase by 25 percent its generation of electricity from renewable sources by 2018. Fourth, Melbourne intends to reduce the use of energy in transportation. In 2009, roughly 50 percent of all trips in the city were made in low-emissions vehicles. The city aims to increase this percentage to 60 by 2018.

The 2014 update to the zero emissions strategy, the latest report, recognizes that government alone cannot put Melbourne on a path to sustainability. The private sector is equally important, so a public-private partnership should be at the core of Melbourne's approach to sustainability. Despite progress, the 2014 update sounds

Solar panels on an office-building roof in Melbourne, Australia, August 20, 2015. The city aims to reduce the cost of electricity in commercial buildings by $108 million by 2020. (Scott Barbour/Getty Images)

a note of caution in admitting that Melbourne is still too dependent on coal to generate electricity, a problem that the rest of Australia shares. The report acknowledges that as of that year, coal remained too large a contributor to energy production and greenhouse gas emission. Part of the problem with coal and traditional sources of energy in the generation of electricity, the report concedes, is the centralized nature of production. A utility operates a turbine at a central location, transmitting electricity along a grid to businesses, government buildings, and homes. This transmission involves the movement of electricity through copper wires. Electricity is simply the flow of electrons through these wires. But transmission is not perfect. As the electrons move through the copper wires, they encounter resistance and so must dissipate some of their energy. This dissipation represents lost energy in the form of heat. The 2014 update estimates that Melbourne loses 10 percent of its electricity from this inefficiency.

The update approaches the problem of electricity loss through transmission by promoting improvements in the grid of power lines, notably the use of information technology to improve the efficiency with which the grid operates. The report appears to gloss over another solution to the problem of electricity loss by encouraging the use of solar energy. Solar photovoltaic cells, often simply known as solar panels, are attractive in this regard, partly because they convert sunlight directly into electricity but also because of their decentralized nature. Solar panels may be placed anywhere in Melbourne so that they may be near consumers. Dispersed solar panels near consumers provide electricity close to the end user, so that little electricity will be lost in transmission. Melbourne looks to private firms like Ingenero and Energy Matters to tailor solar energy to the city's needs.

The report acknowledges an obstacle to the conversion to solar energy given that in Melbourne, coal generates electricity more cheaply than do current solar technologies. Because residents are unwilling to accept an increase in their electric bills, Melbourne continues to rely disproportionately on coal to generate electricity. The

---

Greenhouse Gas

The burning of fossil fuels liberates many gases into the atmosphere. Those that trap the sun's energy as heat are known as greenhouse gases. The term "greenhouse" refers to the action of glass in a greenhouse. On a sunny day, sunlight passes through the glass to warm the interior because the interior traps some of the incoming heat. An analogous warming is occurring in earth's atmosphere because the burning of fossil fuels is changing the composition of gases to include an ever-larger amount of greenhouse gases. Such gases permit sunlight to pass through them on their way to earth just as glass admits sunlight into a greenhouse. Earth absorbs some of the sunlight—for example, plants capture some sunlight for photosynthesis—whereas the rest rebounds into the atmosphere. But this light, now having a longer wavelength than when it entered the atmosphere, does not all escape into space because greenhouse gases capture it in this form. This trapping warms the atmosphere. Humans notice this effect in higher average global temperatures. Climatologists have identified numerous environmental and economic problems from these increasing temperatures, but politicians cannot agree on solutions.

cost of generating solar energy must decrease in Melbourne to make it competitive in the marketplace.

Irrespective of costs, Melbourne must become more efficient in its use of energy. In this context, conservation is key. An important application of this agenda is the improvement in the efficiency with which buildings use energy. Yet Melbourne struggles with an increase in population that has led to the building of more dwellings that in the aggregate use more energy. The problem is conspicuous in the construction of high-rise apartment buildings that tend to waste energy. Hallways and parking garages must be lighted and swimming pools heated. Heat rises in such buildings so that much energy must be used to cool upper floors during summers. To compound problems, the report notes that landlords may resist paying for improvements to their apartments that would enhance energy efficiency.

Commercial buildings present their own challenges, especially since as an aggregate they are the largest consumers of energy in Melbourne. The city aims to reduce the use of electricity in commercial buildings by $108 million by 2020 ("Zero Net Emissions by 2020: Update 2014," 17). The report acknowledges that the owners of commercial buildings will need to upgrade their structures, a process that will not be inexpensive. Nevertheless, the update estimates that such improvements can realize sufficient savings in energy use to repay the initial investment within four years. The financing for such improvements, however, is not always easy to obtain, the report concedes. Government can provide some of the funds for improvements, but private banks must also invest in energy efficiency. Part of the solution may involve an educational campaign in which government and the private sector collaborate in instructing office tenants on the most efficient use of heating and cooling systems. Government and the private sector may contribute to this effort by educating hotels and retailers about the most efficient way to heat and cool their structures.

The report focuses on improving the energy efficiency of roofs on all buildings. Many strategies may be pursued to realize savings. One approach involves the cultivation of green or living roofs, so named because the owner grows plants on them. These plants absorb sunlight before it has a chance to heat the building during summer. Because plants capture this heat in the form of sunlight, the building need not expend so much electricity on air conditioning during summers. The plants also serve to insulate the buildings so they lose less cool air through diffusion during summers. It is also possible to achieve the goal of a cool roof by wetting roofs. The water on a roof will evaporate, liberating heat in the process in a mechanism akin to sweating. Of course, the provision of water to a roof requires the expenditure of energy. The use of a wet roof might involve spraying the roof with water or constructing a shallow pool atop the roof from which water evaporates. The report anticipates that the Sustainable Melbourne Fund, a source of public money, can finance the construction of green or wet roofs. Other avenues of conservation are open, including the use of energy-efficient appliances in commercial structures and residences. In concert with other approaches, Melbourne is taking strides toward sustainability.

Christopher Cumo

See also: Energy and Sustainability: Copenhagen, Denmark: Striving to Be Carbon-Neutral by 2025; London, United Kingdom: Improving Mobility Can Save Energy

Further Reading

City of Melbourne. n.d. "City of Melbourne: Zero Net Emissions Strategy." https://www
.melbourne.vic.gov.au/about-council/vision-goals/eco-city/pages/zero-net
-emissions-strategy.aspx.

Department of Industry, Australian Government. 2016. "Australian Energy Update, 2016." p. 1. https://www.energy.gov.au/publications/australian-energy-update-2016.

Kane, Annie. 2016. "Australia's Greenest City: Adelaide Pulls ahead of Sydney and Melbourne." *Guardian*, February 12. https://www.theguardian.com/sustainable
-business/2016/feb/12/australias-greenest-city-adelaide-pulls-ahead-of-sydney
-and-melbourne.

"Zero Net Emissions by 2020: Update 2014." https://www.melbourne.vic.gov.au/site collectiondocuments/zero-net-emissions-update-2014.pdf.

Mumbai, India: Providing Energy for a City of 21 Million

Mumbai is an Indian megacity located on the western coast of India overlooking the Arabian Sea. It is the state capital of Maharashtra and with a population count of 21 million is the second most populated city in India (after Delhi) and the fourth largest in the world. Mumbai is the financial hub of the nation, with a large number of multinational corporations, banks, and financial institutions headquartered in the city, not to mention the country's two biggest stock exchanges, a thriving and globally recognized film industry, a growing technology sector, and a multitude of scientific institutions and centers of higher learning. In terms of global connectivity, it enjoys the same status as alpha cities of the world like Frankfurt, Mexico City, Los Angeles, Sydney, Johannesburg, and Toronto to name a few.

POPULATION GROWTH AND ENERGY DEMAND

Mumbai is ranked 31st among world cities in terms of gross domestic product (GDP) at purchasing power parity (Koppikar 2016). It is one of the most densely populated cities of the world, and its population is expected to grow to 27.8 million by the end of 2030. A growing population, while a valuable resource in terms of economic progress, also puts incredible pressure on the energy resources and the environment. International Energy Outlook (2016) predicts that world energy consumption will grow by 48 percent from 2012 to 2040, and the majority of the predicted increase in energy demand will arise from the rapidly growing developing nations, who are not part of the Organization for Economic Cooperation and Development (OECD) (International Energy Agency Website 2015). Amongst the non-OECD Asian nations, China and India will be responsible for almost 50 percent of the increase in energy consumption by 2040. Currently, India is the third-largest consumer of primary energy at 882 million tons of oil equivalent (Mtoe), after China (3,101 Mtoe) and the United States (2,196 Mtoe). India's plan to extend electric power to 240 million citizens who currently do not have access to electricity, coupled with India's renewed focus on the manufacturing sector–led growth ("Make in India" campaign), guarantees that the energy demand will quickly escalate.

India faces major challenges when it comes to energy access, energy security, and environmental sustainability. The World Economic Forum ranked India 87th out of 127 countries, in its Global Energy Architecture Performance Index Report, 2017. India's power generation capacity is disproportionately reliant on coal-fueled thermal power plants, and is a major contributor to atmospheric pollution. India's reliance on imports to meet its energy needs—whether it is oil and natural gas or coal (India is the third-largest importer of crude oil and the largest importer of coal in the world)—is a major impediment in its future growth prospects as well as in energy security and sustainability.

Even though India is the third-largest producer and consumer of electricity after China and the United States, the country's per capita energy consumption is very low: around one-third of the world's average, as a large portion of its population do not have access to power and energy. The nation also grapples with large transmission and distribution losses. Martin (2016) reported that India loses as much as 25 percent of the power generated (on average) during transmission. This is alarming, since in developed countries the power loss due to transmission doesn't exceed 10 percent. India needs to improve its power generation capacity, lower its dependence on fossil fuels, and embrace renewable energy sources, not to mention modernize and drastically improve the financial health as well as operational efficiencies of its power distribution and transmission to move toward a more sustainable and energy-secure future.

ENERGY AND THE ENVIRONMENT

As the second-largest city in India, Mumbai is not immune to the problems in the power sector and faces a steep challenge when it comes to energy and atmospheric pollution. The Brihanmumbai Electricity Supply and Transport (BEST) is one of the providers of domestic, infrastructure, and industrial electricity in the Greater Mumbai region. Additional coverage is provided by the private-sector utilities Tata Power and Reliance Infrastructure. Mumbai and Mumbai Suburban District consumed 17,360 million kilowatt hours (kWh) of electrical energy in 2014–15. In annual per capita terms, Mumbai's electricity consumption was 1,318 kWh in 2014 (Infrastructure Statistics of Maharashtra State 2013–2014 & 2014–2015). This is reflective of the city's high urbanization and mercantile nature. While Mumbai's per capita electricity consumption was much higher than the national average (India's per capita annual consumption of electricity was 804.7 kWh in 2014), it was still one-tenth that of the United States. In 2014, India had one of the lowest per capita power consumption rates relative to other developed and emerging nations, namely, Brazil (2,577.8 kWh), China (3,927 kWh), and the United States (12,972.7 kWh). However, India's annual per capita electricity consumption is increasing rapidly and is projected to grow to 2,000 kWh by 2040 (India Energy Outlook 2015).

In Mumbai, the daily peak electricity demand can rise up to 3,400 megawatts (MW) in the summer months, but the city is well equipped to provide power supply without load shedding as its power supply companies are able to improve power transmission and reduce transmission and distribution losses. Mumbai electricity supply is the most efficient among the three Indian megacities (Sridhar and Kashyap 2012). Between the periods of 2007–08 and 2009–10, the average transmission and distribution losses for the city of Mumbai were just 8 percent compared to 13 percent in Kolkata and 23 percent in Delhi.

Mumbai's daily peak electricity consumption is higher than Kolkata (2,100 MW), but it pales in comparison to Delhi's daily peak power consumption of 6,000 MW. Electricity consumption in Indian megacities is higher than in rural regions, but compared to the world's cities they are still quite low. In Shanghai, peak summer load reached 30,000 MW in August 2015, almost 10 times that of Mumbai and 5 times that of Delhi. This is an indication of low accessibility to reliable sources of power in India, though the situation has been improving steadily over the years.

Rising income and increased demand for household appliances are a major contributor of electricity demand in India, and Mumbai is no exception. Nationwide, the domestic (24 percent) and commercial sectors (9 percent) currently account for one-third of the total electricity consumption, second only to the industrial sector, which accounts for 42 percent of the total electricity consumption. In Mumbai, the domestic and commercial sectors are the dominant consumers of electricity, collectively responsible for almost 60 percent of total electricity consumption (Sreekumar and Josey 2012).

Mumbai is currently able to meet its electricity demand without major interruptions, but electricity generation and consumption are responsible for high levels of greenhouse gas emission (GHGS), namely, carbon dioxide (CO_2) and nitrous dioxide (N_2O), not to mention particulate matter ($PM_{2.5}$) and sulfur dioxide (SO_2). Guttikunda et al. (2015) reported that nationwide emissions from coal-based thermal power plants in India were responsible for more than 80,000 premature deaths and 20 million asthma cases due to exposure to particulate matter in 2011. Mumbai receives its power primarily from a coal-fired power plant nearby in Trombay. Coal-based thermal power plants constituted 60 percent of the total state's capacity, with only 20 percent from renewable sources. The composition is slightly better than national power composition, where the share of thermal power generation in overall national capacity was more than 73 percent, followed by renewables at 12 percent (Energy Statistics 2017). India and China are the two largest users of coal in electricity generation. In these countries, coal accounted for 67 percent and 72 percent of the total electricity production, respectively, compared to only 31 percent for OECD nations and 38 percent for the United States in 2014.

India's reliance on coal for power generation is neither sustainable nor environmentally safe. India is the third-largest emitter of GHG emissions in the world after China and the United States, and the energy sector in India is responsible for 71 percent of the total GHG emissions. Power plants are responsible for poor air quality in Mumbai, and are the biggest contributor of suspended particulate matter (SPM); 37 percent of the city's SPM is generated by power plants in Mumbai (Kaur 2017). Mumbai's SPM levels were reported to be 13 times the safe limit, leading to higher incidences of respiratory and pulmonary diseases (Chatterjee 2017a). Coal power generation in India is estimated to triple between 2013 and 2030. With no emission restriction currently in place for nitrous oxide (NO_x) and sulfur dioxide (SO_2), their levels are projected to double; and consequently, premature deaths due to air pollution will increase two to three times during the same period (Conservation Action Trust India 2014). In Mumbai, electricity consumption was the dominant source of carbon dioxide emission at 73 percent, followed by the transportation sector at 22 percent. Domestic, commercial/business sectors, the two biggest consumers of electricity in Mumbai, are responsible for high levels of GHG emissions. The domestic sector's energy needs are rising in proportion to India's economic growth and prosperity. Indian household appliance ownership per capita is still quite low compared to many developed and developing nations, but it is growing rapidly, and electricity demand for lighting, refrigeration, space conditioning, communication, and entertainment are on the rise. Chunekar et al. (2016) reported that residential electricity consumption in India has grown 8 percent annually, compared to only 5 percent and 1 percent growth in South Korea and the United States respectively. The rate of growth is expected to be high in India and other similarly emerging economies like China (whose rate of growth during the same decade was 12 percent), with increasing income and higher rates of electrification. The state of Maharashtra itself has a higher per capita residential electricity consumption compared to the national average, attributed to its higher standard of living. Mumbai should implement energy-efficiency measures especially for the building sectors (commercial and residential) and advocate the use of energy-efficient appliances for a sustainable growth.

The second-biggest contributor to GHG emissions in Mumbai is the transportation sector, even though its transport-sector emissions are just one-third of Delhi, and less than that of many Indian cities like Chennai, Hyderabad, Ahmedabad, and Bangalore. One of the reasons for this relatively low GHG emissions is that Mumbai has a robust public transportation system. However, as with most urban cities in India, personal vehicle ownership is on the rise, and the number of vehicles in Mumbai increased by 55 percent in the seven years between 2007 and 2014 (Sen 2014).

Mumbai's transportation system currently accounts for 36 percent of its total end use energy consumption. According to India Energy Outlook (Birol 2015), India's transportation fuel demand is going to triple between 2013 and 2040, and 90 percent of the increase will be generated by oil demand from road transport. The transportation sector is the fastest-growing sector in terms of energy consumption in India and will further exacerbate the country's dependence on oil imports. Apart from pressure on energy resources, the transportation sector is also the major contributor to air pollution in Indian cities. It is also a major contributor of carbon monoxide (CO), nitrogen oxides (NO_x), sulfur dioxide (SO_2), hydrocarbons (HC), and suspended particulate matter (SPM), which cause grave health issues ranging from respiratory and cardiovascular to long-term cellular and metabolic disorders. This has direct public health consequences—one study estimated that air pollution contributed to more than 80,000 premature deaths in Mumbai and New Delhi in 2015, almost double that from 1995. Mumbai in particular recorded 32,000 premature deaths from ingestion of PM_{10} (particulate matter sized less than 10 microns) in 2015, up from 19,290 in 1995 (*Economic Times* 2017).

MUMBAI TAKES STEPS TOWARD ENERGY SUSTAINABILITY

The Mumbai Pollution Control Board has prioritized certain areas to reduce vehicular pollution. Aside from tighter emission controls, these include fuel quality control to ensure that adulterated fuels do not make their way into vehicle fuel supplies—leading to greater pollution; the implementation of alternative fuel sources such as compressed natural gas (CNG), liquefied petroleum gas (LPG), other biofuels, all of which can be used in existing engines, better mass transit systems, and congestion control mechanisms such as surcharges.

However, one problem with biofuels in the Indian context is that, per capita, there is far less available land than in the United States and Brazil, two countries where biofuels are meeting with success. Further, given India's large population and food grain requirements, land that is currently used for agricultural food production cannot be repurposed for growing fuel crops. Thus, while the central government made the first steps in drafting a national biofuel policy in 2009, implementation using first-generation biofuels (sourced from molasses and non-edible vegetable oils) has been slow. Second-generation biofuels or 2G (which do not impact human or animal food chains), however, show promise (Lali 2016). The national outlook is optimistic, with 15,000 crore (Indian rupee or INR) of projected investment over the next few years, including a 300 crore INR biodiesel plant in Mumbai planned by Munzer Biofuels, an Austrian private firm. Indian industrial giant Tata Chemicals is also planning its entry into the biofuels market. Interestingly, the Tata Group, the parent company of Tata Chemicals, has also leveraged internal synergies with Tata Motors, one of India's biggest automakers, to use biofuels in public transport buses.

While the use of biofuels is a modern development, India has a long history of using biogas derived from biowaste, especially in rural areas. This idea of converting waste to energy (WTE) has been scaled up in the context of Mumbai—where 9,000 tons of municipal solid waste (MSW) are generated per day (Pandit 2016). Proposals have been made to use solar water heaters and fermenters/bioreactors to convert this solid waste into methane and electricity. The Brihanmumbai Municipal Corporation (BMC) has announced plans to set up the nation's first such biomethanization plant in Mumbai.

The Mumbai Pollution Control Board also makes recommendations for energy sustainability and pollution reductions from ancillary sources—such as promoting energy efficiency and use of cleaner fuels like LPG and electricity in its domestic sector and enacting a complete ban on open burning of refuse at landfills. Additionally, implementation of Bharat Stage V emission standards, implementation of tax rebates for purchase of electric cars (which are currently offered in New Delhi but not in Mumbai), along with a growing network of community charging stations could speed up electric vehicle adoption in India.

India has taken an important step toward a sustainable future by joining the Paris agreement on tackling climate change. The country has pledged to reduce its carbon intensity of GDP by 33 percent relative to 2005 levels by 2030 and to increase the share of renewable energy in electricity generation to 40 percent. Leveraging solar power is an obvious solution not just for large-scale projects, but also for individuals and smaller institutions. Mumbai has numerous success stories, such as the Siddhivinayak Ganapati Temple, which generates 20 KW from roof-mounted panels and has managed to reduce its electricity bill by 30 percent. There are various other technical developments that are helping to improve power output and reduce power consumption—such as nationally linked smart grids, carbon capture and sequestration systems, more efficient transportation systems, more efficient HVAC systems in large residential complexes and office buildings, the gradual adoption of green-architectural practices and promotion, and so on.

The Maharashtra State Government has set itself the ambitious target of generating an additional 11 gigawatts (GW) of energy from renewable sources, of which 67 percent is slated to be derived from solar power. This trend toward harnessing solar power is not just limited to large-scale projects; smaller end-users including 60 housing societies and commercial buildings in Mumbai have installed rooftop solar panels. Inroads are also being made in the transport sector. Mumbai Metro One Private Limited, which operates an urban rapid transport train system, has plans to source 30 percent of its 11 MW non-traction energy needs from solar panels installed atop train stations. A recent study by the Indian Institutes of Technology, commissioned by the Union Ministry for New and Renewable Energy estimates that Mumbai alone has the potential to develop 1.7 GW of solar power (Ramachandran 2017). The National Solar Mission of the Government of India envisions that up to 40 percent of solar power generated will come from small installations on rooftops and not from large plants. In this context, Mumbai shows the potential for growth and development.

The next couple of decades are crucial periods in human history, and anthropogenic climate change is one of the most significant challenges to ever face our species. Mumbai has taken important first steps in its journey toward energy sustainability and environmental conservation. These measures will undoubtedly contribute to a better quality of lives for its citizens in the future.

Moumita Roy

See also: Energy and Sustainability: Beijing, China: Battling Water Shortage

Further Reading

Anonymous. 2014. "Coal Kills: Health Impacts of Air Pollution from India's Coal Power Expansion." Conservation Action Trust. http://cat.org.in/wp-content/uploads/2017/05/Coal-Kills-Health-Impacts-of-Air-Pollution-from-India's-Coal-Power-Expansion.pdf.

Anonymous. 2017. "India Ranks 87th on Energy Architecture Performance: WEF." https://economictimes.indiatimes.com/industry/energy/india-ranks-87th-on-energy-architecture-performance-wef/articleshow/57778171.cms.

Ashar, Sandeep A. 2015. "Maharashtra Bets Big on Solar Power." *Indian Express*. http://indianexpress.com/article/cities/mumbai/maharashtra-bets-big-on-solar-power.

Australian Broadcasting Corporation. 2016. "World's Third Largest Emitter India Formally Joins Paris Agreement on Climate Change, UN Says." http://www.abc.net.au/news/2016-10-03/india-ratifies-paris-climate-change-deal/7897082.

Bhalerao, Sanjana. 2017. "Mumbai to Get One More Biogas Plant, Reduce Load on Dumping Grounds." *Hindustan Times.* http://www.hindustantimes.com/mumbai-news

/mumbai-to-get-one-more-biogas-plant-reduce-load-on-dumping-grounds/story-q7P4t3dPNEbtQTRGub5ZTI.html.
Birol, F. 2016. "India Energy Outlook, World Energy Outlook Special Report, 2015." International Energy Agency. https://www.iea.org/publications/freepublications/publication/india-energy-outlook-2015.html.
Census of India Website. 2011. Census Data. Office of the Registrar General & Census Commissioner, India. Ministry of Home Affairs, Government of India.
Chatterjee, Badri. 2017a. "Deadly Pollutants in Mumbai's Air Have Soared in Past 10 Years." *Hindustan Times*. http://www.hindustantimes.com/mumbai-news/deadly-pollutants-in-mumbai-s-air-have-soared-in-past-10-years/story-6SmHgOAAYk7r8nQyu8KWII.html.
Chatterjee, Badri. 2017b. "Mumbai Temple to Reduce Annual Power Bills by Rs8 Lakh Using Solar Energy." *Hindustan Times*. http://www.hindustantimes.com/mumbai-news/mumbai-temple-to-reduce-annual-power-bills-by-rs8-lakh-using-solar-energy/story-JEEJGRIfIUgXTxXiV3DU6I.html.
Chunekar, Aditya, Sapekshya Varshney, and Shantanu Dixit. 2016. "Residential Electricity Consumption in India: What Do We Know?" December. Prayas Energy Group. http://www.prayaspune.org/peg/publications/item/331-residential-electricity-consumption-in-india-what-do-we-know.html.
Cohen, Aaron J., et al. 2017. "Estimates and 25-Year Trends of the Global Burden of Disease Attributable to Ambient Air Pollution: An Analysis of Data from the Global Burden of Diseases Study 2015." *Lancet*, 389, 10082: 1907–18. http://www.thelancet.com/journals/lancet/article/PIIS0140-6736(17)30505-6/fulltext.
Conservation Action Trust and Urban Emissions India. 2014. "Coal Kills: Health Impacts of Air Pollution from India's Coal Power Expansion." http://www.indiaairquality.info/wp-content/uploads/docs/Air%20Pollution%20from%20India%20Coal%20TPPs%20-%20LowRes.pdf.
Eco Enviro Post. 2016. "India at 90th Rank in Terms of Energy Security, Access." https://www.thehindubusinessline.com/economy/india-at-90th-rank-in-terms-of-energy-security-access-wef/article8304837.ece.
Economic Times. 2016. "India's Looming Power Crisis." http://economictimes.indiatimes.com/indias-looming-power-crisis/articleshow/51051903.cms.
Economic Times. 2017. "Air Pollution Killed 81,000 in Delhi & Mumbai, Cost Rs 70,000 Crore in 2015." http://economictimes.indiatimes.com/news/politics-and-nation/air-pollution-killed-81000-in-delhi-mumbai-cost-rs-70000-crore-in-2015/articleshow/56658488.cms.
Enerdata. 2017. *Global Energy Statistical Yearbook 2017*. https://yearbook.enerdata.net/world-electricity-production-map-graph-and-data.html.
Energy Statistics. 2017. *Central Statistics Office, Ministry of Statistics and Programme Implementation of Government of India*. http://www.mospi.nic.in/sites/default/files/publication_reports/Energy_Statistics_2017r.pdf.pdf.
Fairless, Daemon. 2007. "Biofuel: The Little Shrub That Could—Maybe." *Nature* 449, 7163: 652–55. PMID 17968401. doi:10.1038/449652a.
Federico, Tobias. 2015. "Heat Wave in Shanghai Leads to Record Peak Demand." *Energy BrainBlog*. https://blog.energybrainpool.com/en/heat-wave-in-shanghai-leads-to-record-peak-demand.
Ge, Mengpin, Johannes Friedrich, and Thomas Damassa. 2014. "6 Graphs Explain the World's Top 10 Emitters." *World Resources Institute*. http://www.wri.org/blog/2014/11/6-graphs-explain-world%E2%80%99s-top-10-emitters.

Globalization and World Cities (GaWC) Research Network. 2016. "The World According to GaWC 2016." http://www.lboro.ac.uk/gawc/world2016t.html.

Goswami, Sweta. 2016. "It's Official: Delhi Is India's 'Power' Capital." *Hindu.* http://www.thehindu.com/news/cities/Delhi/its-official-delhi-is-indias-power-capital/article8623110.ece.

Guttikunda, Sarath K., Puja Jawahar, and Debi Goenka. 2015. "Regulating Air Pollution from Coal-Fired Power Plants in India." *Economic and Political Weekly* https://www.epw.in/journal/2015/1/notes/regulating-air-pollution-coal-fired-power-plants-india.html.

"India: First Biennial Update Report to the United Nations Framework Convention on Climate Change." 2015. *Ministry of Environment, Forest and Climate Change, Government of India.* December. http://unfccc.int/resource/docs/natc/indbur1.pdf.

India Today in Education. 2016. "India Ranks 90th in Terms of Energy Security: World Economic Forum Report." http://indiatoday.intoday.in/education/story/world-economic-forum/1/611046.html.

Infrastructure Statistics of Maharashtra State. 2013–2014 & 2014–2015. Directorate of Economics and Statistics. Planning Department. Government of Maharashtra, Mumbai.

International Energy Agency Website. 2015. "India Energy Outlook, World Energy Outlook Special Report." https://www.iea.org/publications/freepublications/publication/IndiaEnergyOutlook_WEO2015.pdf.

The International Energy Outlook. 2016. U.S. Energy Information Administration. Office of Energy Analysis, U.S. Department of Energy.

Jacob, Shine. 2016. "Biofuel Industry to See Rs 15,000-cr Investments." *Business Standard.* http://www.business-standard.com/article/companies/biofuel-industry-to-see-rs-15-000-cr-investments-116081001079_1.html.

Jog, Sanjay. 2018. "Mumbai Power Arrangement Should Suffice for a Decade." *Business Standard.* http://www.business-standard.com/article/companies/mumbai-power-arrangement-should-suffice-for-a-decade-116011800325_1.html.

Kaur, Narinder. 2017. "Changing Air Quality and Its Impact: A Case Study of Mumbai." *International Journal of Scientific Research.* 6, 1.

Koppikar, Smruti. 2016. "Mumbai Not the Economic Capital of India? Think Again." *Hindustan Times.* https://www.hindustantimes.com/mumbai-news/mumbai-not-the-economic-capital-of-india-think-again/story-dsVhGrgQd6ggE35JiKK7GK.html.

Lali, A. 2016. "Biofuels for India: What, When and How." *Current Science* 110, 4.

Mallapur, Chaitanya. 2015. "Delhi's Transport Sector 3 Times More Polluting Than Mumbai's." *IndiaSpend.* http://www.indiaspend.com/cover-story/delhis-transport-sector-3-times-more-polluting-than-mumbais-95198.

Martin, Richard. 2015. "India's Energy Crisis." *MIT Technology Review.* https://www.technologyreview.com/s/542091/indias-energy-crisis.

Mehta, Manthank. 2017. "30 Per Cent of Total Power Usage for Mumbai Metro from Solar Panels Now." *Times of India.* http://timesofindia.indiatimes.com/city/mumbai/30-of-total-power-usage-for-metro-from-solar-panels-now/articleshow/58439960.cms.

Ministry of Statistics and Programme Implementation of Government of India. 2017. "Energy Statistics." http://www.mospi.nic.in/sites/default/files/publication_reports/Energy_Statistics_2017r.pdf.pdf.

Mohan, Vishwa. 2015. "Greenhouse Gases: India Fourth Biggest Emitter, but Lags Far behind Top Three." *Times of India.* http://timesofindia.indiatimes.com/home

/environment/global-warming/Greenhouse-gases-India-fourth-biggest-emitter-but-lags-far-behind-top-three/articleshow/47807927.cms.

Pandit, Aniruddha. 2016. "Fixing Mumbai: Electricity from Waste." *Hindu*. http://www.thehindu.com/news/cities/mumbai/Fixing-Mumbai-Electricity-from-waste/article14308409.ece.

Ramachandra, Thejaswini V., and Shwetmala. 2009. "Emissions from India's Transport Sector: Statewise Synthesis." *Atmospheric Environment* November. doi:10.1016/j.atmosenv.2009.07.015. http://adsabs.harvard.edu/abs/2009AtmEn..43.5510R.

Ramachandra, Thejaswini V., B. H. Aithal, and K. Sreejith. 2015. "GHG Footprint of Major Cities in India." *Renewable and Sustainable Energy Reviews*. 44: 473–95. https://doi.org/10.1016/j.rser.2014.12.036.

Ramachandran, Shreya. 2017. "Mumbai Has 1.7 GW Solar Energy Potential: IIT Study." *Hindu*. http://www.thehindu.com/news/cities/mumbai/mumbai-has-17-gw-solar-energy-potential-iit-study/article17914545.ece.

Rane, P. K. 2016. "Survey Predicts 3000% Rise in Vehicles from 2015 to 2050." *Hindustan Times*. http://www.hindustantimes.com/mumbai-news/survey-predicts-3000-rise-in-vehicles-from-2015-to-2050/story-jN7HPF65SFIdZaxZtW4lJN.html.

Sen, Somit. 2014. "Vehicles in Mumbai Increase by More Than Half in Seven Years." *Times of India*. http://timesofindia.indiatimes.com/city/mumbai/Vehicles-in-Mumbai-increase-by-more-than-half-in-seven-years/articleshow/33570794.cms.

Sen, Somit. 2017. "Demand for Power in Mumbai Soars as Mercury Climbs." *Times of India*. http://timesofindia.indiatimes.com/city/mumbai/demand-for-power-in-mumbai-soars-as-mercury-climbs/articleshow/58184525.cms.

The Shift Project Data Portal. 2017. "Breakdown of Electricity Generation by Energy Source." Data sourced from the World Bank—World Development Indicators. Data Generated: June 2017. http://www.tsp-data-portal.org/Breakdown-of-Electricity-Generation-by-Energy-Source#tspQvChart.

Sohale, P. D., et al. 2017. "Infrastructure Statistics of Maharashtra State, 2013–2014 & 2014–2015." Directorate of Economics and Statistics. Planning Department. Government of Maharashtra, Mumbai. https://mahades.maharashtra.gov.in/files/publication/Infrast_Statistics2013-14_2014-15.pdf.

Sreekumar, N., and Ann Josey. 2012. "Electricity in Megacities." *Prayas Energy Group*. http://www.prayaspune.org/peg/publications/item/176-electricity-in-megacities.html.

Sridhar, Kala Seetharam, and Nivedita Kashyap. 2012. "State of Indian Cities: An Assessment of Urban Conditions in Four Mega Cities." *Public Affairs Centre India*.

Tembhekari, Chitaranjan. 2017. "Use of Solar Panels for Green Power on Rise in Mumbai." *Times of India*. http://timesofindia.indiatimes.com/city/mumbai/use-of-solar-panels-for-green-power-on-rise-in-mumbai/articleshow/57763527.cms.

United Nations, Department of Economic and Social Affairs, Population Division. 2014. "Atmospheric Environment (ST/ESA/SER.A/352)." https://www.compassion.com/multimedia/world-urbanization-prospects.pdf.

United Nations, Department of Economic and Social Affairs, Population Division. 2016. "The World's Cities in 2016—Data Booklet (ST/ESA/ SER.A/392)." http://www.un.org/en/development/desa/population/publications/pdf/urbanization/the_worlds_cities_in_2016_data_booklet.pdf.

United Nations Framework Convention on Climate Change Website. 2015. "India: First Biennial Update Report to the United Nations Framework Convention on Climate Change." Ministry of Environment, Forest and Climate Change, Government of India. http://unfccc.int/resource/docs/natc/indbur1.pdf.

Unnikrishnan, C. H. 2007. "Tata Chemicals Plans Foray into Biodiesel." *Livemint.* http://www.livemint.com/Companies/3qijsuXJnm1wUJObX25U1I/Tata-Chemicals-plans-foray-into-biodiesel.html.

The U.S. Energy Information Administration Website. 2016. The International Energy Outlook 2016. https://www.eia.gov/outlooks/archive/ieo16.

Williams, D. 2017. "Report Identifies Mumbai Solar Power Potential." Decentralized Energy. http://www.decentralized-energy.com/articles/2017/04/report-identifies-mumbai-solar-power-potential.html.

The World Bank. 2014. "Electric Power Consumption (kWh per capita)." IEA/OECD Statistics 2014. http://data.worldbank.org/indicator/EG.USE.ELEC.KH.PC?locations=IN-CN-US-BR.

The World Economic Forum Website. 2017. "Global Energy Architecture Performance Index Report 2017." https://www.weforum.org/reports/global-energy-architecture-performance-index-report-2017.

Pittsburgh, United States: Air Quality Is a Work in Progress

Pittsburgh was once known for its dirty air, much like Beijing today, with its "Orange-level" smog, or New Delhi, with its asphyxiating winter air pollution. Today the air in Pittsburgh is relatively clean. What happened to the city's infamous smog, which once provoked visitors to characterize it as "hell with the lid off" (Madrigal 2013)? While Pittsburgh's National Football League team is still called the Steelers, and their helmets still carry the trademark of U.S. Steel, much of the steel-making that used to foul its atmosphere is now being made in places such as Beijing and Shanghai, thus their dirty air. While China is moving full speed ahead into solar, it is also burning more coal for electricity than ever before.

By 2016, China was producing more steel than any other country, half of the world total, and 200 percent of domestic demand. The United States produced 5 percent of the world supply, 25 percent below its consumption, and less than the European Union (10 percent), Japan (6.4 percent), and India (5.9 percent) (Turner 2017).

A CITY ONCE POWERED BY COAL

Until the 1940s, as Alexis C. Madrigal wrote in the *Atlantic* (2013): "Pittsburgh emerged as the seat of metalworking, iron and then steel. This was a city powered by coal. Soot and smoke covered the city. There was no blue sky. Travelers from around the world visited Pittsburgh to see the wonder of American capitalism. The stories they tell are like—exactly like—the ones you hear today about China." A traveler recalled: "Everybody who has heard of Pittsburgh knows that it is the city of perpetual smoke, and looks as if it were built above the descent to 'the bottomless pit.'"

Pittsburgh's carbon dioxide-infused smog hasn't vanished. It's merely been exported, and is still a factor in global warming. About 2007, China as a whole passed the United States as the world's largest emitter of greenhouse gases from

Pittsburgh, Pennsylvania, ranked among the worst cities in the world for air pollution in the 1950s. Since then, the collapse of the city's coal-burning iron and steel industries, coupled with municipal environmental protection policies, has resulted in cleaner air. (Tupungato/Dreamstime.com)

such things as manufacturing, vehicle exhaust, and coal-fired power plants. In 2016, China produced twice as much carbon dioxide (and accompanying air pollution) as the United States.

Until the proportion of carbon dioxide and other greenhouse gases in the atmosphere starts to decline worldwide, because of thermal inertia, the atmosphere will continue to heat up for at least 50 years after our energy sources change from fossil fuels to renewables.

PITTSBURGH'S AIR IS HARDLY PRISTINE

Pittsburgh has been working on its air pollution at least since 1941, when its city government passed a law requiring the use of low-sulfur, cleaner-burning coal in steel mills and other industries. The law was phased in after World War II. Natural gas, which produces less pollution and carbon dioxide, was substituted for coal when possible, and railroad companies used diesel fuel instead of coal in their locomotives. However, wrote Mark Byrnes in CityLab (an online forum on urban issues), "Ultimately, the collapse of the iron and steel production industries in the 1980s led to rapidly improved air quality leading into the 21st century. . . . Control of coal smoke made it possible to clean soot-covered buildings and to re-plant hillsides, helping provide the city a look it could hardly envision in the depths of its industrial heyday" (Byrnes 2012).

Even today, the air in Pittsburgh and nearby areas is hardly pristine all of the time, especially when atmospheric inversions cause the air to stagnate in valleys, topography that is also a factor in other large urban areas, such as Mexico City and Beijing. According to a report in the Huffington Post: "There is a lot to love about Pittsburgh: top-rated universities, world-class health care, abundant cultural and natural amenities, and winning sports teams. Unfortunately, air quality is not something Pittsburghers love or brag about" ("The Reality" 2017).

SOME STEEL WORKS CLOSE, BUT NOT ALL

Many steel-industry plants have closed, reducing emissions. For example, the Shenango Coke Works was one of the biggest and most visible polluters in the Pittsburgh region.

The coke plant's pervasive pollution was bad enough for the EPA to make it a priority issue, focusing considerable community pressure, cooperating with a community group, Allegheny County Clean Air Now (ACCAN), "to elevate awareness among local and federal authorities of the threat Shenango posed to public health. After meeting with ACCAN and community members, the EPA made Shenango a priority, often deploying staff to Pittsburgh to check up on the situation and ensure that all violations were being addressed properly. EPA's scrutiny of the plant and their involvement with the local community was instrumental in keeping pressure on the plant" (Pittsburgh 2017). The Shenango plant degraded the Pittsburgh area's atmosphere until it was shuttered in January 2016, citing "global overcapacity in the steel industry" (Pittsburgh 2017).

Coke, which is refined from coal, is an essential component in steel making. Coke's manufacture is a very dirty process that produces several noxious air pollutants that are classified as carcinogenic by the U.S. Environmental Protection Agency (EPA). According to a Clean Air Council report (Pittsburgh 2017): "Not only were Shenango's emissions already some of the worst, but the facility regularly violated the regulations that were in place. Most shockingly, over a 432-day period from the summer of 2012 to the fall of 2013 the facility violated air pollution laws on 330 days" (Pittsburgh 2017).

Pollution has sometimes become more serious in some of Pittsburgh's suburbs as it has eased in its urban core. For example, residents in and near Clairton, Pennsylvania, 15 miles south of Pittsburgh, in 2017 filed a class-action lawsuit against U.S. Steel, which still maintains some industrial plants in the area, asserting that air pollution from its coke works has had a negative effect on their property values. Attitudes have changed in that area since the steel industry's pollution was tolerated because it brought good-paying jobs. Julie Grant of PRI's (Public Radio International) series "Living on Earth" described this change:

> Many members of Richard Ford's family have worked at Clairton Coke Works, including both his grandfathers, his father, his wife, his brother and sister-in-law, and two uncles. "These were good jobs, too," Ford said, "and no one wanted to give them up or see them go away." So, when people from nearby wealthier communities, like Mount Lebanon and Upper St. Clair, came to Clairton to talk about pollution

from the mill, "We ran them out of here," Ford said. "We said, 'How are you going to tell us? We live here. You go to Upper St. Clair and keep living like you're living and we're going to stay right here,'" Ford related. "As long as there's smoke coming from the mills, we're eating, we're drinking and we're driving good [cars]. We're sending kids to college. We thought that was all right."

The toll of pollution on people's health became too acute to accept, however. "In my own family," said Ford, "My dad died of cancer of the trachea. I had a daughter that died at the age of 25 with scleroderma," a form of auto-immune rheumatic disease. "My son passed away this past October [2016] from prostate cancer" (Grant 2017). Neighbors compared notes about family members who had died of various cancers, and began to associate their illnesses with air pollution from the coke works, which had violated restrictions on pollution 6,700 times between 2012 and 2015 (Grant 2017).

The Allegheny County Health Department negotiated a consent decree with U.S. Steel to reduce pollution in 2016. Even so, the plant was still violating federal air-quality standards for fine particulates (those most likely to injure people's lungs), as well as sulfur dioxide. However, proving a legal connection between specific cases of cancer and one source of air pollution is very difficult.

Jim Kelly, deputy director of environmental health at the Allegheny County Health Department, told Grant: "There are so many reasons people get cancer, especially in low-income areas. You have high smoking rates. You've got old housing stock, with lots of asbestos—lung cancer right there. You have low education. You have high unemployment. You have high obesity rates. All of these things are correlated with [increased cancer rates]" (Grant 2016). Even so, air pollution likely plays a role. Children in Clairton who live near smokestacks who have never smoked tobacco experience exceptionally high rates of asthma, three times the national average (Grant 2017).

STAGNANT AIR IN THE MONONGAHELA RIVER VALLEY

When the atmosphere is stagnant in the Monongahela River Valley, the air quality in and around Pittsburgh can still become polluted from vehicle exhaust as well as industrial emissions, although nowhere near the acrid conditions prevalent until the 1940s. The Clean Air Council reported in 2017 that given atmospheric inversion, the air in Allegheny County can be the eighth worst in the United States, something that the local Chamber of Commerce does not brag about.

In the [Clean Air Council's] 2016 State of the Air report, Western Pennsylvania was the 8th worst in the United States for year-round measures on fine particle pollution (or soot), and the 14th worst for short-term particle pollution (the number of days with unhealthy particle levels when air quality is especially dangerous). Pittsburgh also ranked 26th worst in the nation for smog from ground-level ozone. Asthma rates for the Pittsburgh region, especially children, exceed the national average and air pollution plays a big role, the Clean Air Council said (Pittsburgh 2017). The Clairton Coke Works is only one of several potent polluters in the area. Others include the Edgar Thomson Steel Works and the Irvin Plant, also a steel producer.

> ### The Export of Pollution
>
> Pittsburgh's air is much cleaner today not because pollution has been eliminated, but because it has been moved, raising issues of environmental racism and justice that intertwine ecology with issues of race and class, frequently involving poor, often racial minority communities whose residents are subjected to a disproportionate level of many kinds of toxicity, while being denied ecological benefits such as clean water and air, as well as sustainable use of resources for a decent and dignified standard of living.
>
> In a worldwide context, "environmental racism" also has been used to describe and explain the movement of polluting industries, with their toxicity, from affluent nations to the third world. Thus, in the last century the worst air quality in the world has moved from urban areas such as Pittsburgh, New York City, and London to such cities as Mexico City, Beijing, and New Delhi.
>
> Pollution also may be exported from urban areas to rural enclaves within state and federal borders. Coal-fired power plants that supply cities often are sited in rural areas, within sight of poor nonwhite communities whose residents rely on easily polluted wells for water. Describing Walnut Tree, a mainly African American town near Duke Energy's Belews Creek Stream Station in North Carolina, Margaret Talbot wrote in the *New Yorker* that "For years, coal ash from the station . . . fell like snow over the town's modest houses and backyard vegetable gardens. Kids wrote their names in the ash that blanketed their parents' cars and corroded the paint" (2018, 41). The plant's power went mainly to urban areas.

In 2005, an Air Toxics Assessment report described Clairton and the neighboring community of Glassport as having the third- and fourth-highest rates of cancer risk, respectively, in the United States. Allegheny County as a whole was in the top 2 percent for cancer risk nationally (Pittsburgh 2017). The bad old days remain in more than memory, especially outside Pittsburgh's showcase urban core. Residents still routinely clean soot from their windowsills in some areas that are adjacent to steel and coking plants. They can only imagine what it is doing to their lungs.

The Clean Air Council also has been monitoring Lawrenceville, a neighborhood in Pittsburgh, regarding the McConway & Torley steel foundry, which is more than 150 years old. That plant has been violating emissions limits not only for carbon dioxide, but also "excesses of benzene and other carcinogenic pollutants [that] escape the plant and enter the surrounding community" (Pittsburgh 2017). Over several decades, this plant has acquired exemptions from many pollution regulations, because it was built long before the regulations existed, a procedure known as "grandfathering." However, pressure from the Allegheny County Health Department has forced the plant to reduce emissions by 77 percent without any impact on production.

Bruce E. Johansen

See also: Pollution: Flint, United States: National and Local Politics in the Creation of a Public Health Emergency

Further Reading

Byrnes, Mark. 2012. "What Pittsburgh Looked Like When It Decided It Had a Pollution Problem." CityLab. June 5. https://www.citylab.com/design/2012/06/what-pitts burgh-looked-when-it-decided-it-had-pollution-problem/2185.

Grant, Julie. 2017. "Residents Sue US Steel over Air Pollution in Western Pennsylvania." PRI (Public Radio International) *Living on Earth*, August 11. https://www.pri.org/stories/2017-08-11/residents-sue-us-steel-over-air-pollution-western-pennsylvania.

Madrigal, Alexis C. 2013. "Aghast over Beijing's Air Pollution? This Was Pittsburgh Not That Long Ago." *Atlantic*, January 16. https://www.theatlantic.com/technology/archive/2013/01/aghast-over-beijings-air-pollution-this-was-pittsburgh-not-that-long-ago/267237.

Pittsburgh Air Pollution. Clean Air Council. 2017. http://cleanair.org/public-health/pittsburgh-air-pollution.

"The Reality of Pittsburgh's Air Quality: We Can't Be Our Best When We Have Some of the Country's Worst Air Quality." 2017. *Huffington Post*, September 28. https://www.huffingtonpost.com/entry/the-reality-of-pittsburghs-air-quality_us_59cd83cee4b09538b5074165.

Talbot, Margaret. 2018. "Dirty Politics: Scott Pruitt's E.P.A. Is Giving Even Ostentatious Polluters a Reprieve." *New Yorker*, April 2, 38–51.

Turner, Zeke. 2017. "China Raises U.S. Ire over Steel." *Wall Street Journal*, December 1, A-10.

Rio de Janeiro, Brazil: A City with a Passion for Conservation and Renewable Energy

Like any modern city, Rio de Janeiro, Brazil, is a consumer of energy. This fact is particularly true because as the income of residents rises, so does their use of energy, putting pressure on all sources of energy. Like other cities, Rio de Janeiro relies to an extent on the fossil fuels oil, coal, and natural gas. Problems exist with this approach. First, although recent discoveries of oil reserves may hold promise, Brazil is not well endowed with fossil fuels. Second, these resources are finite. Once they are exhausted, the world, including Rio de Janeiro, must have alternatives in place. Third, fossil fuels emit greenhouse gases that are warming the planet. Fourth, Rio de Janeiro traditionally has received its electricity some distance from the city so that it is vulnerable to disruptions in supply. In short, a reliance on fossil fuels is not sustainable. Even Rio de Janeiro's traditional reliance on hydroelectric power carries the risks of fluctuations in supply because rainfall is not constant in Brazil. In years of low rainfall, rivers are at their nadir and so are less effective in supplying hydroelectricity. The solution appears to take two forms. First, Rio de Janeiro must conserve energy. Second, the city must transition to renewable sources of energy.

CONSERVATION

The 2016 Summer Olympics stimulated and continues to stimulate the construction of energy-efficient buildings in the host city, Rio de Janeiro. Energy-efficient buildings reduce the consumption of energy for cooling, heating, and lighting. In tropical Rio de Janeiro, cooling is an important consideration, totaling about one-fifth of the city's consumption of electricity, according to a report by riorenewables

.com (Rio de Janeiro 2014). Because of the need to promote cooling, Rio de Janeiro is designing buildings to be more efficient in circulating air to reduce the need for air conditioning. It is possible for these buildings to reduce the consumption of electricity by 30 percent ("National Ventilation"). Along the coast it is feasible to take advantage of sea breezes to improve air circulation in buildings. Yet because sea breezes seldom penetrate inland, this solution is not viable for all of Rio de Janeiro. Air circulation promotes cooling by whisking heat away from the skin. For this solution to be effective, temperatures must be below 35 degrees Celsius and the humidity must be below 80 percent. Above these values, air warms rather than cools skin. Rio de Janeiro satisfies these requirements much of the year. Even during the hottest months of January and February, temperatures are often below 35 degrees Celsius and the humidity is below 80 percent. Vents near the ground allow air to enter a building. In the morning this air may be comparatively cool and so will rise through the building as it warms. As it rises, it will circulate by definition, promoting cooling. Air exits through a chimney atop the building.

Another energy-efficient design promotes the use of shade to cool buildings. This solution is not high tech, but it is effective. Yet shading diminishes the amount of light that enters a building and may cause an overuse in electricity for lighting. Windows, of course, allow light to enter a building, but they must be strategically placed. The larger the window the more sunlight it will allow to enter. Sunlight is a form of heat, so it will warm the building. To compensate for this effect, windows must be comparatively small when they face north, because, being in the Southern Hemisphere, Rio de Janeiro with a northern exposure faces the sun. Windows should also be small when they face east, the direction of the rising sun, and west, the direction of the setting sun. The largest windows should face south to allow the entrance of light to minimize the use of electricity for lighting. In a similar vein the orientation of buildings is also important. Buildings should be oriented to minimize eastern and western exposures. Buildings with circular shapes absorb less heat from

An eco-guesthouse powered by solar energy in Rio de Janeiro, Brazil, July 27, 2016. Rio generates electricity from solar panels at a cost that compares favorably to that of nonrenewable sources. (Ricardo Funari/Brazil Photos/LightRocket via Getty Images)

the sun than traditional rectangular buildings. To minimize the use of electricity for lighting, rooms and shelves should be a light color, preferably white, because white reflects the most light.

It has been noted that air conditioners consume considerable electricity in tropical Rio de Janeiro. The city's geography places a premium on the construction of the most energy-efficient air conditioners, which may reduce the consumption of electricity by 75 percent over less efficient models ("Efficient Air Conditioning"). Where possible, fans should be preferred to an air conditioner because they use less electricity. The consumption of electricity for cooling may be further lessened by turning up the thermostat when the building is unoccupied, another low-tech solution. Air conditioners generate heat as lost energy, but this energy may be captured to heat water for bathing and cooking.

Buildings in Rio de Janeiro should minimize horizontal surfaces. These surfaces absorb the most heat because the city, being near the equator, has the sun positioned high in the sky much of the day. Like the interiors of buildings, roofs should be white to reflect heat. Another possibility lies in the construction of green roofs, roofs upon which plants grow in profusion. These plants absorb sunlight and so promote cooling. These roofs are sometimes known as living roofs and can reduce energy consumption by 28 percent, according to riorenewables.com. These plants also confer benefits by shading a building. Moreover, plants insulate buildings and thereby reduce the loss of cool air supplied by air conditioning. For these reasons a green roof may be 12 degrees Celsius cooler than a concrete roof ("Green Roofs and Walls"). Rio de Janeiro may reduce energy consumption further by wetting roofs. Water absorbs heat, which it dissipates upon evaporation in a mechanism that mirrors the act of sweating.

SUSTAINABLE ENERGY

It was noted earlier that a reliance on fossil fuels is unsustainable for Rio de Janeiro. In this context, the city is making strides in the use of renewables. The reliance on hydroelectricity, not an entirely satisfactory solution, was noted earlier. Rio de Janeiro, like much of Brazil, also relies on biofuels. The most notable must be sugarcane. The residues left after the derivation of sugar from the plant are known as bagasse and are burned to generate electricity. Because sugarcane may be continuously planted, bagasse is a type of renewable energy.

Rio de Janeiro has other advantages. Being in the tropics, it receives much solar radiation. Sunlight is, of course, a form of energy, and the capture of even a small fraction of it can generate electricity. Solar technologies still have much progress to make, but Rio de Janeiro is taking advantage of the abundance of sunlight. The price of solar photovoltaic panels diminishes as the technology improves, making them increasingly attractive to building owners. One may see these panels on the roofs of buildings in Rio de Janeiro. They convert the sunlight that strikes each panel directly into electricity, which is nothing more than the movement of electrons from one location to another. One might recall that the electron is a subatomic particle with a negative charge. Because electricity is negatively charged, it flows from a negatively charged terminal to a positively charged terminal on the principle that like charges repel and opposite charges attract. An advantage of solar photovoltaic panels is that they can be positioned on a building, supplying electricity over very short distances. The shorter the distance, the more efficient the transmission of electricity because over distances the electrons lose energy as they travel through the copper wire. This lost energy is in the form of heat. Moreover, the hydroelectric power system in Brazil is old and costly to maintain. In the long run, solar panels in Rio de Janeiro should be less expensive to maintain, though there is, of course, the cost of installing new panels. Solar panels provide another advantage. As the sun shines intensively, the demand for electricity to run air conditioners increases in this tropical city. Yet such conditions are perfect for deriving the most electricity from solar panels, so that as the demand for electricity increases, so does the supply. Brazil's government encourages the use of solar technologies by subsidizing their construction in Rio de Janeiro and elsewhere. Even now the city can generate electricity from solar panels at a cost that compares favorably with the generation of electricity from nonrenewable sources.

Another option is the use of what is known as concentrated solar power. The idea is to position mirrors to reflect sunlight onto a single point. The concentration of such sunlight produces enormous energy in the form of heat. This heat can boil water. The escaping steam can rotate a turbine, thereby generating electricity. In Rio de Janeiro and many other locations, this concentrated source of power takes the form of a tower to hold water for boiling to generate electricity. This system of generating electricity is particularly efficient, converting almost 30 percent of sunlight into electricity. By contrast, plants convert only a few percent of sunlight into biomass. The generation of electricity is not, however, enormous. Most of the concentrated solar technologies generate 5 to 50 kilowatts of electricity.

Solar energy is also useful in Rio de Janeiro in heating water for bathing and cooking. This system produces solar thermal energy. Typically, buildings in the city have collectors on the roofs. These collectors absorb the sun's energy for heating water. This energy collects in a reservoir of water, heating it. The tank is insulated to conserve heat from being lost when the sun is not shining. This technology holds promise in Rio de Janeiro, where bathing accounts for more than 20 percent of the city's electricity consumption. By one estimate, solar thermal heating systems could save the residents of Rio de Janeiro 35 percent of their electricity consumption ("Solar Thermal Heating"). Because of these savings, Rio de Janeiro has since 2008 required the installation of solar thermal collection tanks on all government buildings. The city aims to use solar thermal collection systems to save 40 percent of the electricity that would otherwise be necessary to heat water ("Solar Thermal Heating"). The neighborhood of Mangueira in Rio de Janeiro has made vigorous strides in the direction of heating water with solar thermal collection tanks. These solar units may cost as much as $2,000 to install, but over time they will more than cover the cost of installation in reducing the use of electricity. Recent studies indicate that solar collection tanks can repay the cost of their installation in Rio de Janeiro in as little as four years ("Solar Thermal Heating"). Care must be taken, however, during the winter when temperatures in these tanks are not as high as in summer because warm but not hot conditions can hasten the growth of the bacterium that causes Legionnaire's disease. The temperature in these tanks must

> ### Sugarcane
>
> A source of renewable energy through burning its residues to generate electricity, sugarcane is a perennial because it regenerates after being harvested. Farmers seldom allow it to regrow more than once or twice because yields decline in subsequent harvests. A tropical grass, sugarcane likely originated on or near the island of Papua New Guinea, which lies just south of the equator in the Pacific Ocean. The island's people probably first used sugarcane, which produces abundant foliage, to thatch their homes, discovering in the process that juice from the stems is sweet. Sweetness is a function of the juice's sucrose, a chemical commonly known as sugar, though sucrose is not the only sugar in plants. These people chewed the pith of sugarcane stems to derive the juice. An ancient plant, sugarcane was likely domesticated about 8,000 to 10,000 years ago on Papua New Guinea or a nearby island, thereafter spreading throughout tropical Asia. In the Atlantic world, sugarcane became the source of a plantation economy in islands off Africa's coast and in the Americas after Italian-Spanish mariner Christopher Columbus planted it on the Caribbean island of Hispaniola (Haiti and the Dominican Republic) in 1493. The Portuguese introduced sugarcane into Brazil about 1530.

rise to at least 60 degrees Celsius for not less than one hour per day to kill the bacterium.

Whereas conditions in Rio de Janeiro favor the use of solar energy, the generation of electricity from wind turbines may not prove fruitful because winds in the city are often too weak to turn them. The possibility exists of mounting wind turbines on the city's tall buildings, where the wind typically blows with greater strength, but even in these instances the winds may not suffice to generate a steady flow of electricity. Another possibility is the installation of wind turbines on the shore, where sea breezes are notable, but the appeal of the seacoast is its relatively pristine condition. Wind turbines would mar the aesthetic appeal of this area. The tides and heat from geothermal sources are other avenues for generating renewable energy for Rio de Janeiro. The city's future depends on a transition from fossil fuels to renewable energies.

Christopher Cumo

See also: Traffic and Transportation: Mexico City, Mexico: Improving Governance Is Key to Solving Traffic Challenges

Further Reading
"Efficient Air Conditioning." https://riorenewables.com/efficient-design/efficient-air-conditioning.
Rio De Janeiro. 2014. "Energy Toolkit for Buildings." https://riorenewables.com/.
Riorenewables.com. "Energy Toolkit for Buildings: Rio de Janeiro." https://riorenewables.com/about-us.
Riorenewables.com. "Green Roofs & Walls: Energy Efficient Buildings in Rio de Janeiro." https://riorenewables.com/efficient-design/green-roofs-walls.
Riorenewables.com. "National Ventilation: A Review for Buildings in Rio de Janeiro." https://riorenewables.com/efficient-design/ventilation-airflow.
Riorenewables.com. "Renewable Technologies." https://riorenewables.com/renewable-technologies.

Singapore City, Singapore: Go Solar!

An island nation in the tropics of Southeast Asia, Singapore is both a city and a state. Highly urbanized, its largest metropolis is Singapore City. Its modern economy shares many features with the industrial West, including a reliance on fossil fuels. Oil and coal play a role in the energy sector, though the chief fuel is natural gas, which supplies more than 90 percent of the city's electricity. Singapore City has steered a course in the direction of natural gas because it is a cleaner fuel than oil or coal. That is, natural gas spews fewer pollutants and fewer greenhouse gases into the air than the burning of oil or coal. Yet a reliance on natural gas or any fossil fuel is unsustainable because these resources are finite. Once they are exhausted, Singapore City will need to have transitioned to renewable sources of energy. The city is pursuing two avenues toward the future. The first emphasizes conservation of energy as a movement toward sustainability, whereas the second promotes the transition from fossil fuels to renewable sources of energy. Because of its proximity to the equator, Singapore City has ample sunshine. This sunshine is a form of energy and a boon to the generation of electricity from solar power.

CONSERVATION

Being urbanized, Singapore, like the West, depends on the automobile. This dependence may be unsustainable at least given current technologies that rely on gasoline, diesel, and other fossil fuels. Even electric cars may not be viable in the long term if this electricity must be generated from the burning of coal, oil, or natural gas. In Singapore City, the tendency toward few riders per car exacerbates the problems of the automobile. By one estimate some 80 percent of automobiles have a driver and no passengers. Such an allocation tends toward maximum wastefulness of fossil fuels and maximum pollution of the environment. Singapore City is attempting to reduce waste and pollution by encouraging people to carpool or ride a bicycle to work. Such solutions are not high tech, but they can be implemented immediately with little change to the city. In concert with these efforts is the government's commitment to mass transit. Singapore City aims by 2030 to have some three-quarters of its residents travel to work by public transportation during peak commuting hours. To the degree that the automobile remains an important feature of Singapore City, government has mandated the derivation of more fuel-efficient cars. In the same vein, Singapore in 2013 enacted the Carbon Emissions-based Vehicle Scheme to reduce the emission of greenhouse gases from cars. Energy conservation and greener vehicles have thus emerged as twin goals. In 2017, Singapore replaced the Carbon Emissions-based Vehicle Scheme with the Vehicular Emissions Scheme to implement a tax on the least efficient models of cars. The measure took effect on January 1, 2018.

Singapore City also attempts to conserve energy by promoting the construction of energy-efficient buildings. One approach to conservation lies in the topping of buildings with green roofs. These roofs are sometimes known as living roofs because they harbor live plants. Plants absorb sunlight, capturing heat before it can penetrate the roof. This strategy keeps roofs naturally cool. Plants also serve to insulate roofs, helping buildings keep indoors the cool air from air conditioning. The maintenance of cool air in buildings is important in Singapore City, lying as close as it does to the equator. By insulating buildings, green roofs reduce the demands on air conditioning and in this way conserve electricity. Inside buildings, the residents of Singapore City are using energy-efficient refrigerators, washing machines, and other appliances. Government mandates the use of such appliances as another way of conserving electricity.

RENEWABLE SOURCES OF ENERGY

Conservation is one way of reducing the demands on fossil fuels. Another is the use of renewable sources of energy in place of fossil fuels. One promising avenue along this highway of energy is the use of solar photovoltaic cells, often known simply as solar panels. These solar panels are an attractive option because they convert sunlight directly into electricity. The harnessing of sunlight to generate electricity is important in Singapore City. Located as it is only one-degree latitude north of the equator, Singapore City has the sun high overhead much of the day and year round. Because of this, its rays reach Singapore City directly and with greater intensity than is the case in the temperate zone. By one estimate the city receives approximately 50 percent more sunlight per year than do countries in the temperate zone. This rich harvest of sunlight powers solar panels efficiently. In fact, the more intense the sunlight, the greater is the conversion into electricity. This phenomenon is important given the demand curve for electricity. When the sun is most intense, the demand for electricity is greatest for air conditioning. Yet this is the very moment when solar panels generate the most electricity, meeting the demand for electricity.

Another benefit of solar panels is their nearness to the sources that consume electricity. A solar panel on the roof of a building powers the appliances within that building. Because there is only a short distance to traverse, solar panels deliver electricity without loss. This scheme contrasts to traditional power sources that must deliver electricity over distance. Electricity is by definition the flow of electrons. As electrons flow for a distance through a copper wire, they lose some of their power in the form of heat during transit. Solar panels minimize this loss. The criticism of solar panels is that they do not deliver electricity as cheaply as does the burning of fossil fuels. This critique has become less relevant over time. As the technology for delivering electricity by solar panels improves, solar panels have become more efficient in their generation of electricity. Already solar panels are nearly as cost-effective as a modern turbine powered by cheap natural gas. This cost-effectiveness stems from a reduction in the cost of generating electricity from solar panels by 70 percent in the past six years. The transition to solar panels holds promise for freeing Singapore City from a reliance on fossil fuels, at least in the generation of electricity.

Yet the use of solar energy in Singapore City faces challenges. Perhaps the most pressing is the city's compact size and high population density. Little land remains idle for the creation of solar farms. Solar panels must instead be placed atop buildings to maximize the efficient use of horizontal space. The second problem is also difficult to solve. It is clear that solar power is effective only when the sun is shining. During night, solar panels cannot generate electricity. Improvements are therefore necessary in the storage capacity of batteries to provide electricity throughout the day. Another possibility is the marriage of solar panels with traditional sources of energy, so that when clouds are numerous or the sun sets, consumers can secure electricity from the burning of fossil fuels.

Despite these limitations, Singapore City is pursuing the generation of electricity from solar panels. In 2014, the government projected an increase in the capacity to generate solar power to 350 megawatts by 2020. Such capacity would give the city 5 percent surplus over current peak demand. Obviously, the danger is that peak demand will rise by 2020 so that solar panels may not be able to meet all the demand, but even a partial fulfillment of the city's demand for electricity will lessen the reliance on fossil fuels for generating electricity. In 2015, Singapore's government took a second step in the promotion of solar power by empowering residents who adopt solar powers to sell capacity back to the utilities when supply exceeds the demand for electricity.

In 2008, Singapore City could count just 30 solar panels. In 2016, the number approached 1,500. At this rate of adoption, solar panels should allow Singapore City to generate 5 percent of its electricity by 2020. Admittedly, this number still leaves fossil fuels to generate the majority of the city's electricity, but even small steps mark progress in the transition to renewable sources of energy.

Yet it is possible that rising incomes and population will outrun the capacity of solar power to meet Singapore City's demands for electricity in the future. Other options may not suit the island nation. Singapore does not have winds of sufficient strength and duration to power wind turbines. Rivers do not move fast enough to generate hydroelectric power on a vast scale. Given these shortcomings, Singapore City is grappling with the prospect of generating electricity from nuclear sources to meets its energy needs. Nuclear power may be attractive given Singapore's vulnerability to reductions in the supply of fossil fuels, particularly natural gas. Currently, Singapore generates about 95 percent of its electricity from natural gas. Yet the nation produces little natural gas and must rely heavily on imports from Malaysia and Indonesia. National security issues mandate that Singapore become less dependent on foreign sources of natural gas.

The adoption of nuclear power would be one way of reducing Singapore's reliance on natural gas in the generation of electricity. Singapore City's supporters of nuclear power point to the fact that by weight, the radioactive element uranium can generate 50 times more energy than can fossil fuels. Because of the energy density of nuclear power, it generates electricity more cheaply than any current source of renewable energy. The technology of nuclear power has progressed to a point that small reactors can generate enormous amounts of electricity. With land at a premium, small nuclear power plants may be the antidote for overcrowding in the city. Moreover, nuclear power is a clean technology, generating no greenhouse gases. This feature is important in Singapore City, which produces large amounts of greenhouse gases per capita. The question for the residents of Singapore City may be whether nuclear power is sustainable. The past has been littered with high-profile

> ### Coal
>
> Coal being an important fuel, companies in Singapore City are exploring the entire island for additional deposits to generate electricity. Coal formed on what is today Singapore and worldwide during the Carboniferous period (360–300 million years ago). The climate, being warmer and wetter than today, supported vast stretches of swampy forests whose plants, many being woody, captured the sun's energy through photosynthesis. When the plants died, their wood fossilized rather than decayed because mushrooms and other specialized fungi had not yet evolved to decompose the bark. Fossilization preserved the plants' energy. Being fossilized, coal is known as a fossil fuel. This resource, having formed during the 60 million years of the Carboniferous, is being unearthed and burned in only centuries. In this sense, humans are squandering what cannot be replaced. Today's biota has the decomposers that prevent coal's re-formation. In any case, the formation of coal or any fossil fuel takes too long because people need energy now. Estimates of how much coal remains to be mined vary, but even the World Coal Association doubts that the world has much more than 150 years of reserves at current rates of consumption.

accidents that worry Singapore's public. Critics worry that nuclear power must be made safe before questions of sustainability can be broached.

Two possibilities may address the lack of space for a nuclear power plant in dense Singapore City. The first is to build a nuclear power plant underground. An underground nuclear power plant would not leak above ground if an accident occurred. Should an accident occur, a leak should therefore be easier to contain below ground than above ground. An underground nuclear power plant should be easier to defend against terrorism than an above-ground plant. A second possibility might be to build a nuclear power plant offshore in the way that oil companies position a derrick offshore. Should an accident occur, it might be possible for a tugboat to pull the plant farther out to sea so that radioactive leaks might not poison the residents of Singapore City.

Yet government is sensitive to public hand-wringing over the potential dangers of nuclear power. Given such constraints, government and the private sector continue to promote renewable sources of energy. Singapore's government notes that between 2007 and 2015 the number of private firms researching clean energy has risen from almost none to roughly 100. Singapore's government appears to believe that it and the private sector can leverage technology to meet the demands for energy and sustainability. Clean technologies appear to be at the forefront of research in Singapore City. In 2016, Singapore announced the allocation of $900 million for research into renewable sources of energy. In addition, the National University of Singapore funds the Solar Energy Research Institute of Singapore in an effort to create and use the latest technologies in the generation and delivery of solar energy. Singapore City also conducts research in fuel cells and other alternatives to fossil fuels.

Christopher Cumo

See also: Energy and Sustainability: Rio de Janeiro, Brazil: A City with a Passion for Conservation and Renewable Energy; *Waste Management:* Singapore City, Singapore: Managing Food Waste

Further Reading

"Conversations on Sustainable Singapore: Energy and Climate Change." 2013. http://www.greenfuture.sg/wp-content/uploads/downloads/2014/05/Conversations-on-Sustainable-Singapore-Energy-and-Climate-Change.pdf.

Khew, Carolyn. 2016. "Spike in Number of Solar Panel Installations." *Singapore Times*, October 17. https://www.straitstimes.com/singapore/environment/spike-in-number-of-solar-panel-installations.

Peloso, Matthew. 2016. "Why You Should Go Solar in Singapore." Sun Electric, 2016. https://sunelectric.com.sg/why-you-should-go-solar-in-singapore/.

Singapore Government. 2018. "Urban Solutions & Sustainability." https://www.edb.gov.sg/en/our-industries/urban-solutions-and-sustainability.html.

"Solar Photovoltaic Systems." https://www.ema.gov.sg/solar_photovoltaic_systems.aspx.

"Sustainable Singapore Blueprint 2015—Highlights and Thoughts." 2014. www.greenfuture.sg/2014/11/11/sustainable-singapore-blueprint-2015-highlights-and-thoughts.

Toronto, Canada: A City with a Passion for Energy Conservation

Toronto scores multiple "firsts" in many different categories. It is the largest city in Canada, the safest city in North America, and the most diverse urban center on earth. On the North American continent, Toronto additionally claims to have the largest underground pedestrian system (known as PATH), to be the largest urban car-free community, and to operate the second-largest public transit system. According to the Economist Intelligence Unit, Toronto is the fourth most livable city in the world in such categories as health care, education, and stability. Ontario's capital has also been ranked highly on its business climate (the second most business-friendly city in the world), environment, and infrastructure.

It is not surprising, therefore, that when it comes to energy and sustainability, Toronto is likewise among the leaders. The city is known for its eco-projects, seven-generation stewardship, and smart use of energy resources. By and large, Toronto's policies are threefold and include 1) measures to conserve energy; 2) measures to reduce emissions; and 3) measures to increase energy supply. Careful situation analysis and masterfully drafted long-term strategic energy initiatives for the city continually promote the above-mentioned policies.

ENERGY CONSERVATION

Toronto conserves energy primarily via reductions in consumption of electricity and natural gas, as well as through growth in renewable energy usage. Of all the city's initiatives in this direction, three seem to have been the most successful:

1. The Toronto Green Standard;
2. Community Energy Planning (CEP);
3. Home Energy Loan Program (HELP).

Implemented in 2014, the Toronto Green Standard is described by the city as "a two-tier set of performance measures for sustainable site and building design. Tier

1 is required for new construction in Toronto; Tier 2 is a step higher, it is the voluntary level of performance with a financial incentive. Projects that achieve Tier 2 may be eligible for a partial reimbursement on Development Charges paid to the City" ("Toronto Green Standard" n.d.). In plain language, this is the carrot-and-stick approach. In accordance with the standard, the newly constructed mid-to-high-rise buildings are encouraged (and expected) to achieve 25 percent higher energy efficiency than what is required by the existing Ontario Building Code. In addition, all the newly constructed buildings with a square footage of 600 square meters or more must utilize at least 5 percent renewable energy. That is the stick. And here is the carrot: if the construction companies exceed those levels, they become eligible for financial stimuli from the municipal government.

The Green Standard has received mixed reactions. While some of the developers do aim at higher-than-required levels of energy efficiency, many feel that the initiative comes "too quickly and is not rooted in fulsome consultation and/or thought for implementation [and that] the industry is still playing catch-up on the recent (Ontario Building) Code changes" (Viola 2013). At the same time, green policy activists applaud the city's efforts. Thus, Sustainia, a leading global sustainable energy organization, has recognized the Toronto Green Standard as one of the world's most successful city projects.

Another initiative, the Community Energy Planning (CEP), is, in fact, a strategy that has been successfully adopted by not only the city of Toronto, but also by many other Canadian municipalities. The program calls for analysis of two "hows": how the city uses energy and how that energy usage affects the city. Along with the analysis, the CEP prudently requires early projections on energy, water, and waste needs. Mount Dennis, a neighborhood located in northern Toronto, can serve as an example of the effective implementation of the Community Energy Planning program. Even though the neighborhood is rapidly growing (in the next 25 years, approximately 1,000 residential units will be added and the population will significantly increase), it is expected that the total energy consumption will remain at approximately the same level as it is currently. Economy will be achieved via retrofitting existing buildings (e.g., heating and heat exchange retrofits, low-flow showerheads and faucets, solar hot water boilers, window insulation and refurbishment, etc.) and designing new high-performance residences. Having made energy planning an important consideration at the stage of construction design, the city avoids potential problems in future.

Finally, the Home Energy Loan Program (HELP), a logical extension of the CEP, provides incentives to the general population to improve the energy efficiency of their homes. The low-interest loan it offers is paid back as a part of property tax, and it allows the homeowner to reduce natural gas and electricity bills. What makes the program unique is the fact that the loaned amount is attached to the property and not to the property owner. Thus, when the house is sold, a new homeowner takes the responsibility to repay the loan. The initiative has been successful, as, according to The *Environment and Energy Division: 2015 Annual Report*, "on average, home energy retrofit projects are valued at $18,000 and have achieved deep-energy savings by cutting natural gas bills by 30%, saving an average of almost $800 on energy bills per year, and avoiding an estimated 3 tons of greenhouse gas emissions annually."

In general, these three initiatives demonstrate that Toronto's energy conservation strategies are cutting-edge and often serve as a model for other municipalities.

EMISSION REDUCTION

Similar to any large city, Toronto aims at finding a fine balance between its high demands in energy and the necessity of lowering the emissions. In recent years, a number of different programs have been introduced. Thus, the city's *Environment and Energy Division: 2015 Annual Report* lists several strategies that collectively address environmental policies, transportation and traffic congestion management, and education of the general public. Some of these programs—for example, Smart Commute, Green Taxis, Congestion Management Plan 2014–2018, and Zero Waste Building—can undoubtedly be named among the city's most distinctive strategies. As can be observed, three of the programs deal with transportation, since it alone is responsible for nearly 40 percent of Toronto's greenhouse gas emissions.

As mentioned earlier, Toronto has one of the best public transit systems in North America. Yet, in order to remain relevant amid the rapid population growth and development of new neighborhoods, the public transportation infrastructure requires constant update and expansion, measures that are both costly and slow. To provide a short-term solution to the problem, the city of Toronto encourages sustainable transportation use through its Smart Commute Program. The program offers the city employers carpool matching, discounted transit passes, flexible work

An electric streetcar in Toronto, Canada, November 13, 2018. The city encourages residents to use public transportation, carpool, and ride bikes. (Jerome Cid /Dreamstime.com)

arrangements, as well as walking and cycling programs. Environmentally conscious business owners enthusiastically support the program. Thus, as of 2014, 94 major firms and corporations (which employ approximately 331,000 commuters) participated, and, in doing so, greatly contributed to the reduction in traffic emissions.

The city also invests heavily in its cycling infrastructure. Currently, there are 200 biking stations with a total of over 2,000 bicycles (2016), and the number is constantly growing. According to some studies, more than 20 percent of Torontonians get to work either walking or biking.

The Green Taxis is another interesting program. According to this initiative, by 2021, all the city cabs must be replaced either with hybrids or by vehicles on alternative fuel. In addition, the new taxis must have a fuel efficiency of at least 33.6 miles per gallon. The expected outcome will be the reduction of greenhouse emissions from the current annual 99,000 tons to 79,000 tons. Toronto is, in fact, the first municipality in Canada to introduce such an idea and even turned it into a bylaw. The initiative first materialized in 2007, when Eco Taxi, the first fully green cab company, was founded in Toronto. With a small fleet of Toyota Priuses, the company nowadays serves the needs of many Torontonians and city visitors, while contributing almost 50 percent less to greenhouse gas emissions.

Along with addressing the means of transportation, Toronto pays much attention to traffic congestion problems. The major improvements in that area, however, are achieved not so much through expanding the existing infrastructure, but through development of new technologies that prevent traffic jams. These technologies are multifactorial and consider eight different areas:

1. Intelligent Transportation Systems, which allow for effective traffic monitoring;
2. Congestion and Engineering Studies, aiming at finding the best possible engineering solutions for traffic management;
3. Incident and Event Response Systems, dealing with emergencies;
4. Construction Coordination, seeking the ways to manage traffic congestions during road construction and repair;
5. Curbside Management, developing parking solutions;
6. Support of All Models of Transportation, examining the ways of making it possible to keep on the road differently performing vehicles;
7. Traveler Information, proving both drivers and pedestrians with the traffic updates;
8. Traffic Operations Centre, coordinating all the aspects of traffic.

The *Congestion Management Plan 2014–2018* has a main idea that is rather simple—as the number of stops on the roads decreases, level of greenhouse gas emission will decline.

When it comes to non-transport-related initiatives, Toronto's Zero Waste Building Program deserves a closer look. The history of the problem is well known to any Torontonian—approximately 15 years ago, the city faced a severe garbage crisis. As residents discarded more waste and as available landfill areas continuously shrank, the cost of garbage disposal increased dramatically. Purchase of the new

Green Lane landfill near London (Ontario) provided a viable, albeit temporary, solution. By 2029, that landfill will be completely full, and the city will again need to cope with the issue. In this situation, it is only logical that Toronto City Hall takes preventive measures to avoid a possible future disaster.

Thus, to divert the waste from rapidly filling landfills, Zero Waste Building Program has been introduced. The program aims at achieving the maximum efficiency in garbage recycling. According to some estimates, approximately 54 percent of organic waste, 24 percent recyclables, 4 percent electronic ad hazardous waste, and 6 percent reusables (e.g., clothing, toys, or furniture) can be diverted from a typical residential garbage bag.

And the city achieved those levels! In some instances, the results are even more impressive—recently, it was reported that Toronto's eight largest buildings managed to divert 88 percent of their waste from going into the landfill, which ultimately saved the city a significant amount of money. Nowadays, Toronto's average garbage diversion rates are about 90 percent, the accomplishment officially recognized by Zero Waste International.

Generally, the city pays much attention to emission problems, constantly works with all the major stakeholders, and educates the public on the importance of the sustainable energy policies.

ENERGY SUPPLY

In recent years, Toronto has been actively working on the development of different innovative and alternative sources of energy. The most prominent ones are district energy (DE) systems and microFIT solar photovoltaic programs.

The idea of DE systems consisting of "a heating and cooling center and a thermal network of pipes connecting multiple buildings" ("District Energy") is not entirely new. For decades, it has been used in many European countries and has proved its efficiency. The positive results are achieved through economies of scale, since big energy plants are more cost-effective and administratively simpler than numerous small stand-alone stations. Given the obvious benefits of DE systems, Toronto attempts to include as many residential buildings as possible into the DE networks.

The microFIT program (FIT stands for "feed-in-tariff") provides support and incentives for residents wishing to install small solar panels on the roofs of their houses. Such panels generate up to 10 kilowatts of energy, and homeowners sell the produced power to the municipality at a guaranteed rate. Despite the high cost of installation (often $20,000–$30,000), relatively low return on investment (currently, about $400 per year), and uncertainty about the future of the solar panels, many Torontonians opt for the program, as they are willing to contribute to a cleaner environment.

By combining the efforts of cutting-edge engineering and green activities, the Toronto government confidently implements new technologies that allow the city to remain one of the world's leading industrial and cultural centers.

Mykola Polyuha

See also: Green Spaces: Halifax, Canada: Near-Urban Wilderness Protection; *Waste Management:* Calgary, Canada: Waste Management Is a National Effort and Calgary's Priority

Further Reading

Congestion Management Plan 2014–2018. 2013. Toronto City Hall. https://www.toronto.ca/wp-content/uploads/2017/08/963e-congetion-managment-plan-2014-2018.pdf.

"District Energy." (n.d.). Toronto City Hall. Accessed February 1, 2019. https://www.toronto.ca/services-payments/water-environment/environmentally-friendly-city-initiatives/district-energy/.

"Draft Mount Dennis Community Energy Plan." 2016. City of Toronto: Environment & Energy Division. http://www.toronto.ca/legdocs/mmis/2016/pe/bgrd/backgroundfile-95624.pdf.

The Environment and Energy Division: Five Year Business Plan (2014–18). 2013. Toronto City Hall: The Environment and Energy Division. http://www.toronto.ca/legdocs/mmis/2013/pe/bgrd/backgroundfile-62457.pdf.

The Environment and Energy Division: 2017 Annual Report. 2017. Toronto City Hall: The Environment and Energy Division. https://www.toronto.ca/wp-content/uploads/2018/11/9a76-EED-AnnualReport2017-AODA.pdf.

Myllyvirta, Lauri. 2013. *Silent Killers: Why Europe Must Replace Coal Power with Green Energy.* Green Peace International. https://www.greenpeace.org/slovenia/Global/international/publications/climate/2013/Silent-Killers.pdf.

Novakovic, Stefan. 2015. "An Inside Look at Toronto's New Home Energy Loan Program." *Urban Toronto*, August 27. http://urbantoronto.ca/news/2015/08/inside-look-torontos-new-home-energy-loan-program.

"Promoting Efficiency in New Developments." 2015. *Cities 100.* Sustainia. https://issuu.com/sustainia/docs/cities100/97?e=4517615/31305566.

"Toronto Green Standard." n.d. Toronto City Hall. https://www.toronto.ca/city-government/planning-development/official-plan-guidelines/toronto-green-standard/.

Viola, Daniel. 2013. "Toronto's New Green Standard Raises Concerns." *Remi Network*, October 7. https://www.reminetwork.com/articles/torontos-new-green-standard-raises-concerns.

Zero Waste Toronto: A Vision for Our City. 2016. Toronto Environmental Alliance. https://d3n8a8pro7vhmx.cloudfront.net/toenviro/pages/1636/attachments/original/1456190964/TEA_-_Zero_Waste_Toronto_Report_-_2016.pdf?1456190964.

Green Spaces

OVERVIEW

The world is urbanizing at an increasing rate. According to a report by the UN, 54 percent of the world's population live in urban areas today. That number will be nearly 70 percent by 2050. This means that cities are expected to provide more jobs and more livable spaces. A city that can't sustain a livable condition will be entangled in an environmental crisis at the minimum. The most widely embraced solution is to preserve and create green spaces. Urban green spaces typically include parks, gardens, and woodlands. The concept also includes "blue spaces," such as streams, ponds, and coastal zones. There is no doubt that green spaces are necessary for a healthy living environment; they have become an indispensable facility of a modern urban neighborhood. However, the provision of greenery in urban areas bears significant costs and other challenges. Articles in this section review the efforts of 10 world cities.

Preservation

Hong Kong's challenge is its limited dwelling space—too many buyers running after too few flats, as Fornes points out, making Hong Kong the most expensive housing market in the world. Nevertheless, HK is one of the greenest cities in the world: 40 percent of its land is allocated to parks and recreational space, and HK has on average nine square meters of green space per capita, well above the recommended international standard. There are a number of factors that have made this possible. The island's mountainous topography offers a natural protection of green space. Political climate is favorable as well: from the perspective that HK will be fully ruled by Beijing in 2064, land sales are already restricted. The pressure coming from an influx from mainland China, however, will be a tremendous challenge. HK's population will increase by more than half a million between 2014 and 2064, bringing the city's population to over 8 million. Solutions are scanty, but HK is unwilling to build on the green belt that delimits urban zones. The next speculated option is to rezone industrial areas for residential use, pushing industrial facilities into Shenzhen on the China side, then open spaces in communities and vacant office spaces. The ultimate solution, however, appears to be in controlling the influx. In that regard, though, HK will not likely have the final word.

Canada has 9 percent of the forestry in the world. Canadians, however, are unwilling to waste a single tree. Halifax is a mid-sized city with 400,000 residents who enjoy hiking, canoeing, kayaking, swimming, paddleboarding, mountain biking, geocaching, trail running, rock climbing, camping, bird-watching, berry picking, dog walking, and nature appreciation, according to Miller. However, they risk having to give up these activities if urban sprawl deprives them of near-urban wilderness. When that happens, biodiversity will also be disturbed. Urban sprawl grew by 92 percent between 1992 and 2014, in contrast with the population growth of only 19 percent. Most of the development was on the edges of the city (exurbs, suburbs), and predominantly on private lands. To protect the wilderness, residents urged the provincial government and the municipality to take actions against developers. The public pressure succeeded in getting more land included under legal protections. What's important in Halifax's story is that people stepped in to protect the environment. However, whether this success could be duplicated elsewhere is a question.

While creating and preserving green spaces is seen as a moral and financial obligation in many cities, for New York City, it is a legacy. Let every community live near a green space was a wish of the city's founders. The long list of appropriations shown on the website of the Department of Parks and Recreation reflects the city's desire, as well as the citizens' generous contribution, for more green spaces. The major expressways, bridges, and the "city" are built to follow the contour of the natural conditions, which is in contrast with the kind of urban planning solely centered on the planner's wish. Scholars agree that NYC has been successful in not letting urban sprawl run out of control. The challenge, however, is in adapting the green environment to the city's fast-paced life and its critical functions in almost every field. Over the years, NYC has met this challenge by adding roads and transportation facilities to make accessing the green spaces more convenient. On the other hand, NYC has made tremendous efforts in adding recreational and social facilities to existing parks. In other words, the city finds in expanding green spaces a solution to urban inefficiency.

Expansion

Can abandoned industrial spaces be returned to green? The city of Aguascalientes in Mexico says yes. Aguascalientes is a medium-sized industrial city, home to many large information technology firms and the largest Nissan manufacturing plants today. Deregulation in the 1990s led to agrarian lands being urbanized and occupied by office buildings and residential housing. One of the largest projects was an industrial corridor in the valley of Aguascalientes that used a wide stretch of agrarian land. When urban sprawl was stopped as a result of the financial crisis in the 1990s, the municipality was able to redirect focus to sustainable development. Through the La Linea Verde project, the city transformed a 12-kilometer oil pipeline infrastructure into a greenway traversing 23 impoverished neighborhoods. It provides a green space for people to walk, bike, and spend time with family. The greenway attracted neighborhoods and businesses, forming a much larger tax base that facilitated the city's recovery from economic crisis. The Aguascalientes greenway has since been a model of accomplishing three goals at once: economic, environmental, and social. The new challenge is to build affordable housing for the poor and an environment suitable for the elderly.

Rotterdam, the Netherlands, faces challenges from being a low-lying city—slightly below sea level. The geographical condition makes the area vulnerable for trapping pollutants from emission. Being a quintessential port, gas emission is what plagues the city. Heavy traffic of cargo ships from emerging economies in Asia, Americas, and the Middle East make Rotterdam's air twice as polluted as that of Shanghai and London. Rotterdam's solution is to set up regulations to curb carbon emission by 50 percent by 2025. On the other hand, the city has been steadily increasing its green spaces for over a decade, reaching 28.4 square meters per capita currently, far surpassing WHO's recommended level of nine square meters. These green spaces come in many forms, including pocket parks, green roofs, green walls, tree-lined streets, and gardens. "Edible Rotterdam" is probably the most exciting form of greenery: urban agriculture puts real food on the table. The municipality provides guidance and financial incentives to encourage the initiatives.

For Tokyo, a top challenge has been to regain depleted green spaces and make them larger. As of 2011, this most populated city in the world had seen its green areas dwindle to 3.4 percent of its total area, falling far behind the levels of Seoul and the New York City. Aging population, low birth rate, and stagnant economy, as Karsner indicates, were among the factors that prompted environmental actions. Tokyo's strategy is to attack the situation at multiple levels. The municipality constructed *Umi no Mori* or the Sea Forest in Tokyo Bay, a historical dumpsite with tens of thousands of tons of garbage piled up over decades. To involve the citizens, Tokyo launched the *My Tree* program encouraging residents to donate money toward planting trees. Donors receive tax benefits and get their names and tree information recorded on plaques mounted on the trees. A most ingenious move appears to be integrating disaster relief functions with the construction of green spaces. Park areas have charging stations, food storage and supplies stored underneath, and benches that can be turned into stoves. In times of earthquakes, particularly the ones of the scale of the Kanto earthquake of 1923, these green spaces may serve as relief zones for an extended period of time.

Moscow is more than the cultural and political center of Russia. It is an industrial city offering jobs to 12 million people. Overbuilding, CO_2 emissions, and overpopulation have reduced green spaces. To Muscovites, this is a serious issue to be resolved. The municipality sets up laws to require bare lands be covered with vegetation, especially those affected by industrial operations. Moreover, task forces are established to monitor and evaluate green areas and keep strict records. Moscow involves citizens in these efforts through projects such as My Street, One Million Trees, and Active Citizens. Citizens are invited to select trees or shrubs through online voting. The city also uses Internet programs to let citizens report violations and deterioration that needs to be fixed. The Russian standards require a city to have 40 percent of green coverage. Today, Moscow holds a leading position among megalopolises in the world, with 20.2 square meters of green area per person, beating New York City's 19.2 square meters, Paris's 6 square meters, and Tokyo's 5 square meters.

Oil economy has transformed Abu Dhabi from a pearling village into a magnificent modern city. Urbanization crunch has made it necessary to build more green and shaded spaces. Abu Dhabi faces a twofold challenge: on the one hand, there is not much ground for vegetation; on the other hand, expanding public open spaces that reflect traditional aspects of the culture calls for bold actions. In its 2030 Plan, Abu Dhabi endeavors to claim green spaces from the sea and from sandy deserts by building green islands and eco-villages. Some islands are built to preserve biodiversity while others for recreation purposes. To create open spaces in neighborhoods, the city broadens roads for the convenience of traffic and gathering. Promoting vernacular-style landscaping in mosques and turning religious grounds into community centers are considered a bold change. It contributes to making the society more open as well.

Creative Use

Paris is an excellent garden city, not just because its grand royal parks are artistic standards, but more importantly because the city has never stopped investing in preservation and improvement. Paris attracts millions of tourists every year who contribute handsomely to the city's coffers, giving it every incentive to make its gardens more attractive. Additionally, Parisians find every way possible to integrate green spaces with daily living. The royal gardens, for example, are made to seamlessly connect to public transit stops. The trails are embedded with displays and signs for educational purposes. Pocket gardens are abundant all over the city and in a variety of forms, such as green roofs, green walls, and hanging gardens, to let people enjoy a moment of quietude whenever such need is called for. One impressive effort is to develop green spaces in suburban neighborhoods where low-income immigrants reside. Streets are widened and decorated with tree lines. In some neighborhoods, crowded residential compounds are revamped to make room for an open area. The social life in these neighborhoods is improved. The city explores security functions as well: green spaces can make surveillance easier. They allow community members to "see" and "be seen."

For Tel Aviv, greening the city doesn't have to be just for aesthetic purposes; it can bring food to the table and provide jobs. The city allocates gardening plots based on a number of criteria, the fundamental one being equality. The city strives to let as many as possible have access to a garden regardless of their economic, cultural or ethnic status, or sexual orientation. Avid growers and casual growers can all have their fix of gardening fever. Those who have trouble affording groceries are welcome to give a few moments of fieldwork in exchange for vegetables. Community gardening in Israel is rooted in Jewish cultural tradition. "From each according to his ability, to each according to his needs" is the adage that comes with the kibbutzim tradition. Gardening can provide serious jobs, too. When the city deploys hydroponics technology to gardens in immigrant neighborhoods, it creates jobs of urban farming. Immigrants enjoy the opportunity of supplying fresh produce to the neighborhoods. Meanwhile, collective work improves communication. Community gardening has become a unique venue to create green spaces in Tel Aviv.

Further Reading

The Department of Economic and Social Affairs of the United Nations. 2014. *World Urbanization Prospects.* https://www.compassion.com/multimedia/world-urbanization-prospects.pdf.

Jim, C. Y. 2012. "Sustainable Urban Greening Strategies for Compact Cities in Developing and Developed Economies." Springer US. https://doi.org/10.1007/s11252-012-0268-x.

Abu Dhabi, United Arab Emirates (UAE): Building a Greener City with a More Open Culture

Abu Dhabi is the capital city of the Emirate of Abu Dhabi and the federal capital of the United Arab Emirates (UAE). Located on the southern shoreline of the Persian Gulf, its largest and most influential neighbor would be Iran, though separated by the Gulf. Abu Dhabi is the largest of the seven emirates, with more than three-fourths of the area of the entire federation. The contour of the land features island-dotted coastline, sandy deserts in the interior with fertile oases where date palms thrive, scenic wadis of stunning beauty, and sand dunes on the edge of the Rub al Khali that could be as high as a thousand feet. In fact, 85 percent of the land is sandy desert with spectacular dunes in ripple formations. The oasis presents a different scene where mangrove forests are inhabited by a variety of land and seabirds, some migrating from Asia. The temperature in wintertime is around 20 Celsius, while summer temperatures can be as high as 45 Celsius (113 degrees Fahrenheit). Meanwhile, 7 percent of the land is salt-covered flat areas where virtually no vegetation could grow. Overall, 93 percent of the emirate's land mass present challenges to comfortable living (Abu Dhabi Urban Planning Council 2007).

HISTORY

Compared to most megacities in the world, Abu Dhabi's urban crisis has a shorter history. The solution, however, is no less challenging. A hunting and pearling ground in the mid-18th century, Abu Dhabi was known for operating the world's largest pearling fleet around the end of the 19th century. The pearling industry was brought to prosperity by Indian traders. They arrived at the heels of the British in the late 19th century, and exported pearls to Asian markets. Hindu financiers who controlled the pearl trade exported almost all Gulf pearls to Mumbai, the world's largest pearl market. As demand increased, pearl prices rose to the level of gold. By 1917, a single gram of quality Gulf pearl was valued at 320 grams of gold, or 7.7 kilograms of silver. Around the same time, Mikimoto Kokichi successfully cultured pearls in Japan (Mikimoto History Website) and established pearl factories. It did not take long before hundreds of pearl farms in Japan soon flooded world markets with millions of cultured pearls. When Japanese traders arrived in Abu Dhabi with cultured pearls in the 1930s, the local pearling business came to an end. By 1949, the Gulf region had lost 90 percent of the market share and even suffered starvation as a result (Zacharias 2009).

Just as the pearling industry faded out, Abu Dhabi found itself sitting on the world's largest pool of oil. Toward the mid-20th century, oil fields were discovered both in the sea and on land, and everything else was history. Much like the urban scene during the boom days of the pearling era when rich pearl divers and foreign financiers lived in their villas surrounded by deserts, the modern Abu Dhabi has skyscrapers lining its horizons. While emirate citizens rake in handsome incomes from royalty checks, foreign workers arrive in great numbers to find jobs. "I have never seen so many Ferraris (or Starbucks) in my life," a visitor remarked (Lenhart 2015). A critical mechanism that contributed to the economic prosperity, however, turns out to be more than just oil. The formation of the UAE federation in 1971 by Sheikh Zayed bin Sultan Al Nahyan in Abu Dhabi and Sheikh Rashid bin Saeed Al Maktoum in Dubai on the basis of democratic principles was critical in streamlining the oil trade of the seven member emirates (Easterling 2013). Today, with a half a million people (Abu Dhabi Urban Planning Council 2007), Abu Dhabi's combined revenues from oil and overseas investments makes the city home to one of the world's highest per capita incomes (Encyclopaedia Britannica).

Unlike most new capital cities, however, Abu Dhabi was built from scratch and in a brief period—high-rises filled up superblocks in the city during the 1980s and 1990s to accommodate the influx of foreign workers. However, rapid urbanization resulted in the building of crowded neighborhoods with narrow streets. Additionally, high-rise residential buildings were criticized for lacking authenticity and being devoid of life, presenting challenges for the city to improve (Hashim 2012). Local people have been fishing and farming for generations in the region, during which they have developed a rich local cultural tradition. The city council is aware that the tradition will be destroyed if not well cared for. The challenge, however, is how to make a city world class while preserving its cultural traditions.

THE 2030 PLAN

Urban regeneration has been a widespread movement in the Gulf countries during the past decade, with traditional environments being recreated or restored. The goal is to let different cities showcase different styles. Dubai, for example, focuses on creating appeal via building suburban homes through projects such as Arabian Ranches and Falconcity of Wonders. Its downtown area is designed as a community of the world's tallest buildings. Saudi Arabia has plans to develop six metropolises also known as economic cities in undeveloped land, the purpose of which is to accommodate a large and growing population (Velegrinis 2015). To address its urban issues, Abu Dhabi plans to produce more green, public, and shaded spaces. The city wants to be branded with the identity of "heritage, sea, desert and city" (Hashim 2012). The Abu Dhabi Planning Council, chaired by the Crown Prince His Highness Sheikh Mohammed bin Zayed Al Nahyan, puts forward his vision in the Emiri Decree *Abu Dhabi 2030 Urban Structure Framework Plan* (Abu Dhabi

Urban Planning Council 2007). The development will transform Abu Dhabi into a city that showcases a unique environment with an evolving culture, its own identity, and provides excellent livability and connectivity.

The plan highlights sustainable living as a critical objective. It stresses that, while oil has contributed significant wealth to the city, the city must develop renewable resources, both for clean energy and for preserving the natural living spaces. Environment, economy, and culture are identified as three elements that must be reflected in urban features. Therefore, natural sceneries of oases, islands, sand dunes and coastlines, and wild life are at the top of the preservation agenda. The plan stipulates that natural spaces must be protected from the impact of the fast-rising urban population, and protecting green spaces is one of the best ways to preserve cultural identity. The principle of *estidama* ("sustainability" in Arabic) is upheld as the spirit of modern urban design. It is broadly reflected in regulations covering everything from urban design, environmental health and safety, to building and zoning requirements. In implementation, the city council conducts evaluations according to what is known as the Pearl Rating System, which includes five levels of compliance, with "5 pearls" being the highest level (Department of Urban Planning and Municipality undated).

The 2030 Plan's public open space framework policies specifically address the development of green spaces including national and regional parks, landscaped parkways and boulevards, neighborhood parks, and beach parks. One of the requirements is that parks and communities must be connected with green streets. Furthermore, these streets must be convenient for walking and socializing. In describing the capital's cultural characteristics and how the plan integrates them, it states:

> The Capital Boulevard is enhanced to provide a beautiful and dramatic connection between the Presidential Palace, the Grand Mosque, and the new Capital District. The approach to the Capital District is very visual, symbolic and memorable. For example, it is proposed that the Boulevard will travel under seven high arches, representing the seven Emirates of the UAE, and terminate at a main capital square. A rail station is located at the center of the new city, linking Emiratis living across the country to their capital. Inside the central square might be monuments, palm gardens and water features. (Abu Dhabi Urban Planning Council 2007, 13)

According to the plan, Abu Dhabi will build several key districts into iconic precincts, with processional routes, such as the Cultural District on Saadiyat Islan, the Palace Row, and the Embassy District. National government activities will take place in a designated National District.

GREEN SPACES

Abu Dhabi being a coastal city, it includes ecosystems of both marine and desert environments. Preservation involves prevention of urban encroachment through implementation of proper land use. This is to be done by congregating business developments into a new Central Business District adjacent to the old town. This area, however, due to its proximity to the Capital District (also known as Zayed City), is under pressure to develop residential facilities for migrant workers. Here, heavy and light industries are concentrated in inland spaces—the

Mussafah and Mafraq areas. The planned solution is to build marine transportation and high-speed rails linking these areas with a variety of residential areas. Additionally, to improve living quality of densely populated areas, the 2030 Plan intends to connect open green spaces from national parks to city parks and community recreational areas. Mangrove Park, Corniche Beach, and Lulu Island are currently major parks serving as the backbone of green space. Lulu Island is a man-made island of 400 hectares, designed to serve as an environmental sanctuary for cultural tourism.

ECO-VILLAGES

A great advantage of Abu Dhabi is the potential for expanding urban scope into the sea and the sandy desert. The 2030 Plan aims at creating desert eco-villages and island eco-villages outside the urban center. On-land desert villages will be built along Al Ain, also known as a "garden city," and will feature traditional courtyard-style housing in low-density neighborhoods. Island eco-villages are designed to be separated from urban road traffic by allowing only access by ferryboat. The power grid will also be solar-based. Waterfront housing will be developed.

The Environmental Framework Plan is a program to create green spaces by building islands. Some islands will serve to preserve the local biodiversity. Access will be limited to low-impact uses, such as picnicking and hiking. Access will also be limited to nonmotorized boats. Other islands offer horseback riding, golfing, and other forms of entertainment. These islands will be accessible via bridges.

GREEN RELIGIOUS AND RESIDENTIAL SPACES

Green spaces are always an important part of religious life. To provide space for religious practice, Plan 2030 promotes a vernacular style of environment. The design uses traditional-style landscaping to make the mosque a suitable place for meditation and relaxation. As such, the mosque will become a community center for many activities in daily life. The vernacular mosque includes a portal, a *suhan* (an open courtyard), a *riwaq* (semi-open space for prayer), prayer hall, and a *mihrab* (where the imam leads the prayer). Different from the tight-spaced traditional mosque, the vernacular mosque features open spaces that reflect the spirit of modern urban living.

In designing residential housing, the plan intends to preserve the traditional while introducing modernity. To reflect this goal, modern neighborhoods will integrate two key features: 1) a convenient network of neighborhood streets; and 2) plentiful open spaces for meeting and playing. One of the projects is Al Falah, located to the east of the Abu Dhabi International Airport. The project was completed in 2012. The neighborhood includes 4,857 homes across 12.5 million square meters, and community facilities for 60,000 residents. The area is subdivided into five villages, each with shopping center, schools, and a mosque. The town center has more public open spaces for leisure, shopping, and public activities (Abu Dhabi Urban

Planning Council 2015b). Overall, Abu Dhabi's focus on developing green open public spaces is believed to represent the city's next phase of development.

Jing Luo

See also: Employment and Jobs: Riyadh, Saudi Arabia: Creating Jobs in the Post–Oil-Boom Era; *Migration and Demographic Changes:* Tehran, Iran: Toward a More Open and Tolerant Society

Further Reading
"Abu Dhabi Facts." *National Geographic.* http://travel.nationalgeographic.com/travel/countries/abu-dhabi-facts.
Abu Dhabi Urban Planning Council. 2007 "Executive Summary—Plan Abu Dhabi 2030 Urban Structure Framework Plan." https://www.ecouncil.ae/PublicationsEn/plan-abu-dhabi-full-version-EN.pdf.
Abu Dhabi Urban Planning Council. 2015a. "Plan Capital." https://www.upc.gov.ae/en/strategic-framework-plans/capital-plan.
Department of Urban Planning and Municipality. Undated. "The Pearl Rating System for Estidama." https://www.dpm.gov.abudhabi/en/Urban-Planning/The-Pearl-Rating-System-for-Estidama.
Easterling, Keller. 2013. "Abu Dhabi and Dubai—World City Doubles." In Rodolphe El-Khoury and Edward Robbins, eds. *Shaping the City.* 2nd ed. London: Routledge.
Encyclopaedia Britannica. "Abu Dhabi." https://www.britannica.com/place/Abu-Dhabi.
Hashim, Alamira Reem Al Ayedrous Bani. 2012. "Branding the Brand New City: Abu Dhabi, Travelers Welcome." *Place Branding and Public Diplomacy*, 8, 1: 72–82. Macmillan Publishers.
Lenhart, Jennifer. 2015. "Abu Dhabi & Dubai: Far from People-Centered Planning." The Urban Observer. https://exploring-and-observing-cities.org/2015/11/20/abu-dhabi-dubai-a-long-way-from-people-centred-planning.
Mikimoto History Website. https://www.mikimoto.com/en/about-us/history.html.
Valdemar, Wake. 2010. "Abu Dhabi: The City That Grew Out of a Desert." *Australian Quarterly* 82, 1: 32–36.
Velegrinis, Steven and George Katodrytis. 2015. *Architectural Design* 85, 1: 72–79.
Zacharias, Anna. 2009. "For Years, Life in the Gulf Was Dominated by 'Jewels of the Sea': For Some, Pearls Brought Fabulous Wealth." *National, UAE*, June 14. http://www.thenational.ae/uae/heritage/for-some-pearls-brought-fabulous-wealth#page3.

Aguascalientes, Mexico: Returning Industrial Ruin to Green Space

Aguascalientes City is the capital of the state of Aguascalientes in Mexico's north-central region. A mid-sized city, it is home to one of the largest industrial-to-green-space conversions in Latin America. Aguascalientes is internationally regarded as a green city and recognized as one of the cities with the best quality of life in Latin America. Although its sustainable redevelopment is considered a great success story, aging populations pose serious challenges for urban planners. Studies estimate that one out of four people living in Latin America will be 60 years or older by 2050, with the majority living in urban centers (Sanchez Gonzalez 2015; Beard et al. 2012; Plouffe and Kalache 2010). As a result, these studies reveal the need to create elderly-friendly urban areas, especially public spaces that promote active and healthy aging. As cities implement sustainable redevelopment plans, there is a need to evaluate the advantages and disadvantages of new infrastructures for various social groups. The following paragraphs focus on Aguascalientes City as a case study of green urban development through a brief historical introduction and analysis of the advantages and disadvantages from policy change, implementation, and large-scale development projects.

Aguascalientes City was established in 1575 as a rest stop between the cities of Zacatecas and Mexico City. Although the location was not intended to become a major city, it became the capital for the newly formed state of the same name when its territory separated from the neighboring state of Zacatecas in 1835. The name "Aguascalientes," which literally translates to "hot waters," is attributed to the abundance of hot springs in the city. Aguascalientes has a semi-arid climate, with most precipitation concentrated between the months of June through September. The development of Aguascalientes into an urban center was strategically planned since 1936 (Collado 2013). The city developed three major beltway loops to traverse the city, which is a unique feature for a Mexican city. Today, 63 percent of Aguascalientes State's total population resides in Aguascalientes City. Aguascalientes State's urban development accelerated in the 1990s. It is home to companies in information technology and software, as well as two large Nissan manufacturing plants, including the most important outside of Japan. The Aguascalientes Nissan manufacturing plants are responsible for the majority of Mexico's annual production of 850,000 Nissan automobiles. Aguascalientes is also home to eight higher-education institutions, such as the Autonomous University of Aguascalientes (UAA).

Mexico experienced land and agrarian changes in the 20th and 21st centuries through national constitutional reforms and municipal-level policy changes. Most notable are the contributions of architect and urban planner Luis Ortega Douglas (1913–80), whose innovative work as urban planner, local town hall president, and later, governor of Aguascalientes influenced the urban design of the city between 1948 and 1969. Ortega Douglas introduced a concentric circle beltway model to traverse the city. In this way, the development of Aguascalientes in the 20th century was intentionally planned to provide access into the central business district and the heart of arts and culture across three main transportation rings. Furthermore, Ortega Douglas's social networks worked in his favor to transform Aguascalientes into a model Mexican urban center due to his strong ties with political leaders, such as the support of then Mexican president (1952–58), Adolfo Ruiz Cortines (1889–1973).

During the 1990s, Aguascalientes experienced an exponential wave of development as a result of several national and local policies. After the Mexican Revolution (1910–17), the Mexican federal government created the *ejido,* a communal resource-holding institution, to ameliorate the long-standing land-tenure inequality farmers and indigenous peoples experienced during Porfirio Díaz's (1830–1915) dictatorship (1884–1911) (Memorandum 1995; Perramond 2008). Under the government of President Carlos Salinas de Gortari, the reform of Article 27 of the Mexican Constitution in 1992 paved the way to urbanize agrarian lands. The reform no longer protected the institution of ejido as outlined in the 1917 Mexican Constitution. As a result, the 1992 agricultural reform led to the privatization and deregulation of former ejido land, which accounted for 52 percent of Mexico's agricultural land and affected more than 3 million *ejidatarios* (members of the *ejido* land commons) (Memorandum 1995; Perramond 2008). In Aguascalientes City, the reforms opened the way for large-scale development projects, which attracted private investors and real estate speculators (Durán et al. 2007). These projects included an industrial corridor in the valley of Aguascalientes, development of new *fraccionamientos* (city divisions similar to neighborhood boundaries, but refers also to houses or apartment buildings that are similar in style and in year built), condominiums, and luxury housing, built on former agricultural *ejido* lands.

Throughout the mid- to late 1990s, Aguascalientes City found itself challenged as its intention to preserve green spaces from further urban development was at odds with the exponential demand in housing. This resulted in a chaotic urban sprawl, which ultimately stopped environmental preservation of green space in the outskirts of the city (Bassols and Delgadillo 1987). During 1995–2004, the municipal government experienced a change in political parties, which coincided with a period of economic crisis (Durán et al. 2007). This time period prioritized an increase in financialization via economic development projects, which led to the creation of an urban development plan for Aguascalientes City 2000–2020. As a result, Aguascalientes's urban plan placed sustainable development at its core (Durán et al. 2007; Gil-García 2012). Urban planning during the 1990s was significantly influenced by the United Nations Rio Earth Summit in Rio de Janeiro, Brazil. The Rio Earth Summit promoted sustainable development models for municipal financialization through projects and services that attract a larger tax base while simultaneously creating a better quality of life. These models were rapidly implemented in world-class cities such as New York City, Chicago, and London, among others. Influenced by the development of these world-class cities, Aguascalientes attempted to brand its new wave of urban development through the sustainability theme.

One of the ways in which Aguascalientes aims to create a better quality of life is through the implementation and development of La Linea Verde project. La Linea Verde, which translates into "The Green Line," is a 12-kilometer stretch of land with underground oil pipelines, the largest industrial-to-green-space conversion in Mexico. The greenway traverses 26 impoverished neighborhoods in the southeastern region of the city and is considered one of Latin America's most extraordinary urban sustainable redevelopments (Arana 2014). The greenway functions as a city park where families and children gather in the afternoons and weekends for walking, biking, exercising, and using many of the park's recreational spaces, including a gym facility with an Olympic-size swimming pool. In this way, Aguascalientes City works to address all three elements of sustainable development: economic, environmental, and social. In regard to economic development, La Linea Verde has encouraged residential redevelopment and attracted businesses to surrounding neighborhoods, generating a larger tax base. The conversion of industrial land to green spaces provides a pleasant aesthetic to an area that was abandoned and crime ridden. Socially, La Linea Verde provides a safe and clean environment for residents in one of the most marginalized sections of the city, promoting a healthy and active life with recreational programs at the park.

Although public officials at the local, state, national, and international level recognize La Linea Verde as a green redevelopment success story, this land conversion is not without criticism. There are two main critiques: 1) gentrification, the displacement of marginalized low-income groups; and 2) lack of consideration of the aging population (people of age 65 and older). Some scholars believe that the environmental benefits of green redevelopment do not benefit marginalized groups, especially the poor, as higher environmental quality attracts larger housing demands. As a result, housing markets usually raise rent prices and property values in areas that are more environmentally desirable, making the improved neighborhood unaffordable to long-term residents with low socioeconomic status. For example, New York City's High Line and Chicago's 606 Bloomingdale Trail, both industrial conversions from abandoned railroad to greenways, increased the quality of life of the surrounding neighborhoods by providing access to green space, entertainment, and recreational areas (New York City Economic Development Corporation 2017; The 606 2007). However, these developments resulted in an increase in housing values and the construction of high-rise condominiums, which quickly became unaffordable to long-term residents of low socioeconomic status (Moss 2012; Vivanco 2016).

Second, researchers focused on Aguascalientes's rapid urban growth are concerned with the population changes of today's adult labor force (Sanchez Gonzalez and Cortes 2015). Today's adult labor force in Aguascalientes will reach 60 years of age or older by 2050. Similarly, at least one out of four people will be 60 years of age or older in Latin America's urban areas (Sanchez Gonzalez and Cortes 2015). Aguascalientes's sustainable development projects, such as Linea Verde, focus on families and children, but very little on the elderly. Elderly services lacking in Aguascalientes include senior citizen homes, homeless shelters, hospitals, green spaces such as gardens and parks with programming tailored for the elderly. Chicago's La Villita Park, the conversion of a 15-acre industrial lot into a park, promoted park space as a benefit for youth ages 3–18 (United States Environmental Protection Agency 2015). Although La Villita Park primarily focused on the installation of a skate park for youths, it also serves as a meeting space for the elderly population, mostly aging Mexican immigrants with agricultural knowledge, who participate in local urban gardening projects. In this way, La Villita Park functions as an intergenerational space with activities tailored for specific age groups.

In Aguascalientes, Linea Verde has yet to establish itself as a meeting space for the elderly. However, the city's Terán Market is an essential social place for the elderly due to its historic role in cementing strong social networks (Sanchez Gonzalez and Cortes 2015). Terán Market provides access to goods such as fresh produce, food products, housewares, and clothing at affordable prices. The market also functions as a source of entertainment and social interaction with vendors as well as a meeting space for family and friends. Furthermore, the average distance traveled by elderly people to Terán Market is 30 minutes, with most traveling via public transportation or by foot (Sanchez Gonzalez and Cortes 2015). Its design as an indoor and outdoor market with green space and seating areas available make it an accessible and pleasant space. In this way, Terán Market provides an environment where the elderly can enjoy autonomy. Researchers studying urban gerontology (the study of elderly people) encourage the inclusion of the elderly population in urban planning and development. These researchers suggest accessibility is of most importance in building and creating services. As the current adult population is introduced to La Linea Verde, it provides the opportunity to build social networks and engage in placemaking (a process that mutually shapes the identity of a place and individuals), which can serve as a positive asset to meet the social needs of the aging population in 2050. However, in the meantime, it is important to engage urban gerontologists and the elderly population in Aguascalientes City's future urban development plans so that the population's unique needs are met.

As Latin American Cities prepare to face a drastic increase in the aging population by 2050, a participatory approach to urban planning can help mitigate unequal distribution of resources. Participatory planning is an urban planning approach that emphasizes involving community residents in every stage of the urban planning process (Sutton and Kemp 2006). Idea generation in the participatory planning process is usually facilitated by design charrettes, an activity where small groups of community residents collaborate to sketch the development on paper or with props (Sutton and Kemp 2006). After the sketch session, small groups report back to all participants to combine their ideas into two community designs, culminating in a vote by community residents for the best design. This provides urban planners the information necessary to build a development that suits the needs of the community. In this way, participatory planning meaningfully engages a variety of social groups. Successful sustainable redevelopment projects engage diverse populations, government actors, private sector, and developers, prioritizing to meet community needs. Stakeholder collaboration with local community organizations can create more viable solutions based on science and local community knowledge.

Marisol Becerra and Kerry Ard

See also: Green Spaces: Hong Kong, China: Adding Green Spaces to Densely Populated Neighborhoods

Further Reading

Arana, A. 2014. "In Mexico, a City's Scar Becomes Its Most Prized Park, La Línea Verde." *Citiscope*, January 20. http://citiscope.org/story/2014/mexico-citys-scar-becomes-its-most-prized-park-la-linea-verde.

Bassols, M., and J. Delgadillo. 1987. "La ciudad de Aguascalientes: Desarrollo regional y políticas urbanas (1970–1985)." México: Problemas urbano regionales.

Beard, J., A. Kalache, M. Delgado, and T. Hill. 2012. "Ageing and Urbanization." In John R. Beard, Simon Biggs, David E. Bloom, Linda P. Fried, Paul Hogan, Alexandre Kalache, and S. Jay Olshansky, eds., *Global Population Ageing: Peril or Promise?* Chapter 19, 93–96.

Collado, A. A. 2013. Aportaciones artísticas y urbanísticas del ingeniero Ortega Douglas en la ciudad de Aguascalientes, México (1948–1969). Mexico: Arte y Ciudad 3, 1: 847–60.

Durán López, H., J. E. Medellín Lozano, and E. Bernal Ramos. 2007. "La Vialidad en el Área Periférica-Elemento Detonante de la Dispersión Urbana." *Investigación y Ciencia* 15, 38: 25–32.

Gil-García, C. 2012. "Transformando lo local desde el medio ambiente: Las políticas ambientales en las ciudades de Lyon, Francia y Aguascalientes, México (1990–2002)." *Economía, sociedad y territorio* 12, 38: 107–47.

Memorandum, A. (1995). 'The Reform of Article 27 and Urbanization of the Ejido in Mexico." *Bulletin of Latin American Research* 13: 327–35.

Moss, J. 2012. "Disney World on the Hudson." *New York Times*, August 21. http://www.nytimes.com/2012/08/22/opinion/in-the-shadows-of-the-high-line.html.

New York Economic Development Corporation. 2017. Projects: The High Line. https://www.nycedc.com/project/high-line.

Perramond, E. P. 2008. "The Rise, Fall, and Reconfiguration of the Mexican Ejido." *Geographical Review* 98, 3: 356–71.

Plouffe, L., and A. Kalache. 2010. "Towards Global Age-Friendly Cities: Determining Urban Features That Promote Active Aging." *Journal of Urban Health* 87, 5: 733–39.

Sánchez González, D. 2015. "Ambiente físico-social y envejecimiento de la población desde la gerontología ambiental y geografía: Implicaciones socioespaciales en América Latina." *Revista de Geografía Norte Grande* 60: 97–114.

The 606. 2017. "Our Story." http://www.the606.org/about/story/.

Sutton, S. E., and S. P. Kemp. 2006. "Integrating Social Science and Design Inquiry through Interdisciplinary Design Charrettes: An Approach to Participatory Community Problem Solving." *American Journal of Community Psychology* 38, 1–2: 51–62.

United States Environmental Protection Agency. 2015. "Celebrating Success: Celotex Corporation Site Chicago, Illinois." https://semspub.epa.gov/work/05/921104.pdf.

Vivanco, L. 2016. "Marchers Take to the 606 Trail to Protest Gentrification." *Chicago Tribune*, May 17. http://www.chicagotribune.com/news/local/breaking/ct-606-trail-march-gentrification-met-0517-story.html.

Halifax, Canada: Near-Urban Wilderness Protection

Halifax is a mid-sized Canadian city with a population of approximately 400,000 people. It is the capital of the Province of Nova Scotia and the largest city in Atlantic Canada. As a regional hub and port city, Halifax contains many government services, including administration, universities, military, health care, and ocean research institutes. The city is mostly built around a large central harbor, which has played an important role in its history, culture, geography, economy, and transportation.

Like many cities in Canada, Halifax has struggled to deal with the problem of suburban sprawl. Over the last several decades, the city has spread out into new areas on the landscape, often by largely uncontrolled as-of-right development, leading to huge subdivisions on the distant edges of the urban core. Between 1992 and 2014, the development footprint of the city grew by 92 percent, yet the overall population of the city increased by only 19 percent over that same time period (OurHRM Alliance 2015).

It is becoming increasingly difficult for the city to service these suburban developments, and this often results in the need for increased taxes simply to maintain existing infrastructure. A recent study commissioned by the Halifax Regional Municipality has shown that the city can save an estimated $3 billion CAD over the next 18 years by reining in suburban sprawl (Stantec 2013). In response, the city's municipal government has been attempting to concentrate new development within the existing urban core, where roads, sidewalks, public transit, and water and sewage infrastructure are already in place.

Table 1 Protected Areas Established within 25 km of Downtown Halifax to Protect Near-Urban Wilderness Values

Protected Area	Year Established	Size (hectare)
Terrence Bay Wilderness Area	1998	4,429
Waverley–Salmon River Long Lake Wilderness Area	1998	8,621
Clattenburgh Brook Wilderness Area	1998	1,913
McNabs Island Provincial Park	2002	485
Duncan's Cove Nature Reserve	2004	369
Blue Mountain–Birch Cove Lakes Wilderness Area	2009	1,317
Five Bridge Lakes Wilderness Area	2011	8,626
Sackville Lakes Provincial Park	2013	292
Pockwock Wilderness Area	2015	1,900
Rogues Roost Wilderness Area	2015	1,140
Old Annapolis Road Nature Reserve	2015	454
West Dover Provincial Park	2015	1,036
Blue Mountain–Birch Cove Lakes Wilderness Area expansion	2015	451
Terrence Bay Wilderness Area expansion	2015	57
Total		31,090

PROTECTING NEAR-URBAN WILDERNESS

Haligonians (the term for residents of Halifax) place a great deal of importance on the protection of forests near the city. It's not uncommon for the protection of near-urban wilderness to become an election issue for candidates running for mayor and city council. Lots of different community groups have formed in different parts of the city specifically to help protect wilderness that's threatened by suburban sprawl.

This public pressure to protect near-urban wilderness in Halifax is generating results. Over the past 20 years, several large tracts of publicly owned land near Halifax have been established as legally designated protected areas, totaling approximately 31,000 hectares (310 square kilometers). Pre-existing protected areas, created prior to 1998, total approximately 4,000 hectares, bringing the total amount to approximately 35,000 hectares within 25 km of the downtown. No development is allowed to occur in these protected areas. Industrial activities such as forestry and mining are also banned.

Much of these conservation successes are the result of bottom-up grassroots campaigning, rather than top-down decision making from government. This means that when decisions are eventually made by government to support near-urban wilderness protection, it is usually met with overwhelming public support for such measures. In most cases, the local communities are asking for these protections proactively, before they are imminently threatened with sprawling development.

Interestingly enough, much of the progress made in protecting near-urban wilderness in Halifax has been the result of the provincial government, not the local

The residents of Halifax in the province of Nova Scotia, Canada, are avid fans of outdoor life. When Halifax's wilderness was under threat from developers, the citizens pressed the provincial and city governments to take action against them. (Ron Garnett/Getty Images)

municipal city government. That's because much of the forest that still remains intact near the city occurs on public lands controlled by the provincial government. It should be noted, however, that municipal planning efforts often recognize the importance of these forested lands and encourage the provincial government to declare them as legally protected sites. The protection of near-urban wilderness lands is clearly noted in the policies and land-use planning guidelines contained in the Halifax Regional Municipal Regional Plan (HRM Regional Plan) (HRM 2014), which guides overall development within the city. It's also demonstrated by the Halifax Greenbelt Planning Initiative (currently under way), which is examining opportunities to expand protection of forested areas adjacent to the suburban and urban core (HRM 2013).

Although Canada is a very large country with lots of wilderness (9 percent of the total forest on the planet (NRCAN 2016), most Canadians tend to live in the very southernmost parts of the country. Approximately 75 percent of Canadians live within 100 miles of the border with the United States of America (National Geographic 2016), and mostly in suburban and urban areas (81 percent of Canadians) (Statscan 2011). These southern areas are highly settled landscapes, with a large human footprint, compared with the more remote northern parts of Canada. Without the protection of near-urban wilderness, a large proportion of Canadians could lose a direct connection with the forested landscapes that are so important to the country as a whole. In that regard, the steps that Halifax has taken in recent years to protect intact forested areas close to the city are part of a larger effort to ensure Canadians remain connected to the wilderness landscape.

There are similar examples from across the country. The first National Urban Park in Canada was established by Parks Canada near Toronto recently (Parks Canada 2014). The Ottawa/Gatineau region has a very large near-urban wilderness park called Gatineau Park (NCC 2005). The city of Whitehorse has recently developed a municipal plan that calls for the protection of a substantial amount of wilderness close to the city (City of Whitehorse 2014). Protecting near-urban wilderness in Canada is becoming more common. An additional benefit of protecting these forested lands is that it also helps contain sprawling development, which can become quite expensive for a city to service and maintain over the long term.

For Halifax, the landscape setting for our near-urban wilderness protection is extensive coastal forests, containing lots of lakes, peatlands, and small rivers. The city is located within the Atlantic Maritime Ecozone (CCEA 2015), which contains temperate broadleaf-mixed forests of the Acadian forest. Inland areas contain richer soils and support a wider diversity of forest types, whereas the coastline is typically dominated by rocky soils (granite bedrock and metamorphosed sandstone) and influenced by salt spray and high precipitation rates. These coastal areas mostly contain conifer forests, dominated by black spruce, white spruce, and balsam fir, and are more typical of the northern boreal forest than the Acadian forest.

THE SYSTEM OF PROTECTED AREAS NEAR HALIFAX

Over the past 20 years, a large number of protected areas have been established near Halifax, protecting a substantial amount of near-urban wilderness. The parks and protected areas described in Table 1 are located within the near-urban wilderness fringe of the city, mostly within 25 km of the urban core of Halifax. Some, such as Blue Mountain–Birch Cove Lakes Wilderness Area and McNabs Island Provincial Park occur only a few kilometers from the downtown.

Additional protected areas have been established in the more rural parts of the municipality, which covers a very large geographic area (5,490 square kilometers and over 150 km in length), but these areas are too far away from the urban core to be considered near-urban wilderness within the Halifax context. Smaller parks have also been established within newly developed parts of the city, as well, but these are generally neighborhood parks, and are too small and isolated to protect wilderness values. This article focuses only on the larger near-urban wilderness parks and protected areas of Halifax, located in relatively close proximity to the urban core.

Three large protected wilderness areas were established by the Nova Scotia government in 1998, including 1) Terence Bay Wilderness Area (4,429 hectares), 2) Waverley–Salmon River Long Lake Wilderness Area (8,621 hectares), and 3) Clattenburgh Brook Wilderness Area (1,913 hectares) (DNR 1994; DNR 1995; Wilderness Areas Protection Act 1998). A few years later, McNabs Island in Halifax Harbour was declared a provincial park in 2002 (485 hectares) (DNR 2005) and Duncans Cove a nature reserve in 2004 (369 hectares). Protected-area designations stalled after that, until the provincial government established the Blue Mountain–Birch Cove Lakes Wilderness Area in 2009 (1,317 hectares) after a sustained public campaign to protect these near-urban wilderness lands (NS Government 2007).

Many new protected areas occurred in quick succession after the protection of Blue Mountain–Birch Cove Lakes. These include Five Bridge Lakes Wilderness Area in 2011 (8,626 hectares) (NS Government 2011), Sackville Lakes Provincial Park in 2013 (292 hectares), and a commitment from the Nova Scotia government (also in 2013) to legally protect many new areas close to the city (NSE 2013). Many of those promised designations took effect in 2015, including the creation of Pockwock Wilderness Area (1,900 hectares), Rogues Roost Wilderness Area (1,140 hectares), Old Annapolis Road Nature Reserve (454 hectares), West Dover Provincial Park (1,036 hectares) (includes the existing Peggy's Cove Preservation Area plus expansion), as well as an expansion to the protected areas of Blue Mountain–Birch Cove Lakes Wilderness Area and Terence Bay Wilderness Area.

Several other protected areas that were promised by the Nova Scotia government in 2013 are still awaiting legal protection. These sites include an expansion to Waverley–Salmon River Long Lake Wilderness Area (3,328 hectares) that will connect that protected area with the nearby Clattenburgh Brook Wilderness area. It also includes Sackville River Nature Reserve (631 hectares), Little Soldier Lake Nature Reserve (88 hectares), St. Margaret's Bay Islands Nature Reserve (55 hectares), and Blind Bay Provincial Park (338 hectares). Community-led initiatives are also pushing for the completion of a regional park for the Birch Cove Lakes (on the eastern urban core side of the Blue Mountain–Birch Cove Lakes Wilderness Area), the protection of the Purcell's Cove Backlands, and the creation of two new protected areas near the Ingram River watershed.

BENEFITS

The benefits of near-urban wilderness protection are numerous. In addition to the environmental advantages of biodiversity conservation and habitat protection, these green spaces also provide important natural areas for residents of Halifax to access nature close to where they live. Haligonians utilize their near-urban wilderness areas for all sorts of activities, including hiking, canoeing, kayaking, swimming, paddleboarding, mountain biking, geocaching, trail running, rock climbing, camping, bird-watching, berry picking, dog walking, and nature appreciation, among other activities. In wintertime, these areas are used for skating, snowshoeing, cross-country skiing, and winter hiking. The protected wilderness areas near the city also help define the service boundary for the urban/suburban core and encourage land-use policies that prioritize denser developments closer to Halifax Harbour.

The near-urban wilderness protected areas also help maintain water quality in the numerous lakes and rivers close to the city. In many cases, the watersheds near Halifax are quite small, with many contained entirely within the city's boundary. This means that some of the near-urban wilderness areas that have been protected contain the headwater ecosystems and headwater lakes of several watersheds that drain into the more developed parts of the city. This helps maintain water quality downstream and saves the municipality from having to implement expensive solutions to improve water quality. Examples where headwaters are protected include Blue Mountain–Birch Cove Lakes Wilderness Area, Five Bridge Lakes Wilderness Area, and Waverley–Salmon River Long Lake Wilderness Area. The Pockwock Wilderness Area also protects a portion of the drinking water supply area for Halifax.

CHALLENGES

Although Halifax has made important strides to protect near-urban wilderness near the city, most of these achievements occur on public lands administered by the provincial government and are not the direct result of the municipality. The system of protected areas that has been established (and soon to be expanded again) goes a long way in providing protected green space for the residents of Halifax and the associated quality-of-life benefits, but large gaps in the greenbelt system still remain. These gaps occur mostly on private lands between the protected spaces, and some are facing imminent development pressures.

Although the municipal government has prioritized denser development in the urban core over rampant greenfield development in the suburbs, many of those policies are untested, and it remains to be seen if the municipality will truly move to limit sprawling development that's reaching into the near-urban wilderness. The decision to launch a comprehensive greenbelt planning initiative is an important step toward filling some of the gaps in the protected-area system, but the city government has often struggled to implement plans it has previously developed to protect green space.

One such example is Blue Mountain–Birch Cove Lakes. This area was identified as a regional park by the municipal government as far back as the 1970s and has been included in the HRM regional planning document that guides development in the city for the next 25 years, yet the city has consistently failed to acquire the privately owned lands for the park. In sharp contrast are the actions of the provincial government, which has successfully protected nearly all of the public lands within this same wilderness area. The contrast between the two levels of government is striking, with the city government doing lots of innovative planning but often failing to successfully implement.

CONCLUDING REMARKS

Halifax has prioritized the protection of near-urban wilderness within its land-use planning, with a total of approximately 35,000 hectares of land being legally protected within roughly 25 km of the downtown. Much of this progress has occurred over the past 20 years, with the successful implementation of at least 12 substantial protected areas by the provincial government over that time, as well as several park expansions. The benefits to the residents of Halifax from this near-urban wilderness protection are numerous, including habitat protection, cleaner air and water, recreational opportunities, and constraining expensive suburban sprawl.

Gaps remain within the protected-area system, however, particularly on private lands in between the existing protected areas. The city government needs to finalize its greenbelt planning initiative and develop effective constraints on development within these interlying areas crucial for connectivity. The city government also needs to follow through on existing plans to acquire privately owned lands within the Blue Mountain–Birch Cove Lakes wilderness for a long-promised regional park. At the provincial level, the Nova Scotia government needs to finalize the implementation of its protected-areas plan from 2013 that includes a number of yet-to-be-designated protected areas close to the urban core of Halifax. Citizen-led initiatives and grassroots campaigning are the primary reason why Halifax has made such important progress protecting near-urban wilderness.

Christopher A. Miller

See also: Waste Management: Calgary, Canada: Waste Management Is a National Effort and Calgary's Priority

Further Reading

Canadian Council on Ecological Areas (CCEA). 2015. "An Introduction to Canadian Ecozones." http://www.ccea.org/wp-content/uploads/2015/10/RP_Introduction-to-Canadian-Ecozones.pdf.

City of Whitehorse. 2014. Regional Parks Plan: City of Whitehorse. https://www.whitehorse.ca/departments/planning-building-services/plans-and-implementation/regional-parks-plan.

Department of Natural Resources (DNR). 1994. "A Proposed Systems Plan for Parks and Protected Areas in Nova Scotia." https://novascotia.ca/parksandprotectedareas/pdf/Parks-Protected-Areas-Proposed-Plan.pdf.

Department of Natural Resources (DNR). 1995. *Protecting Nova Scotia's Natural Areas: The Report of the Public Review Committee for the Proposed Systems Plan for Parks and Protected Areas in Nova Scotia.*

Department of Natural Resources (DNR). 2005. *Management Plan: McNabs and Lawlow Islands, Halifax Harbour, Nova Scotia.*

Halifax Regional Municipality (HRM). 2013. "RP+5; Regional Plan 5 Year Review: Greenbelting. Information Brief."

Halifax Regional Municipality (HRM). 2014. "Halifax Regional Municipal Planning Strategy."

National Capital Commission (NCC). 2005. *Gatineau Park Master Plan.* http://ncc-ccn.gc.ca/our-plans/gatineau-park-master-plan.

National Geographic. 2016. http://travel.nationalgeographic.com/travel/countries/canada-facts.

Natural Resources Canada (NRCAN). 2016. "How Much Forest Does Canada Have?" http://www.nrcan.gc.ca/forests/report/area/17601.

Nova Scotia Environment (NSE). 2013. "Our Parks and Protected Areas: A Plan for Nova Scotia." https://novascotia.ca/parksandprotectedareas/pdf/Parks-Protected-Plan.pdf.

Nova Scotia Government (NS Government). 2007. "Province Creates Near-Urban Wilderness Area." Press release, October 30. http://novascotia.ca/news/release/?id=20071030002.

Nova Scotia Government (NS Government). 2011. "More Valuable Land Protected." Press release, October 25. http://novascotia.ca/news/release/?id=20111025005.

OurHRM Alliance. 2015. http://ourhrmalliance.ca/halifax-green-network/ Parks Canada. 2014. *Rouge National Urban Park: Draft Management Plan.* http://cpaws.org/uploads/Rouge_PMP_draft.pdf.

Stantec Consulting. 2013. *Quantifying the Costs and Benefits to HRM, Residents and the Environment of Alternate Growth Scenarios: Final Report.* http://legacycontent.halifax.ca/boardscom/documents/HRMGrowthScenariosFinalReportPresentation04192013.pdf.

Statscan. 2011. http://www.statcan.gc.ca/tables-tableaux/sum-som/l01/cst01/demo62a-eng.htm.

Wilderness Areas Protection Act (1998). An Act to Protect Wilderness Areas in Nova Scotia; Chapter 27 of the Acts of 1998.

Hong Kong, China: Adding Green Spaces to Densely Populated Neighborhoods

People all over the world come to compete with Hong Kong residents in the Oxfam Trailwalker or the MacLehose Trail Challenge or many other trail races the city and different institutions organize in Hong Kong's country parks. But there is another race in which Hong Kongers, mainland Chinese, and other foreign investors are competing for, and that is the race to buy an apartment or flat in this prosperous city. Every month, hundreds of prospective apartment buyers gather at the gates of developers' offices to place their offers to acquire a property. However, the supply of land in this small Special Administrative Region of China (SAR) is limited by its geography (mountains and political borders) and land regulations. The combination of high demand for flats and low supply of land makes Hong Kong's property market one of the most expensive in the world. As the demand for apartments in Hong Kong increases, the pressure to develop its parks increases as well. A solution to provide housing to an increasing population with limited supply of land is needed.

It is hard to believe that Hong Kong, one of the world's most cosmopolitan cities, is one of its greenest cities as well. According to the World Bank Group, Hong Kong had the densest urban area in the East Asia region with around 32,000 people per square kilometer in 2010 (World Bank Group 2016). But this high population density doesn't mean that all its land is a metropolis. On the contrary, more than 40 percent of its land is allocated to country parks (Anonymous 2015). These parks, all 24 of them, were established in the late 1970s after the Country Park Ordinance was enacted by Governor Murray MacLehose in 1976 to provide recreational alternatives to an increasing population close to urban areas (Wong 2013). If shrubland and grassland are included, then the amount of green area increases to 66 percent. This amount of green space gives Hong Kong one of the highest green spaces per capita for an urban area worldwide (63 square meters), well above the recommended international standard of 9 square meters per capita (Sorensen 1997).

However, Hong Kong wasn't always a city with vibrant green spaces untouched by infrastructure or uncontrolled development or squatter settlements. The orderly urban development has benefited from a strong legal and justice system and an efficient public service that was developed through its historical experiences.

View of downtown Hong Kong, China, from the Nan Lian Garden, March 30, 2018. Hong Kong has the highest population density of any urban area in East Asia, yet it has allocated 40 percent of its land to green space. (Pmh561/Dreamstime.com)

According to a Heritage Museum document, before 1954, hundreds of thousands of mainland Chinese sought refuge in Hong Kong because of conflicts, such as the Japanese invasion of China in 1937 and the Chinese Civil War between 1947 and 1949. Many of these people settled in squatter areas on the hillsides of Hong Kong. Such settlements ended on Christmas Day, 1953. On that day, a fire destroyed Shek Kip Mei squatter area, leaving 53,000 people homeless. Again, according to the Heritage Museum document already mentioned, this fire forced the government not only to provide immediate housing solutions for the victims but also to come up with long-term and methodical solutions to the squatter problem. In 1954, the Hong Kong Housing Authority was set to develop low-cost housing that provided a better living environment (Anonymous 2014a).

After this experience, other migrant crises have impacted the city's livelihood, but not its green areas. For example, between 1975 and 1979, the city received around 200,000 Vietnamese, who arrived by boat. The city was able to cope with the arrival of foreign migrants in an orderly manner by providing temporary refugee camps (Law 1996). Most of the refugees were resettled to third countries. Many were repatriated to their country of origin, and in a very few cases, some were given local residency after a lengthy process (Gordon 2008), sparing the city from an unexpected population growth with dire consequences to its most valuable resource, land.

An exploration of the issue of limited land supply coupled with the reality of an increasing population is essential to understanding the pressure placed on Hong Kong maintaining its green spaces. Besides the proportion of country parks in relation to the total territory, many factors affect the limited supply of land. Only 20 percent of HK's land is developed (Planning Department 2005). This is mostly due to its rugged topography, with 60 percent of its territory including slopes of 20 degrees or more (CEDD 2012).

Land regulations and the process of land development also impose limitations on new residential projects. Because of its British colonial past and its later handover to China, which will be completed in 2047, all the land in the Hong Kong Special Administrative Region (HKSAR), belongs to the government. Only 50 hectares of land can be disposed for private developments, according to the Sino-British Joint Declaration (Hong Kong Legislative Council 1997). The government holds or leases the land for different purposes (Lands Department: Service Desk 2008). The sale of land and the modification of leases (land premium), as well as the taxes (stamp duty) on property sales or transfers, are two of the five major sources of the HK government's revenues (FSTB 2016). Land development goes through a careful planning process that considers many variables. In order for appropriate living and/or working conditions to be adequately met, transportation, basic services like water supply, provision for electricity, schools, environmental factors, and open spaces intended for recreation require consideration. The bureaucratic process can take from six months to seven years to develop public land and even more than 10 years for private projects (Hong Kong Legislative Council 1997).

Hong Kong's population continues to grow, increasing the need for housing alternatives and increasing the pressure on maintaining the green spaces. The city is currently growing at a rate of 0.4 percent, mainly due to immigrants arriving. The strategic geographical location close to Mainland China, its economic success, and a Western-style legal system with the rule of law as a premise makes the city attractive to outsiders. The government expects an inflow of 0.57 million people from 2014 to 2064, mostly from Mainland China. Currently, the Chinese government has a daily quota of 150 one way permit (OWP) or 54,750 mainland citizens per year who are spouses or children of Hong Kong residents to relocate in the SAR (LCQ2 2013). In addition to those relocating, just in 2006, there were 26,132 newborns in Hong Kong with both parents being Chinese nationals. These children might one day relocate in the city, increasing the demand on services and housing (Anonymous 2007).

On the other hand, Hong Kong's local population shows a lower fertility rate that characterizes developed countries. The fertility rate in 2014 was 1,234 live births per 1,000 women, well below the population replacement rate of 2,100 live births per 1,000 women (Censtatd 2015). The decrease in population growth estimates has also decreased the housing target with the election of each new chief executive. In 1997, Chief Executive Tung Chee-hwa set an annual target of 85,000 residential units for the following 10 years (Policyaddress 1997). In 2001 the Census and Statistics Department had projected 8.72 million people by 2031. However, current Chief Executive Leung Chun-ying has set a target of 460,000 flats for the next decade (Chan 2016). In this new projection, Hong Kong is expected to reach its peak of 8.22 million people in 2043, before it starts to decline (Censtatd 2015). The reduction of estimated future flats suggests the use of the new slower population growth and demographic data.

The obvious, knee-jerk response to the housing challenge would be to develop the country parks. However, there are several wise alternatives that should be considered first. The pressure on the local government to find suitable land to provide housing for its citizens continues and has become a frequent source of friction between different members of Hong Kong society. Therefore, the local government needs to find spaces to develop in order to provide housing for approximately 1 million more people from the current (2016) census of 7.35 million residents. Some ideas proposed and implemented by the current and previous governments are to rezone some green belts, government and industrial sites, as well as to increase the development density of unleased sites. The increase of the areas of islands by reclaiming land from the sea and the development of rural areas have also been proposed and used. Each of these alternatives offer benefits, limitations, and controversies.

The use of greenbelts (GB) to curb land demand for housing development is one of the least controversial proposals because they are close to developed areas and comparatively less expensive. Greenbelts are buffer zones defined to limit urban areas, conserve natural environments, and provide passive recreational uses (Hong Kong Town Planning Board 1991). To encroach on them in a city like Hong Kong, GB take 25 percent, or 12,639 hectares, of the total developed area (Hong Kong Legislative Council 1997). Tang, Wong, and Lee in a research paper examining the evolution, implementation and performance of GB in Hong Kong, concluded that GB are considered a transition zone intended for possible future urban development rather than a conservation zone (Tang, Wong, and Lee 2007). Unfortunately, if urban buffer zones are urbanized, the next area to be developed might logically be the country parks.

The transition of Hong Kong from an industrial city to a service-oriented one has opened the possibility to use industrial sites for residential purposes. Since the creation of the Shenzhen Special Economic Zone (Phillips and Yeh 1983) just across the border with Hong Kong in 1980, many Hong Kong companies moved their factories to this SEZ. One positive consequence is the rezoning of industrial parks into residential areas. In an information note from the Legislative Council in 2012, the HKSAR planned to rezone 16 industrial sites to add 30 hectares of land available for 20,400 flats (Hong Kong Legislative Council 2013). This alternative is more appealing than the development of country parks.

A look at neighboring Asian cities with similar land and housing challenges can be useful. Hong Kong faces similar constraints as Singapore for land and freshwater. Both cities have historical, geographical, and economical similarities, and both have tried similar solutions. A special report by the *Economist* (2015) describes how Singapore, with a forecasted population of 6.9 million in 2030, faces serious land supply shortcomings. Singapore has become more dependent on its neighbor Malaysia for water supply and cheaper housing for citizens that cross the border daily. The city-state, which already has claimed 14,000 hectares from the sea, has planned to increase its land area by 8 percent. Hong Kong has also reclaimed land from the sea. Its new airport was built by leveling a small island, which gave the HKSAR 1,300 hectares more land. Several other smaller reclamations have taken place. For example, the Central Star Ferry Pier Terminal relocation increased the land in 20 hectares (Tsui 2016). Reclamation of land for the purpose of not only housing but the creation of green spaces provides an appealing alternative, though it has economic costs.

In Hong Kong, new land does not imply the creation of new parks. In contrast to Singapore, where the government plans to increase its park space by 900 hectares by 2020 (Index, Asian Green City 2011), the Hong Kong authorities have not planned for new parks for the near future. The last park opened was the 61-hectare Wetland Park in 2006 (Hong Kong Wetland Park 2016). The inclusion of new parks in new urban areas has been urged by some civil organizations. For example, the West Kowloon Cultural Development, a 40-hectare area reclaimed from the sea at the exit of a tunnel crossing Victoria Harbour, was originally slated to be used as an open space (Hong Kong Legislative Council 2005); however, 17 hectares of this site were later rezoned for private residential uses (Anonymous 2014b), but no land was provided for parks.

Are the city residents using open spaces instead of country parks for their recreational activities? Open spaces are planned areas set for active (sport centers) or passive (playgrounds, cultural centers) recreational activities, as well as to allow sunlight penetration, air movement, and visual relief (Anonymous 2015). The SAR government mandates 2 square meters per person of open spaces. Open spaces are usually close to high-density residential complexes, which makes them very convenient, especially for an aging population. As land gets scarcer, people will need to make trade-offs and accept open spaces for recreation as opposed to the luxury of country parks.

At this point, another land-use perspective emerges that demands attention. Some question whether there are truly a housing shortage and land scarcity at all in Hong Kong. Many citizens believe that there is no housing shortage but insist that private owners, companies, and the government are keeping empty flats out of the market to increase profits or to avoid price reductions. In 2012, a private citizen proposed a tax on vacant flats to Hong Kong's Secretary for Transport and Housing, Professor Anthony Cheung Bing-leung. The proposal was based on figures released by the Housing Authority that showed the existence of 2.6 million residential flats and only 2.35 million residential households (LCQ16 2012). The figures implied the existence of more than 200,000 vacant flats in the territory. The secretary answered the question by saying there was an overall low vacancy rate of 4.3 percent.

Examples of empty buildings abound in the city and support doubts about increasing housing needs. A famous luxury building on the south side of Hong Kong Island, The Lily, was kept empty for more than four years before its flats were finally offered for sale and rent (Ma 2006). Another example of how the government and developers keep an artificial housing scarcity is the Hunghom Peninsula Redevelopment project, now called Harbour Place. The government completed the 2,470 flats under a program of subsidized sale in 2002 (Hong Kong Legislative Council 2004). However, it decided not to sell or rent flats to the public under a public housing rental program. Instead, the Housing Authority auctioned the building back to the developers so that they could demolish it and build luxury private flats (Seawright 2004). After a public outcry about the environmental impact of the demolition, the winning consortium decided to redevelop the buildings to be later sold to private buyers (Nws.com.hk 2004).

Finally, when considering the future of green spaces and country parks in Hong Kong, there are several unknown factors that make predictions complicated. For instance, after 2047, there remains the question of whether Beijing via the Guangdong government will administer Hong Kong and change its land-use regulations. Additionally, Beijing may maintain or change the one-way permit policy, affecting population growth. As the Chinese government is already closely working with the Hong Kong government, it is expected that this relationship will continue harmoniously.

Gabriel José Fornes Dutilh

See also: Housing and Infrastructure: Chongqing, China: Chongqing's Ingenuity in Providing Public Housing for a City of 33 Million

Further Reading

AFCD. 2015. Hong Kong: The Facts—Country Parks and Conservation. Agriculture, Fisheries, and Conservation Department, May 27. http://www.afcd.gov.hk/english/country/cou_lea/the_facts.html.

Anonymous. 2007. "Chapter 7." Hong Kong 2030. Planning, Vision, and Strategy. Hong Kong: Planning Department, 2007. Final Report. Developmental Bureau and Planning Department, October. http://www.pland.gov.hk/pland_en/p_study/comp_s/hk2030/eng/finalreport.

Anonymous. 2014a. "Memories of Home—50 Years of Public Housing in Hong Kong." Hong Kong Heritage Museum. Leisure and Cultural Services Department. http://www.heritagemuseum.gov.hk/documents/2199315/2199693/Public_Housing-E.pdf.

Anonymous. 2014b. "Minor Relaxation of the Development of the West Kowloon Site." Yau Tsim Mong District Council, Paper No. 12. Hong Kong, February. http://www.districtcouncils.gov.hk/ytm/doc/2012_2015/en/dc_meetings_doc/356/YTM_DC_12_2014_E.pdf.

Anonymous. 2015. "Chapter 4: Recreation, Open Space and Greening." Planning Department. The Government of the Hong Kong Special Administrative Region., October. http://www.pland.gov.hk/pland_en/tech_doc/hkpsg/full/ch4/ch4_text.htm#1.6.

Anonymous. 2015. "Seven Million Is a Crowd." *Economist*, July 18. http://www.economist.com/node/21657607/print.

CEDD. 2012. "Natural Terrain in Hong Kong." *Hong Kong Slope Safety Website of Geotechnical Engineering Office (GEO), CEDD*. Geotechnical Engineering Office, Civil Engineering and Development Department. http://hkss.cedd.gov.hk/hkss/eng/natural_terrain.aspx.

Censtatd. 2015. "Hong Kong Population Projections 2015–2064." Press Release, September 25. Census and Statistics Department. Census and Statistics Department. The Government of the Hong Kong Special Administrative Region. http://www.censtatd.gov.hk/press_release/pressReleaseDetail.jsp?charsetID=1&pressRID=3799.

Chan, Paul. 2016. "Gov't Committed to Land Supply." Hong Kong's Information Services Department, April 7. http://www.news.gov.hk/en/record/html/2016/04/20160407_191035.shtml.

Financial Services and Treasury Bureau (FSTB). 2016. "Major Revenue Sources of the Government." The Treasury Branch, Financial Services and the Treasury Bureau. The Government of the Hong Kong Special Administrative Region. September 30. https://www.legco.gov.hk/research-publications/english/1617issf02-major-sources-of-government-revenue-20170606-e.pdf.

Gordon, Jon. 2008. "FYI: What Happened to Hong Kong's Vietnamese Refugee Community?" *South China Morning Post,* June 15. http://www.scmp.com/article/641644/fyi-what-happened-hong-kongs-vietnamese-refugee-community.

Hong Kong Legislative Council. 1997. Research and Library Services Division. "Land Supply in Hong Kong." By Eva Liu, Jackie Wu, and Vicky Lee. Legco. http://www.legco.gov.hk/yr97-98/english/sec/library/967rp08.pdf.

Hong Kong Legislative Council. 2005. "Is Hong Kong Really Asia's World City?" *Hong Kong Alternatives.* http://www.legco.gov.hk/yr04-05/english/hc/sub_com/hs02/papers/hs020913cb1-wkcd182-e.pdf.

Hong Kong Legislative Council. 2013. "Information Note. Land Supply in Hong Kong." IN21/12-13. Legco. http://www.legco.gov.hk/yr12-13/english/sec/library/1213in21-e.pdf.

Hong Kong Legislative Council. 2016. "Hunghom Peninsula Private Sector Participation Scheme Flats." Legco. http://www.legco.gov.hk/yr03-04/english/panels/hg/papers/hgplw0217cb1-1000-1e.pdf.

Hong Kong Town Planning Board. 1991. "Town Planning Board Guidelines for Application for Development within Green Belt Zone Under Section 16 of the Town Planning Ordinance." http://www.info.gov.hk/tpb/en/forms/Guidelines/pg10_e.pdf.

Hong Kong Wetland Park. 2016 "Hong Kong Wetland Park." http://www.wetlandpark.gov.hk/en/aboutus/index.asp.

Index, Asian Green City. 2011. "Asian Green City Index." Siemens AG Corporate Communications and Government Affairs. http://www.siemens.com/entry/cc/features/greencityindex_international/all/en/pdf/report_asia.pdf.

Lands Department: Service Desk. 2008. "Lands Department: Service Desk." The Government of the Hong Kong Special Administrative Region. November 28. http://www.landsd.gov.hk/en/service/landpolicy.htm.

Law, Preeta. 1996. "Refugees Magazine Issue 106 (Focus: 1996 in Review)—Leaving Hong Kong." The UN Refugee Agency. December 1. http://www.unhcr.org/publications/refugeemag/3b5841391/refugees-magazine-issue-106-focus-1996-review-leaving-hong-kong.html.

LCQ2: One-way Permit Scheme. 2013. "LCQ2: One-way Permit Scheme." Press Releases. The Government of the Hong Kong Special Administrative Region. March 20. http://www.info.gov.hk/gia/general/201303/20/P201303200372.htm.

LCQ16: Vacant Private Residential Flats. 2012. "LCQ16: Vacant Private Residential Flats." Press Releases. The Government of the Hong Kong Special Administrative Region. December 19. http://www.info.gov.hk/gia/general/201212/19/P201212190309.htm.

Ma, Raymond. 2006. "$8b Foster Landmark Empty Four Years On." *South China Morning Post*, July 2. http://www.scmp.com/article/555112/8b-foster-landmark-empty-four-years.

Nws.com.hk. 2004. Hunghom Peninsula Development Plan Consortium Sets New Environmental Standards with Waste Recycling Reaching 95%. Hong Kong, November 29. http://www.nws.com.hk/html/eng/pdf/PR2004112901E.pdf.

Phillips, D. R., and A. G. O. Yeh. 1983. "China Experiments with Modernisation: The Shenzhen Special Economic Zone." *Geography* 68, 4: 289–300. http://www.jstor.org/stable/40570723?seq=3#page_scan_tab_contents.

Planning Department. 2005. "Ch5 Analysis of the Hong Kong Landscape." http://www.pland.gov.hk/pland_en/p_study/prog_s/landscape/tech_report/ch5.htm.

Policyaddress. 1997. "1997 Policy Address." The Government of the Hong Kong Special Administrative Region. http://www.policyaddress.gov.hk/pa97/english/light_e.htm.

Seawright, Stephen. 2004. "Controversy Clouds Hunghom Property Sale." *South China Morning Post*, February 16. http://www.scmp.com/article/444685/controversy-clouds-hunghom-property-sale.

Tang, Bo-Sing, Siu-Wai Wong, Anton King-wah Lee. 2007. "Green Belt in a Compact City: A Zone for Conservation or Transition? Landscape and Urban Planning." *Science Direct*. https://www.sciencedirect.com/science/article/pii/S0169204606000788.

Tsui, Enid. 2016. "HK$12b Transformation of Hong Kong's Central Waterfront: What's about to Happen." *South China Morning Post*, May 31. http://www.scmp.com/culture/article/1959391/hk12b-transformation-hong-kongs-central-waterfront-whats-about-happen.

Wong, Olga. 2013. "The Uphill Battle for Our Green Havens—Hong Kong's Country Parks." *South China Morning Post*, September 20. http://www.scmp.com/news/hong-kong/article/1313224/uphill-battle-our-green-havens-hong-kongs-country-parks.

World Bank Group. 2016. "East Asia's Changing Urban Landscape: Measuring a Decade of Spatial Growth." World Bank, September 20. http://www.worldbank.org/en/topic/urbandevelopment/publication/east-asias-changing-urban-landscape-measuring-a-decade-of-spatial-growth.

Moscow, Russia: Planting 1 Million Trees

Quality of life in a city in many respects depends on the level of coverage of green space. This is especially important for such a megalopolis as Moscow. Ecological safety and environmental protection define the level of health and quality of life of Moscow's citizens and visitors. Moscow is not only the capital of the Russian Federation, it's also the economic, political, scientific, and cultural center of Russia. Moscow is one of the unique capitals in the world, and includes one of the biggest urban area of 2,561.5 square kilometers, which has more than doubled from the 1,078.17 square kilometers in 2012, and is the most inhabited city in Russia with more than 12 million people. Among all Russian cities, Moscow has the highest cost of living and the highest density of cars on the road. However, the highest salaries are also found in Moscow.

Green space, in the form of bushes, forests, houseplants, and lawns, helps reduce the level of pollution of dust and noise. Protecting the environment and making a city more comfortable and beautiful for its citizens is of primary importance for a city's management. According to statistics, more than half of Moscow's old territory is covered by vegetation. The green space is twice that of London, two and a half times more than in Paris, and 14 times more than in Beijing (Mayor's Office of Moscow 2016). According to the norms in Russia, the amount of green space shouldn't be lower than 40 percent. According to Anton Kulbachevsky, the head of the Department of Environmental Protection, Moscow is one of the top three megalopolises in the world by the number of trees (Kulbachevsky 2015). World experts (PWC 2015) noted that Moscow holds a leading position in the world among large megalopolises by the number of square meters of vegetation per person. For comparison, Moscow has 20.2 square meters of greens per person, New York 19.2 square meters, Paris 6 square meters, and Tokyo 5 square meters. Moscow is attracting more visitors each year, thanks to the citizens' efforts in improving the city's environment.

MAIN CHALLENGES

Like any megalopolises, Moscow faces many challenges such as pollution, noise, climate changes, over urbanization, global warming, and density of population. With a population of more than 12 million, it is necessary to increase the awareness of clean air, enhance green spaces, and preserve nature to create a comfortable environment for the people. Solving global and local environmental problems during intensive economic development is the main challenge of the contemporary Moscow.

As an industrial powerhouse, Moscow suffers from pollution and has to deal with pollution control aggressively. The Moscow area is home to a great number of businesses and production facilities. Industrial enterprises include chemical, mechanical, power engineering, food, and construction companies. Furthermore, Moscow has several seaports, airports, multiple metro stations, and railroads. Such a high concentration of population and versatile industrial activities on a limited city territory impact the environmental conditions of Moscow and nearby areas. According to Mosgorstat, in the territory of Moscow, over 630 enterprises are registered with more than 30,000 stationary sources of emissions of pollutants in atmospheric air (Mosgorstat 2015).

Climate changes contribute to difficulties for expanding green space. Even though compared to other European capitals, Moscow's climate is moderately continental, it has the highest range of annual temperature. Its winters are longer and more severe. Global warming makes the climate even more unstable, and triggers abnormal hot or cold temperatures. Multiple fires in wooded areas in Moscow and surrounding areas in 2010 cost over 1 percent of GDP of the Russian economy, or $15 billion (Kommersant 2010). In an interview, a scientist, Lupan, stated that around 40,000 hectares, including 18,000 hectares covered by forests, were burned in Moscow's region. According to him, restoration of completely burned down woods will require more than just one decade. For example, birch wood reaches the peak of its growth cycle in about 60 years, and the coniferous forest needs about 20 years (RIA Novosti 2010). Additional factors that pollute the atmosphere are greenhouse gases and auto emission, which are comparable to the level of European capitals.

These economic activities affect the environment of the capital. Recent development in Moscow triggers new economic activities, which create further environmental issues. The goal of the city is to balance economic development and environmental protection. These circumstances demand a competent approach to protecting nature in the territory of the megalopolis.

CURRENT SITUATION OF GREEN SPACE

Green spaces are monitored regularly through a system of constant points of observations (CPO). Moscow's CPO network is located evenly, embracing all types of green territories such as squares, boulevards, and parks ("About the State" 2015). The quality of green coverage is assessed according to criteria set by the government of Moscow, as stipulated in Law #822. According to a survey of inspection of 100 CPOs, 72.9 percent of green plants are in satisfactory condition.

According to the norms mentioned above, the trees with greatest viability are linden, larch, and chestnut. The most weakened breeds are poplar, ash tree, and mountain ash. The most favorable conditions for these trees are in parks (39.4 percent), gardens and squares (26 percent), followed by micro regions (22.1 percent), urban streets (19.9 percent), and boulevards (18.3 percent). Poor growth conditions for trees and green plants are found in industrial zones (6.5 percent), yards (11.1 percent), and highways (16.1 percent). In new micro regions of Moscow, the number of green plants increased by 22.1 percent during 2012–15, due to compensation requirements for planting for construction of new roads, buildings, and micro regions.

The number of trees in satisfactory condition in the last three years is stable, and varies within 69–73 percent. However, the number in good condition declined in 2015 compared to 2012 from 35 percent to 20 percent, and that of unsatisfactory condition increased from 3 percent to 5 percent. According to *GeoCenter—Moscow* (GeoCenter—Moscow 2015), the main reasons for such a deterioration of growth condition were climate changes of 2014–15, such as droughts of 2014, plentiful rains of 2015, and warm winters of 2014 and 2015; and a related decrease in the level of groundwater. As a result, weakened trees and vegetation were wiped out by diseases.

MOSCOW TAKING ACTION

Even though Moscow takes the leading position on gardening and planting in the world, the government and citizens of Moscow strive to improve their city and make it more beautiful and green. During last two years, several programs related to green planting were started, such as My Street, A Million Trees, *Active Citizens*, and Hole to Hole.

The purpose of the My Street program is to create a comfortable environment for both pedestrians and motorists. The program embraces 50 streets and includes about 100 kilometers (Arguments and Facts 2015). Every fall and spring, thousands of trees and bushes are planted in Moscow. About 4,000 trees and 200,000 shrubs were planted in Moscow as of spring 2016 (Green Megalopolis 2016).

Anton Kulbachevsky states that vegetation is distributed unevenly and the central part of the city has the least coverage of green plants (Kulbachevsky 2015). The density of Moscow's streets, roads, and underground engineering communications limits the space of a grass cover in the center of Moscow. To solve this problem, experimental containers with trees and bushes were established on a central street in 2013, which made it possible to considerably improve the ecological and aesthetic state of Tverskaya Street ("About State of Environment" 2015).

Green Spaces

Workers plant trees along a street in central Moscow. Some 3,000 trees were planted in 2017 as part of the city's *Moya Ulitsa* ("My Street") program. (Alexander Shcherbak/TASS via Getty Images)

The government simplifies the procedure for ordering green plants. Muscovites can order a planting of trees in their yards simply by submitting an online application on a portal, Active Citizen, per Law #743-PP (2002). Simplification of the process has accelerated the process of restoration of lost trees and shrubs. The plans of the municipality are to revive an old tradition related to green space in Moscow. For example, in the 19th century, one of the requirements to construct a mansion within the Garden Ring area of Moscow was to plant an orchard (Kubachevsky 2015). According to the results of voting on the Active Citizen portal, 4,000 trees and 200,000 bushes were planted in Moscow's yards in the fall of 2016. Additionally, 850 trees and 30,000 bushes were planted in 160 public spaces. To replace lost trees and bushes after the hurricane of 2016, about 3,000 trees and 20,000 bushes were planted according to the program Hole in a Hole (Mosru 2016).

There are other programs related to green space in Moscow. One of them is A Million Trees. Since 2015, more than 11,200 Moscow yards were planted with trees and shrubs. In the spring of 2016 alone, about 4,800 trees and 153,000 bushes were planted. Additionally, on the grounds of such public places as day care, schools, and hospitals (totaling 182), about 500 trees and 60,000 bushes were planted. Furthermore, about 50 educational actions for children and teenagers were devoted to ecology and the care of green plantings in Moscow in 2015 (Mosru 2016). Students and their parents, representatives of public organizations, and volunteers are participating in planting the trees.

The list of trees picked by Muscovites included more than 80 kinds. Among the most popular are birch, maple, linden, chestnut, and oak. Among bushes, barberry, mock orange, sweetheart plant, silverweed, and lilac are the most popular choices. Additionally, in 2016, Moscow was decorated with 61 million flowers, including balsam, begonias, petunias, dahlias, and summer phloxes, covering almost 448 square meters. The assortment was chosen by more than 211,000 citizens (Mosru 2016).

According to a report on the state of the environment in the city of Moscow in 2015, the results of A Million Trees and Active Citizen initiatives, the share of planted trees increased by 10.2 percent, the share of bushes by 50 percent, and the number of yards with planted vegetation increased by 23.4 percent, compared to 2014.

FUTURE PLANS

Regardless of multiple initiatives that were conducted in the past, the government should continue to maintain and improve planting and gardening, and to monitor green plantings growth conditions. Additionally, the municipality needs to provide compensation for gardening. Also important is controlling emissions of greenhouse gases. Involving citizens in decision processes related to the gardening of Moscow and the Moscow region is critically important.

All information about green planting in Moscow is located in a "roster of green plants" of Moscow. Currently the government is working on transferring all data to a portal, Our City, so citizens may report offenses against the nature protection legislation.

Every time a new micro region, road, or building is constructed, compensation planting is carried out for the restoration of affected green coverage. The department keeps records of all cut-down and planted trees and bushes. Cutting down of trees and bushes is only allowed for sanitary reasons. Efforts in compensation planting have been shown to improve the ecological and environmental situation, and increase the comfort of residents in the city of Moscow. In addition, the dynamics of the condition of the city's vegetation and the influence of climatic factors should be researched.

The economic, social, and demographic development of Moscow, paired with rapid urbanization, makes the enhancement of green spaces one of the most important tasks. Priority should be given to protecting the interests of citizens, and to maintaining the balance between green plantings and improvement of the ecological situation and economic development.

Dina Clark

See also: Green Spaces: New York City, United States: Pursuit of More Green; *Traffic and Transportation:* Saint Petersburg, Russia: Swamped with Traffic

Further Reading

"About the State of the Environment in the City of Moscow in 2015" (in Russian). 2015. http://eco.mos.ru/legislation/report.

Anonymous. 2015a. "Common Knowledge about Moscow" (in Russian). Ne ciditca.ru. September 10. http://nesiditsa.ru/city/moscow.

Anonymous. 2015b. "In Moscow, Gardening Program 'My Street' Begins." Arguments and Facts News (in Russian). October 15. http://www.aif.ru/realty/city/v_moskve_nachinaetsya_ozelenenie_po_programme_moya_ulica.

Arguments and Facts (in Russian). 2015.

Kommersant. 2010. "Smog over Moscow and the Fires in Central Russia" (in Russian). Kommersant.ru. August 25. http://www.etoday.ru/2010/08/fires-russia-moscow-smoke.phpl.

Kubachevsky, A. 2015. "Greens Make Moscow More Comfortable and Friendly." https://www.mos.ru/news/item/9845073.

Law #743-PP. 2002. "About the Approval of Rules of Creation, Contents and Protection of Green Plantings and Natural Communities of the City of Moscow." September 10. http://www.dpioos.ru/eco/ru/million_dereviev.

Law #822-PP. 2003. "About Methodical Recommendations about Viability Assessment of Trees and Rules of Their Selection and Appointment to Cutting Down and Change." September 30. http://www.znaytovar.ru/gost/2/Postanovlenie_822PP_Metodiches.html.

Mayor's Office of Moscow. 2016. "Muscovites Have Chosen Trees for Landscaping Their Yards" (in Russian). MOS.ru. March 23. https://www.mos.ru/news/item/8962073.

Moscow Municipality. 2015. "The Report About the State of the Environment in the City of Moscow in 2015" (in Russian). Eco.mos.ru. September 10. http://eco.mos.ru/legislation/report.

Mosgorstat. 2015. http://moscow.gks.ru.

Ne ciditca. 2015. "Common Knowledge about Moscow." http://nesiditsa.ru/city/moscow.

Official Website of Mayor of Moscow. 2016. "Green Megalopolis: What Trees and Flowers Are Planted in Moscow" (in Russian). https://www.mos.ru/news/item/11754073.

PWC. 2015. "Cities of Opportunities." PWC.ru. December 2. https://www.pwc.ru/en/doing-business-in-russia/assets/doing-business-and-invest-in-russia_fin.pdf.

Riamo. 2015. "Moscow Is in the Top 3 Ranking of Megacities of the World in Greening." https://riamo.ru/article/66343/moskva-vhodit-v-top-3-rejtinga-megapolisov-mira-po-ozeleneniyu.xl.

RIA Novosti. 2010. "In the Summer of 2010 Russia Burned Two Times Less Forests Than in 2008" (in Russian). RIA.ru. October 29. https://ria.ru/discovery/20101129/302272139.html.

Rosstat, R. F. 2015. "Official Numbers" (in Russian). GKS.ru. December 4. http://www.gks.ru/wps/wcm/connect/rosstat_main/rosstat/ru/statistics/enterprise.

New York City, United States: Pursuit of More Green

With more than 8.5 million people living in its five boroughs—Brooklyn, Queens, Manhattan, The Bronx, and Staten Island—New York City (NYC) is the most populous city in the United States. Globally, it is a powerhouse in every aspect of modern life, from art, fashion, entertainment, education, and science, to political and diplomatic functions. New York City is also recognized for its excellence in maintaining citizens' physical and mental health through developing green spaces. Fourteen percent of the land in New York City, or 30,000 acres, are green spaces, according to the city's Department of Parks and Recreation (NYC Parks); the more than 5,000 properties designated as green space include such well-known sites as Central Park in Manhattan and Coney Island Beach as well as many small green streets and community gardens. The city operates some 800 athletic fields, as well as 1,000 playgrounds, 1,800 basketball courts, 550 tennis courts, 65 public pools, 51 recreational facilities, 15 nature centers, 14 golf courses, and 14 miles of beaches (NYC Parks). This is an admirable record few world cities could match.

THE VILLAGE GREEN

Green spaces are as dear to New Yorkers today as they were to the European settlers in the 17th century. Building a city around green spaces has been in the European tradition for centuries. However, New Yorkers did not follow this tradition in the same way that was done in Europe, which was to build grandiose royal gardens like those in Paris. Rather, the New Yorkers built small to medium-size parks in great numbers, evenly distributed across the city, and with free access. The philosophy behind this is simple: let everybody live near a patch of the village green. When the Trinity Church sold a lot in 1797 to the City of New York that became Duane Park in Manhattan today, the condition was that it be landscaped as "promotive of health and recreation" (NYC Parks). So was the wish of the Stuyvesant family, who sold a four-acre family farm in mid-Manhattan to the City of New York in 1836 for five dollars.

BUILD MORE, BUILD LESS

It may be difficult to accept, given the great number of high-rises in Manhattan today, that NYC has been trying to build more green spaces and fewer structures on the ground. In a sense, New Yorkers are obsessed with developing more green spaces, which is shown through a long list of acquisitions, donations, and expansions. Compare this with some other world cities, such as Chinese cities where "handshake buildings" and "line-sky alleys" (to be explained a bit later) that reveal a runaway urbanization that builds every inch of the ground, leaving little room for greenery.

The oldest parks of NYC, Bowling Green Park, Battery Park, and City Hall Park, were built on the lots granted by the Dongan Charter in 1686. Thomas Dongan, then governor of the Province of New York, put "waste, vacant, unpatented and unappropriated lands" (NYC Parks) in municipal care and made them available for public use. In 1733, the Common Council established the first official park of the city, Bowling Green Park, planted grass and trees in it and a wooden fence all around, "for the Beauty and Ornament of the Said Street as well as for the Recreation & Delight of the Inhabitants of this City" (NYC Parks). Subsequently, in 1733 and 1736, the Common Council founded Battery Park and City Hall Park, barring any structures to be built on these grounds. Years later, these parks meant more in New Yorkers' lives than just being places of recreation. In 1776, following a reading of the Declaration of Independence in City Hall Park, a patriotic mob marched down the street and toppled the statue of George III in Bowling Green Park, and made musket balls with the metal. In subsequent years, Battery Park was a center of celebrations of the Evacuation Day and many other events, and became George Washington's favorite park while he was residing in New York City.

By the 1840s, the population in NYC had increased to 312,710 (U.S. Bureau of the Census), making it the most populous city in the United States. In an effort to relieve urban pressure, the city acquired 770 acres of land in 1853 for the creation of Central Park. The acquisition of Central Park was also accredited to activists like William Cullen Bryant, editor of the *New York Evening Post*, who, together with landscape designers and politicians, promoted public park programs. To commemorate his contribution, Reservoir Square, which opened in 1847, was renamed Bryant Park in 1884. When C. S. Woodhull and A. C. Kingsland campaigned for New York mayor, both put the appropriation of large public green spaces at the top of their agenda. Following the building of Central Park and under its influence, the American Museum of Natural History was opened in 1877 in Manhattan Square (Theodore Roosevelt Park) and the Metropolitan Museum of Art in 1880. In the 1890s, parks were increasingly decorated with statues and monuments to commemorate historical figures and events. Major parks in New York City had more and more educational content featured in the setting.

After Staten Island, Brooklyn, and Queens were incorporated in 1898 to form Greater New York, the city's population swelled to 3.5 million. The city began to acquire a great number of smaller parks and playgrounds in congested neighborhoods, taking advantage of the Small Parks Act passed by the State Legislature in 1887. Recreation pavilions, running tracks, and outdoor gymnasia were added to these parks. The Playground Association of America was founded in 1906. The organization strengthened social functions for parks and improved facilities in parks across the country. Subsequently, thanks to the economic boom following WWI and population growth in the new boroughs, large parks of hundreds of acres were built, including Cunningham Park (350 acres) and Alley Pond Park (654 acres) in Queens. Clove Lakes Park (195 acres), Wolfe's Pond (317 acres), and LaTourette Park (550 acres) were acquired in Staten Island in the 1920s. In 1928, Staten Island opened New York City's first wildlife refuge, the William T. Davis Wildlife Refuge.

MODERNIZING THE PARKS

NYC is not satisfied with the green spaces as they are, but keeps investing in their upgrades. In the 1930s, a new wave of green expansion of the city's park system was underway following Franklin D. Roosevelt's New Deal for the American people. Thousands of engineers, supervisors, and some 70,000 workers were employed by the federal government to work on park projects in 1934 alone (NYC Parks). These projects added multiple zoos, golf courses, beaches, and swimming pools. Parkways and bridges, such as the Grand Central, Inter-borough, and Laurelton Parkways opened in 1936, became predecessors of modern highways. They were part of the new road system that connected the parks. Henry Hudson Bridge was built at this time to extend Henry Hudson Parkway over Spuyten Duyvil Creek through a series of parks sitting on the Hudson River bank. Other well-known projects included the Flushing Meadows Park (later Flushing Meadow-Corona) in 1939 that used to be 1,200-acre swamp and ash dump site, the 35-mile Belt Parkway from Owl's Head Park in Brooklyn to the Bronx-Whitestone Bridge in Queens in 1940. Post-WWII constructions added Jamaica Bay Park in 1954 and the Coney Island Aquarium in

1955. In the 1970s and 1980s, the City of New York funded restoration programs to improve facilities of existing parks and playgrounds, preserve historical monuments, and reseed underdeveloped forests and wetlands. Since 1994, the Department of Transportation resumed the Green Streets project established in 1986 to turn thousands of paved streets into green spaces. Additionally, the city worked to enrich the parks' social functions. In 1984, Flushing Meadow-Corona Park opened the Playground for All Children, the first play space in the United States that is fully accessible. In 1997, the city reopened the Tisch Children's Zoo in Central Park to which the Tisch family had donated $4.5 million in renovation.

In NYC's urban framework, it appears that green spaces have been the backbone that gives urban expansion a blueprint. In practice, acquisition of green spaces typically precedes the building of neighborhoods. In 2003, the U.S. Coast Guard transferred 150 acres in Governor's Island to New York State for $1 to build a public park, in addition to a 22-acre lot the organization had given to the National Park Service. Free ferries transport visitors to concerts and health programs held in the park. In 2005, the city opened a 5,000-seat Olympic-size track-and-field arena on Randall's Island, and Fort Totten Park, a 49.5-acre ground where a Civil War fortress is preserved. Fort Totten is a Civil War-era battery located on Bayside. It was transferred from the U.S. Army to NYC by the National Park Service in 2004. Mayor Bloomberg provided $12 million in the executive budget to renovate the property, transforming it into a public park in 2005 (NYC 2005). In 2008, a 2,200-acre landfill was transformed into Freshkills Park, which is three times the size of Central Park (NYC Parks). These transactions were made without preset commercial or urban outcomes in mind, except for the concept of preserving the natural environment. These green projects, however, will eventually attract businesses and new communities to the vicinity.

NEW BEIJING STRIVING TO CATCH UP WITH NEW YORK

Comparisons can be helpful for understanding. Admittedly, not all world cities can afford to let urban expansion yield to green spaces the way New York City does; many have to use every inch of land to build residential or commercial spaces. A recent report by the *Beijing Daily* reveals that a number of high-rises were found in violation of building codes. These are apartment buildings that are so densely packed that there is only 1 meter of space between them (Luo and Qinglin 2015). They are popularly known as "handshake buildings," as residents can shake hands between two neighboring buildings. The narrow walkways between buildings have a name too: "skyline alleys," after the strip of sky on top. Handshake buildings are typically seen in "urban villages" in China's southern cities. Now, they have made their way into Beijing to be part of the housing solution. The challenge of providing living space for 21.5 million residents apparently provided a market for some risky choices. When living space is in desperate shortage, public spaces are expectedly underdeveloped. The reality is, the parks listed on the website of the Beijing Municipal Administration Center of Parks are mostly heritage parks built in dynastic times, such as Forbidden City, Summer Palace, Tiantan, Beihai, Jingshan, among others. The Olympic Village that was built to host the 2008 Olympics is the only large space recently constructed. Moreover, almost all of these parks charge entrance fees.

In Beijing's defense, the current shortage of public spaces can be blamed on historical circumstances. For a long time, the Chinese tradition has been one that stresses utility. The top-down decision-making process made mistakes difficult to correct and negative impacts last longer. Beijing's first master plan of 1953, for example, stipulates the city's function as both China's cultural center and an industrial base for the country. As such, preservation of heritage buildings and sites was only selectively granted. Many historical places, including the old city walls and traditional neighborhoods, were subsequently demolished and replaced with office buildings and streets. During the 1960s and 1970s, the Great Cultural Revolution did much more to further this trend. The post-Mao economic reforms in the 1980s stopped such practices. However, drastic economic development and the lack of an effective legal system only led to more severe environmental damage. From the 1990s to the early 2000s, 20 to 30 million square meters were built per year in Beijing (Gu et al. 2010). Migrant influx, congested roads, and air pollution have become top urban problems. Environmental deterioration and pollution cost the Chinese economy the equivalent of 8–12 percent of GDP annually according to a Chinese government's report (Gov.cn 2006). The good news is, Beijing's 2004–2020 master plan finally started to address sustainability issues and put emphasis on transforming Beijing into a humanistic city, with ecological and habitable qualities, and increased walkable space. Terms such as "eco-city," "low-carbon city," "zero-pollution economy," "renewable energy," and "green spaces" have become common in daily life. Beijing is catching up on the environmental front, and there is every reason to believe that the progress will be in great leaps. Meanwhile, NYC can be thankful for its founders' obsession with creating more "village green."

Jing Luo

See also: Green Spaces: Moscow, Russia: Planting 1 Million Trees; Paris, France: Returning to Nature

Further Reading

Beijing Municipal Administration Center of Parks (in Chinese). http://www.bjmacp.gov.cn.

Chen, Sijia. 2016. "Beijing's Best Urban Green Spaces to Make the Most of Spring." https://www.thebeijinger.com/blog/2016/05/09/beijings-best-urban-green-spaces-make-most-spring.

Crowley-Hughes, Andrea. 2017. "New York City's Unique Urban Green Spaces." Culture Trip, February 9. https://theculturetrip.com/north-america/usa/new-york/articles/8-unique-urban-green-spaces-in-new-york-city.

Fangzheng Li, Yinan Sun, Xiong Li, Xinhua Hao, Wanyi Li, Yu Qian, Haimeng Liu, and Haiyan Sun. 2016. "Research on the Sustainable Development of Green-Space in Beijing Using the Dynamic Systems Model." http://www.mdpi.com/2071-1050/8/10/965/pdf.

Farquhar, Judith. 2009. "The Park Pass: Peopling and Civilizing a New Old Beijing." *Public Culture* 21, 3. http://publicculture.dukejournals.org/content/21/3/551.full.pdf+html.

Gov.cn. 2006. "Green GDP Accounting Study Report 2004 Issued." Gov.cn, September 11. http://www.gov.cn/english/2006-09/11/content_384596.htm.

Gu Chaolin, Yuan Xiaohui, and Guo Jing. 2010. "China's Master Planning System in Transition: Case Study on Beijing." http://www.isocarp.net/data/case_studies/1657.pdf.

Luo Qiaoxin, and Chang Qinglin. 2015. "Beijing Builds 'CBD Youth Apartments' within Only 1 Meter Space between Buildings" (in Chinese). *Beijing Daily.* http://www.chinanews.com/sh/2015/07-27/7428624.shtml.

NYC—The Official Website of the City of New York. 2005. "Mayor Bloomberg Opens Fort Totten Park to the Public." https://www1.nyc.gov/office-of-the-mayor/news/228-05/mayor-bloomberg-opens-fort-totten-park-the-public.

NYC Parks. "The Earliest New York City Parks." https://www.nycgovparks.org/about/history/earliest-parks.

Staff Writer. 2015. "Park Life: A Day in the Life of One of the Capital's Few Green Spaces." *Economist,* December 16. http://www.economist.com/news/christmas-specials/21683978-day-life-one-capitals-few-green-spaces-park-life.

U.S. Bureau of the Census. 1998. "Population of the 100 Largest Urban Places: 1840." https://www.census.gov/population/www/documentation/twps0027/tab07.txt.

Xu Xuegong, Xiaofeng Duan, Haiqing Sun, and Qiang Sun. 2011. "Green Space Changes and Planning in the Capital Region of China." *Environmental Management* 47, 3 (March). https://link.springer.com/article/10.1007/s00267-011-9626-3.

Paris, France: Returning to Nature

Paris is an ancient city that has its origin along the Seine River. Archaeological findings on l'Ile de la Cité trace human occupation back some 10,000 years. The city became a garrison town under the Roman Empire in the third century BCE, probably the earliest urban development of Paris on the record. It was Clovis I, the King of the Franks, who first turned Paris into a governing center in 508 (Combeau 1999). During the Middle Ages, Paris became the largest city in Europe. It weathered the fierce bubonic plague in the 14th century and devastations of wars between the Catholics and the Protestants. Under King Louis XIV (1638–1715), also known as the Sun King, Paris became Europe's cultural center, with grand palaces built in the center of an exquisite urban layout. In the ensuing century, known as the Age of Enlightenment, great minds in art, philosophy, and science gathered in Paris and established the most important principles of science and democracy. In a sense, the city's intellectual heritage serves as its most important achievement. That being said, Parisians have always been worshipers of nature. In fact, the idea of beautifying the city for all, rather than focusing on grandiose representations of royal power, arose during the Age of Enlightenment. Philosophers, such as Voltaire and Montesquieu, were promoters of green spaces (Roche 1987). "Return to nature" remains a dominant theme in French culture. Integrating gardens into the texture of urban life has been a feature of Paris's long history, reflected by more than 450 gardens today scattered across the city (Paris Visitors Bureau). Paris is arguably just as memorable, perhaps more so, for its green spaces as for its food and wine.

HISTORICAL GARDENS

A satellite view from Google Maps shows that the royal gardens constitute Paris's center, from which the entire city radiates outward. Jardin des Champs Élysées was originally a royal garden commissioned by King Louis XIV in the mid-17th century. Nearly all of the major components were added, redesigned, and upgraded in the ensuing centuries. La Place de la Concorde was redesigned under Louis Philippe in 1834, Arc de Triomphe was built by Napoleon after the victory of the Battle of Austerlitz in 1805, and the Grand Palais and Petit Palais were constructed around 1900.

These historical parks have been witness to some important moments. The avenue of Champs-Élysées has been the stage of several famous military parades, the most notable being the march of German troops celebrating the Fall of France on June 14, 1940, and the parade of French and American military forces celebrating the liberation of Paris on August 25, 1944. The park serves as a sports field for major athletic events, including the annual Paris Marathon and the Tour de France.

But Paris has only been beautified gradually thanks to the efforts of generations of nature-loving Parisians, particularly during the 20th century. Those who have read Victor Hugo's *Les Misérables* must remember that the city was notorious for its substandard conditions in poor neighborhoods. Research indicates that waste removal remained problematic until the late 1800s. Cemetery of the Innocents, by one account, was a mysterious source of pungent odors seeping into people's homes. Human waste was seen on the streets, and rotting garbage was left on every corner. It was the development of science and education that made people aware of germs as the cause of many diseases (Barnes 2006). The contemporary concept of nature in the form of broad-based green infrastructures had to wait until the late 20th century to finally take hold. As a result, contemporary gardens and parks rose in abundance, culminating in contemporary Paris as a showcase for public green space (Van der Velde 2015).

The scale of traditional gardens has always been admired. The two most magnificent green spaces are Jardin des Champs-Élysées, as mentioned earlier, and Champ de Mars (Alba 2013a). They are located next to each other. Jardin des Champs-Élysées stretches approximately 74 acres along the banks of the Seine River. The Avenue of Champs Élysées stretches 3 kilometers along the east-west axis between Palais du Louvre and Arc de Triomphe. This is the place where national celebrations and other major events take place. In the layout of the land, the avenue appears to be a land bridge connecting neighboring gardens to the east of approximately 54 acres, known as Jardin des Tuileries. The two gardens jointly showcase a grand green area decorating central Paris. Jardin du Champ de Mars, on the other hand, is an elongated public garden of approximately 29 acres that lies along a north-south axis. At its southern end and behind Place Joffre are located some important government compounds, such as UNESCO and the Ministry of Social and Health Affairs. At its northern tip sits the Eiffel Tower, right on the bank of the Seine River.

AN ESCAPE FROM THE BUSTLING CITY

A lesser-known design marvel of the Jardin des Champs-Élysées is that its lawns are intentionally shaped slightly concaved, such that rainwater is preserved and noises are also reduced as a result. This feature comes from a tradition dating back to the 19th century. The formation allows sufficient underground and surface water to accumulate to sustain 17 fountains, 2 ponds, and an artificial stream through underground channels.

A contemporary function of the Champs Élysées is that it breaks the busy flow of traffic at the urban center in a seamless manner. Tourists as well as residents going about their daily lives can traverse the park to their destinations. Without the park, one could imagine, roads would be inundated with cars and pedestrians as the east-west axis line in this area is the location of the most important monuments of Paris including Grand Palais, Petit Palais, Place de la Concorde, and Musée du Louvre. The park blends into the urban texture naturally without fences or roadblocks. At any time, pedestrians may walk into the park and enjoy shaded alleys that offer a relaxing promenade. By following the trails, one may view a variety of monuments, sit down at open-air cafés or crepe stands, or join the audience of national and international athletic, musical, or commercial events. These events are held 170 days throughout the year (Alba 2013a). The trails are smoothly connected to street sidewalks on both sides of the park. This is done by gradually changing pavement from sand or gravel stones to cement near entrances to streets.

Champ de Mars hosts one of the most important landmarks of the industrial age: the Eiffel Tower. Built in 1889, the monument alone attracts 7 million visitors every year. One of the park's main functions is to provide visitors with the best vantage point for viewing the tower. The square area at the riverside front surrounding the tower is the most frequented area. Structurally, Champ de Mars is composed of three segments: the Eiffel Tower park, the diamond-shaped central segment, and the plateau area where the Military School is located. The rectangular-shaped park has a 360-meter-long riverfront on the Seine and connects to a variety of tourist sites. The park welcomes approximately 21 million visitors per year (Alba 2013b). Like Champs Élysées, Champ de Mars plays an important role in reducing urban tension and, therefore, improves people's well-being. To that end, the park has gone through many projects aimed at optimizing traffic, protecting the quality of underground water, and making waste management more efficient.

GREEN CORNERS FOR EVERYONE EVERYWHERE

Champs Élysées and Champ de Mars are good examples of how the traditional serves modern needs. Parisians understand, however, that as urban sprawl continues, the grand parks are insufficient; green spaces should be maximally present in all forms. In fact, a prominent feature of Paris is the abundance of small patches of green spaces interwoven into the urban texture, also known as "tucked away gardens" (Sisson 2015). They offer convenient escape from bustling city life. These mini parks naturally fit the space among buildings and streets. In a sense, it is these green spaces that give Paris its identity, shape, and the feel of life. Here are a few examples. Jardin Catherine-Labouré is on Rue de Babylone near the very center of Paris. Its vine-shaded pergolas offer a nice spot of relaxation from walking. Going eastward, one encounters Square René Viviani, located next to the Seine River. The garden offers a nice view of Notre Dame and one of Paris's oldest trees, planted in the 18th century. Strolling further eastward, one arrives at Jardin Alpin, named for its pine trees and hilly scenery reminiscent of the Alps, Pyrenees, and Himalayas.

View of Square René Viviani in Paris, France. The city's many green spaces offer Parisians a welcome break from the bustle of urban life. (Natalia Bratslavsky /Dreamstime.com)

Jardin de l'Atlantique was built in 1994, located approximately a 20-minute walk to the south of Jardin Catherine Labouré. The garden is situated on the rooftop of the railway station la Gare de Montparnasse, with walkways and lampposts representing gangways and ship's masts. Surrounded by high-rises, the tiny green space offers a unique corner of peace. Additionally, one finds "vertical gardens." These are facades of buildings covered with green plants. A famous one is located in the Musée du Quai Branly near the Eiffel Tower. Completed in 2005, the garden features about 150 species of plants, all hanging on the walls of the museum. A similar vertical garden is located between two train stations of Paris, Gare de l'Est and Gare du Nord, along the alley way of Rue D'Alsace (Patrick Whatman 2016).

Green spaces are not only widely present in downtown Paris, they are developed in the *banlieues* (suburbs) as well, including in some working neighborhoods. Suburbs around Paris can be quite varied; some are wealthy, known as *banlieue aisées,* with gated living compounds, such as those in the districts of Versailles and Neuilly-sur-Seine. Some are occupied by blue-collar communities living in low-income apartment complexes (HLMs), such as those in la Courneuve and Clichy-sous-bois. These are residential quarters where most immigrants from Africa reside. The disadvantaged suburbs have a special name—*banlieues défavorisées*. Parisians have a subtle way of referring to the underprivileged neighborhoods, by resorting to the beltway known as *Périphérique*. Thus, going into Paris is to "cross the *Périphérique*." Suburban dwellers often jokingly say that crossing into Paris would require a visa and immunization card (Packer 2015).

SEE AND BE SEEN

For the municipality, improving conditions in these suburbs is a challenge of high priority. The French government put in place an urban renewal program in 2004 with a threefold objective: to change the image of social-housing neighborhoods, to transform the living conditions of inhabitants, and to re-create social diversity. As such, creating public spaces is not only a way of improving the quality of urban living, it carries a function of urban safety through "natural surveillance." Two urban renewal projects were initiated to satisfy a requirement known as "see and be seen." The two communities were the Colbert neighborhood of Meaux, which is a commune located approximately 25 miles east of Paris, and the Val d'Argent neighborhood in the commune Argenteuil about 8 miles northwest of Paris. In these neighborhoods, narrow alleys were widened and broad public green spaces were built (Gosselin 2016).

Overall, Paris has been striving to be a model of the greenest city in the world. It has put forward a plan to make it greener by the end of 2014–20. The program includes developing more than 800 acres of new park areas and 2,400 acres of gardens on walls and rooftops; planting 20,000 trees; and offering teaching gardens and farms in schools. The municipality provides information, tips, and hotlines through its website. The goal of making Paris greener is embraced by every Parisian.

Jing Luo

See also: Green Spaces: New York City, United States: Pursuit of More Green; Tokyo, Japan: Making the City More Livable

Further Reading

Alba, Dominique. 2013a. "Deux grands espaces verts parisiens—Champ de Mars et Champs-Elysées, diagnostic prospectif 1: Les Jardins des Champs Élysées" (in French). http://www.apur.org/etude/grands-espaces-verts-parisiens-champ-mars-champs-elysees-diagnostic-prospectif-1-jardins-champ.

Alba, Dominique. 2013b. "Deux grands espaces verts parisiens—Champ de Mars et Champs-Elysées, diagnostic prospectif 2: Les Jardins du Champ de Mars" (in French). http://www.apur.org/sites/default/files/documents/jardins_champ_mars.pdf.

Barnes, David S. 2006. *The Great Stink of Paris and the Nineteenth-Century Struggle against Filth and Germs.* Baltimore: Johns Hopkins University Press.

Combeau, Yvan. 1999. *Histoire de Paris* (in French). Paris: Presses Universitaires de France.

Gosselin, Camille. 2016. "Urban Renewal and the 'Defensible Space' Model: The Growing Impact of Security Issues on the Way Our Cities Develop." *Metropolitique.* http://www.metropolitiques.eu/Urban-renewal-and-the-defensible.html.

Packer, George. 2015. "The Other France." *New Yorker,* August 31. http://www.newyorker.com/magazine/2015/08/31/the-other-france.

Paris Municipal Website. "Végétalisons la ville" (in French). http://www.paris.fr/duvertpresdechezmoi.

Paris Official Website of the Convention and Visitors Bureau. "Parks, Gardens and Fountains: Green Paris." http://en.parisinfo.com/discovering-paris/themed-guides/Paris-a-fabulous-heritage/classic-paris/Parks-gardens-and-fountains-green-Paris.

Roche, Daniel. 1987. *The People of Paris.* Berkeley: University of California Press.

Sisson, Patrick. 2015. "15 Secret Gardens and Green Spaces Hidden around Paris." http://www.curbed.com/maps/paris-secret-garden-map.

Van der Velde, J. R. T., and S. I. De Wit. 2015. "Representing Nature: Late Twentieth Century Green Infrastructures in Paris." https://journals.open.tudelft.nl/index.php/rius/article/view/838.

Whatman, Patrick. 2016. "Patrick Blanc and the Hanging Gardens of Paris." https://theculturetrip.com/europe/france/paris/articles/patrick-blanc-the-hanging-gardens-of-paris.

Rotterdam, The Netherlands: Building an Edible City

A rising trend in cities around the world is the decline in green spaces to make way for development projects geared toward handling urban population growth. The impact of declining urban green space has been a topic of interest from a wide array of scholars around the world. Increasingly, researchers are identifying the mental and physical health benefits of green spaces for humans, as well as the ecological services they provide for human and nonhuman species. To that effect, many cities across the world are developing policies to incorporate green spaces throughout the city. As one of the greenest cities in the Netherlands, Rotterdam is no exception.

Rotterdam is a coastal city positioned along the Rhine-Meuse Delta of the North Sea. It is considered to be a booming metropolitan area and is home to over 600,000 people from over 170 countries (IUCN 2017). At 48 square miles, Port Rotterdam is the largest port in Europe in terms of cargo volume. Rotterdam is a prime international trade center and is also considered a gateway for the emerging economies in Asia, the Middle East, and South America (IUCN 2017). However, being a bustling, international shipping hub does not come without cost. The environmental impact of thousands of vessels migrating through a port is extraordinarily high. In addition to harmful pollutants, Rotterdam has one of the highest emissions of carbon dioxide per capita in the world. At 29.8 tons of carbon per capita, it is more than double that of Shanghai and London, respectively 11.7 tons and 9.6 tons (Soffel and Maguder 2013).

Most of Rotterdam is below sea level, making climate change and rising sea levels a great concern for the city's future. In the past century, Rotterdam has experienced a sea-level rise of roughly 20 centimeters (Hirst and McGoewn 2009). As the threat of climate change becomes more salient, cities throughout the world have been working to mitigate greenhouse gas emissions. Officials in Rotterdam and other port cities have set major goals toward the reduction of carbon dioxide emissions. In 2007, the Rotterdam Climate Initiative (RCI) was started with the goal to cut and offset carbon emissions by 50 percent by 2025 (RCI 2017a). Though a significant part of the initiative is directed at the Port Authority for carbon capture and sequestration, there are many policies geared toward infrastructural changes in the city as well.

The infrastructural changes in Rotterdam entail both mitigation strategies and adaptive management. The goal is to develop a more sustainable, livable city for the future and decrease vulnerability to a changing climate. One example of infrastructural changes in the city is the development of sustainable urban water systems, such as parks with integrated surface water drainage systems. Waterscaping plays a pivotal role for future adaptation, but the expansion of green spaces is also important for Rotterdam to offset carbon emissions, protect from excess water damage, and keep the city cool. The 2010–14 Rotterdam Programme for Sustainability and Climate Change report identified increasing green space as a key task for making the city sustainable (RCI 2017b).

There is no doubt green spaces beautify urban environments, but they also improve health for people and the planet. In the most basic classification, green spaces can be defined as areas covered with vegetation. In the urban context, green spaces often entail vegetated spaces available to the general public for recreation, including parks, greenbelts, green roofs, green walls, botanical gardens, and urban agriculture. Studies have shown that exposure to, and time in, natural environments and green spaces have both physical and psychological benefits for children and adults alike. Urban green spaces also provide ecosystem services, such as air filtration, habitat for other species, mitigation of urban heat island effect, attenuation of storm water runoff, and carbon sequestration.

The World Health Organization (WHO) recommends a minimum of nine square meters per person of green space (Karayannis 2014). Rotterdam has been steadily increasing green space across the city for over a decade, and at 28.4 square meters per capita, it has more than triple the WHO recommendation. By comparison, Curitiba, Brazil (one of the world's leading cities when it comes to incorporating urban green space) had a population of almost 1.9 million in 2009 and still managed to provide 52 square meters of green space per capita (Danish Architecture Center 2017). In Rotterdam, green spaces come in many forms, including parks, canals bordered with green buffers, botanical gardens, green roofs, and urban agriculture projects.

Parks, small and large, play an integral role in urban green space development. Rotterdam has many pocket parks and large open space parks, including Zuiderpark, which is the largest urban park in the Netherlands. Kralingse Bos is considered by some to be the most popular park in the Netherlands and is known for its beautiful forest cover. Other open space parks include Het Park, Vroesenpark, Museumpark, and Park Schoonoord. The Trompenburg Arboretum is a botanical garden spanning seven hectares; it boasts a diverse plant and animal collection and is open year-round to the general public for a small fee. Dakpark, though only one kilometer long, boasts playgrounds, community gardens, and a Mediterranean garden. New parks are being developed every year, including tidal parks that partially flood when the tide is high to create novel ecosystems. When the tide is in, visitors can enjoy the view of the water; when it is out, children can play in that space. In 2014, the Green Gateway Tidal Park project began under the auspices of the City of Rotterdam, which worked in partnership with the Port Authority. Other completed and projected tidal parks in Rotterdam include Mallegatpark, Nassauhaven, and Maashaven tidal park.

Completed in 2014, Roofpark Vierhavenstrip is considered one of the more interesting parks in Rotterdam. At 80,000 square meters, it is the largest green roof in

Rotterdam and the largest roof park in the Netherlands/Europe (RCI 2017c). The project integrates outdoor green space on top of an indoor, retail strip mall located along the harbor. It has a playground, community gardens, recreational opportunities, and plenty of green space. In addition to improving the quality of life for people, this roof park serves as flood and storm water protection.

Rotterdam has been supporting the installation of green roofs throughout the city using various strategies for almost a decade. Where applicable, it is mandatory for all municipal properties to have green roofs. To date, green roofs have been developed on the central library, municipal archives building, several hospitals, and a museum. Additionally, in 2008, the Rotterdam Climate Proof (RCP) project began a subsidy scheme for the installation of green roofs on nonmunicipal property (RCP 2014). The subsidy has been very successful at encouraging green roof expansion. In 2012, Rotterdam had over 100,000 square meters of green roof coverage; by 2017, over 220,000 square meters of green space could be found on Rotterdam roofscapes (RCP 2014, 36; RCI 2017d).

Living green walls are one more project that sets Rotterdam apart from other cities. In 2010, a 5,000 square meters green façade at the Westblaak car garage was launched. When densely covered with English ivy, the façade surface is meant to filter particulate matter and offset carbon emissions from cars parking in the garage. The greening of neighborhoods is yet another project the Rotterdam Climate Initiative has under way. Green infrastructure projects including green walls, tree-lined streets, garden squares, and vegetable gardens have been proceeding in some of the most brick-dense areas of the city. Between 2014 and 2018, the city municipal office has been tasked to facilitate the installation of these projects in the following districts: Tarwewijk, Bloemhof, Hillesluis, Nieuwe Westen/Middelland, and Oude Noorden. Citizen participation and engagement is encouraged through Green Tables, a platform for people to share ideas and express their needs.

In conjunction with green roofs and garden squares, urban agriculture has been on the rise in Rotterdam. In 2010, the municipal government of Rotterdam established a think tank on urban agriculture to increase the number of gardens producing food in the city, with an emphasis on districts with the least green space. The municipality supports urban agriculture efforts through various means from disseminating information to citizens, providing expert knowledge from university researchers, to marketing the importance of regional production. Additionally, the municipality has been encouraging young farmers through the installation of educational gardens at schools throughout the city. Alexandra van Huffelen, the alderman in 2012 for Sustainability, Inner City and Outdoor Space, said, "It is my ambition that, in ten years, a significant part of the fruit and vegetables eaten by the Rotterdam inhabitants will be grown in this region. . . . It is my dream that we will have several urban farmers by then who have taken up the challenge of producing food in the outskirts of the city for the city dwellers" (Town Planning, Urban Planning 2012, 5).

Rotterdam is part of an international movement seeking to increase urban food production in cities around the world. Eetbaar Rotterdam, or Edible Rotterdam, is one of many initiatives exploring the possibilities of expanding urban agriculture. Room for Urban Agriculture in Rotterdam, a mapping project spearheaded on behalf of Eetbaar Rotterdam, has a wide array of partners looking to realize the full potential of food production in the city (Viljoen and Wiskerke 2012). Another project, the Food Bank Garden, or Stichting Voedselbanktuin, is an all-organic garden employing permaculture techniques to grow food behind a food bank (a place that provides basic food provisions free of charge to people in need). Dakakker was the first urban rooftop farm in Rotterdam. The project was started by an architecture firm as a test site and produces vegetables and herbs that are sold to local restaurants and shops. Another interesting urban agriculture project, Uit je Eigen Stad, or "From your Own City," has been operating an urban farm-to-table project in an abandoned railway yard in a harbor. Equipped with greenhouses, tunnels, and aquaculture, the project was created to reconnect people of Rotterdam with food from their city.

The growth in urban agriculture is not limited to entrepreneurial pursuits of business owners; Rotterdam has a thriving community of guerrilla gardeners, community gardeners, and permaculture enthusiasts. A simple online search will link a user to a variety of community groups trying to grow the urban agriculture movement in Rotterdam. Online forums provide a rich community for those interested in farming the city and can guide people on how to obtain free mulch from the municipality or which businesses provide waste streams for composting. In 2014, a committed group of volunteers called Foodforest Kralingen saw their vision of a food forest in the city come to fruition. The development of the 800 square meters food forest in Nieuwe Plantage park began with plantings in 2013 (Voedselbos Kralingen 2017).

Though much of Rotterdam's efforts to green the city have been achievements, there are still concerns in terms of ensured future success. The green roof subsidy offered to citizens will expire, and many wonder whether people will continue to manage their existing green roofs and if green roof expansion will stall. Unlike other cities with mandatory policies, Rotterdam has relied solely on incentives for its citizens. Another concern expressed by some scholars and city planners is the potential for gentrification as neighborhoods continue to expand green infrastructure. In some areas, planners have even contemplated setting a limit to beautification in poorer neighborhoods to prevent displacement of locals. While gentrification is a widespread problem in cities around the world, it is progressive for planners to explicitly recognize such concerns. That said, Rotterdam can still be considered a model for other delta port cities.

Thelma I. Velez and Kerry Ard

See also: Energy and Sustainability: Copenhagen, Denmark: Striving to Be Carbon-Neutral by 2025; *Green Spaces:* Tel Aviv, Israel: Community Gardening

Further Reading

Danish Architecture Center. 2017. "Sustainable Cities, Curitiba: The Green Capital." http://www.dac.dk/en/dac-cities/sustainable-cities/all-cases/green-city/curitiba-the-green-capital.

Hirst, Michael, and Kate McGeown. 2009. "Rising Sea Levels: A Tale of Two Cities." BBC News, November 24. http://news.bbc.co.uk/2/hi/science/nature/8369236.stm.

International Union for Conservation of Nature (IUCN). 2017. "City Focus." https://www.iucn.org/regions/europe/projects/completed-projects/urbes/city-focus.

Karayannis, George. 2014. "Dissecting ISO 37120: Why Shady Planning Is Good for Smart Cities." SmartCitiesCouncil, November 19. http://smartcitiescouncil.com/article/dissecting-iso-37120-why-shady-planning-good-smart-cities.

Rotterdam Climate Initiative. 2017a. *Full Steam Ahead!* 2008 Report—Summary. http://www.rotterdamclimateinitiative.nl/documents/2015-en-ouder/samenvatting%20Op%20Stoom%20EN.pdf.

Rotterdam Climate Initiative. 2017b. "Rotterdam Programme on Sustainability and Climate Change 2015–2018. Making Sustainability a Way of Life for Rotterdam." http://www.rotterdamclimateinitiative.nl/documents/2015-en-ouder/Documenten/Rotterdam%20Programme%20on%20Sustainaibilty%20and%20Climate%20Change%202015-2018.pdf.

Rotterdam Climate Initiative. 2017c. "Roof Park Rotterdam." http://www.rotterdamclimateinitiative.nl/uk/city/ongoing-projects/roof-park-rotterdam?project_id=99&global_subcategory_id=2&p=1.

Rotterdam Climate Initiative. 2017d. "Green Roofs Programme." http://www.rotterdamclimateinitiative.nl/uk/city/ongoing-projects/green-roofs-programme?project_id=249&global_subcategory_id=2&p=1.

Rotterdam Climate Proof and the City of Rotterdam. 2014. "Delta Rotterdam: Connecting Water with Opportunities." http://www.urbanisten.nl/wp/wp-content/uploads/publication_UB_RCI_Delta_Magazine.pdf.

Soffel, Jenny, and Natasha Maguder. 2013. "Can Rotterdam Become the World's Most Sustainable Port City?" CNN, August 26. http://www.cnn.com/2013/08/19/world/europe/can-rotterdam-become-the-sustainable/.

Town Planning, Urban Planning Rotterdam. 2012 "Food & the City: Stimulating Urban Agriculture in and around Rotterdam." February. https://www.rotterdam.nl/wonen-leven/stadslandbouw/FoodTheCityEngels.pdf.

Viljoen, André, and Johannes S. C. Wiskerke. 2012. "Sustainable Food Planning: Evolving Theory and Practice." Wageningen, The Netherlands: Wageningen Academic.

Voedselbos Kralingen. 2017. https://voedselboskralingen.wordpress.com/english.

Tel Aviv, Israel: Community Gardening

Tel Aviv-Yafo, popularly known as Tel Aviv, is Israel's second-largest city, next to Jerusalem, with a population of about 440,000 residents in 2016 (Municipality of Tel Aviv-Yafo). Founded in 1909, Tel Aviv was developed as a metropolitan city under the British Mandate in Palestine. Located on Israel's west coastal plain and mostly built on sandy terrain, Tel Aviv enjoys easy access to the Mediterranean Sea on the west side, and to land resources on its eastern side. The city has a mild Mediterranean climate, with average temperatures between 86 degrees Fahrenheit in August and 75 degrees Fahrenheit in January, which is the most pleasant month of the year. Precipitation falls largely in winter months; snowfalls are quite rare. There are multiple attractions, one of which is the Yarqon River. The river was heavily polluted in the 1990s and successfully treated through a series of environmental projects. Another attraction is the International Style buildings constructed in the 1930s–40s influenced by the Bauhaus School. The abundance of these structures won for Tel Aviv the title of "White City," due to the typical color of these buildings. Tel Aviv was also granted, as a result, UNESCO World Heritage Site status in 2003 (Razin 2008).

Historically, according to the description of the *Jewish Virtual Library,* Tel Aviv started as a small Jewish settlement as had many others. In the early 1900s, a small number of Jewish migrants founded a community to the north of Jaffa, the main port of entry to Ottoman Palestine. The name "Tel Aviv" was adopted by the founders in 1910; it means "Spring Hill." During the 1920s and under the British occupation, Tel Aviv's population and territorial scope rapidly expanded. As a result, Tel Aviv gained municipality status by the early 1930s. By the time of the Arab-Israeli war of 1948 that led to Israel's independence, the city's population had swelled to 210,000. In 1950, Tel Aviv and Jaffa merged into a single municipality, and adopted Tel Aviv-Yafo as its official name.

In 2017, Tel Aviv won the title of the world's seventh-greenest city in the list of model cities selected by researchers of the Massachusetts Institute of Technology and the World Economic Forum for creating green spaces and clean air in urban environment. The top three cities are Vancouver (Canada), Sacramento (United States), and Geneva (Switzerland) (Paz-Frankel 2017).

COMMUNITY GARDENS

The municipality and residents of Tel Aviv give creating green spaces a high priority. This is reflected in the city's fever for creating community gardens and various other forms of urban farming. Tel Aviv's green spaces vary in sizes, vegetation cover, and proximity to neighborhoods. Many believe that public green spaces should be less than five minutes' walk from residential neighborhoods, shopping malls, or public buildings, since accessibility is essential to the benefits. Such benefits typically include provision of facilities for recreation, physical exercises, and social interaction, all of which contribute to mental well-being. Moreover, residents of Tel Aviv engage in developing green spaces for economic reasons as well, as they contribute to economic returns. Using vegetation as an environmental cooling mechanism saves much of the city's energy expenses. Property values tend to be higher where green spaces are properly maintained (Haq 2011). Tel Aviv has invested in facilitating community gardening since 2000, on the theory that community gardens are part of the mechanisms that contribute to social stability. Vegetable gardens are intended to express the city's character in aesthetics, culture, and politics (Eizenberg and Fenster 2015).

Community gardening in Tel Aviv is believed to reflect at a certain level a Jewish cultural tradition of the Kibbutzim movement. Kibbutzim (plural of "kibbutz") are farming communities based on joint ownership of property, equality, cooperation of production, and consumption. The first kibbutz was established in 1909 in Ottoman Palestine on the bank of Jordan River just south of the Sea of Galilee (Rifkin 2010). Members of the kibbutz follow the principle of "From each according to his ability, to each according to his needs" (Jewish Virtual Library).

The first community garden in Tel Aviv is recognized as Florentin community garden built in 2005 in southern Tel Aviv. While there are only five avid members and 15 casual growers, the garden attracts many visitors. Anyone who experiences financial hardship may come to the garden to pick vegetables and offer some field work in return and whenever time permits. The garden has been sustained with success. The main reason, as members believe, is that it offers an opportunity for neighbors to establish a close relationship. What the garden's manager, Harel, said reflects what participants share: "It is so nice to go back home with a bag of tomatoes, but the main thing is the sense of community." Sharon Greenblatt of the Tel Aviv municipality who is in charge of coordinating community gardens expresses the municipality's perspective: "It enables a dialogue between the municipality and the residents that does not revolve around parking tickets or municipal taxes. And there is another bonus as it encourages residents to grow food for self-consumption, taking into consideration the ecological aspect. In recent years, the awareness of sustainability in Israel has grown. This is also a celebration for the children, as healthy ways of living are promoted. There are lots of events surrounding the community gardens: give and take markets, LGBT garden, and joint Jewish-Arab garden. Our experience shows that it is up to the local community to get organized and to approach us for guidance. If we ourselves try to create a neighborhood community, it will never work out" (Avivi 2015).

The municipality takes a central planning approach in developing the city's community gardens. The top-down approach aims at utilizing public funds to invest strategically and efficiently. A political consideration behind this approach is that under-privileged locations are not deprived from green spaces. An advantage of public funding s that, without favoring groups or individuals, it could prevent unfair restrictions to residents due to ethnic and cultural differences. Control is intended to integrate open community spaces in a manner that supports economic strength of space and of the city, according to the municipality. In actual practice, the municipality of Tel Aviv imposes a tedious approval process that sometimes lasts months during which community residents go through a rigorous process of petition for their garden project. The municipality selectively approves only groups that not only have required resources, but also meet organizational requirements.

Like in every metropolitan city, Tel Aviv's residential neighborhoods come in different economic conditions. Affluent neighborhoods are located mostly in Northern Tel Aviv, middle class neighborhoods are scattered in the central area, while Southern Tel Aviv is home to many communities of African immigrants who are often economically stressed. Since 2004, 14 gardens have been opened in the upscale Northern Tel Aviv, of which 8 are located to the north of Yarqon River. Three have been opened in middle class communities in the central area, and nine in lower middle- to lower-class areas in Southern Tel Aviv. The current allocation of community gardens shows an effort to maintain a balance between the northern and the southern areas. Without government's interventions, this could not have been achieved, according the municipality (Eizenberg and Fenster 2015). As of 2015, the Tel Aviv municipality supports approximately 27 community gardens across the city. These gardens are required to be open to the public, and to avoid using insecticides or harmful chemicals (Avivi 2015).

In general, for Tel Aviv residents, gardening is more of a sociocultural engagement than a necessity for making a living. They believe that when residents of a community exercise their responsibility over public spaces and employ them creatively and responsibly to pursue their own ideals, they can contribute both to the city and the neighborhood. Moreover, where neighbors seek to communicate with one another and collaborate to strengthen a harmonious living environment, people tend to perceive their life as more fulfilled. Community gardens contribute to collective awareness and prevent alienation and intolerance (Rifkin 2010, Avivi 2015).

HYDROPONICS FARMING

Urban agriculture requires less water than traditional farming, since it uses all nutrient-based irrigation and no soil. Tel Aviv promotes a "Green in the City" ("Yarok Bair" in Hebrew) project from the rooftops of the Dizengoff Center, the city's central mall complex. LivinGreen is a company that provides training to locals. The project serves both the goals of creating more green spaces in the city and bringing organic produce to the family's table. Hydroponics technology grows plants using a nutrient-rich watering system that pumps water directly to the roots. Vegetables and fruits grown in this environment have higher yields that in soil and are pesticide-free (Lim 2015).

Tel Aviv's top environmental organization, Life and Environment, awarded Dizengoff Center the *Green Globes* award 12 years in a row. The award was created to honor the greenest businesses. The Dizengoff Center operates 40,000 square meters (430,556 square feet) of shopping area for more than 400 stores. The rooftop farm provides space for participants to grow vegetables and fruits of various kinds all year round using aquaponics and hydroponics systems. The produce is sold to local restaurants and food services. The aquaponics system connects a watering pipeline with fish tanks from where water is naturally fertilized by fishes' discharge. An advantage of this type of farming is its small space, water saving, and higher quantity of production. A rooftop vertical pipe system can produce eight times the amount of vegetables in a traditional garden, since water and nutrients are efficiently sent to the roots. As such, aquaponics is popular among urban farmers.

Today, hydroponic farming at Dizengoff's has expanded to 8,000 square feet of space from 1,100 square feet at the beginning, and includes multiple greenhouses and several types of growing systems. Training programs reach schools and urban residents (Callie 2016). The urban farm produces 10,000 heads of lettuce per month year-round, and grows 17 different varieties of greens and herbs, using a variety of hydroponics systems, both vertical and horizontal, where plants grow twice as fast as in a soil environment. Technically, the system is easy to manage, not requiring regular cleaning, since the system controls oxygen flow and lighting, reducing rot (Martinko 2016).

A NEW OPPORTUNITY FOR LOW-INCOME COMMUNITIES

Tel Aviv has found in rooftop gardening a way to support gentrification. Over the years, South Tel Aviv has received a great number of African migrants, from

> ### The Kibbutzim Movement
>
> Kibbutzim have been a mainstay in the Israeli cultural tradition. The movement embraces the ideal of "from each according to his ability, to each according to his needs." The term "kibbutz" (pl. "kibbutzim") in Hebrew means "communal settlement," typically in rural areas, on the principle of joint ownership of property, collective production, and equity in consumption and education. The first kibbutz was founded in 1909. By 2000, there were 268 units (Jewish Virtual Library). According to some estimates, the kibbutzim population today is between 126,000 (Rifkin 2010) and 130,000 (Jewish Virtual Library), or approximately 2.5 percent of the Israeli population.
>
> In broader ideological and historical terms, the ideal of "from each according to his ability, to each according to his needs" was fundamental to Communist theory. The goal of eliminating class differences and the exploitation of the poor by the rich was essential to Communist indoctrination. Communist regimes of the 20th century utilized this concept to impose deprivation and dictatorship. For example, in the 1950s, China's farmers were forced to give up their land and work in "People's Communes." The system failed to boost agriculture production. Three decades later, in the early 1980s, the People's Communes were finally disbanded; farmland was allotted back to families based on the "Contractual Responsibility System." The new system allowed farmers to keep the excess produced over the submission quota for themselves. The new motto became "to be rich is glorious," and China experienced an unprecedented economic boom. Arguably, however, "from each according to his ability, to each according to his needs" has been an influential idea that has affected the world in profound ways.

Ethiopia, Nigeria, Sudan, and Darfur, and has become home to 50,000 African migrants, the group that makes up the majority of immigrants of Israel. Most of the immigrant population reside in communities in South Tel Aviv, and most are males between 18 and 35. The area is plagued with poverty, rising crime rates, xenophobia, and violence (Kamin 2013).

Immigrant communities are typically dependent on the government for residential as well as employment support. To meet the demand, the Tel Aviv municipality opened up gardening spaces near the city's New Central Bus Station, an area where the immigrant population is concentrated. The government provides training to the growers. Hydroponics farming seems to have opened up a new job opportunity, which is to supply produce to the neighborhoods. Additionally, the program connects the immigrants of different cultural and language backgrounds with the greens they grow together.

Jing Luo

See also: *Energy and Sustainability:* Copenhagen, Denmark: Striving to Be Carbon-Neutral by 2025; *Green Spaces:* Rotterdam, The Netherlands: Building an Edible City

Further Reading

Avivi, Yuval. 2015. "Israel's Community Gardens Bloom." *Al-monitor*, July 28. http://www.al-monitor.com/pulse/originals/2015/07/israel-tel-aviv-urban-farming-organic-vegetables-community.html.

Callie. 2016. "Rooftop Hydroponic Farms in Tel Aviv, Israel." *Garden Culture Magazine*, December 31. https://www.gardenculturemagazine.com/techno-gardens/hydroponics/rooftop-hydroponic-farming-tel-aviv.

Eizenberg, Efrat, and Tovi Fenster. 2015. "Reframing Urban Controlled Spaces: Community Gardens in Jerusalem and Tel Aviv-Jaffa." *ACME: An International E-Journal for Critical Geographies* 14, 4: 1132–60.

Haq, Shah. 2011. "Urban Green Spaces and an Integrative Approach to Sustainable Environment." *Journal of Environmental Protection* 2: 601–8.

Jewish Virtual Library. "Tel Aviv: From Spring Hill to Independence." http://www.jewishvirtuallibrary.org/tel-aviv-from-spring-hill-to-independence.

Kamin, Debra. 2013. "South Tel Aviv Is South Sudan Now." *Times of Israel*, December 2. http://www.timesofisrael.com/south-tel-aviv-is-south-sudan-now.

Kamin, Debra. 2015. "Gentrification—via Gardening—Slowly Comes to Derelict South Tel Aviv." http://www.jta.org/2015/12/09/life-religion/gentrification-via-gardening-slowly-comes-to-derelict-south-tel-aviv.

Kloosterman, Karin. 2017. "Refugees Plan Roots in World's First Hydroponic Community Garden in Tel Aviv." Greenprophet.com, January 4. https://www.greenprophet.com/2017/01/refugees-plant-roots-in-worlds-first-hydroponic-community-garden-in-tel-aviv.

Lidman, Melanie. 2015. "High-Tech Farmer Turn Mall Roof into Bed of Lettuce." *Times of Israel*, July 22. http://www.timesofisrael.com/hi-tech-farmer-turns-mall-roof-into-bed-of-lettuce.

Lim, Eunice. 2015. "Revolutionary Rooftop Farm Grows Organic Veggies Sans Soil in the Heart of Tel Aviv." Nocamels.com, August 16. http://nocamels.com/2015/08/urban-farm-organic-produce-mall-rooftop.

Martinko, Katherine. 2016. "Tel Aviv's Rooftop Farm Grows Fresh Food for Thousands." Treehugger.com, December 19. http://www.treehugger.com/green-food/tel-avivs-rooftop-farm-grows-vegetables-thousands-people.html.

Municipality of Tel Aviv-Yafo. Undated. "City in Numbers." https://www.tel-aviv.gov.il/en/abouttheCity/Pages/CityinNumbers.aspx.

Paz-Frankel, Einat. 2017. "Urban Jungle: Tel Aviv Named World's 7th Greenest City." Nocamels.com, March 21. http://nocamels.com/2017/03/tel-aviv-seventh-greenest-city/.

Razin, Eran. 2008. "Tel Aviv-Yafo." https://www.britannica.com/place/Tel-Aviv-Yafo.

Rifkin, Lawrence. 2010. "Adult Children of the Dream." *Jerusalem Post*. http://www.jpost.com/Jerusalem-Report/Adult-Children-of-the-Dream.

UN Demographic Statistics 2017. http://data.un.org/Data.aspx?q=tel+aviv&d=POP&f=tableCode%3a240%3bareaCode%3a0%3bsexCode%3a0%3bvarCode3%3a023560%3bvarCode4%3a000001.

Tokyo, Japan: Making the City More Livable

Beginning in the 1990s, Tokyo—the most populated city in the world—has endeavored to reverse the loss of green spaces. This is a major challenge as massive postwar economic and urban growth significantly depleted the amount of greenery. As of 2011, only 3.4 percent of Tokyo's total area was comprised of public green space—far less than many other major cities such as Seoul's 26.5 percent and New York's 27 percent (BOP Consulting 2016). However, the city government, private organizations, regular citizens, and an expanding environmental consciousness have inspired efforts to address this situation and make Tokyo a more livable city.

HISTORICAL BACKGROUND

Formal planning for green space in Tokyo started in 1939. Bureaucrats proposed a greenbelt outside the city center as well as green spaces and parks within the city. Before this plan could be realized, World War II erupted. This led to a new plan in 1940—the air-raid green space plan. Between the end of the war and the early 1960s, more than 60 percent of the green space that had been set aside as wartime evacuation areas had disappeared due to pressures from rapid economic and population growth. Addressing the housing shortage carried far more weight with politicians than preserving green spaces. Several factors in recent decades, such as the oil crises of the 1970s, growing citizen concern about the environment, a stagnating economy in the 1990s, and an aging population and declining birth rate in the early 2000s, opened the door for creating a more sustainable city with greater emphasis on green spaces (Kumagai et al. 2015; Havens 2011; Morita et al. 2012).

RECENT DEVELOPMENTS

While a number of laws enacted over the years by the central government, the Tokyo Metropolitan Government (TMG), and municipalities shaped policies toward green spaces, major policy change began in 2003 when the Ministry of Land, Infrastructure and Transportation decided it was necessary to preserve existing and create new green spaces. This led the TMG in 2006 to create the 10-Year Project for Green Tokyo. The plan listed eight goals, including "recover beautiful Tokyo embraced by water and green corridors," "realize the city with least environmental load in the world," and "reinforce reliance on Tokyo by creating disaster-proof city" (Okata and Murayama 2010, 38).

According to official sources, the green campaign would be led by TMG bureaucrats, private citizens, and corporations. Their efforts would significantly increase roadside trees, "create a hub for greening in each community mainly through the promotion of turf-covered school yards," and preserve existing and create new green spaces. According to a TMG document, "190,000 roadside trees were newly planted" between 2008 and 2011 (Bureau of the Environment 2012, 35). The city also seeks to encourage "voluntary greening" by private corporations and citizens in areas such as new building developments, alongside railroad tracks, next to parking lots, on rooftops, and "wall surface greening" such as at Omotesando Hills. An example of this effort is the My Tree program. Initiated by the Bureau of Construction, My Tree encourages Tokyo residents to donate money for the planting of trees. Donors' trees will have plaques stating their name, tree type, and message they wish to post. By 2014, some 4,700 plaques had been mounted on trees. TMG intends to use tax incentives to foster these efforts (Tokyo Metropolitan Government 2007; Bureau of Construction 2015). Green spaces will also mitigate flooding—a hazard in a city with extensive hard surfaces. Policy recommendations included creating green infrastructure alongside streets and alleys such as planter boxes and bioswales to absorb and evapotranspire stormwater (Tanji and Shinno 2014, 15–16).

A key element of creating more green space is *Umi no Mori*—or the Sea Forest—situated in Tokyo Bay. When architect and environmentalist Tadao Ando joined a panel established to improve the city's image as part of Tokyo's application to hold the 2016 Olympics, among his earliest recommendations was planting more trees. This led to the Sea Forest—an island built atop more than 100,000 tons of garbage collected during the 1970s and 1980s. Rather than rely on government funding or corporate donations, Ando encouraged people of all backgrounds—from elementary school children to famous U2 singer Bono—to donate money and plant thousands of trees with the goal of creating "an oxygen-producing, carbon-trapping lung for the world's most populated city." *Umi no Mori* is central to the city's revised green plan, an element of Tokyo Vision 2020. Its connection to the world of sports continued as it was part of Tokyo's successful bid for the 2020 Olympics. Some of the games will be held on the island (Japan for Sustainability 2007; Knight 2009; Tadao 2009; Cwiertka 2015).

A unique aspect of Tokyo's green policy that differentiates it from many other major cities is that green spaces also serve as disaster evacuation spaces. The origins of this policy go back to the aftermath of the 1923 Great Kanto Earthquake when it was realized that existing green spaces such as Ueno Park helped citizens escape the fires that raged downtown. As a result, thousands of small neighborhood parks were built (Xu 2013, 139, 141). Minister of Home Affairs Shinpei Goto played a key role in this reconstruction plan, "incorporating refuge parks" as an integral part of his vision for an improved capital (Mckean 2014). Thus, in Tokyo, planning for green spaces took on the added role of disaster prevention.

The March 11, 2011, the Great East Japan earthquake furthered this emphasis on "securing places to evacuate to in the event of disaster." Before the year ended, the TMG formalized this in a revised Development Policy for City-planned Parks and Green Spaces (Tokyo Metropolitan Government 2015). Cameron Allan Mckean asserts that "these parks are a precise extension of Goto's original redevelopment." Yet, hidden underneath these green spaces are all sorts of equipment and supplies—for example, charging stations, benches that can be turned into stoves, and food storehouses—to help city residents survive a catastrophe. The city intends to build many more disaster-survival parks throughout the metropolis (Mckean 2014).

There is, however, some evidence that the central and city governments are not achieving as many results in the greening of Tokyo as all the laws and programs suggest. For example, in the Tokyo Metropolitan Government's 2007 policy statement for Green Tokyo, significant focus is centered on grassing school grounds. In addition to listing the benefits of the program, the policy paper notes that "it is important . . . to obtain the understanding and cooperation of parents, neighborhood associations and other local community members." The TMG also planned to "organize 'lawn supporters.'" This discussion suggests that there is resistance to the program (Tokyo Metropolitan Government 2007). Moreover, Jared Braiterman, a design anthropologist living and working in Tokyo and the author of the blog *Tokyo Green Space*, contended in a 2012 interview that "the city as a whole, the Tokyo government, doesn't do much about renewable energy and is not focused on being green" (*Japan Times* 2012). Furthermore, a private research firm that did an environmental study for the city government stated in 2013 that the proposed arenas for the 2020 Tokyo Olympics would "destroy the city's green spaces," which, they asserted, would conflict with the goals of the TMG's green plans (*Japan Press*

An urban park in Tokyo, Japan. In 2006, Tokyo's municipal government adopted a policy to create more green spaces and preserve existing ones. (Phuong Photo/Dreamstime.com)

Weekly 2013). A related conflict emerged over the proposed new stadium to replace the 1964 National Olympic Stadium. In a 2014 *Japan Times* article, Professor Jeff Kingston of Temple University Japan asserted that if the proposed stadium was built it would be a "mammoth monstrosity" that would reduce "one of Tokyo's largest greenbelts" (Kingston 2014).

CONCLUSION

Though some question how committed the Tokyo Metropolitan Government is in creating a more sustainable city with expanding green spaces, and though there is still much work to do, clearly Tokyo is making progress. Government, business, environmentally minded organizations, and common citizens are working toward making one of the great cities of the world a more livable city for the early 21st century.

Douglas Karsner

See also: Energy and Sustainability: Frankfurt, Germany: Protecting the City from Climate Changes; *Traffic and Transportation:* Osaka, Japan: Attracting Private Investments to Public Transportation

Further Reading

BOP Consulting. 2016. "Percentage of Public Green Space (Parks and Gardens)." Global Leadership on Culture in Cities. http://www.worldcitiescultureforum.com/data/of-public-green-space-parks-and-gardens.

Bureau of Construction. 2015. "My Tree Program." The Bureau of Construction, Tokyo Metropolitan Government. http://www.metro.tokyo.jp/english/.

Bureau of the Environment. 2012. "Creation of Greenery and Natural Environment Conservation." Environmental Policy Section, Environmental Policy Division, Bureau of the Environment, Tokyo Metropolitan Government, March. http://www.kankyo.metro.tokyo.jp/en/.

Cwiertka, Katarzyna. 2015. "Talk: Dream Island and Sea Forest: The Afterlife of Tokyo's Landfills." http://www.sustainability.ucsb.edu/event/dream-island-and-sea-forest-the-afterlife-of-tokyos-landfills-katarzyna-cwiertka-modern-japan-studiesleiden-university/.

Havens, Thomas. 2011. *Parkscapes: Green Spaces in Modern Japan.* Honolulu: University of Hawaii Press.

Japan for Sustainability. 2007. "Tokyo Gov't Launches 10-Year Project for Green Metropolis." https://japanfs.org/en/news/archives/news_id026807.html.

Japan Press Weekly. 2013. "Construction of Arenas for 2020 Tokyo Olympics Will Destroy Green Spaces." *Japan Press Weekly,* November 6. http://www.japan-press.co.jp/modules/news/index.php?id=6644. .

Japan Times. 2012. "Tokyo Green Space." *Japan Times,* May 16. https://www.japantimes.co.jp/life/2012/05/16/digital/tokyo-green-space/#.W-NHtJNKhPY.

Kingston, Jeff. 2014. "Hadid's Curse: Mammoth Monstrosity Threatens Tokyo's Greenbelt." *Japan Times,* June 14. https://www.japantimes.co.jp/opinion/2014/06/14/commentary/japan-commentary/hadids-curse-mammoth-monstrosity-threatens-tokyos-greenbelt/#.W-NIB5NKhPY.

Knight, Gordon Kanki. 2009. "Fab 40: The Sea Forest, Tokyo Bay." *Architecture,* October 14. https://www.wallpaper.com/architecture/fab-40-the-sea-forest-tokyo-bay.

Kumagai, Yoichi, Robert Gibson, and Pierre Filion. 2015. "Evaluating Long-Term Urban Resilience through an Examination of the History of Green Spaces in Tokyo." *Local Environment: The International Journal of Justice and Sustainability* 20: 1018–39. dx.doi.org/10.1080.13549839.2014.887060.

Mckean, Cameron Allan. 2014. "Tokyo's Disaster Parks: Hi-Tech Survival Bunkers Hidden under Green Spaces." *The Guardian.com,* August 19. https://www.theguardian.com/cities/2014/aug/19/tokyo-disaster-parks-hi-tech-survival-bunkers-hidden-green-spaces-earthquake.

Morita, Tetsuo, Yoshihide Nakagawa, Akinori Morimoto, Masateru Maruyama, and Yoshimi Hosokawa. 2012. "Changes and Issues in Green Space Planning in the Tokyo Metropolitan Area: Focusing on the 'Capital Region Plan.'" *International Journal of GEOMATE* 2: 191–96. gi-j.com/serial%203/191-196-1253.tmorita.pdf.

Okata, Junichiro, and Akito Murayama. 2010. "Tokyo's Urban Growth, Urban Form and Sustainability." In Andre Sorensen and Junichiro Okata, eds. *Megacities: Urban Form, Governance, and Sustainability.* Tokyo: Springer. https://link.springer.com/book/10.1007/978-4-431-99267-7.

Tadao, Ando. 2009. "Umi no Mori: What if a Forest Is Created and No One Knows?" *Tokyo greenspace.com.* April 7. https://tokyogreenspace.com/2009/04/07/umi-no-mori-what-if-a-forest-is-created-and-no-one-knows/.

Tanji, Kazunori, and Hayato Shinno. 2014. "The Green Infrastructure to Control Urban Flooding in Tokyo." Presentation at the 5th Global Forum on Urban Resilience and Adaptation. Bonn, Germany. http://resilient-cities.iclei.org/fileadmin/sites/resilient-cities/files/Resilient_Cities_2014/PPTs/D/D1_Tanji.pdf.

Tokyo Metropolitan Government. 2007. *Basic Policies for the 10-Year Project for Green Tokyo: Regenerating Tokyo's Abundant Greenery.* http://www.kankyo.metro.tokyo.jp/en/about_us/videos_documents/documents_1.files/10-year_project.pdf.

Tokyo Metropolitan Government. 2015. *Creation of a Comfortable Urban Environment: Creating a city rich in greenery.* http://www.toshiseibi.metro.tokyo.jp/eng/pdf/2015-5.pdf.

Xu, Hao. 2013. "The Evolution and Characteristics of the Green Space System Planning in Japan." *Modern Landscape Architecture.* Proceedings of the 6th WSEAS International Conference on Landscape Architecture, Nanjing, China, November 17–19. Edited by Jon B. Burley. http://www.wseas.us/e-library/conferences/2013/Nanjing/LA/LA-18.pdf.

Housing and Infrastructure

OVERVIEW

Possibly more than other markets, urban housing and infrastructure is more vulnerable to overpopulation. As the global urban population crosses over the current 54 percent line and inches higher, the pressure on housing and infrastructure is materially felt. According to a report by the McKinsey Global Institute, by 2025, a third of urban dwellers—1.6 billion people—will face the struggle to secure decent housing; housing construction cost would be in the $9 to $11 trillion range, without counting land costs that could run $5 to $7 trillion more. Moreover, public funding will likely pay only one-third of the bill (Woetzel et al. 2014). In a sense, a sustainable housing provision is threatened by affordability. Articles in this section attest to a strong correlation between the overall economic well-being of a city and its housing provision. Furthermore, these articles identify economic standing and efficiency of governance to be essential to challenges and solutions.

Land and Economy

Sydney is Australia's largest city with 5.5 million people, and known for extremely high rents. A 2016 survey shows that Sydney ranks second, just after Hong Kong, in the most unaffordable housing index. One cause, Jorgensen argues, is that most people live within 12 percent of the territory where most immigrants reside. Providing affordable housing to the incoming population while balancing the needs of multiple interest groups is a complex challenge. Historically, the strategy of lowering the mortgage rate, instead of helping the lower-income group, has resulted in speculative investment. The municipality now has changed its strategy by turning to lower-density regions to develop family-size social housing and by building a transportation network for convenience in commuting. However, analysts are concerned that improved transportation infrastructure will likely cause housing prices to rise further. To resolve these complex issues, Sydney has established the Sustainable Sydney 2030 project to study various options.

In addition to supply and demand, ideological legacy could be an impediment to sustainable housing as well—Chongqing City is a good case. In China, natural resources are state-owned, and diversion of farmland for nonagricultural purposes is forbidden. Farmers and rural collective units own fixed-term "use rights" only. This situation, however, creates an ownership war: land is doubly owned by the government and the individual, despite the fact that the state has more say. With this complexity in the backdrop, Chongqing struggles to find space to build affordable housing for a population of over 30 million. Chongqing's ingenuity is in creating a market to let farmers and rural collectives trade land leases while leaving the state-mandated farmland quota unaffected. In short, the trade of a credit instrument known as *dipiao* (land ticket) serves as a bypass over the state ownership. It allows the city to acquire building zones and the individual farmer to have access to an opportunity to trade unused or the entire land (lease) for cash or for the city *hukou* (urban residential status). The system is dubbed "the Chongqing Model" and has been piloted for a decade with a potential future of national adoption.

When there is land but few jobs, the situation could be worse. Detroit, Michigan, has been associated with the auto industry since the 1920s. The story of Detroit is one of an ongoing reversal of a prolonged urban decay. Known as the "Motor City," Detroit's urban sprawl reflects a dominant form of housing—the freestanding single-family home. As the auto industry decentralized in the 1960s, the local economy declined, a great number of jobs were lost, and houses and factories were abandoned. The racial divide intensified as most black workers stayed at center-city, while white workers moved to suburbs nearer to the factories. The oil crisis of the 1970s further reduced automobile production, resulting in more unemployment. The job situation deteriorated further in the early 2000s with the bankruptcies of GM and Chrysler. In 2013, under the pressure $18 billion debt and a 16.9 percent unemployment rate, and 80,000 abandoned single-family homes, Detroit initiated the largest municipal bankruptcy in history. After emerging from bankruptcy in 2014, Detroit faces a housing crisis as tens of thousands of houses lie vacant and the urban infrastructure, including the street lighting system, fell out of functional service. Even water supply, a critical provision for people's health and the city's sanitation, falls short. While some analysts argue that Detroit has survived what many thought to be terminal, others believe it is too early yet to tell.

Governance

A city's governance plays an intrinsic part in housing provision. When the governance is creative and the corruption level is low, more solutions can be found. On the other hand, an ineffective governance can worsen the situation.

Vienna, the capital and the largest city of Austria, is regarded as one of the best cities in the world to live in. Its cultural environment and the affordable housing are primary attractions. The municipality works hard to avoid segregation whereby public housing is primarily allocated to the low-income groups. Vienna fosters economically mixed communities through the offering of public housing to people of all social strata. The practice is backed by the concept that dwellings should be made available by society to its citizens, and without being overly limited by the market mechanism. While the Austrian government protects private housing property, not many residents own their homes, due to the lack of tax incentives. Sixty percent of the city's residents reside in subsidized apartments; most residents are renters of units in multi-floored apartment buildings. A drawback appears to be that these housing benefits have a boosting effect on migration, as Polyuha indicates, and accelerated population growth leads to housing shortages.

Is there a large city in the world that is free from land and housing worries? The answer is Touba, the second-largest city of Senegal. Touba is an Islamic holy city with a population of 753,313. Touba and a neighboring community, MBacké, form an urban agglomeration with a combined population of close to 1 million. The governance is controlled by a Sufi religious order, the Murid, rather than by a municipal bureaucracy. Touba stands out in Africa as a city without shantytowns, and where inhabitants enjoy affordable housing and supply of water. Housing is allocated based on the dweller's religious tie with his sheikhs, and taking into account such factors as tuition contribution and housing needs. The dweller invests in the construction, but does not own the land on which the property is built. Water is supplied with pipes to each dwelling and free of charge. According to the spiritual order, water is a necessity of life and should be free. However, water safety is problematic, especially during the pilgrimage season when the city receives more than a million pilgrims. The absence of a sewage system and the use of open dumps are another problem that carries health consequences. Many residents consider it a religious obligation to build a dwelling in Touba. The dwellings tend to be spacious for polygamous households that are typical in Senegal. Touba's residential density stands at 42 persons per hectare or one-fifth that of the capital city of Dakar. Touba's unique housing provisions are attracting more scholarly attention today.

A most noticeable and dynamic change of the 20th and 21st centuries is communism being phased out. However, the former ideological constraints continue to impede liberalization and economic development. Reforms progress unevenly; as a result, cities with weaker economies tend to transform at a slower pace. Havana, Almaty, and Caracas are three cities where housing and infrastructure continue to suffer from neglect as they were in the communist era.

Havana is the capital of Cuba with a population of 2.2 million. Tourism is the backbone of its economy. The colonial history has left Cuba with an infrastructure that defines the city's layout. The 1959 Cuban Revolution ended private ownership and nationalized residential housing construction and distribution. Under Fidel Castro's central planning, improving people's living conditions was not a top priority. The overall built environment was poorly maintained, and new housing was built with low-quality materials and workmanship. Moreover, hurricanes and salty ocean winds cause further damage to the structures. Influx increasingly stresses the neighborhoods. Underdeveloped transportation limits the potential of developing suburbs where residential density is lower. The challenge of providing 2.2 million residents with adequate housing is tremendous. Since 2011, Cuba's market reform has made some people homeowners. The dual economy—with the coexistence of a public sector and a private sector, however, has only caused an economic divide between those who have power and those who don't, as Jorgensen indicates, with little in the way of improvement in quality of life. Additionally, the Cuban economic liberalization has not gotten a boost from the Trump administration, which has shown a renewed commitment to the embargo. Analysts suspect that the resource-dependent Cuba may be pushed to deepen economic ties with China.

Likewise, Almaty, the most populous city of Kazakhstan, struggles to break out of the communist tradition. To improve housing and infrastructure for a population of more than 17 million is by no means easy. Economically, the city produces 27 percent of the country's GDP. However, improving the housing and infrastructure, most of which was built in the Soviet era, is a challenge. Under the former government plan, families were allocated to "micro-districts." These Corbusier-style communities provide some public facilities, such as green space, and shared toilet and kitchen. However, these houses built with premade concrete panels have a tight living area. With the progression of communism from the 1950s to the 1970s, housing comfort improved, but can't match current expectation and can hardly be remodeled. According to Polyuha, the current challenge is twofold: on the one hand, a sluggish economy and low income make houses unaffordable to most people; on the other hand, conservative policy hampers housing market liberalization, barring migrants and noncitizens from purchasing homes. As a result, illegal shanty dwellings are built in suburbs, and residents are constantly threatened by eviction. The Affordable Housing 2020 plan of Almaty allegedly will bring improvement.

Caracas, the capital of Venezuela, has a population of more than 3 million. Once an energy powerhouse attracting tens of thousands of migrant workers from surrounding towns and countries, Venezuela is plagued today by a housing crisis as the oil boom fades. Slums and shantytowns are the only option for the low-income masses. During the years of oil boom under Hugo Chávez, the socialist government was able to provide welfare that sustained slums and shantytowns. As oil declined, communities living in informal dwellings found themselves in severe hardship and vulnerable to rampant crime. Caracas has climbed to the top of the most dangerous cities list. Even skyscrapers in Caracas downtown were turned into slums during the recent economic crisis. The municipality recognizes that the challenge is to transform informal settlement to affordable housing, or "dignified units," with adequate sanitation and access to social services. Experts have proposed changes in zoning regulations to facilitate affordable housing. President Maduro announced a plan of adding 5 million affordable housing units in conjunction with expanded social welfare in 2019. It is unclear how such as plan could be achieved given the economic sanctions by the United States and skyrocketing inflation.

Geo Political Impact

Globalization has created an environment where a city can be directly affected by global events. One example is Dandong, the largest border city in China's Liaoning Province with land connection to North Korea. The city has a population of 2.44 million. Since the late 1990s, Dandong's economic growth has been a function of the bilateral trade. With the agreement of a new North Korean free-trade zone of *Wihwa-Do Island* and *Hwanggumpyong Island* in 2009, a construction boom in Dandong took off. Hundreds of millions were invested by the Chinese government and private investors. The New Yalu River Bridge was built, and skyscrapers rose in the New

Town. Many saw a golden opportunity in the "one bridge, two islands" project for China's low-margin and labor-intensive manufacturing industries. Meanwhile, traders saw in North Korea a hopeful venue for China's surplus goods. Many local residents invested life's savings in real estate deals in the new town, expecting a fast track to wealth. The dream went bust, with the one bridge, two islands project scratched. The U.S.-led international embargo is believed to be the main cause. However, failures of North Korea's long-lasting but unsuccessful efforts in learning from China suggest that the infrastructure's boom and bust reveal deeper woes.

Another example of a city bearing the brunt of international tidal waves is Munich, Germany. Migration in recent years is believed to have a demographic impact on many cities in the EU. Since the Syrian civil war broke out in 2011, millions of Syrian refugees entered Europe, making Munich suddenly a major city of destination. Accommodating too many too soon is a challenge at multiple levels. Resources can be stretched thin; however, a greater challenge seems to be cultural integration. The construction in 2016 of the Munich Wall separating a Munich community from an upcoming neighborhood of refugees has been the topic of heated debate. Some denounce it as a new Berlin Wall, while others approve it as a legitimate representation of democratic rights. For most Germans, the Munich Wall may be just a small physical divider, or it may be the tip of the iceberg. Many issues have come to light in the debates, ranging from the fear of insecurity to nationalism and the right-wing anti-immigration sentiment. The future of the Munich Wall will likely provide a window into Germany's sociocultural changes.

Overall, these articles show that while housing and infrastructure constitute a main pillar to a sustainable urban life, they are also a fragile part of the urban foundation. It is obvious that housing and infrastructure can be negatively affected by climate change, poverty, affordability, availability of services, social equity, and the global situation. Houses are no longer just roofs over our heads; they represent relationships among people and between human society and the natural environment. It is only through coordinated solutions that sustainability can be achieved.

Further Reading

The Department of Economic and Social Affairs of the United Nations. 2014. *World Urbanization Prospects.* https://www.compassion.com/multimedia/world-urbanization-prospects.pdf.

Woetzel, Jonathan, Sangeeth Ram, Jan Mischke, Nicklas Garemo, and Shirish Sankhe. 2014. "Tackling the Worlds Affordable Housing Challenge." McKinsey Global Institute, October. https://www.mckinsey.com/global-themes/urbanization/tackling-the-worlds-affordable-housing-challenge.

Almaty, Kazakhstan: Housing Reform

Known as "the Southern capital" of Kazakhstan, Almaty is presently the biggest city in the republic and an important center of commerce and culture. With a population of 1,716,779 inhabitants (April 2016), Almaty is an ethnically mixed metropolis composed of almost 50 percent Kazakhs, over 30 percent Russians, and

5 percent Uyghurs. Despite the fact that the city has only about 9 percent of country's inhabitants, it contributes significantly to the economy of the region, producing approximately 27 percent of the national GDP. Unlike during the Soviet times, when the economics of the city was largely based on food, and light and heavy industries, Almaty nowadays is a modern center with substantial focus on financial markets. The city is *de facto* a financial capital of the Central Asian region, as it has headquarters and regional offices of many banks and other monetary institutions (BTA Bank, People's Bank, Kazkommertsbank, and Kaspi Bank to name just a few).

According to the Worldwide Quality of Living Survey rating published by Mercer Human Resources Consulting Company, Almaty placed 176th among 230 participating cities (2016), just slightly below St. Petersburg and Moscow, but ahead of capitals of other former Soviet republics such as Minsk, Baku, or Yerevan ("Quality of Living City Ranking" 2016). In the last decade, Kazakhstan's southern capital has noticeably improved its rating, moving up almost 10 positions. Even though geographically distant from the United States, Almaty has economic and cultural ties that reach across the ocean, cooperating through Sister Cities International with other world cities (Tucson, Arizona, for example).

Administratively, Almaty is divided into eight districts: Alatau, Almaty, Auezov, Bostandyk, Medeu, Nauryzbay, Turksib, and Zhetisu. As with most urban centers, the districts are not homogenously developed, have different cityscapes, and dissimilar levels of access to available infrastructure or services. Consequently, not all the districts enjoy the same reputation among the inhabitants, potential buyers, or developers. Southeasterly located Medeu is considered to be the most prestigious part, and Bostandyk (westerly adjacent to Medeu) is the commercial quarter. Each of the districts is managed through a borough *akimat* (council), which is, in turn, a branch of the city *akimat*.

ALMATY: HISTORY

By regional standards, Almaty is a relatively young metropolis. Founded by the Russian Cossacks in 1854 as Fort Verny (Russian for "faithful"), the locality remained scarcely populated and peripheral until the late 1920s. Only in 1927, when Soviet authorities moved the Kazakh capital there from Kyzyl-Orda, the town (which, in 1921, changed its name to Almaty) began to expand. Almaty was selected to serve as the capital primarily because of its location, conveniently sited on the Turkestan–Siberian Railway that connected Siberia with Central Asia.

Yet it was also the very location that initially prevented Almaty from intense growth. Situated in a seismologically unstable region and bordered by the Tian Shan mountains, which constantly threatened the southern side of the town with mudflows, the new capital had to overcome many obstacles on its way to metropolis. Thus, after the devastating earthquake of 1887, construction of stone and brick houses was banned, and only wood and cane structures were allowed. Literally, geography forced the new capital to keep a low profile.

From the 1930s until 1960, mostly two- or three-story buildings were erected. During that time, the center of the city was formed in the rectangle between Gogol

Street, Dostyk Avenue, Kabanday Batyr Street, and Nauryzbay Batyr Street. Between the 1930s and 1950s, numerous administrative, cultural, and commercial buildings were designed (Government House, House of Academy of Sciences, Central Stadium, Central Universal Store, etc.).

Following the vision of an ideal communist city, Soviet architects and engineers developed projects that would emphasize collectivism, ergonomics, and blissful coexistence of man and the natural environment. To achieve that vision, planners advanced the concepts of micro-districts for areas as well as multi-family apartments for buildings. According to the definition, a micro-district was "a municipal area with the comprehensive complex of public and cultural amenities. It [did] not have highways. But it [had] much green spaces and flowers, stores, a school, kindergartens, sports facilities, and swimming pools. Everything [was] in close proximity to the residential buildings" (Sokolova 2014). Every city had several such micro-districts, connected by broad avenues. Parks inside the micro-districts were called to provide idyllic oases amidst the fast-paced urban life.

Even though the micro-districts became the visiting card of the Soviet Union, they in fact were first designed in France by famous Swiss-French architect Charles-Édouard Jeanneret (more known as Le Corbusier). Le Corbusier cherished the idea of the Radiant City (la Ville Radieuse), which he poetically described in the following way: "The radiant city, inspired by physical and human laws, proposes to bring machine age man *essential pleasures*" (Guiton 1981, 104).

In the 1930s, he visited the Soviet Union, attracting enormous public interest. It is not surprising, therefore, that his ideas, which corresponded to communist ideals, were readily adopted.

In the micro-districts, all the buildings were similar. A house was supposed to be an industrial product, not a piece of art. The social-realist architects were thus fascinated with concepts of buildings that featured straight lines and angles, simplicity, a utilitarian approach, and low cost. Taking Le Corbusier's ideas further, Soviet engineers designed the type of buildings that could be constructed with prefabricated concrete panels. The first buildings of such type were made during Stalin's era (they became known as "stalinka"), then during Nikita Khrushchev's years ("khrushchevka"), and, finally, under Leonid Brezhnev ("brezhnevka"). Five-storied khrushchevkas were (and still remain) the most widespread and most recognized.

For economy reasons, the first residential block buildings did not have elevators, balconies, or basements. Ceilings were relatively low (8.5 feet, i.e., almost 8 inches lower than the previous norm); kitchens, toilets, and bathrooms were shared; and rooms were small. It is interesting to note that, in accordance with early standards, shared kitchen space was deemed to be unnecessary—while living in communes, Soviet people were expected to eat in collective dining rooms located outside of residential buildings. Yet, after Leon Trotsky (who was one of the main proponents of the idea of the "kitchenless" houses) was exiled, that standard was abandoned. Until 2011, however, there was a small housing complex in Almaty called "the skew houses" (for some unknown reason—some say due to seismic considerations—the houses were put not parallel to the street, but at an angle) that did not have kitchens.

Five-storied khrushchevkas, made with prefabricated panels, were normally constructed within 15 days and were ready for the dwellers within approximately 1.5 months or even less. Yet, because of the desire to achieve the lowest cost possible, these buildings had many noticeable problems, especially with insulation and soundproofing. While insulation was considered to be less of a problem (heating was central and heating costs were negligible), complete absence of privacy was a cause of many domestic arguments. In Almaty, the first buildings used cane as insulation material, and, interestingly enough, there are currently still several structures with this insulation type.

In the late 1950s, the size of newly constructed houses was further reduced, and the emphasis was put on the most rational usage of space. According to the Soviet Project Office's calculations, an average person needed about 16 inches between the wall and the kitchen table to be able to sit down. Thus, the kitchens became smaller. Under the kitchen window, a closet was designed to serve as a natural fridge. Staircases became narrower (according to some, they were expected to be just big enough to carry a casket with a deceased person), and bathrooms were combined with toilets. People jokingly observed that Khrushchev combined everything—roofs with attics, villages with cities, and bathrooms with toilets—and speculated that his next project would likely be a combination of water supply pipes with sewage pipes.

Khrushchevkas were erected most intensively after 1957, when the Almaty Concrete Plant was launched, and prefabricated concrete blocks became available in close proximity to the construction sites. As the city's population grew, the demand for housing increased, and Soviet architect Vitaly Lagutenko successfully developed a concept of stable nine-story buildings. In Almaty, given the region's seismic activity, the first buildings of that type were tested by conducting controlled explosions in the vicinity.

In the 1960s, the city expanded mainly westward, and many of its famous apple orchards fell victim to the construction boom. New micro-districts were created in record time. Numbered chronologically (i.e., in the order they were constructed), the buildings within those micro-districts are nowadays a source of confusion for a casual observer, as building number 48 can be next to building number 11. Even though there are presently 12 districts in Almaty, many inhabitants also described a 13th district located outside of Kazakhstan. According to the city history, in 1967, builders from the Kazakhstan capital were invited to Cuba, and, in Santiago de Cuba, they erected a micro-district that Cubans nowadays call "Almaty."

In 1967, khrushchevka projects were replaced with brezhnevkas, more modern multistoried building types that featured balconies, separate bathrooms and toilets, bigger kitchens, and a chute. Nowadays, khrushchevkas along with brezhnevkas constitute the largest portion of Almaty's housing stock.

CURRENT SITUATION: DEMAND

Almaty's level of housing demand is somewhat difficult to estimate. Low density and low income are two factors that make such an assessment challenging. Generally, Kazakhstan is one of the least densely populated countries (15 people per square mile), and, although the situation in Almaty differs from the rest of the country, the city mostly satisfies the needs of its long-term permanent inhabitants. From 500,000 to 1 million newcomers and foreign workers (mostly from China) are in a disadvantageous position largely due to peculiarities of the national law (for more information, please see the section on housing policies).

Young people frequently do not have enough financial resources to purchase an apartment. With an average monthly salary of approximately $500, average housing price of $1,750 per square meter, and virtual absence of low-interest bank credits, it is very hard to save enough to secure the purchase. It is also not surprising, consequently, that the current house market is dominated by "swappers"—people who look for an opportunity to upsize their apartments (e.g., to exchange a two-bedroom apartment for a three-bedroom apartment).

In addition, inflation rates have recently been relatively high, which discourages activity in the housing market. Even though the government creates policies that make low-interest credits more available and prices for properties have decreased, Almaty's situation can nowadays be characterized as buyer- and tenant-oriented, meaning that sellers and property owners have to be more flexible and willing to discuss options in order to attract buyers and tenants to their properties. However, according to real estate experts, the housing demand is likely to increase by 2019 (Kuchma 2016).

CURRENT SITUATION: SUPPLY

Given the relatively low demand, volatility of national currency, and buyer-oriented market, construction and real estate businesses are regarded as one of the riskiest investments. The government of Kazakhstan did much to attract foreign capital to the building sector, but the companies are still very cautious. Without governmental support, it would, therefore, be difficult to revive the housing market. That is why in 2012, a residential construction program, Affordable Housing—2020, was launched.

The program aims at a gradual increase in the volume of construction, so that by 2020, it can be at the level of 10 million square meters per year. According to housing market analysts from Scot Holland Professional Services, Affordable Housing—2020s focuses on three main areas:

- construction of affordable housing by local authorities using the residential savings system,
- allocation of funds to second-tier banks for the subsequent financing of construction and mortgage lending,
- construction of utility infrastructure.

In addition, one of the goals of the State Program for the Development of Residential Construction in the Republic of Kazakhstan is to increase the affordability of housing for wider public through a better development of housing saving system. In particular, this program stipulates that JSC "Housing Construction Saving Bank" ("Zhilstroysberbank") will grant loans to the special-priority groups of the population at an interest rate as low as 4% per annum. (Scot Holland Professional Services 2015)

It is expected that this program will greatly stimulate both supply and demand, since the potential buyers are not only given an opportunity of obtaining low-interest credits, they are also provided with the lease-with-subsequent-buyout option.

Some results of the program are palpable even now. During the period from January to September 2016, almost 1 million additional square meters were added to the housing market, a 1.3 percent increase compared to the same period of 2015.

HOUSING POLICIES

Property rights represent an area of concern in Kazakhstan. According to the Property Rights Index, Kazakhstan has scored 30, which means that "property ownership is weakly protected. The court system is highly inefficient. Corruption is extensive, and the judiciary is strongly influenced by other branches of government. Expropriation, which is considered intrusion in private rights in many places of the world, is possible" ("Property Rights" 2019). Indeed, there are many problems in the realm of housing policies. Even though the Constitution of the Republic guarantees housing for all its citizens, the details are not elaborated, and the quality of homes is not assured. Standards for newly constructed buildings are outdated, the quality of construction materials is questionable, and the old Soviet-style buildings are frequently decrepit.

The situation is especially worrisome when it comes to noncitizens and poor people. Many migrant workers, who come to Kazakhstan in search of a better life and higher income, cannot legally purchase houses and do not have the right to reside in social housing. According to the Housing Relations Act of 1997, only citizens have such privileges. Migrants as well as poor people also often cannot afford to rent decent apartments and are essentially forced to live in the outskirts of the city in informal dwellings lacking basic amenities, such as toilets or running water. The municipal authorities consider those dwellings illegal, and the inhabitants live under constant threat of eviction. In fact, in 2006, more than 100 houses were demolished in Shanyrak on the outskirts of Almaty. As expected, the population resisted the demolition—several people were killed, and more than 100 were arrested. At the same time, the law does little to protect people who have lost their homes. In fact, current laws in the Republic of Kazakhstan do not even contain a definition for "homeless person" (Rolnik 2011, 18).

Yet it would be unfair to say that the government does not look for solutions. Slowly but steadily, the housing situation is getting better, and, if the current trends continue, within several years, Almaty will greatly improve its image, becoming one of the most attractive cities in the region.

Mykola Polyuha

See also: Housing and Infrastructure: Havana, Cuba: Facing Challenges of Housing and Infrastructure in Economic Transition; *Pollution:* Baku, Azerbaijan: A Tainted Reputation

Further Reading

Aubakirov, Erik. (2013). "Residents of 'Khrushchevkas' Had Their Night Pots with Handles Inward" (in Russian). *Express-K* 29. Accessed November 23, 2016. http://old.express-k.kz/show_article.php?art_id=79192.

Azhiev, Adil and Adilzhan Psiaev. (2016). "Microdistrics" (Микрорайоны) (in Russian). Vlast: Internet Zhurnal so Svoim Mneniem. Accessed November 23, 2016. https://vlast.kz/gorod/18589-mikrorajony.html.

Boyko, Boris. 2004. "Urban Planning of Almaty on the Threshold of Its 150-Year Anniversary" (in Russian). *Kumbez* 3–4. http://vernoye-almaty.kz/others/grados.shtml.

Galat, Irina. 2016. "Kazakhstan Real Estate Market: Nerves Pass" (in Russian). *Vlast: Internet Zhurnal so Svoim Mneniem.* https://vlast.kz/jekonomika/19102-rynok-nedvizimosti-kazahstana-nervy-sdaut.html.

Guiton, Jacques, ed. 1981. *The Ideas of Le Corbusier on Architecture and Urban Planning.* New York: G. Braziller.

Kuchma, Viktoria. 2016. "Experts: The Housing Market in Almaty Has Become Inadequate" (in Russian). *Kapital.* https://kapital.kz/economic/47241/eksperty-rynok-zhilya-v-almaty-stal-neadekvatnym.html.

Nazarov, Alois. 2013. "'Skewed Houses' in Almaty" (in Russian). http://alnaz.ru/almaty/kosye-doma.html.

"Property Rights." 2019. *2019 Index of Economic Freedom.* The Heritage Foundation. http://www.heritage.org/index/property-rights

"Quality of Living City Ranking." 2016. https://www.imercer.com/content/mobility/quality-of-living-city-rankings.html.

Rolnik, Raquel. 2011. *Report of the Special Rapporteur on Adequate Housing as a Component of the Right to an Adequate Standard of Living, and on the Right to Non-discrimination in This Context. Mission to Kazakhstan.* United Nations General Assembly: Human Rights Council. http://www2.ohchr.org/english/bodies/hrcouncil/docs/16session/A-HRC-16-42-Add3.pdf.

Scot Holland Professional Services. 2015. "Residential Market Overview: Almaty." http://cbre.kz/news/residential-market-overview-almaty.html?lang=en.

Sokolova, Tatiana. 2014. "How Almaty Micro-districts Were Built (Notes of Local Historian . . .)" (in Russian). *Komsomolskaya Pravda: Kazakhstan.* http://www.kp.kz/1148.

Caracas, Venezuela: Will Informal Settlement Be Forever?

Caracas, the capital of Venezuela, is a historical city founded in 1567. Located in the north-central part of the country and home to 3.2 million people, or about 10 percent of Venezuela's population today, Caracas is one of the most populous cities in Latin America. Its environment features the mountain range of El Avila offering stunning natural beauty, the rich downtown nightlife, and historical sites that visitors can't pass up. Caracas was little known until 1914 when oil was discovered in the Maracaibo Basin. The oil boom started in the 1970s and lasted until the early 2000s, attracting millions of migrant workers. During this time, the Caracas Valley became the cultural and economic center of Venezuela, and was gradually encircled by densely populated slums and shantytowns.

While easy oil money made Caracas one of the most modern cities in Latin America in a short period of time, tragically, the sudden bear market of oil brought down the city's economy much faster. When the global financial crisis hit in 2008, Venezuela found itself devastated by poverty, high inflation, and political turmoil. Slums deteriorated, as President Hugo Chávez's welfare money dried up, and even high-rises in downtown business districts were turned into slums. The murder rate rose and deterred tourists. People living in slums who had been beneficiaries of social welfare saw their income diminished. They had supported former president Chávez (1999–2013); now they rose up to protest against his successor, current president Nicolas Maduro Moros, who vowed to continue Chávez's policies. Housing and infrastructure that used to be at the core of the state-managed social welfare have become a hotbed of unrest today.

ECONOMY

Venezuela holds the world's largest supply of crude oil, which made it the energy powerhouse of South America. The country could rely on oil alone to provide a comfortable living for its citizens, or so it seemed. Venezuela turned to socialism with the election of Hugo Chávez as president in the late 1990s. A populist leader, Chávez relied on Russia, China, and Cuba for guidance and support, and took a hostile stance toward the United States. Implementing a socialist system, Chávez was mandated to create and approve laws, and run the economy however he wanted. A grave mistake he made was to let the economy depend excessively on oil trade to the detriment of other sectors. The policy of nationalizing farmlands and neglecting agriculture is a glaring example. By controlling the price of goods, Chávez amassed political power as well as the ballots of the masses, whom he made dependent on his socialist welfare. Power engendered corruption—there was no shortage of administrative officials accepting millions in bribes. However, during the Chávez administration, poverty fell from 50 percent in 1999 to about 27 percent in 2011 (CIA 2018), school enrollment went up, child mortality rate fell, and health care and sanitation were improved, thanks to oil revenues.

World experience shows that the "Dutch disease," an economic phenomenon involving the sharp inflow of foreign currency as a result of excessive dependence on a single resource, also known as "resource curse," tends to negatively impact the economy in the long run. It typically makes the economy vulnerable when the market falls, and there is no alternative capacity to make up for the loss. In the short term, politicians may find reliance on natural resources such as oil and gas a convenient tool to strengthen their control. This has been proven true once again by Venezuela's experience: oil earnings that provided 95 percent of the country's foreign exchange earnings (*Economist* 2016) allowed Chávez to strengthen his political control, crack down on private businesses, and suppress opponents' influence. Since 1999, nearly 2 million people, mostly upper and middle class, have left Venezuela. The brain drain slowed down the economic recovery tremendously (Gillespie 2017).

In 2008, the world oil price reached $147 per barrel. The global financial crisis and an oversupply of oil led to a precipitous price drop. By 2016, the price dipped to as low as $26 per barrel, or less than 20 percent of the 2008 level. As a result, the Venezuelan economy collapsed. Despite a recovery to $50 per barrel by 2017, the earnings were not sufficient for Venezuela to fund its welfare provisions and pay off debt owed to Chinese and Russian investors. American drilling companies operating in Venezuela refused to pump more oil until their invoices were paid.

There was a concern that a debt downgrade by international assessment firms would further raise the cost of borrowing. As such, President Maduro chose to pay back debt to Chinese, Russian, and other foreign investors rather than using the cash, a meager sum of US$9 billion, to buy food and medicine from abroad and alleviate a domestic crisis. As a result of a shortage of food, medicine, and items necessary for daily living, inflation skyrocketed, resulting in a humanitarian crisis. Venezuela's money became worthless due to hyperinflation by summer 2017. Back in 2013, $20 could still buy 629 bolivars; in 2017, $20 was worth 195,755 bolivars (Gillespie and Zamora 2017). To quell the unrest, Maduro raised the minimum salary three times, but such measures could hardly catch up with inflation. In July 2017, the Maduro government held a constituent assembly vote to allow the president to amend the constitution and concentrate more power in his hands. The voting results, although in favor of the president, were suspected by the protesters of having been rigged and were questioned by Western media.

UNSAFE NEIGHBORHOODS

Economic distress, government corruption, and a weak justice system made Caracas the number one most violent city in the world. There were 130 homicides per 100,000 in Caracas in 2016 (World Facts 2017). According to Mexico's Citizens Council for Public Safety, of the 50 most violent cities in the world, 43 are in Latin America and 7 in Venezuela (Woody 2017). Unsurprisingly, most homicides happened in the poorest neighborhoods. Reportedly, a typical scenario in which people are attacked is when they wait in long lines carrying a lot of money, they become targets of robbery. Weak law enforcement in slum neighborhoods allows murderers to go unpunished. Drug trafficking and gang-related killings are higher in urban zones, where law enforcement is paralyzed. Also, the country's prison system has failed: the 30 prison facilities throughout the country house 45,000 inmates, while their capacity is only one-third of that number. In some cases, the government pays armed gangs to help run prisons (Anderson 2013).

INFORMAL SETTLEMENTS

One of the first things visitors see in Caracas is the city's informal settlements which primarily consist of slums sprawling over a vast area. The best known would be the Tower of David, a 45-story skyscraper in the center of Caracas built by a private banker to glorify the country's oil boom. Named after the oil investor David Brillembourg, the tower was intended to be an office building for world-class companies. However, construction was halted when Brillembourg died in 1993, and has never been resumed. The 1994 banking crisis in Venezuela wiped out much of the country's banking sector. Squatters moved in around 2007, turning the tower into the world's tallest slum. The leaders of the first group of residents soon began selling access to latecomers. After all, the tower was more livable than the hillside slums, despite the fact that gangsters, thugs, murderers, and kidnappers found home in the tower as well (Anderson 2013).

Over the years, the tower's resident population increased, as the local community gradually stabilized. A management system was instituted, and the government provided utilities at subsidized prices. To use electricity, for example, residents no longer needed to steal from the grid. Today, the tower is home to between 2,000 and 3,000 residents. A BBC video about life in the tower can be seen on Youtube (BBC Newsnight 2014). The Tower of David is not the only high-rise turned slum; hundreds of buildings in Caracas downtown were invaded during the prolonged economic downturn. In 2011, Chávez extended an "invitation" to the homeless in his revolutionary rhetoric: "I invite people. Look for your own *galpones* (abandoned warehouses). Look for your own *galpones* and tell me where it is. Everyone should go find a *galpone*. Let's go get us a *galpone*! There are a thousand, two thousand abandoned *galpones* in Caracas. Let's go for them! Chávez will expropriate them and put them at the service of the people" (Anderson 2013).

Most of Caracas's slums are constructed on hillsides using rudimentary building materials. Most of the dwellings are under 3 stories, although some reach 10 stories high. Some old neighborhoods date back to the 1950s, built by rural migrant workers. In some cases, the municipal government provided subsidies. For example, "23 *de Enero*" was one of the projects the government built to provide affordable housing. It was soon extended by self-built dwellings that formed *barrios* (neighborhoods) expanding into adjacent hillsides. From the perspective of urbanization in its natural form, the *barrios* offer a good example of how informal urban settlements develop in economic, cultural, and socioeconomic contexts. A prominent characteristic is that the expansion follows no planning, design, or zoning guidance. They reflect individual creativity, adaptability, neighborhood coordination, and the pressure of densification (Gouverneur 2015).

During the oil boom years, the Venezuelan government spent some of the profits to improve the *barrios'* living conditions. However, from the 1990s to the early 2000s, an influx of migrants made the *barrios'* densification worse, and Chávez's socialist revolution was one of the causes. The widening economic gap, lack of police to protect people's safety, worsening hygiene conditions, and drug trafficking made life miserable. However, the population demonstrated support for Chávista programs, seeing no better choice.

One of the welfare programs Chávez launched in the early 2000s was *Barrio adentro* ("inside the neighborhood"). It is a system of neighborhood clinics providing free health care to the residents in the slums. The clinics covered basic primary care and dental care. After their launch in Caracas, similar programs sprang up across Venezuela. There were rumors of building full-fledged hospitals with Chinese and Cuban support. Indeed, training programs were set up by Cuban medical personnel to train Venezuelan medical students. For the Cubans, analysts believe, supporting Venezuela was a viable venue to access world markets. Despite the grandeur of political rhetoric about "serving the people," *Barrio adentro* disappointed. It failed to provide procedures to help patients with simple symptoms. Many believe that *Barrio adentro* was a fraud by the national treasury, which sustained a budget equivalent to 9 percent of the 2004 GDP and an investment of $6.36 billion by the state oil company PDVSA from 2003 to 2011. Due to its failure, 14,000 Cuban medical staff returned home, existing hospitals ran short of funds, and the staff of *Barrio adentro* clinics eventually quit to open private services (Mahjar-Barducci 2011).

SOLUTIONS

Challenges faced by the Caracas municipal government are complex. However, there is no question that problems in housing infrastructure need urgent action. Sprawling slums brew social unrest, and taint the image of Venezuelan socialism. In fact, during Chávez's term, efforts were already being made to address these problems. Two solutions were proposed: 1) improve existing *barrios* by strengthening housing structure and preventing overbuilding; and 2) construct tens of thousands of new low-cost "dignified units" in a short period of time on vacant tracts of land outside the capital city. The latter proposal was favored by the government, given that it appeared to promise a better political payoff. The outcome proved, however, that it was unachievable for two reasons: 1) the investment was too high, and the number of houses actually built was too low, in fact, even lower than the period of 1960s–70s; and 2) new housing units are unaffordable for a great number of poor people who can't afford the down payment. Urban designers have since proposed a third and more holistic plan aimed at advancing both solutions on the same time (Gouverneur 2015). As of this writing, the Maduro government's strategy appears to be building more public housing units—the goal being "at least 5 million homes"—and expanding social welfare to cover more families (TeleSUR English 2019). Whether continuing with offering socialist welfare solutions will improve the Venezuelan economy and Caracas's housing crisis remains to be seen.

Jing Luo

See also: Employment and Jobs: Riyadh, Saudi Arabia: Creating Jobs in the Post–Oil-Boom Era; *Housing and Infrastructure:* Havana, Cuba: Facing Challenges of Housing and Infrastructure in Economic Transition; *Migration and Demographic Changes:* Lima, Peru: Migration and Demographic Changes Driven by Climate Changes

Further Reading

Anderson, Jon Lee. 2013. "Slumlord—What Has Hugo Chávez Wrought in Venezuela?" *New Yorker.* http://www.newyorker.com/magazine/2013/01/28/slumlord.

BBC Newsnight. 2014. "The Tower of David: Venezuela's Vertical Slum—Newsnight." https://www.youtube.com/watch?v=4ZrCzgprPT8&feature=youtube.

Cawthorne, Andre, and Jorge Silva. 2014. "Venezuela's Skyscraper Slum Provides Haven for Poor." Reuters, April 2. http://www.reuters.com/article/us-venezuela-slum-idUSBREA310NU20140402.

CIA. 2018. "The World Factbook: South America: Venezuela." *The CIA World Factbook.* https://www.cia.gov/library/publications/the-world-factbook/geos/print_ve.html.

Clavel, Tristan. 2017. "Latin America Again Dominates World's 50 Deadliest Cities Ranking." *Insight Crime*, April 7. http://www.insightcrime.org/news-briefs/latin-america-dominates-world-50-deadliest-cities.

ComentYT. 2016. "Los Lugares Mas Horribles Del Mundo: Petare." *Youtube.com.* https://www.youtube.com/watch?v=9H8V0aNF7gs.

Fisher, Max, and Amanda Taub. 2017. "How Venezuela Stumbled to the Brink of Collapse." *New York Times*, May 14. https://www.nytimes.com/2017/05/14/world/americas/venezuela-collapse-analysis-interpreter.html.

Gillespie, Patrick. 2017. *CNN Money.* "Venezuela Brain Drain: I Miss Mom, but Don't Want to Go Back." CNN, April 4. http://money.cnn.com/2017/04/04/news/economy/venezuela-crisis-brain-drain/index.html?iid=EL.

Gillespie, Patrick, and Rhonny Zamora. 2017. *CNN Money.* "Venezuela's Hyperinflation Is Jaw-Dropping. See for Yourself." CNN, August 3. https://money.cnn.com/2017/07/28/news/economy/venezuela-cash-crisis/index.html.

Gouverneur, David. 2015. *Planning and Design for Future Informal Settlements—Shaping the Self-Constructed City.* London: Routledge.

Mahjar-Barducci, Anna. 2011. "The Failure of Chavez's Socialist Health Care." https://www.gatestoneinstitute.org/2371/chavez-socialist-health-care.

Mallett-Outtrim, Ryan. 2018. "New Venezuelan Welfare Scheme to Benefit 4 Million Homes." *VenezuelanAnalysis.com.* https://venezuelanalysis.com/news/13605.

Shuford, Charmaine. 2015. "More People More Slum: Venezuela's Struggle with Urbanization." *International Affairs Review,* Spring. University of San Francisco. https://www.usfca.edu/journal/international-affairs-review/spring-2015/venezuelas-struggle-with-urbanization.

Staff Writer. "Venezuela: A Nation in a State." 2016. *Economist.* http://proxy-bloomu.klnpa.org/login?url=https://search.proquest.com/docview/1766984440?accountid=26459.

TeleSUR English. 2019. "Venezuelan Housing Mission Passes 'Milestone' with 2.5M Homes." January 2. *Venezuelan Analysis.* https://venezuelanalysis.com/news/14198.

Woody, Christopher. 2017. "The 50 Most Violent Cities in the World." *Business Insider,* April 8. http://www.businessinsider.com/most-violent-cities-in-the-world-2017-4/#50-durban-south-africa-had-3443-homicides-per-100000-residents-1.

The World Bank. 2017. "Venezuela: Overview." http://www.worldbank.org/en/country/venezuela/overview#1.

World Facts. 2017 (last modified). "Most Dangerous Cities in the World." http://www.worldatlas.com/articles/most-dangerous-cities-in-the-world.html.

Chongqing, China: Chongqing's Ingenuity in Providing Public Housing for a City of 33 Million

Located in the Midwest of China, Chongqing is a sprawling city built on a mountainous terrain. The total area is estimated to be 31,700 square miles (Kuo et al. 2018), just slightly smaller than that of South Carolina. Chongqing's population is 33.7 million (CSB 2017), of which 30 million are permanent residents, which ranks Chongqing the second most populous city in the world, after Tokyo. It should be understood, however, that Chongqing is a provincial-level city; its urbanized space is only 60.9 percent. However, compared to just 20 years ago, the urbanized area has doubled in size (Wu 2016). What has contributed to the economic growth has been the government's policy of developing the western regions. The construction of the Three Gorges Dam and development of local tourism are two of the factors that have boosted Chongqing's GDP to within the top 10 in China.

The challenge is obvious: the pressure of influx is a fundamental challenge. Millions of migrants and low-income families struggle with increasing rental costs; continuing market reform drives more state-owned factories into bankruptcy, leading to more layoffs and early retirement; insufficient health care and education for children add to the expanding budget. As China's economic growth slows down, the government is hoping that improvement in public housing could offer an avenue to revive the economy. Moreover, improving public welfare for the low-income group and providing more opportunities for them to join the middle class are seen as necessary to prevent social unrest. An angry resident says, "If they (young people) work in a factory now, they need to work for 100 years to buy a house" (Coonan 2016).

While providing affordable housing is an urgent need, the complexity of housing regulations does not make solutions easy to find. Typically, the provision of affordable housing involves government intervention and the market mechanism. What the government can do to help is to create a favorable tax structure and financing guarantees. This environment will encourage private developers to be willing to bid on and engage in construction with confidence. However, government-backing is nonexistent in Chongqing. Since China's 1998 housing reform that made housing virtually a commodity, the government has given up its monopoly in housing provision. The government does have control over housing subsidies, particularly to help employees of state-owned enterprises. The problem is that government policies tend to be arbitrary and deficient in many ways. One example is the appearance of a sizable "sandwich population" whose incomes are not high enough to purchase subsidized housing, nor low enough to qualify for low-rent housing. This group therefore find themselves excluded from housing support (Ying et al. 2013). Chongqing's former mayor, Bo Xilai, was known to proactively address the public housing dilemma through a plan called the Chongqing Model (*Economist* 2016). Despite Bo being ousted due to corruption, the Chongqing Model made Bo a most popular political figure of Chinese new left-wing politics.

THE "CHONGQING MODEL"

Essentially, the Chongqing Model aims at experimenting with ways to provide public rental housing (PRH) by making available rental properties that also carry an option for purchase. The plan is projected to develop 40 million square meters of rental property by 2020 for people who earn less than 1,500 yuan, or $230 per month. Additionally, the city also planned to provide *hukou* (urban residential status) to 10 million migrants, a major percentage of the tenants, with benefits such as health care and education (*Economist* 2016). To do this, the municipality needed to resolve barriers in land acquisition and raising funds.

LAND

To understand Chongqing's land solution, a revisit to the land tenure history can be helpful. From 1958 to 1979, China's rural population were organized into what's known as *People's Communes*. During this period, land belonged to the collectives; individuals had no land ownership nor usage rights. Individual peasants could only work on the collective land as members of "production teams." Their daily labor was recorded in "work credit points" convertible to cash payment. To the detriment of the rural population, the state collected most of the crop yield and paid the peasants with meager rations. By doing so, the state was able to allocate the majority of resources to the industrial sector, particularly, the "heavy industry" that produces machinery and weaponry. Parallel to this policy, the government put in place a migration control system—the *hukou system* (residential status) that tied residents to their birthplaces. People with rural *hukou* were not permitted to settle down and work in cities. This socioeconomic framework finally started to crumble in the early 1980s at the onset of Deng Xiaoping's economic reform. The *People's Communes* were disbanded, replaced with a contractual responsibility system whereby peasants were given a land lease on plots of farmland. These plots were allocated in proportion to the headcount in a household. Peasants were now allowed to retain surplus grains after the state collected its share. This policy, also known as the "household responsibility system," was a reversal of the legacy of state monopoly, and, as a result, China's agricultural production skyrocketed. The Sichuan Province became the nation's "rice bowl" in less than a decade. A by-product of this policy was also born: millions of peasants became surplus laborers and were on the lookout for urban jobs. But a troubling by-product, from the perspective of the state, is that rural residents today have claim to the use-right of a plot they are unwilling to give up for nothing (to be explained further).

Economic liberalization in urban cities led to a construction boom in the early 1990s. Urbanization and availability of surplus rural labor created China's unprecedented scale of in-migration. As a result, the city's *hukou* system was loosened—while rural people were not even allowed to stay overnight in cities in the 1970s, now they could stay for the long term. Today, the *hukou* system is only loosely implemented in first-line cities in the area of benefits provision, such as schools and health care. Selection of school districts, for example, is a priority of *hukou* holders. However, in most cases, money can buy most welfare services that are provided free to *hukou* holders. That said, basic urban welfare and rights are important to the majority of migrants, and can be critical to the newly arriving migrants.

The economic liberalization, however, also generated a new obstacle that cities must overcome to expand—the *double ownership* of rural land. More specifically, by the land law of China, the farmland is a state property. Thanks to the reform, the individual families or collectives (e.g., villages) also own the land through control of the usage rights or "land lease." Those rights, today, are worth a lot of money, so much that the holders are not willing to easily part with them. Additionally, to guarantee the nation's food supply, the law stipulates that farmland must not be diverted to nonfarming purposes. In summary, for the local government and urban developers to seek land for building rental spaces, there must be a new policy that would make land sales allowable.

Chongqing's solution is to let rural people trade their land rights, more specifically their rights to the portion of the land that is unused for farming purposes, such as abandoned home base, obsolete space occupied by village industries, and so on. The urban developer will buy this lease and return an equitable piece of land back to farming conditions, in exchange for the right to a space to build in the outskirt. This exchange allows the total balance of farmland space to be sustained at the provincial account. It also bypasses the land sale taboo, thanks to the swap of leases. The seller does not have to be the one that owns a piece of land in the urbanization path; his/her land can be anywhere in a faraway village. In other words, it is the land quota that the developer is interested in acquiring and the rural family in selling.

The trade is in the form of auction of a "land ticket," or *dipiao*. The *dipiao* is bid on in the open market; the vendor retains 85 percent of the proceeds, and 15 percent goes to the village collective where the vendor resides. The developer/buyer must pay the costs to restore farming conditions to the underlying farmland. The seller may choose to continue to till the land he or she sold, or to migrate to the city to acquire the urban *hukou* and find a salary-based job. Between 2008 and 2011, the trading of *dipiao* rose from 0 to over 3,500 hectares in 2011 at its peak. Since 2014, the quantity has leveled out at around 1,300 hectares per year, worth roughly 4 billion yuan (*Economist* 2016).

Apartment buildings and skyscrapers in Chongqing City, China, 2012. The city struggles to provide affordable housing given its large population and limited space. (Pytyczech/Dreamstime.com)

The *dipiao* system is praised as a breakthrough in China's property ownership system in a way both the Party and the private seller could accept, according to observers. On the one hand, it allows the city to encroach into rural areas without reducing the total farmland balance; on the other hand, it allows rural people to make a profit and use the money to either live a better life locally or join the urban middle class by switching to the Chongqing *hukou*. In fact, the Chongqing municipality incentivizes rural people with subsidized housing and other benefits to give up their land assets in exchange for Chongqing *hukou* (Zhou and Ronald 2017). *Dipiao* sellers who have cash in hand are reportedly particularly welcome. According to Chongqing media, *dipiao* opens up an avenue to allow the city to give back some of its profits to remote regions. A Chongqing farmer says, "In the past, farmland was dead property, now, one *mu* (.1647 acre) of land brings in 140,000 yuan." Another says, "In my village, there are more than 700 sets of dwellings that have not been lived in for years, out of which 240 are in hazardous conditions. Most folks find it a nice option to make money on these properties through *dipiao* trading" (Qiu 2016). According to Mayor Huang Qifan, it is a proven trend in other countries that as rural population migrate to cities, more land becomes available, due to the fact that rural dwellings tend to be sparsely located, and hence less efficient than urban housing. He believes that the reason this did not happen in China is that the law permits rural families to keep their land and dwelling even after they have moved to the city. The property couldn't be sold and bought, since the tenants are only leaseholders; now it can (Jia 2015).

However, many migrant families hold onto their land documents, so that if it doesn't work out in the city, they'll have a place to call home. This did happen in 2008 when the global financial crisis shut down China's export businesses in the east coast. Laid-off migrant workers returned to farmlands in droves (Branigan 2009). To those who are reluctant, Chongqing offers a further concession—the new rule says that those who switch to city *hukou* will enjoy a three-year grace period during which they may continue to hold onto rural property, and if it doesn't work out in the city, they can go back to their roots (Xu 2010).

A BREAKTHROUGH IN FINANCING?

The 1997 Asian financial crisis sent tidal waves to the Chinese economy. In 1998, China's housing reform put an end to the government-monopolized housing provision system. However, the reform brought more confusion than balance in the public housing area (Hui 2009). The public housing provision is intrinsically a welfare cause, which is different from high-profit projects such as hotels, resorts, office buildings, and shopping malls. As a result, the government plays a main role. The Chinese social environment, however, is more complex: unlike in many Western countries where the government guarantees bank loans to public housing projects, Chinese developers receive no government guarantee; they have to mortgage their own assets of houses and land stock as collateral for bank loans to fund construction. Hence, developers run a high risk. Chongqing's municipal government, however, took a particular interest in helping developers to get loans. The Chongqing Model made noticeable achievements by creating a financial mechanism called finance and construction enterprises (FCEs). These FCEs are intermediaries between the local government and private developers. They receive loans and land from the local government and national banks. Their expenses are covered up to 70 percent by bank loans, 20 percent by the municipality, and 10 percent by state funding (Zhou and Ronald 2017). The interesting part is, the FCEs are not the traditional "state-owned" units, nor are they private enterprises. Their funding is guaranteed by the powerful local government, which is even willing to encourage mortgage banks to provide favorable rates; and they are permitted to build profitable commercial properties around the public rental housing. Additionally, since the rental properties can be purchased by the tenants after five years of rental, the FCEs stand to make more than enough to cover construction costs (Zhou and Ronald 2017).

Some believe that Chongqing's FCEs received exceptionally strong backing from Bo Xilai, the city's powerful Communist Party secretary from 2007 to 2012. Bo, a politician known for fighting corruption and his phenomenal push to revive the red culture of the Mao era, is believed to have intended to use public housing programs to rally support from the masses of Chongqing to further his political advancement

(Zhou and Ronald 2017). At a time when the widening gap fueled increasing protests in Chongqing, Bo's Chongqing Model was welcomed.

TRANSFERABILITY

The Chongqing Model entered the pilot stage in 2008. As of 2016, 15 million square meters (out of the 40 million projected to be completed by 2020) of public housing had been built, a project that is believed to be slower than planned. Fifty billion yuan, or 50 percent of the budget, has been spent; and, by the time of completion, investment in health care and education will add 100,000 yuan for receiving each migrant, or 100 billion yuan for 1 million migrants, according to estimates by the Chinese Academy of Science (*Economist* 2016). One question that has been raised is whether Chongqing is realistically ready to absorb rural people. Chongqing's large land stock and the overwhelming pressure on public housing coming from the biggest urban population appear to make the Chongqing Model unique. Whether the model is transferable nationwide is an open question. As of this writing, the model's pilot stage continues.

Jing Luo

See also: Employment and Jobs: Shenzhen, China: Struggle to Leave Shanzhai Behind; *Green Spaces:* Hong Kong, China: Adding Green Spaces to Densely Populated Neighborhoods

Further Reading

Branigan, Tania. 2009. "Unemployment Forces Chinese Migrants Back to the Countryside." *Guardian*, May 17. https://www.theguardian.com/world/2009/may/17/china-crossroads-migrants-tania-branigan.

Chandrasekhar, C. P., and Jayati Ghosh. 2016. "Why China's Housing Market Is a Frenzy." *BusinessLine*. http://www.thehindubusinessline.com/opinion/columns/c-p-chandrasekhar/china-is-witnessing-a-housing-price-bubble/article9208342.ece.

Chongqing Bureau of Statistics (CSB). 2017. *Chongqing Statistical Yearbook 2017* (in Chinese). http://www.cqtj.gov.cn/tjnj/2017/zk/indexeh.htm.

Coonan, Clifford. 2016. "Demise of 'Iron Rice Bowl' Brings Social Change in Chongqing." *Irish Times*, April 28. http://www.irishtimes.com/news/world/asia-pacific/demise-of-iron-rice-bowl-brings-social-change-in-chongqing-1.2626926.

Hui, Xiao-xi. 2009. "The Chinese Housing Reform and the Following New Urban Question." *The 4th International Conference of the International Forum on Urbanism, 2009*. http://newurbanquestion.ifou.org/proceedings/3%20The%20Urbanized%20Society/full%20papers/B008_Xiaoxi_The%20Chinese%20Housing%20Reform%20and%20the%20following%20New%20Urban%20Questions-fullpaper_revised.pdf.

Jia, Huajie. 2015. "Huang Qifan Talks about Chongqing's Urbanization Reform" (in Chinese). Caixin Weekly Online, March 23. http://special.caixin.com/2015-03-23/100793769.html.

Jing Zhou, and Richard Ronald. 2017. "The Resurgence of Public Housing Provision in China: The Chongqing Program." *Housing Studies Journal* 4. http://www.tandfonline.com/doi/full/10.1080/02673037.2016.1210097.

Kuo, Ping-chia and Wang Mingye. 2018. "Chongqing, China." *Encyclopaedia Britannica* (online). Accessed February 19, 2018. https://www.britannica.com/place/Chongqing.

Qiu Yue. 2016. "Dipiao Wakes Up Sleeping Capital in the Countryside" (in Chinese). *Guangming Daily*. http://epaper.gmw.cn/gmrb/html/2016-06/02/nw.D110000gmrb_20160602_1-13.htm.

Staff Writer. 2016. "Urbanization: Reform's Big Taboo." *Economist* (online), March 26. http://www.economist.com/news/china/21695556-ambitious-plan-social-change-has-run-trouble-reformu2019s-big-taboo.

Wu, Xinwei. 2016. "Chongqing's Urbanization Rate Exceeds 60%, as the Nation's Migration to First-Line Cities Accelerates" (in Chinese). *Xinhuanet*. http://news.xinhuanet.com/politics/2016-05/30/c_129026647.htm.

Xu, Qiyong. 2010. "Chongqing *Hukou* Reform: Within Three Years Urban *Hukou* Holders May Resume Rural *Hukou* and Land Rights" (in Chinese). *Chongqing Evening News*. http://www.ce.cn/xwzx/gnsz/gdxw/201009/20/t20100920_21833696.shtml.

Ying, Q., D. Luo, and J. Chen. 2013. "The Determinants of Homeownership Affordability among the 'Sandwich Class': Empirical Findings from Guangzhou, China." *Urban Studies* 50, 9. https://www.jstor.org/stable/26144334?seq=1#page_scan_tab_contents.

Dandong, China: One Bridge, Two Islands

Dandong is the largest border city of the Liaoning Province of China. The 2010 census shows that the city's population was 2.44 million with a diverse ethnic composition. Located along the Yalu River, Dandong is a next-door neighbor of the city of Sinuiju of the Democratic People's Republic of North Korea; Dandong plays an important role in bilateral trade. Forty percent of Dandong's import and export is with North Korea, and 70 percent of China's export goods goes through Dandong (Zhang 2012). On the side of North Korea, 90 percent of its foreign trade is with China, and over 50 percent of the goods flows through Dandong. While North Korea trades with other countries, such as India, Pakistan, and Russia, China with $5.4 billion in trade in 2016 is by far its biggest trade partner. The *New York Times* depicts Dandong as "a boom-and-bust city whose fortunes are tied to trade with North Korea" (Perlez and Huang 2016).

One of the historical landmarks of Dandong is the 589-meter-long Sino-Korean Friendship Bridge, also known as the Old Yalu River Bridge. In August 1950, tens of thousands of Chinese Volunteer troops crossed the bridge and into North Korea to fight in the Korean War. Built more than 80 years ago by the Japanese and destroyed multiple times by war and natural disasters, the Old Bridge is of limited economic function today other than being a tourist spot. In 2009, China and North Korea agreed to build the New Yalu River Bridge (New Bridge) to connect the New District of Dandong with North Korea's Sinuiju City. The New Bridge and Sinuiju's two islands, *Wihwa-Do* and *Hwanggumpyong*, constituted a package deal known as "one bridge, two islands." These islands were to open to Chinese investors as free trade zones. However, after $338 million having been invested by Chinese investors, the one bridge, two islands dream has yet to come true. The reality is, instead of seeing a "North Korea Hong Kong" (Cathcart 2012) growing into shape by the planned bridge opening date in 2014, Dandong found itself struggling with tons of debt. As of this writing, the grand New Bridge is lying in the mud of North Korea's farmlands, waiting to be connected to some form of road extension.

ONE BRIDGE, TWO ISLANDS

The New Yalu River Bridge was a joint venture in which the Chinese side was responsible for most of the construction and financial investment. The bridge, as completed, is 3 kilometers long, with 1.4 kilometers in China and 1.6 kilometers in North Korea. The suspended bridge body over the Yalu River is 636 meters long and 194 meters high. The bridge deck is 28 meters wide, allowing for four lanes of traffic. The construction started on December 31, 2010, with a planned opening on October 30, 2014. However, the North Korean government has allegedly delayed the construction of the connecting roads for a variety of reasons. Experts believe that international sanctions may have been the main cause (Lee 2017, BW40 2015).

North Korea not only suspended the New Yalu River Bridge, it has blocked access to the new island economic zone as well. Online photos show that accesses to *Hwanggumpyong Island* and *Wihwa-Do Island* are barb-wired and guarded by North Korean soldiers. In 2009 when Wen Jiabao, the former premier of China, signed the joint venture agreement, both sides hailed the plan as a historical event. North Korea's Supreme People's Assembly stated that these islands to be jointly developed will serve "the purpose of strengthening friendship and expansion of foreign trade" (Zhang 2011). Both sides further agreed that the guiding principle would be government led, company centered, market oriented, and mutually beneficial, reflecting a high level of trust and confidence. The document "Law of Hwanggumpyong Island and Wihwa-Do Island Economic Zone" includes the following stipulations:

1. *Wanggumpyong Island* will focus on information technology, light industry, agriculture, commerce, and tourism.

2. The North Korean government will provide land, labor and tax incentives to foreign companies, and reward those companies that produce world-class competitive products.

3. Foreign investments will be protected by the Law and will not be subjected to nationalization. If any property must be recalled due to national interest, the government will issue an announcement ahead of time and compensate the business owner according to the assessed value and in a timely manner.

4. Profit from operation will be taxed at 14 percent; or at 10 percent if the company qualifies for a category of rewarded projects. Investments longer than 10 years will be exempted from taxation; companies who reinvest profit will enjoy 50 percent tax refund on the portion of reinvestment (Xinhuanet 2012).

The failure of one bridge, two islands has a serious impact on Dandong. In Wujin, a commercial area of Dandong's New Town, two-thirds of shops are closed. The New Town was originally planned to accommodate a population of 400,000 by 2014's end; it barely had 60,000 residents in 2016. During the period of 2009–2012 when the ribbon was cut and the project entered the construction phase, the local media hyped New Town as a "once-in-a-century opportunity." Many individual investors pitched personal savings in real-estate investments that eventually had no renters; and some even borrowed money to invest in the rosy opportunity. China's official newspaper the *Global Times* reports:

> Dozens of modern skyscrapers form an impressive skyline on the Yalu River, which demarcates the China-North Korea border. The city also boasts a massive government building, a large commercial complex and a riverside park with a ferry wheel. But there is one thing that the district is short of: people. During the day, few cars travel on the 10-lane, 70 meter-wide main road; not a single store is open on its commercial pedestrian street, and the ferry wheel never moves. When night falls, the emptiness of Dandong New City is eerie as neon lights illuminate the hollow skyscrapers. (Zhang 2016)

WHY NORTH KOREA AND CHINA PURSUE SPECIAL ECONOMIC ZONES?

The concept of the "special economic zone" (SEZ) was an invention by former Chinese leader Deng Xiaoping in the early 1980s. Seeing that the Soviet-style central economy had failed, Deng opened up four SEZs in the Guangdong Province to piloted Western management—Shenzhen, Zhuhai, Shantou, and Xiamen. These zones were between 1,000 and 2,000 square kilometers in space area; access was limited to select Chinese workers and managers. The success of the SEZs soon led to the opening of more cities for Western-style management, and eventually the rest of the country was open to foreign investment. The concept of SEZ was expanded to a higher level, known as "special administrative region" (SAR). In 1997 and 1999, Hong Kong and Macau were returned to China under the SAR provision that allows them to continue without interruption their existing governing structure and life style. Looking back, China being the number two economy in the world today owes much to the successful SEZ experiment. As a result, North Korea decided to test the China model.

Experience shows, however, that duplicating may not necessarily result in a successful transfer. North Korea's experience has not been successful, although it is still too early to declare failure. Here are some intrinsic barriers: On the one hand, North Korea is concerned about China's economic encroachment and wary about China's political penetration; on the other hand, the top-down governing structure under Kim Jong-un generates countless bureaucratic barriers that are toxic to trade. As a result, North Korea's first SEZ, the Rason Economic and Trade Zone opened in 1991 suffers from diminishing foreign investors today, despite its prime location that borders China and Russia. Rason offers an ice-free port that China could use to connect its landlocked northeastern provinces to the sea. However, it has not been easy to get business going there. According to reports, 80 percent of investors in Rason are from China, and they are "tearing their hair out as their efforts are being resisted by official decisions or diluted by corruption" (Potter 2014). The Sinuiju Special Administrative Zone is another case. Established in 2002, the SEZ was intended to operate with a higher degree of tolerance. Its governor, Yang Bin, a Sino-Dutch businessman, was arrested in China one year after the opening for tax fraud and received an 18-year jail sentence. The incident put an end to much of the SAR's operation (Tertitskiy 2015). Likewise, joint ventures between North Korea and South Korea have not gone well. The Mount Kumgang Tourist Zone opened in 1998 and the Kaesong Industrial Complex (KIC) initiated in 2000 have gone through frequent interruptions due to tensions between the two Koreas. In 2013, North Korea's Central News Agency announced the establishment of a dozen more SEZs covering most of the provinces of North Korea; however, little is known about the real motivation and outcomes of these operations.

Chinese scholars attribute North Korea's pursuit of SEZs with China to economic and political stress. In the 1960s, North Korea followed China's example to implement "political independence, economic self-reliance, and capability in national defense," also known as the *Juche ideology*. As in China, the closed-door policy failed to alleviate poverty. The 1970s and 1980s saw moderate economic recovery thanks to increased weight on light industry and ramp-up of consumer goods. However, North Korea had no intention to engage in political and economic reform. In the 1990s, the country's economy fell into a prolonged recession. A shortage of petroleum, rubber, and other basic materials crippled most of the industrial sector. During the same period, however, China's economy was on a fast rise. In the 2000s, to reverse its economic downturn, North Korea appears to have no other choice than modeling China. The government refocused it guidance by stressing "developing economic strength," "building a big country of prosperity," "stressing science and technology," and "improving economic management." The size of North Korea's economy today, however, remains "paltry" (Bremmer 2017). North Korea's oil consumption averaged 15,000 barrels a day in 2016, which is insignificant compared to the consumption of 2.6 million barrels a day in South Korea and 12.5 million barrels a day in China. In 2012, the government under Kim Jong-un adopted a 10-year National Economic Plan, also called "the Great Leap Plan," aimed at opening up to the world, and catching up with developed nations by 2020. In that spirit, the New Yalu River Bridge and the *Hwanggumpyong* and *Wihwa-Do* economic zone were projected to become a primary zone of trade, finance, and warehouse storage (Jiao 2012; Man 2011; Ping and Zhang 2012).

China's motivation in building economic zones with North Korea has multiple dimensions. First, since 2000, import products from North Korea have gradually expanded from seafood, coal, and iron ore to machinery, artificial fabrics, and industrial and home electronic equipment. This structural shift is creating a market for struggling senior industries of the Liaoning Province. Secondly, the *Hwanggumpyong* and *Wihwa-Do* economic zone could be an avenue for China to transfer its labor-intensive factories to North Korea, where labor costs are at the level of China's early 1980s. Thirdly, energizing North Korea's economy could be a way to wean it off its dependence on China's "blood transfusion" (Man 2011). Finally, the one bridge, two islands project is an integral part of President Xi Jinping's grand "one belt, one road" mega plan. For China, theoretically speaking, there is little to lose, but much to gain. The newly established trade zones mean easier trade for China's surplus products. In fact, in addition to Dandong, China is building free-trade zones in Tumen and Hunchun encompassing connections with Russia, North Korea, and surrounding countries. As such, despite the fact that the bilateral trade with North Korea is a minimal portion of China's foreign trade as a whole, it is intrinsic to China's goal. Additionally, experts contend that the potential of extending transportation through the New Yalu River Bridge to North Korea's hinterland, including Pyongyang, means a lot for Chinese influence (Jiao 2012; Choi 2015).

WHY THE ONE BRIDGE, TWO ISLANDS PLAN HAS BEEN ALL BUT A SMOOTH RIDE

Economic sanctions are believed to be a major distraction. North Korea's relentless pursuit of nuclear capability has created deep concerns in Beijing. A denuclearized Korean Peninsula is of fundamental importance to China's safety and security. In a speech to commemorate the fourth "Six-party Talks" held on September 19, 2005, China's foreign minister Wang Yi had this to say:

> The *September 19 Joint Statement* by the six parties is an open and solemn promise to the world. Every party must be committed to the promise, implement the promise, and not betray the promise. More importantly, no party should lose its trustworthiness to the world community. The *Statement* serves as the groundwork to six-party talks, its goals and principles represent our common interests. We must strive to let these principles and goals take root and grow, we must not shelve them away, and moreover, we must not conveniently deny and discard them. We call on all parties to take this opportunity and make a political determination to return to the promised responsibilities, duties, and obligations. (Wang 2015)

Not only has North Korea ignored China's complaint, but it went further to test an intercontinental ballistic missile (ICBM) delivery system in 2017, increasing fears globally. As a result, China has further tightened sanctions. Since North Korea's first nuclear test in 2006, China has gradually turned to being supportive of the UN's economic sanctions. Recent measures include banning coal imports in April 2016 with exceptions for goods for basic needs, suspending coal

---

The Six-Party Talks

Six-party talks, also known as six-party nuclear talks, are held by representatives of North Korea, South Korea, Japan, the United States, China, and Russia. The goal of these talks is to convince North Korea to give up its nuclear weapons and programs. The first round of talks was held in 2003, after North Korea withdrew from the Nuclear Non-Proliferation Treaty (NPT). The sixth round, the latest, was held in 2007. The fourth round, held on September 19, 2005, in Beijing, achieved the first breakthrough in resolving the North Korean nuclear crisis. The "Joint Statement of the Fourth Round of the Six-Party Talks" produced agreed-upon steps toward denuclearization of the Korean Peninsula. North Korea committed to abandoning nuclear programs and weapons, returning to the NPT and accepting IAEA inspections. However, the parties respected peaceful uses of nuclear energy by North Korea and agreed to later talks regarding the provision of a light-water reactor to North Korea. In return for this commitment, the United States and South Korea both affirmed that they would not deploy nuclear weapons on the peninsula, and stated, along with Russia, China, and Japan, their willingness to supply North Korea with energy aid. The United States and Japan also committed to working toward normalizing relations with North Korea.

On June 12, 2018, President Donald Trump met with North Korean leader Kim Jong-un in Singapore and signed a joint "historic document" that includes a commitment to working toward complete denuclearization of the Korean Peninsula. Experts cast doubt, however, on whether the commitment will be met, despite the promise being made by the top leaders.

imports from February 2017 through the rest of year, and threatening to ban oil export to North Korea (Albert 2017). While economic sanctions have failed to stop the nuclear and missile tests, they appear to have drained North Korea's coffers. Experts believe that the sanctions are directly related to the discontinuation of the one bridge, two islands program.

In a broader context, ideological differences generate constraints as well. Clearly, China and North Korea have drifted apart on the socialist road. Since Deng Xiaoping's reform, the Chinese have finally accepted that the market mechanism is a ubiquitous economic tool serving both capitalism and socialism. One can believe in socialism, but in doing business, one must respect the market mechanism. To most North Koreans, however, the market mechanism is synonymous with capitalism, which is a menace to the regime. As such, North Korea puts strengthening its military ahead of anything else. Not surprisingly, political dissidents are cruelly purged. One example is the 2013 execution of Jang Song-thaek, a powerful government official and Kim Jong-un's uncle, with anti-aircraft guns. The charges included "traitor" and "worse than a dog" (Choe 2013). The Chinese, however, sorely remember Jang as the founder of the New Yalu River Bridge project in 2009. Ideological differences can result in heated exchanges at the business negotiation table too. North Korean representatives may readily resort to the use of such hurtful terms as "traitors of socialism," generating hard feelings in their Chinese counterparts (Dongsihang 2013).

Despite failed investments, many in Dandong remain hopeful that the one bridge, two islands project may be revived someday, and some merchants dream of opening stores in North Korea when the good times come (Zhang Yu 2016). With respect to sanctions against North Korea, what Professor Lu at the Liaoning Academy of Social Sciences says may reflect the mood of some local Chinese: "We believe that wrongdoings deserve punishment, but punishment should not be seizing them by the throat and trying to choke them to death" (Denyer 2017).

Jing Luo

See also: Employment and Jobs: Mumbai, India: Exploring Employment Solutions in Temporary Jobs; Shenzhen, China: Struggle to Leave Shanzhai Behind

Further Reading

Albert, Eleanor. 2017. "The China-North Korea Relationship." *Council on Foreign Relations*. https://www.cfr.org/backgrounder/china-north-korea-relationship.

Bremmer, Ian. 2017. "China's Oil Lifeline to North Korea Targeted after Nuclear Blast." Interview by Bloomberg News. *Bloomberg News*, September 4. https://www.bloomberg.com/news/articles/2017-09-04/china-s-oil-lifeline-to-north-korea-targeted-after-nuclear-blast.

BW40.net. 2015. "New China-DPRK Failed to Open on Time" (in Chinese). June 18. http://www.bw40.net/5343.html.

Cathcart, Adam. 2012. "Building a 'North Korean Hong Kong': Tang Longwen on the Sinuiju SEZs." *SinoNK*, April 29. http://sinonk.com/2012/04/29/building-a-north-korean-hong-kong-tang-longwen-on-the-sinuiju-sezs.

Choe Sang-Hun. 2013. "North Korea Says Leader's Uncle Was Executed as a Traitor." *New York Times*, December 13. http://www.nytimes.com/2013/12/13/world/asia/north-korea-says-uncle-of-executed.html.

Choi, Ha-young. 2015. "China-N. Korea Border Bustling and Evolving: Expert." *NK-News On-line*. https://www.nknews.org/2015/11/china-n-korea-border-bustling-and-evolving-expert.

CNN Library. 2017. "North Korea Nuclear Timeline Fast Facts." http://www.cnn.com/2013/10/29/world/asia/north-korea-nuclear-timeline--fast-facts/index.html.

Daily NK News Crew. 2014. "Hwanggumpyong Economic Zone after Three Years: Only North Korean Soldiers Were Seen Ploughing the Land" (in Chinese). *DailyNK*. http://dailynk.com/chinese/read.php?num=13823&cataId=nk00600.

Denyer, Simon. 2017. "On China's Border with North Korea, a Constricted Economic Lifeline Is Still a Lifeline." *Washington Post*, September 28. https://www.washingtonpost.com/world/asia_pacific/on-chinas-border-with-north-korea-a-reduced-trade-lifeline-is-still-a-lifeline/2017/09/28/bbc6eefc-a2c4-11e7-b573-8ec86cdfe1ed_story.html.

Dongsihang. 2013. "Analyzing China's North Korean Policy in Light of 'Yang Bin' Event" (in Chinese). *Douban.com*. https://www.douban.com/group/topic/37796298.

DPRK. "Law of *Hwanggumpyong* Island and *Wihwa Do* Island Economic Zone" (in Chinese). http://www.naenara.com.kp/ch/trade/?law+7.

International Atomic Energy Agency (IAEA). "Fact Sheet on DPRK Nuclear Safeguards." https://www.iaea.org/newscenter/focus/dprk/fact-sheet-on-dprk-nuclear-safeguards.

Jiao Zhaoxia. 2012. "Analysis of DPRK's Special Economic Region and Its Impact on Sino-DPRK Economic Collaboration" (in Chinese). *Journal of Shanghai Business School* (Shanghai Shangxueyuan Xuebao) 5: 17–19.

Lee, Nathaniel. 2017. "China Built a $350 Million Bridge That Ends in a Dirt Field in North Korea." *Business Insider*. May 5. http://www.businessinsider.com/china-built-bridge-north-korea-new-yalu-bridge-trade-2017-5.

liuliudadakanshije. 2017. "China's Longest Cross-Border Bridge, Total Investment 2 Billion Yuan, Remains Closed to Traffic" (in Chinese). Tencent Travel. May 24. http://ly.qq.com/a/20170524/021122.htm.

Man Haifeng. 2011. "Defining Sino-DPRK Relationship and Development of Border Economy" (in Chinese). *Journal of Eastern Liaoning University (Social Sciences)*. http://www.hprc.org.cn/gsyj/wjs/dwgx/201206/P020120605556004279356.pdf.

National Bureau of Statistics of the People's Republic of China (NBS). 2011. "The 6th Census of the Liaoning Province—Selected Indicators" (in Chinese). http://www.stats.gov.cn/tjsj/tjgb/rkpcgb/dfrkpcgb/201202/t20120228_30396.html.

Parker, Clive. 2016. "Delayed Opening of $338m Bridge Hurting Dandong Economy and China-DPRK Ties." NKNews.org, July 11. https://www.nknews.org/2016/07/delayed-opening-of-338m-bridge-hurting-dandong-economy-and-china-dprk-ties.

Perlez, Jane, and Yufan Huang. 2016. "A Hole in North Korean Sanctions Big Enough for Coal, Oil and Used Pianos." *New York Times*, March 31. https://www.nytimes.com/2016/04/01/world/asia/north-korea-china-sanctions-trade.html.

Perlez, Jane, and Yufan Huang. 2017. "China Says Its Trade with North Korea Has Increased." *New York Times*, April 13. https://www.nytimes.com/2017/04/13/world/asia/china-north-korea-trade-coal-nuclear.html.

Ping, E., and Zhang Jiacheng. 2012. "Analysis of the Model of Sino-DPRK Border Region Economic Collaboration" (in Chinese). *Industrial & Science Tribune*. Issue 12, pages 54–55. http://caod.oriprobe.com/articles/found.htm?keyword=%E4%B8%AD%E6%9C%9D%E8%BE%B9%E5%A2%83%E8%B4%B8%E6%98%93+%E6

%96%B0%E4%B9%89%E5%B7%9E&package=&key_author=&key_qkname=&key_year=&key_volumn=&key_issue=.

Potter, Robert. 2014. "The Perils of Investing in North Korea." *Diplomat*, February 11. http://thediplomat.com/2014/02/the-perils-of-investing-in-north-korea.

Tertitskiy, Fyokor. 2015. "The Ill-Fated Sinuiju Special Region." NK-News, January 27. https://www.nknews.org/2015/01/the-ill-fated-sinuiju-special-region.

U.S. Department of State. *Joint Statement of the Fourth Round of the Six-Party Talks Beijing*. 2015. https://web.archive.org/web/20070313233046/http://www.state.gov/r/pa/prs/ps/2005/53490.htm.

Wang Yi. 2015. "Revisiting the September 19 Common Declaration, Safeguarding the Peace and Stability of the Korean Peninsula and East Asia" (in Chinese). Ministry of Foreign Affairs of the PRC, September 19. http://www.fmprc.gov.cn/web/wjbzhd/t1298236.shtml.

Xinhuanet. 2012. "DPRK Announces Law of Huanggumping and Wihwado Economic District," March 17. http://www.chinanews.com/gj/2012/03-17/3751864.shtml.

Zhang Ying. 2012. "A Study of Characteristics of Dangong-DPRK Trade" (in Chinese). *Foreign Economic Relations and Trade*. https://wenku.baidu.com/view/d9e4681952d380eb62946d9c.html.

Zhang Yu. 2016. "Chinese Town on North Korean Border Faces Bleak Business Prospects." *Global Times*, March 16. http://www.globaltimes.cn/content/974210.shtml.

Zhang, Zhe. 2011. "North Korea Approves Plans for the New Special Economic Zone, Citing Strengthened China-DPRK Relationship" (in Chinese). *Global Times*, June 7. http://world.huanqiu.com/roll/2011-06/1740973.html?test=1.

Detroit, United States: Housing and Infrastructure after the Auto Boom

In 2017, there was a widespread perception among Americans that Detroit was a disaster area. This image was fostered by TV, newspaper and magazine articles, blogs, websites with photographs of the city's ruins, and even bands like The Rumpshakers who lamented "what happened to the Motor City" in their evocatively titled blues song "Urban Decay" (The Rumpshakers 2009). Yet, in recent years the people of Detroit have been trying to counteract this negative image and reverse the long-term trends that fostered their current predicament. This article will focus in particular on Detroit's housing and infrastructure—two key elements of the urban crisis.

HISTORICAL BACKGROUND

Starting in the second half of the 19th century, Detroit's economy grew rapidly. By the turn of the 20th century, the city had a varied economic base. Detroit's connection to the growing railroad network, interior waterways, and central geographic location, as well as the efforts of key individuals such as Henry Ford and Albert Kahn, helped foster the rise of the automobile industry, which dominated the city's economy by the 1920s. The need for more workers led to huge in-migration. In the mid-1940s, the growing power of the United Auto Workers led to union contracts that enabled blue-collar workers to afford to buy homes. White-collar workers took advantage of various government-backed mortgages to also become homeowners (Sugrue 2004; Jackson and Leary 2016).

In Detroit, more than any other city in the United States, the preferred housing choice was the single-family, detached home. There were two building booms: from 1915 to 1930, corresponding to the rise of mass automobility; and from 1945 to 1960, during the early postwar economic boom. By the early 1960s, about two-thirds of all residents lived in freestanding, single-family homes—in sharp contrast to most other industrial cities where row houses and tenements were more common. Two key factors stimulated this trend: an increasingly auto-dependent workforce and "flat buildable land in nearly every direction." This led to massive urban sprawl, which created a low-rise, low-density landscape (Grunow 2015). The city could afford to provide the infrastructure for this sprawling metropolis—lighting, sewers, and so on—as long as the economy continued to grow.

During World War II, Detroit became known as the "Arsenal of Democracy" as auto and related firms mass-produced weapons of war for the Allies. This development led to a huge influx of workers. More and more rural Southern black and white workers moved to the Motor City, bringing with them their cultural traits and attitudes. Adequate housing and competition for good jobs became increasingly contentious issues between black and white workers. The conflict that erupted between them in 1942 over which group would live in the new federal government-sponsored Sojourner Truth Housing Project and the subsequent 1943 race riot revealed the racial tensions that would intensify over the next several decades (Russ 2012). Simultaneously, white neighborhood associations began to draw up restrictive neighborhood covenants to prevent blacks from moving into their communities (DeRuiter-Williams 2007).

The early postwar period initially appeared to signal continued rapid economic expansion. The late 1940s and 1950s, however, saw the beginnings of developments that would eventually undermine much of the city's economy, which would negatively affect Detroit's housing stock and infrastructure. Though many residents did not notice these trends at the time, scholars have since analyzed this process in detail. Historian Thomas Sugrue argues in *The Origins of the Urban Crisis* that several factors undermined the local economy, especially deindustrialization, the decentralization of automobile production—"between 1947 and 1958, the Big Three built twenty-five new plants . . . in suburban communities"—and automation. As a result, "Detroit lost 134,000 manufacturing jobs . . . between 1947 and 1963." This huge job loss had many negative ramifications, including making "homeownership in the city all the more insecure" and undermining the tax base, thereby sowing the seeds of insufficient funding to maintain infrastructure. By the early 1960s, the number of abandoned factories, small businesses, and deteriorating housing stock began to multiply. These developments hurt African American auto workers the worst (Sugrue 1996). Historian Kevin Boyle notes another key issue—that conservative and liberal city governments failed to address the growing problems (Boyle 2001).

Other factors further undermined Detroit's economy. The construction of the interstate highway system decimated inner-city, primarily black neighborhoods while fostering suburbanization. While higher-paid white workers could move to the suburbs near the new plants, lower-paid black workers could not. As Thomas Sugrue observed, increasingly "two separate cities" emerged, "one black and one white." Those "blacks who attempted to cross the city's invisible racial boundaries regularly faced violence" (Sugrue 2004). In "Why Detroit Matters," Betsy Jackson and Margaret Leary argue that "the stresses of urban crime, unemployment and inadequate housing stock" led to the massive 1967 urban uprising or race riot that saw more than 40 deaths, thousands of buildings burned, and millions of dollars in property damage (Jackson and Leary 2016).

Negative developments seemed to spiral out of control. In 1973, the oil embargo sent gasoline prices soaring. Ford, GM, and Chrysler made few fuel-efficient cars, so consumers increasingly purchased Japanese and German automobiles that got much better gas mileage. As American automobile production plummeted, more people left the city, further undermining its economy, housing stock, and infrastructure. Detroit's population collapsed from a peak of more than 1.8 million in 1950—when it was the fourth-largest city in the nation—to 1.2 million in 1980 (Jackson and Leary 2016). The Motor City's dependency on the auto industry—which fostered its rapid growth in the first half of the 20th century—became a crucial factor in its decline when the car companies took too long to adapt to changing international competition (Cohen 2013). During the Great Recession of 2008, the giant General Motors Corporation filed for bankruptcy. The next year Chrysler Corporation joined GM (Sugrue 2004; Carter 2015). At the turn of the 21st century, Detroit was the most segregated big city in America, with about one-third of its population living below the poverty line—more than any other major city (Boyle 2001). By 2010, barely 700,000 residents made the Motor City their home. It was now the eleventh-largest American city.

RECENT DEVELOPMENTS

As Detroit's situation grew more desperate, Michigan Governor Rick Snyder intervened in March 2013 and appointed lawyer Kevyn Orr as the city's emergency financial manager with "extra-governmental powers." With debts totaling some $18 billion, unemployment at 16.9 percent, and some 80,000 abandoned single-family homes, Orr recommended the city file for bankruptcy (Jackson and Leary 2016; Murembya and Guthrie 2015; Kosmowski 2014). In July, city officials initiated "the largest municipal bankruptcy in history" (Carter 2015).

Why did this happen? At the time, many commentators offered their analysis. According to a 2013 *New York Times* article, Detroit's collapse was "six decades in the making." Numerous factors led to this crisis, including trying to maintain the infrastructure for a "139-square mile city" on a shrinking tax base and efforts to pay down the debt by borrowing more money (Davey and Walsh 2013). AP national writer Sharon Cohen argued in another 2013 article that two key factors had the biggest impact on Detroit: overreliance on one industry and the city's "long history of racial strife." She interviewed Professor Sugrue for the article, who added that "the racial divisions between the city and the suburbs" so influenced Michigan's politics that "there's very little political will . . . by suburbanites and other parts of the state to provide financial support" for the city (Cohen 2013).

Detroit, Michigan, 2016. The city was once the center of America's automobile industry. Today, its economic decline is reflected in neighborhoods full of abandoned houses. (Chris Boswell/Dreamstime.com)

In a remarkably short period of time, Detroit emerged from bankruptcy in November 2014. According to Leary and Jackson, this rapid "exit from bankruptcy was the result of a 'perfect storm' of timing, judicial and management talent, creative mediation, and philanthropic and corporate spirit" (Leary and Jackson 2017). Mayor Mike Duggan and other city boosters immediately began initiating revitalization plans, but they faced serious challenges (Trickey 2017).

One overwhelming challenge was the continuing housing crisis. Tens of thousands of houses lie vacant. From 2014 through 2016, the city demolished more than 10,000, asserting that "property values seem to increase when demolition is strategically targeted." This expensive process, however, was marred by corruption within the Detroit Land Bank Authority tasked with blight removal (Leary and Jackson 2017).

A related housing problem was the foreclosure crisis that began after the 2008 Great Recession and continued into 2017. In this period, "more than 100,000 Detroit homeowners [fell] into foreclosure" (Gallagher 2017). To make matters worse, the city—according to Edmund Zagorin—has not "updated many property tax assessments in two decades, but still uses them to kick people out of their homes." Many houses have not been assessed in 20 years, but in the interim the housing market has collapsed. Ted Phillips, the United Community Housing Coalition's executive director, pointed out that people are "getting taxes assessed on a $30,000 or $40,000 property value for a house that probably couldn't sell for more than $5,000." When owners could not pay their taxes, the city took the property and auctioned it "to collect tax revenue." African American homeowners have been disproportionately hurt by this process. In response, in July 2016 the NAACP Legal Defense and Education Fund and the ACLU "filed a class action lawsuit seeking an injunction against tax foreclosures of owner-occupied property." They argued that this policy was counterproductive, destabilizing neighborhoods and violating federal law. Moreover, wealthy property speculators have taken advantage of the tax foreclosure sales (Zagorin 2016). Detroit People's Platform, an advocacy group, asserted in early 2017 that the city's revitalization plan targeted only select areas for expanded investment, which primarily benefitted "wealthier and whiter" neighborhoods, while concluding that many communities—primarily poorer and blacker neighborhoods—were "no longer 'viable'" and should have their city services slashed to save money. In response, the advocacy group recommended the creation of a housing trust fund to help those residents who made less than $20,070 a year. Since 33 percent of Detroit residents fit this category, it was extremely difficult for them to find "affordable housing options" (Detroit People's Platform 2017).

Though many were in various states of disrepair, Detroit had a large number of historic brick homes that could be an asset if restored. To rehabilitate such homes would be costly. Moreover, high property tax rates were another impediment to restoration. Daniel Kosmowski in a *Wayne Law Review* article advocated changing the historic preservation laws so as to encourage individuals to purchase and upgrade these substantial structures (Kosmowski 2014).

Recent efforts to improve public infrastructure included successes and failures. Regarding transportation, the city bus system had precipitously declined in recent decades. The system lacked sufficient numbers of drivers, buses, and maintenance facilities. The bankruptcy's Plan of Adjustment pumped $10 million into hiring more drivers, purchasing more buses, and instituting other improvements. A public-private venture—which began before the bankruptcy—opened the first light-rail line in Detroit in 60 years. The QLine paralleled Woodward Avenue for 3.3 miles, linking downtown Detroit with midtown—two sections of the city that were already attracting investment, especially from Quicken Loans founder Dan Gilbert. The goal of linking this line with a broader regional network failed when suburbanites voted against a requested millage increase (Leary and Jackson 2017; Huffman 2017; Goldstein 2017).

Lighting was another immediate infrastructure issue. At the time of bankruptcy, some 40 percent of Detroit's streetlights did not function as the city could not maintain the system. Walking dark city streets at night increased citizens' fears and fostered crime. In 2013, the city government relinquished control of lighting to a new independent agency, the Detroit Public Lighting Authority (PLA). The PLA initiated a major overhaul of the city's lights, installing 65,000 new LED streetlights that were brighter and used less energy than the old fixtures (Leary and Jackson 2017; Reitz 2017).

The Detroit Water and Sewerage Department (DWSD) is responsible for providing water to city residents and maintaining thousands of miles of sewer lines. Under Emergency Manager Kevyn Orr, in July 2013, the DWSD began shutting off water to residents who had not paid their bills. Though the city initiated a program to help citizens set up payment plans so they could maintain their service, some 70,000 people had their water shut off from 2014 to 2016. Many severely criticized this program. John Nichols in the *Nation* condemned it as a brutal austerity program, adding that access to water is a basic human right according to the United Nations. Writing in the *Progressive*, Abayomi Azikiwe stressed that the program was imposed by an "unelected emergency manager" and was thus an attack on "democratic control" and the poorest residents of the city. Moreover, the city added a new charge on "impervious surfaces" such as paved parking lots that produced much water runoff into the storm drains. Churches and small businesses, for example, experienced huge increases in their water bills. Ironically, according to Leary and Jackson, just as the city was improving neighborhoods by installing new lights, they destabilized them by instituting draconian water and sewerage charges (Leary and Jackson 2017; Nichols 2014; Azikiwe 2014).

Rebuilding a water and sewer system that had been neglected for years would cost millions of dollars that the city could not afford. A new nonprofit agency, the Detroit Future City Implementation Office, began working with the DWSD to institute less costly green infrastructure projects that would also make the city more sustainable. "Residents that install green infrastructure such as rain gardens and pervious pavers on their property can earn credits on their water and sewer bills." Vast areas of vacant land—where houses once stood—could actually be an advantage when installing rain gardens and bioswales. As John Gallagher noted in the *Detroit Free Press*, "by keeping water out of the sewer system, the city in theory could save hundreds of millions of dollars by not having to invest in more big-pipe gray infrastructure to treat the mix of sewerage and storm runoff" (ICIC 2017; NYC 2017; Gallagher 2015).

Not surprisingly, Detroit's miseries have attracted political commentary. In a 2013 article, Ruth Conniff asserted that "the rightwing argument that public employees bankrupted Detroit" is not tenable. She countered that "Detroit has been hollowed out by job-exporting trade policies, deindustrialization, and American auto manufacturers' poor business decisions" (Conniff 2013). During the 2016 presidential campaign, Republican candidate Donald Trump claimed that "excessive taxes and regulation led to the decline of Detroit." An August 9, 2016, *Detroit Free Press* article entitled "Trump Fact-Check: Over-regulation Didn't Kill Detroit," the authors interviewed Professor Thomas Sugrue who pointed out that "the loss of a manufacturing base in Detroit proper had been under way for much of the 20th century and had nothing to do with federal regulations" (Spangler et al. 2016). Recently, Detroit has served as a "political football" between right and left-wing commentators.

DETROIT RISING?

In their 2017 study of the Motor City in the appropriately named *Journal of Urban Regeneration and Renewal*, Leary and Jackson conclude that "Detroit survived what many thought terminal: it came out of an asset-less bankruptcy with renewed optimism and potential." Revitalization projects are occurring downtown, in the neighborhoods, and in city services. Despite this relatively positive assessment, they argue that the future is uncertain as "daunting challenges . . . remain." Detroit, they conclude, "could go either way."

Douglas Karsner

See also: Employment and Jobs: Seattle, United States: Have Job, Going Homeless

Further Reading

Azikiwe, Abayomi. 2014. "Fighting Back in Detroit." *Progressive*, September, 78, 9: 40–42.

Boyle, Kevin. 2001. "The Ruins of Detroit: Exploring the Urban Crisis in the Motor City." *Michigan Historical Review* 27, 1 (Spring): 109–27. https://www.jstor.org/stable/20173897.

Carter, Keith Allen. 2015. "General Motors and the City of Detroit: A Study in Urban Decline." Forum on Public Policy, February. forumonpublicpolicy.com/wp-content/uploads/2015/02/Carter.pdf.

Cohen, Sharon. 2013. "Detroit's Downfall: Decline of Autos, Troubled Racial History Blamed for City's Decline." *Minneapolis Star Tribune*, July 21. http://www.startribune.com/autos-troubles-race-at-root-of-detroit-collapse/216349491/.

Conniff, Ruth. 2013. "A Nation of Detroits." *Progressive*, September. https://trove.nla.gov.au/work/187206258?q&versionId=203769813.

Davey, Monica, and Mary Williams Walsh. 2013. "Billions in Debt, Detroit Tumbles into Insolvency." *New York Times*, July 19, A1, A3.

DeRuiter-Williams, Danielle. 2007. "The Critical Nexus: Deindustrialization, Racism, and Urban Crisis in Post-1967 Detroit." *McNair Scholars Journal* 11, 1. https://scholarworks.gvsu.edu/mcnair/vol11/iss1/5.

Detroit People's Platform. 2017. "Red Alert—Detroit's Housing Crisis." January 19. detroitpeoplesplatform.org/2017/01/red-alert-detroits-housing-crisis.

Gallagher, John. 2015. "Detroit to Test Innovative 'Blue Infrastructure' Project." *Detroit Free Press*, May 16. https://www.freep.com/story/money/business/michigan/2015/05/16/detroit-infrastructure-water-sewerage-wetlands-environment/27243935/.

Gallagher, John. 2017. "Foreclosure Crisis Makes Detroit a City of Renters, Not Homeowners." *USA Today*, March 20. https://www.usatoday.com/story/money/nation-now/2017/03/20/foreclosure-crisis-makes-detroit-city-renters-not-homeowners/99433002.

Goldstein, Matthew. 2017. "Detroit: From Motor City to Housing Incubator." *New York Times*, November 4. https://www.nytimes.com/2017/11/04/business/detroit-housing.html.

Grunow, Francis. 2015. "A Brief History of Housing in Detroit." http://www.modelmedia.com/features/detroit-housing-pt1-111715.aspx.

Huffman, Bryce. 2017. "Detroit's QLine Is Officially Open to Public." *Michigan Radio*, May 12. http://www.michiganradio.org/post/detroits-qline-officially-open-public.

Initiative for a Competitive Inner City (ICIC). 2017. "Detroit Revitalizes Neighborhoods with Green Infrastructure and Workforce Training." Research and Advisory Practice, Urban Business Initiatives, Blog. http://icic.org/blog/revitalization-detroit-through-green-infrastructure-workforce-training/.

Jackson, Betsy, and Margaret Leary. 2016. "Practice Papers: Why Detroit Matters: Part 1." *Journal of Urban Regeneration and Renewal* 9, 4 (May 13): 325–38.

Kosmowski, Daniel. 2014. "Restoring Detroit One Historic Home at a Time: A New Look at Old Historic Preservation Laws." *Wayne Law Review* (Winter).

Leary, Margaret, and Betsy Jackson. 2017. "Detroit: Part 3—Two Years On." *Journal of Urban Regeneration and Renewal* 10, 3 (February 24): 240–65.

Murembya, Leonidas, and Eric Guthrie. 2015. "Demographic and Labor Market Profile: Detroit City." State of Michigan, Department of Technology, Management, and Budget, April. http://milmi.org/Portals/198/publications/Detroit_City_Demographic_and_Labor_Mkt_Profile.pdf.

New York City Soil & Water Conservation District. 2017. "Green Infrastructure Series: Detroit, MI," March 14. https://www.soilandwater.nyc/whats-new/green-infrastructure-series-detroit-mi.

Nichols, John. 2014. "Wringing Detroit Dry: What We Can Learn from the Water Shutoff." *Nation*, August 18/25, 6, 8.

Reitz, Richard. 2017. "Lights Ahead: Rejuvenating Detroit Starts with Street Illumination." *Roads&Bridges*, August.

The Rumpshakers. 2009. "Urban Decay" from the CD *Urban Decay*. Funky D Records.

Russ, Johanna. 2012. "The 1943 Detroit Race Riot." Walter P. Reuther Library, Archives of Labor and Urban Affairs, Wayne State University, June 12. reuther.wayne.edu/node/8738.

Spangler, Todd, John Wisely, Brent Snavely, and Kristi Tanner. 2016. "Trump Fact-Check: Over-Regulation Didn't Kill Detroit." *Detroit Free Press*, August 9. https://www.freep.com/story/news/politics/2016/08/08/trump-detroit-factcheck/88391672/.

Sugrue, Thomas. 1996. *The Origins of the Urban Crisis: Race and Inequality in Postwar Detroit*. Princeton, NJ: Princeton University Press. See especially Chapter 5.

Sugrue, Thomas. 2004. "From Motor City to Motor Metropolis: How the Automobile Industry Reshaped Urban America." *Automobile in American Life and Society*. http://www.autolife.umd.umich.edu/Race/R_Overview/R_Overview1.htm.

Trickey, Erick. 2017. "Detroit's DIY Cure for Urban Blight." *Politico*, May 18. https://www.politico.com/magazine/story/2017/05/18/how-detroit-is-beating-its-blight-215160.

Zagorin, Edmund. 2016. "Detroit's Housing Disaster Is Its Leaders' Fault." *Huffington Post*, October 11. https://www.huffingtonpost.com/entry/detroit-tax-forclosure_us_57e18a91e4b0e80b1b9ec242.

Havana, Cuba: Facing Challenges of Housing and Infrastructure in Economic Transition

Havana is internationally recognized as a historic city. UNESCO designated its colonial-era fortifications along the Bay of Havana and its old city of squares and narrow streets as a World Heritage Site in 1982. The surrounding neighborhoods display architectural styles ranging from Moorish colonial to Baroque, Beaux Arts, and Art Deco, the legacy of connections built by four centuries of Spanish rule followed by 60 years of American influence. These links were broken by Cuba's 1959 revolution, which removed Havana from the mainstream of Western urban planning. By insulating the city from the ravages of mid-century urban renewal and the glass-tower redevelopment of the late 20th and early 21st centuries, Cuban communism helped to create the illusion that Havana is a city frozen in time.

Beneath its picturesque exterior, however, Havana is a city of 2.2 million people facing the challenge of inhabiting an antiquated built environment. Cuba's state control of housing policy and the American embargo that has been in place since 1960 have shaped a system that prioritized access to housing, but lacked the resources to meaningfully expand or update Havana's housing stock. As a result, the city's

A Cuban flag hangs over a street in Havana, 2015. Beneath its picturesque exterior, Havana is a city falling into disrepair. (Julian Peters/Dreamstime.com)

residents have faced long-term housing shortages, overcrowding, and deteriorating conditions. Recent Cuban attempts to ameliorate these problems have created new challenges: an expanding tourist presence in Havana, encouraged by the government as a source of hard currency, places additional stress on the city's fragile infrastructure, while the growth of a tourist economy and the reintroduction in 2011 of private home sales have threatened the egalitarian foundations of Cuba's social structure without offering an effective replacement. Finally, Havana's location on the Gulf of Mexico leaves it vulnerable to damage from the climate and from hurricanes such as 2017's Irma, a threat that will only increase with warming seas and to which Cuba is ill-equipped to respond.

THE EVOLUTION OF HAVANA'S BUILT ENVIRONMENT

Havana's challenges stem from the combination of its physical evolution over the five centuries since its founding as a Spanish colonial outpost in 1519, and its politically driven development since Cuba's establishment of a centralized one-party system in 1959. Havana lies on the west side of Havana Bay, a large pocket bay on Cuba's northern coast. As a strategic port within the Spanish Empire, it initially developed as a fortified city, today's Old Havana. During the 19th century, the city outgrew its walls, which were demolished in 1863, and the first suburbs were established in what are now parts of the adjacent Centro Habana, Vededo, and Cerro districts. This established a pattern of outward expansion to the west, along the coast, and to the south. The bay and its 15 miles of coastline posed a major obstacle to eastward expansion; not until 1958 would a tunnel beneath the mouth of Havana Bay provide a direct link between the east coast and the city center.

Cuba waged a long struggle for independence from Spain during the last third of the 19th century, even as its economy became enmeshed with the United States. These processes collided in the Spanish-American War (1898), during which the United States pushed Spain from Cuba but also used its military power to further its economic and political interests. After a brief American occupation (1899–1902), Cuba entered its republican period (1902–1958), marked by political instability and American economic domination. Havana's built environment prospered under this regime. American infrastructure investments included a streetcar network and a sewer system, which came on line in 1915. Havana's wealth and status as the national capital were reflected in the opulence of its architecture; in today's Havana, the term "capitalist construction," meaning pre-revolution, remains synonymous with high quality.

After the 1959 revolution, the new communist government radically redistributed the city's assets. Housing reforms forbade Cubans from owning more than one urban property, and real estate belonging to wealthy or middle-class Cubans who fled to the United States was nationalized. Now Havana's sole landlord, the government provided housing to poorer Cubans, capped rents, and created a system that allowed renters to transition into homeownership. In revolutionary Cuba, ownership granted the right to make improvements, pass property to one's heirs, and swap one property for another. However, buying and selling of real estate was illegal at some points, and even when it was allowed, the state set prices and retained the right of first refusal for itself.

During the 1960s, a baby boom and internal migration combined to cause a housing shortage in Havana. Its severity was increased by the American embargo beginning in 1960. Cuba turned to the Soviet Union and Eastern Bloc for support and supplies, including oil and building materials. Cuba did not undertake large-scale slum clearance in central Havana, instead reusing or replacing individual buildings, but it did clear many of the shantytowns that had grown up on the city's fringes during the republican period, providing the residents with other housing or encouraging them to build their own. In the 1970s, Cuban leader Fidel Castro undertook to solve the city's housing problem on a large scale by deploying microbrigades of volunteer workers to build large Soviet-style housing projects on Havana's fringes, including the satellite city of Alamar on the east side of the bay. The combination of isolation, poor planning, unskilled labor, and low-quality materials, however, limited the desirability of these areas. During the 1980s, the state resumed its earlier pattern of working within the city's framework, legalizing the self-built homes to which some residents had resorted in response to the housing shortage. At the beginning of the 1990s, some 85 percent of Cubans were considered homeowners.

The end of the Cold War upset this relative equilibrium. With the collapse of the Soviet Union, Cuba lost its access to Eastern Bloc markets and raw materials, falling into an economic crisis described euphemistically as the "Special Period." The only new building in the early 1990s was designed to attract foreign tourists. In addition to new hotels and condos, this meant redevelopment in Havana's historic center; working with Havana's Office of the City Historian, a government department, the state established Habaguanex, a tourism company empowered to restore historic buildings and develop restaurants, hotels, and other destinations. Although construction resumed in the mid-1990s, Cuba remained unable to meet Havana's needs for new housing and repairs; in the late 1990s, it was estimated that over half of its housing was in poor condition, with almost 100,000 people living in unsafe circumstances and more than 20,000 in shelters without access to permanent housing (Thompson 1998). Increased migration to the capital, a result of the country's difficult economic conditions, led to growing slums and shantytowns on the city's outskirts, with the number of slum housing units in Havana increasing by some 50 percent between 1987 and 2001 (Díaz-Briquets 436).

In 2006, Fidel Castro retired and was succeeded by his brother, Raúl Castro, who in 2011 legalized private real estate markets. This policy encouraged Havana's residents, many of whom had lived in the same family homes for generations, to become more mobile, but it was not able to resolve the underlying problem of housing and infrastructure. Much of the city's built environment still predates the 1959 revolution; as of 2016, some 200,000 of Havana's 2.2 million people lived in *solares*—substantial single-family homes, hotels, or public buildings subdivided into small units as part of the revolutionary reforms (Ruhfus 2016). They have deteriorated from age and lack of maintenance, but remain occupied. Outside the restored tourist zones of Old Havana, many *solares* are in very poor condition and collapse is a common problem, while much of the newer housing stock is of poor quality. Other aspects of the city's built environment are similarly fragile, including the sewer system constructed in 1915 to serve a city of about 300,000 inhabitants. Although the government is working to update the system and expand its capacity, a 2007 estimate suggested that an investment of some $30 billion would be needed to fully modernize it.

CHALLENGES OF CUBA'S DUAL ECONOMY

Cuba's encouragement of foreign tourism and liberalization of real estate regulation were carried out in hopes of rejuvenating the economy. However, they have created new challenges for housing in Havana. Like the rest of Cuba, Havana now operates within a unique dual economy. There are two currencies, the Cuban peso (CUP) and a convertible peso (CUC) pegged to the U.S. dollar. One CUC is worth about 25 CUPs. Foreign visitors are required to use CUCs, and Cubans who work in industries catering to tourists are often paid in this currency. The system was designed to protect ordinary Cubans from tourist-generated inflation. In practice, however, it has opened a gulf between workers with access to CUCs and those stuck in the CUP economy who can afford neither to purchase desirable real estate nor to maintain their homes. By one 2015 estimate, for example, a new toilet fixture cost twice the annual average salary in CUPs. Many Cubans also receive regular remittances from family or friends living abroad; in 2015, Cubans received an estimated total of $3.4 billion in remittances. With average Cuban government salaries (paid in CUPs) equivalent to about $20 per month in 2015, a remittance of $100 per month, while modest by American standards, greatly expands the buying power of their recipients in comparison to other Cubans.

These income streams have distorted the relationship between Havana's housing market and the economy as a whole. In desirable districts close to the tourist centers, houses may sell for over $100,000. Workers who received such properties during the revolution can now sell them for cash that allows them to relocate to less expensive areas and retain a cushion for investment in the tourist-based CUC economy. Those without such assets have no equivalent path to wealth; and, of course, the market for such properties is limited to participants in the CUC economy and those with access to foreign funds. As a result, social and economic stratification are re-emerging as problems in Havana. State-led rehabilitation of historic buildings also contributes, since many former *solares* are refurbished into public buildings or higher-quality housing that is unaffordable for their former residents. Along with others who have lost their housing through collapse or condemnation, they are often relocated to Havana's Soviet-era outer suburbs, which offer available cheap housing because of their lack of connectivity to the city center, lack of amenities, and poor design. Prerevolutionary class divisions based on race are also re-emerging, since lighter-skinned Cubans predominated among those who fled after the revolution and are now in a position to provide remittances to their families. As of this writing, the Cuban state has not responded to these structural issues.

CHALLENGES OF FRAGILE INFRASTRUCTURE

The developing Cuban tourist economy also challenges Havana's infrastructure by stressing its capacity. The state is actively working to add to its supply of tourist accommodation, but the projected increase in visitors will add stress to other parts of the city's built environment that have received little maintenance under the chronically underfunded communist government. For example, most of Havana's water facilities are at least 75 years old, putting them well over their normal lifespan of 50 years. The water main system in central Havana has not received significant updates since the 1920s, and some 50 percent of the water is estimated to be lost to leakages. Overall, access to water in Havana is erratic, and in some parts of the city it is only available by truck.

Transportation is another challenge. While it is known for its iconic mid-century American cars, Havana has low rates of private vehicle ownership, an estimated 37 cars per thousand people (Warren et al. 2015), and high reliance on transit. However, the austerity of the Special Period included cuts to public transportation service, which continue to be felt. In 2012, passenger levels were about half of what they had been in 1984–85, a high point during the Cold War era. Some demand has been absorbed by bicycling, taxis, and minibuses, but residents of the city's outskirts and especially the east side of Havana Bay remain isolated. Analysts have suggested that the addition of a bus rapid transit (BRT) trunk line to the city's network, accessible to local routes and feeder services in low-density areas, could increase connectivity and service levels in the city.

GLOBAL CHALLENGES TO HAVANA'S HOUSING AND INFRASTRUCTURE

In addition to the range of complex challenges posed by national economic policies and the age of the built environment, the condition of Havana's housing and infrastructure is shaped by Cuba's geographical and geopolitical positions. An island nation with no oil reserves and an economy heavily dependent on raw materials production, Cuba has historically depended on its relations with other countries. During the early 2010s, relations between the United States and Cuba began to thaw after 50 years of hostility, raising the possibility of normalized relations and increased American tourism with its challenges and opportunities for Havana's built environment. As of late 2017, however, a change in American administration had led to renewed commitment to the embargo, calling this scenario into question. China has emerged as Cuba's largest creditor, funding infrastructure, manufacturing, and tourism projects. Cuba is also encouraging Chinese tourism; if it succeeds, the influx could add to the stress placed on Havana's housing and infrastructure by the city's dual economy.

Havana's location along the coast of the Gulf of Mexico also poses challenges for the city. While Cuba's poverty and isolation have contributed to the deterioration of the city's housing through lack of maintenance, the climate has increased the impact of neglect. Heat, high humidity, and the salt spray from the coast mean that Havana's buildings need constant maintenance to remain functional, and in its absence the impact of neglect is felt in crumbling walls and corrosion that leads to collapse. Havana is also vulnerable to hurricanes like the category-five hurricane Irma, which struck Havana in September 2017 and caused flooding, blackouts, and building collapses. Cuba's strong hurricane preparedness policies have historically resulted in relatively few deaths from these storms, and its state-run economy allows the government to divert human and other resources to rapid responses. However, as of this writing it is clear that the effects of Irma will challenge Havana's overall ability to improve its housing and infrastructure. Its impact on tourist facilities, a growing part of Cuba's economy, will limit the country's ability to earn the hard currency it needs to finance recovery. With the American embargo renewed, many sources of international materials and support will be cut off. Cuba may respond by increasing its dependence on China. By maintaining its long-standing pattern of global engagement, however, the country will maintain the complex web of social, economic, and political assumptions that has shaped Havana's housing and infrastructure.

Sara C. Jorgensen

See also: Employment and Jobs: San Juan, Puerto Rico, United States: A Stronger Local Government Is Key to Job Creation

Further Reading

Coyula Cowley, Mario, and Jill Hamberg. 2003. "The Case of Havana, Cuba." In *UN-Habitat Global Report on Human Settlements 2003, The Challenge of Slums*. London: Earthscan, 195–228. http://www.ucl.ac.uk/dpu-projects/Global_Report/cities/havana.htm.

Díaz-Briquets, Sergio. 2009. "The Enduring Cuban Housing Crisis: The Impact of Hurricanes." *Cuba in Transition.* Papers and Proceedings of the Fifth Annual Meeting

of the Association for the Study of the Cuban Economy (ASCE), 429–41. https://ascecuba.org//c/wp-content/uploads/2014/09/v19-diazbriquets.pdf.
- Francis, Ted. 2017. "Cuba's Crumbling Infrastructure No Match for Might of Irma." *Guardian,* September 13. https://www.theguardian.com/world/2017/sep/13/hurricane-irma-cuba-havana-flooding-government-response.
- Freeman, Belmont. 2014. "History of the Present: Havana." *Places.* https://placesjournal.org/article/history-of-the-present-havana.
- Hamberg, Jill. 2012. "Cuba Opens to Private Housing but Preserves Housing Rights." *New Political Spaces* 19, 1. http://www.reimaginerpe.org/node/6930.
- Miroff, Nick. 2015a. "A Socialist Vision Fades in Cuba's Biggest Housing Project: Inequality Is Growing in Cuba, Threatening the Legacy of Castro's Revolution." *Washington Post,* December 29. http://www.washingtonpost.com/sf/world/2015/12/29/a-socialist-vision-fades-in-cubas-biggest-housing-project.
- Miroff, Nick. 2015b. "$75,000 Will Get You a Lot of House in Havana—If You're Cuban." *Washington Post,* May 25. https://www.washingtonpost.com/world/75000-will-get-you-a-lot-of-house-in-havana--if-youre-cuban/2015/05/25/bbed3d78-fd8f-11e4-8c77-bf274685e1df_story.html.
- Peters, Philip. 2014. "Cuba's New Real Estate Market: Latin America Initiative Working Paper." Washington, DC: Latin America Institute, Foreign Policy at BROOKINGS, February 21. https://www.brookings.edu/research/cubas-new-real-estate-market.
- Rainsford, Sarah. 2012. "Cuba's Crumbling Buildings Mean Havana Housing Shortage." *BBC News,* May 17. http://www.bbc.com/news/world-latin-america-17935769.
- Ruhfus, Juliana. 2016. "Cuba for Sale" *Al Jazeera,* February 19. http://www.aljazeera.com/programmes/peopleandpower/2016/02/cuba-sale-160215095947647.html.
- Scarpaci, Joseph L., Roberto Segre, and Mario Coyula. 2002. *Havana: Two Faces of the Antillean Metropolis.* Rev. ed. Chapel Hill: University of North Carolina Press.
- Siegel, Robert. 2015. "A Fraying Promise: Exploring Race and Inequality in Havana." *Parallels: Many Stories, One World.* NPR, March 26. http://www.npr.org/sections/parallels/2015/03/26/395530735/a-fraying-promise-exploring-race-and-inequality-in-havana.
- Thompson, Ginger. 1998. "Cuban Housing a Tight Squeeze: Many Complain Prime Land Targeted for Tourists" *Chicago Tribune,* August 16. http://www.latinamericanstudies.org/cuba/housing-98.htm.
- Wainwright, Oliver. 2016. "Cuba for Sale: 'Havana Is Now the Big Cake—and Everyone Is Trying to Get a Slice.'" *Guardian,* February 1. https://www.theguardian.com/cities/2016/feb/01/cuba-for-sale-havana-is-now-the-big-cake-and-everyone-is-trying-to-get-a-slice.
- Warren, James, et al. 2015. "Developing an Equitable and Sustainable Mobility Strategy for Havana." *Cities* 45: 133–41. http://www.sciencedirect.com/science/article/pii/S0264275115000220.

Munich, Germany: The Munich Wall

Munich is the third-largest city in Germany, after Berlin and Hamburg. It is also the capital of the state of Bavaria, the largest state of Germany. The city's population is 1.35 million in the city proper, and 2.3 million in the metropolitan region (New World Encyclopedia 2014). Munich is an ancient city with a history dating back to the 12th century when the Wittelsbach family ruled Bavaria from the area.

The "Munich Wall" is built to separate a refugee shelter from the surrounding neighborhood in suburban Munich, Germany, 2016. Local residents petitioned successfully for the wall, citing noise concerns. Critics see the wall as an anti-immigrant statement. (David Speier/NurPhoto via Getty Images)

The city was a leader in Germany's industrialization in the mid-19th century that transformed the energy structure from coal to fossil fuel. This enabled the economy to shift from heavy industry that produces machinery to light industry that produces precision instruments and consumer goods. Munich has since grown into a major international center of business, engineering, research, and medicine (Encyclopaedia Britannica 2017).

Additionally, located about 30 miles from the northern tip of the Alps, on the banks of the Isar River, Munich is a tourist city, receiving millions of visitors every year. The Old Town showcases Baroque- and Rococo-style churches, and buildings of the 14th century, attracting 300,000 visitors a day. Bogenhausen and Haidhausen enjoy the reputation of the prettiest districts with 19th-century buildings, modern skyscrapers, creperies, and pubs that no visitor would skip. The well-known October Fest, a major event of the city, attracts millions to the beer tents during the two weeks of celebration in September each year. Munich's appeal is also related to some infamous events in world history. In the early 20th century, Munich was the "Haupstadt der Bewegung" (Capital of the Movement) where the Nazi Party was founded. Throughout the Third Reich, it remained the center of the Nazi movement. The historical sites where Nazi gatherings were held have become popular tourist destinations (New World Encyclopedia 2014).

In recent years, a growing number of visitors come to Munich to witness a new piece of infrastructure known as "the Munich Wall." Standing between a planned home for 160 refugees and the rest of Neuperlach, a suburban district in the southeastern suburb of Munich, the Munich Wall was built in 2016. Some compare it to the Berlin Wall; others accept it as a legitimate representation of democracy. One thing is for sure: it is a divider. Its social impact is of interest in this discussion.

A "SOUND BARRIER"

The 13-foot-tall and 300-foot-long stone wall was approved by a Munich court at the petitions of local residents, its purpose being to separate their neighborhood from a scheduled refugee complex. Its function is to serve as a "sound barrier" shielding the community from the noise of the upcoming soccer games. "When the refugees come they are a bit loud, and that's why the wall is there," says a local resident, "We are not evil Germans . . . it's a quiet neighborhood, it's nothing against the refugees" (HBO: *The Munich Wall*). The petition eventually got approved. The process, however, lasted for months. According to the court's decision, ball games will be banned near the wall; the wall, however, would not be built in a way to enclose the refugee camp. Opponents compare the wall to the Berlin Wall, and indicate that it even exceeds the Berlin Wall by one foot in height. They argue that it is not about the noise of soccer games, rather it is "a monster against refugees," a "symbol of marginalization," and "the opposite of integration." Moreover, they ask how loud could the soccer games be that would warrant a high stone wall, plus 50 yards of leafy space between the wall and the nearest residential house (Telesurtv 2016)?

THE COMING OF IMMIGRANTS

Since the early 2000s, Germany has become a major destination of immigration. After Syria's civil war broke out in 2011, waves of immigrants have traveled through Greece, Macedonia, Serbia, and Hungary into Germany, and Munich has been the main entry point for them. According to the Brookings Institution, Munich hosts the second-largest immigrant population by density just after Berlin. As a result, logistically, it is difficult to provide long-term housing in a short period; and some local communities object to such housing projects in their neighborhoods for safety reasons. These concerns were further aggravated by crimes such as the sexual assaults that happened during New Year's Eve of 2015 in Cologne, Germany. An article titled "Can Germany Be Honest about Its Refugee Problems" published in the Opinion section of the *New York Times* states: "The issue is not the one-million-plus refugees who have come to us in the first place. It is how to deal with problems that immigrants might be, are or will be causing" (Bittner 2016). Additionally, the influx puts more strain on the city's resources for providing educational, medical, and emergency services.

WILLKOMMENSKULTUR (THE WELCOMING CULTURE)

Many factors have contributed to Germany's openness to immigration. To some experts, changes in the country's immigration policy reflect the current demographic structure: 15 percent of the 80 million German population are foreign born, and that number rises to 20 percent if the children of immigrants are included (Rietig and Müller 2016). Moreover, the German government implemented a series of policy shifts in the early 2000s that magnified the demographic impact. Chancellor Angela Merkel responded favorably to migrant inflows by famously saying "Wir schaffen das" (We can manage). *Time* magazine chose Merkel as the 2015 person of the year, and lauded her as "Chancellor of the free world" (Vick and Shuster 2015). Societal support for immigration was enthusiastic at the arrival of the first wave. Many German citizens rushed to offer housing, material, and psychological support. However, recent tides of arrivals appear to have been a lot faster and greater than many Germans had anticipated, giving rise to a restrictionist movement. In 2015 alone, 1 million migrants and asylum seekers arrived in Germany, more than 15,000 settling in Munich (Telesurtv 2016). As a result, the country is struggling to absorb migrants and help them integrate. These efforts have been hampered, however, by terrorist attacks in Europe and violent acts committed by asylum seekers or those with recent immigration background. Far-right anti-immigrant and anti-Islamic political forces have taken advantage of these events and gained more seats in the parliament. The *Alternative for German* (AfD) party won 13 percent of the seats in parliament in the 2017 election to become the third-largest party. It was the first time in over 50 years that a far-right party entered the German parliament (Hagen 2017). Right-wing attacks on asylum shelters increased measurably in 2015 and 2016. A question that can be heard across the country is "Is Germany's door closed to refugees?"

FROM JUS SANGUINIS TO JUS SOLI

To understand how Munich turned into a major hub of immigration, it helps to examine Germany's evolving immigration policy. Until the early 20th century, the country had been a country known for emigration, as many Germans left for other European nations and the United States to seek better life or to avoid the domestic political turmoil. In the years between World War I and World War II, the German economy was on a fast track of industrialization, attracting seasonal immigrant workers, particularly from Poland. However, it was the post-World War II economic recovery that prompted the German government to proactively establish guest-worker programs with neighboring countries such as Italy (1955), Spain (1960), Turkey (1961), Portugal (1964), and Yugoslavia (1968) to resolve its labor shortage. By 1973, when the oil crisis struck and the economy fell into recession, the foreign population had grown to 6.7 percent of the German population (Oezcan 2004). To discourage guest workers from settling in Germany permanently, the government adopted a rotation plan that required them to return home after one or two years to make room for new workers. During the period between the 1980s and the 1990s, the Balkan War produced millions of refugees. Under humanitarian programs, migrants from Yugoslavia and Romania became the majority of the incoming population. The German government was able to reduce the inflow by restricting admissions policies. Additionally, it worked to slow the process of overseas ethnic

Germans from returning by investing in the construction of German communities in the countries where they resided, such as the former Soviet Union, Poland, and Romania (Rietig and Müller 2016). Generally speaking, for most of the 20th century, Germany's attitude toward immigration was one of restriction and pragmatism. Migrant workers were allowed entry when there was a labor shortage and required to leave when the need was met. German citizenship was granted strictly on a heritage basis, known as the rule of *jus sanguinis*, regardless of achievement or service to the country. As such, integration was ranked low on the governmental agenda.

The trend turned in the early 2000s, when the coalition of Social Democrats and the Green Party rose to power, leading to the immediate passage of several new immigration legislations. In 2000, reforms to the "Act on Foreigners" expanded the traditional *jus sanguinis* principle by phasing in *jus soli* (citizenship by place of birth). The act offered citizenship to foreign children born in Germany, provided that one parent has been a legal resident for at least eight years. As a result, 80,000 children of immigrants born in Germany from 2000 to 2011 received German citizenship. In the same year, the country introduced a green card system that allows highly qualified technical personnel to stay for five years (Oezcan 2014). The green card added mobility, allowing immigrants with professional expertise to travel more freely in the European Union. Furthermore, back in 2001, research commissioned by the Interior Ministry to assess the country's need for skilled labor concluded that "Germany needs immigration." The report, as well as accompanying proposals, led to an overhaul of the migration law in 2005. The new law simplified residence status to two categories: 1) short-term stay for visit, work, or education purposes; and 2) permanent settlement. An important change, however, is reflected in the requirement that the federal government must take up the charge of integration. For example, courses of the German language, law, and culture must be made freely available at federal expense and be required to some extent for immigrants. As a result of these new legislations, more than 1 million immigrants and asylum seekers have arrived in Germany every year since 2012, the yearly number reaching 1.5 million in 2014. In 2015, close to half million people requested asylum in Germany, a tenfold increase over the number of 2010, and which represented 36 percent of the total asylum claims of the EU (Rietig and Müller 2016).

Experts believe a less advertised factor that triggered these changes was Germany's benefit programs being in risk of shortfalls. Since the 1990s, academics have warned that as more people retire and the working-age population continues to shrink, the country's health care and pay-as-you-go pension system will be in jeopardy. Moreover, to maintain its economic strength in the world, Germany needs more skilled labor sooner than later. Demographers from OECD also warned that Germany can only preserve its economic strength if immigration exceeds emigration by 400,000 people per year. Germany's working population will otherwise shrink more dramatically than anywhere else in Europe (*Der Spiegel* 2013). One of the strengths of the new generation of refugees is that about 50 percent of the immigrants reaching Europe from Syria have university degrees, according to UNHCR, the UN Refugee Agency, contributing to Germany not just labor but skilled workforce (*Economist* 2016).

INTEGRATION

Never in German history has the federal government been more concerned with immigrant integration. It had been the immigrants' responsibility to adapt. This situation has since changed. In 2016, the federal government approved a generous budget to reimburse states for costs of accommodation and integration incurred between 2016 and 2018. This includes 2 billion euros per year for integration efforts, 500 million euros per year for developing new housing facilities, and 6 billion euros per year for initial accommodation costs (Katz et al. 2016). These efforts symbolize that Germany has committed to fulfilling its new identity as a country of immigration. They further suggest that it is more confident in demanding that newcomers learn the German language and adopt German values than at any time since World War II (Rietig and Müller 2016).

However, integration is not guaranteed smooth sailing. It will not be successful, analysts believe, until German society abandons the traditional concept of "guest workers for odd jobs," but welcomes immigrants as equals. "We asked for workers, we got people instead," a line by Max Frisch, remains representative of a traditional mentality. Understandably, there is worry that Germany's democratic values and safety could be compromised, which is why many put more trust in a physical wall than in the good faith of those on the other side. However, most Germans seem confident in their future with their new neighbors. An article in *Der Spiegel* captures the optimistic view of the new immigrants:

> This time, members of the new wave of immigrants are working in university laboratories rather on assembly lines. Instead of doing the work that others won't, they are moving into corner offices, becoming senior physicians and designing products for others to assemble. They have a better education and are more self-confident than previous immigrant generations, and for this reason see themselves as neither guests nor workers. Instead, they feel that they are European citizens and take it for granted that they belong anywhere in Europe, and that they will leave again if they find that they like it better someplace else. They constitute an elite that is now immigrating and changing society's image of immigrants. (*Der Spiegel* 2013)

TOWARD A CONCERTED EFFORT

Despite Germany's welcoming culture, the unprecedented influx has put the level of hospitality to the test. The Munich Wall implies a fear at the community level. However, in the end, building land barriers will not quell the concerns. On the political front, AfD's advancement in 2017 represents a rise of xenophobia, political populism, and right-wing nationalism. Integration pressure may push up political confrontations and force Chancellor Merkel to close Germany's door. Such a scenario will likely trigger a domino effect, setting off border closures across the continent, as the *Economist* magazine warned in February 2016.

A survey conducted in 2017 by researchers at Stanford University found that the concept of promotional equality is, in effect, deeply ingrained in the public's understanding across the EU member countries. They found that regardless of political affiliations, voters were willing to welcome more asylum seekers to their countries, as long as there is a fair share of the responsibility. The current lack of an effective

> **The Syrian War**
>
> The Syrian War erupted in 2011 on the heels of the Arab Spring protests. The major warring sides are the opposition forces, also known as "rebel groups," and forces loyal to the government led by President Bashar al-Assad. As of 2018, the government forces, backed by Russia and Iran, are winning over the rebels backed by the United States and its allies. In this complex situation, however, the U.S. is supporting Kurdish fighters to combat the Islamic State, which seeks to expand its territory through fighting the Assad regime. The war is a brutal one: evidence has been found of chemical weapons being used by the rebel side and the Assad regime. The West has strongly condemned Assad for using chemical weapons in 2013 and the alleged attack in April 2018 (being investigated as of this writing) on civilians. The United States and Israel have launched bombing campaigns on facilities of the government. The war has forced tens of thousands of innocent civilians to flee Syria into neighboring countries and Europe. The future of Syria is uncertain at best. While Russia provides strong backing to the Assad regime, pushing for a secular and independent country, the United States insists that Assad has no place in the future transitional government. In the meantime, the humanitarian crisis continues to worsen in Syria, resulting in extremely harsh living conditions.

coordination mechanism, as the analysts note, generates an environment where every country tries to take as few asylum seekers as possible. Some countries even reinforce their border crossing controls to stay on as free-riders, evading their responsibility of admitting immigrants. The consequence is obvious—on the one hand, there is overwhelming pressure on receiving countries; on the other hand, it leads to more suffering by asylum seekers waiting in temporary refugee camps, and higher costs (Martinovich 2017). The findings suggest that policymakers should work together and establish a responsibility-sharing system as soon as possible.

The concept of building a land barrier is nothing new in human history. From China's Great Wall to the Berlin Wall and to President Donald Trump's project at the Mexican border, walls have been conceived as a solution to problems of migration. What functionalities physical barriers will play in the 21st century, history will tell.

Jing Luo

See also: Migration and Demographic Changes: Tokyo, Japan: Sustainable Growth Calls for Immigration Reform; Vancouver, Canada: The Most Asian City in the Western World

Further Reading

BBC News. 2018. "Syria Profile—Timeline." April 24. http://www.bbc.com/news/world-middle-east-14703995.

Bittner, Jochen. 2016. "Can Germany Be Honest about Its Refugee Problems?" *New York Times*, January 16. https://www.nytimes.com/2016/01/16/opinion/can-germany-be-honest-about-its-refugee-problems.html.

Encyclopaedia Britannica Contributors. 2017. "Munich." *Encyclopædia Britannica*. https://www.britannica.com/place/Munich-Bavaria-Germany.

Federal Government of Germany. 2007. "National Integration Plan: New Paths, New Chances" (in German). https://www.bundesregierung.de/Content/DE/Archiv16/Artikel/2007/07/Anlage/2007-10-18-nationaler-integrationsplan.pdf.

Hagen, Lisa. 2017. "How the AfD Won." *Atlantic Daily*, September 26. https://www.theatlantic.com/international/archive/2017/09/afd-germany-right-wing-merkel-petry/541089.

Katz, Bruce, Luise Noring, and Natke Garrelts. 2016. "Cities and Refugees: The German Experience." Brookings, September 18. https://www.brookings.edu/research/cities-and-refugees-the-german-experience/.

Martinovich, Milenko. 2017. "Survey Finds Europeans Favor Fairness in Allocating Asylum Seekers, Stanford Researchers Say." *Stanford News*, June 28. http://news.stanford.edu/press-releases/2017/06/28/fairness-favoreds-refugee-crisis.

"The Munich Wall: Vice News Tonight on HBO." 2017. HBO. https://www.youtube.com/watch?v=9DIlkmUWxJI.

New World Encyclopedia Contributors. 2014. "Munich." Accessed September 20, 2017. http://www.newworldencyclopedia.org/entry/Munich.

Oezcan, Veysel. 2004. "Germany: Immigration in Transition." *MPI*. http://www.migrationpolicy.org/article/germany-immigration-transition.

Rietig, Victoria, and Andreas Müller. 2016. "The New Reality: Germany Adapts to Its Role as a Major Migrant Magnet." *MPI*. http://www.migrationpolicy.org/article/new-reality-germany-adapts-its-role-major-migrant-magnet.

Staff Writer. 2013. "The New Guest Workers: A German Dream for Crisis Refugees." *Der Spiegel Online*, February 28. http://www.spiegel.de/international/germany/elite-young-immigrants-could-provide-future-stability-for-german-economy-a-885647.html.

Staff Writer. 2016a. "Forming an Orderly Queue; Europe's Migrant Crisis." *Economist*, February 6. https://www.economist.com/news/briefing/21690066-europe-desperately-needs-control-wave-migrants-breaking-over-its-borders-how.

Staff Writer. 2016b. "Learning the Hard Way: Educating Refugees." *Economist*, January 2. https://www.economist.com/europe/2016/01/02/learning-the-hard-way.

Telesurtv. 2017. "Munich Wall: 1 Foot Higher Than Berlin Wall, Keeps Refugees Out." *Telesurtv.net*, February 13. https://www.telesurtv.net/english/news/Munich-Wall-1-Foot-Higher-Than-Berlin-Wall-Keeps-Refugees-Out-20170213-0026.html.

Vick, Karl, and Simon Shuster. 2015. "Chancellor of the Free World—Angela Merkel's Journey from Daughter of a Lutheran Pastor in East Germany to De Factor Leader of a Continent." *Time*. http://time.com/time-person-of-the-year-2015-angela-merkel/.

Sydney, Australia: Struggle for Affordable Housing

Sydney, Australia's largest city, is a growing conurbation composed of 40 local governments overseeing more than 600 individual suburbs, located on the Pacific Ocean on Australia's east coast. Founded in 1788 as a British colonial outpost, the city now encompasses an area of 12,367 square kilometers (approximately 4,775 square miles, or about nine-tenths the size of the state of Connecticut). Its size means that Sydney, like other Australian cities, is much less densely populated than comparable cities elsewhere in the world. However, density is beginning to increase as it nears the natural limits of its ability to expand outward, raising the challenge of providing appropriate infrastructure for its dispersed population.

The city is distinguished by its extremely high housing costs, which in 2016 were identified as the second most unaffordable in the world (Cox and Pavletich 2017,

14), and it struggles with the need to provide enough housing for its growing population. In addition, Sydney faces challenges related to providing appropriate and accessible accommodation for its people. It is the least affordable city for renters in Australia, a problem that especially affects single people, the elderly, and lower-income households. Redevelopment of its central areas and a declining stock of public housing exacerbate the situation by uprooting established communities. The city, along with the state government of New South Wales and the Australian national government, faces the complex task of calming housing costs while balancing the needs of multiple interest groups in a far-flung metropolis.

COMPONENTS OF SYDNEY'S BUILT ENVIRONMENT AND HOUSING MARKET

The environment of Sydney has been shaped by sprawl and rapid population growth. The metropolis of Greater Sydney had a population of 4,391,674 at the time of Australia's 2011 national census, estimated to have risen to around 5.57 million as of June 2017. Despite Australia's large size, its population is concentrated in relatively few areas, with almost 60 percent residing in one of the country's five largest cities. Those cities, however, have not developed conventional levels of urban density. With an overall density level of 400 people per square kilometer (1,036 per square mile), Sydney is Australia's third-densest city after Melbourne and Adelaide, yet the population of much of its territory does not reach four people per hectare (about 2.5 acres), a basic threshold for urban status. As of 2011, 96 percent

View of the harbor in Sydney, Australia, 2014. Sydney's housing prices are among the highest globally. (Byvalet/Dreamstime.com)

of the city's population inhabited just 12 percent of its area (Spencer et al. 2015, 3–4). Like Australia as a whole, Sydney is characterized by a predominance of detached houses on large lots, which supporters argue provide more privacy, affordability, and choice for residents. Only as the city, which is constrained by national parks on its north and south edges and the Blue Mountains to its west, reaches the limits of its geographic ability to expand has density begun to rise in areas other than the city center and along established transit corridors.

Despite its low density, Sydney is among the world's most expensive housing markets. This problem has a long history, but although policymakers and analysts recognized and sought to ameliorate it as early as the 1970s, it has proved difficult to resolve. Between 1997 and 2010, the country's average housing cost increased by 220 percent; for comparison, prices in the United States increased by 70 percent during that period (Worthington 2012, 2). Since 2012, prices in Sydney and Melbourne, Australia's second-largest city, have increased much more quickly than those in other parts of the country. Incomes have not kept pace. In 2016, all of the country's major housing markets were ranked as "severely unaffordable" by the urban consultancy firm Demographia, measured according to the ratio of the city's median housing price divided by its median household income. Demographia concluded that cities with a "median multiple" of 5.1 or higher were severely unaffordable. Even by these standards, however, Sydney's prices are extreme. Its 2016 median multiple was 12.2, a figure surpassed only by Hong Kong (Cox and Pavletich 2017, 2, 14). Australia's Rental Affordability Index for November 2016 reached similar conclusions for that sector of the housing market, finding that with median rents of AUS$480 per week, Sydney was the least affordable city in the country for renters and had reached a "crisis level" of unaffordability (Australian Associated Press 2016).

The crisis of affordability reflects the convergence of economic trends and policy decisions ranging from the local to the global. In the early 2010s, Australia's reserve bank, seeking to help the country as a whole recover from declines in its extractive industries, lowered interest rates to 1.5 percent, a poor fit for Sydney because the low rates encouraged speculative buying. Australia's loose mortgage lending standards and the excess liquidity generated by the global economy are also contributing factors, as both encourage speculative investment in real estate. A 2016 study found that the number of vacant properties in Sydney was growing, and included some 68,000 long-term "speculative vacancies" (Pawson 2017). In 2017, New South Wales enacted a set of measures designed to calm Sydney's real estate market, including rules meant to curb speculative investing by making Sydney real estate less attractive to foreign investors. However, the long-standing nature of the problem adds to the difficulty of finding a solution, since the large numbers of current homeowners and investors for whom housing has become a valuable asset form an interest group that benefits from the status quo.

CHALLENGES OF PROVIDING SUFFICIENT AND AFFORDABLE HOUSING

Sydney's sprawling footprint and high housing costs have complicated the task of providing housing for lower- and middle-income residents. According to a 2017 estimate, Sydney will need to generate 725,000 new units of housing over the next 20 years. Although there was an increase in construction during the mid-2010s, the continued rise in housing prices indicated that builders were focusing their efforts on the higher end of the market. Even at the lower end of the market costs were rising rapidly, as higher earners competed with lower earners for a limited supply of rental housing and housing accessible to transit and other public services. Furthermore, much new development is taking place along the city's western edge, but job growth in that part of Greater Sydney is slower than in other areas, approximately .5 percent per year versus 2 percent for the city as a whole (Pawson 2017). The city's challenge is not merely to encourage housing development but to ensure that it meets the needs of a broad spectrum of residents, a complex undertaking that can create problems as well as solve them.

The lack of affordable housing has been identified as a potential threat to the functionality of the city. It is feared that members of essential professions including educators, health-care workers, and first responders may find themselves priced out of Sydney, and workers in many service industries are also affected by high housing costs. The elderly are another group affected by the housing market; many are unable to secure stable, affordable long-term housing, making it difficult to plan for the future or to age in place. Public housing—called social housing in Australia—has historically provided affordable options in Sydney, but the stock is aging and often designed to accommodate larger households than those currently in need. Government funding for social housing has declined, and in many cases it has been succeeded by public-private partnerships focused on affordable housing, a legal designation that offers reduced or capped rents to those with qualifying incomes but provides less security of tenure or focus on the poor than does the social housing system.

One strategy employed to increase the supply of social housing has been to leverage the value of aging developments in now-desirable locations by opening the sites for redevelopment and using the proceeds to build larger numbers of new public units in more affordable areas. This policy has been criticized as an aggressive form of gentrification, as it pushes poor and elderly residents from their established homes in favor of newcomers with more resources. It also threatens long-standing communities. Aboriginal Australians have long clustered in the inner suburbs near the city center, particularly the suburb of Redfern. During 2014 and 2015, activists fought to ensure that the Aboriginal Housing Company (AHC), a nonprofit administrator of social housing in the neighborhood, would include housing for Aboriginal people in planned redevelopment of a complex called The Block, which originally called for retail, offices, and student housing with the understanding that profits would be used to fund social housing development elsewhere in the city. They established a Tent Embassy to pressure the AHC, a form of sustained protest that uses the term "embassy" to emphasize Aboriginal feelings of lack of representation in their homeland, and received assurances that housing would be provided, although as of mid-2017 the situation remained unresolved.

More broadly, governments are beginning to commit to ensuring that affordable and social housing are included in development throughout the metropolis. The City of Sydney, one of its local government units, has developed a program called

Sustainable Sydney 2030 that calls for 7.5 percent of new housing to be social housing and 7.5 percent affordable housing by that date, and requires developers to either include such units in new construction or pay a fee. In 2016, the government of New South Wales established the Greater Sydney Commission to create a city-wide housing policy focused on increasing affordability. In 2017, Australia's federal government also revamped its mechanism for encouraging social and affordable housing in the states, the National Affordable Housing Agreement, and established a new funding mechanism for rental housing development.

Initiatives have also been proposed for Sydney's low-density regions, where, as of 2017, zoning regulations limited the supply of new housing by specifying single-family or two-family homes and large lot sizes. For these areas, zoning revisions have been suggested in order to allow construction of what is often termed "missing middle" housing, ranging from accessory dwellings alongside single-family homes through courtyard apartment buildings, triplex and fourplex housing, town houses, and small low-rise apartment buildings. Such housing can be smoothly integrated into single-family residential neighborhoods, minimizing the disruption of the built environment for current residents.

CHALLENGES OF INFRASTRUCTURE AND TRANSPORTATION NETWORKS

Apart from housing, the largest infrastructure challenge facing Sydney and its region is the provision of sufficient transportation networks for the city and its people. In 2015, Australia's first national infrastructure audit concluded that seven of the country's eight worst road corridors, measured in terms of congestion and delays, were in Sydney. Traffic congestion is a major concern for the city due to its financial as well as human costs. Between 2010 and 2015, the estimated financial cost of congestion rose by 30 percent, to an estimated AUS$16.5 billion, leading to predictions that employers could eventually choose to relocate to places without such problems.

Sydney does offer public transit via bus, light rail, train and ferry networks, and as of 2017 was constructing an additional train line, Sydney Metro, to complement its Sydney Trains network. The project was designed to add capacity for an additional 100,000 commuters to Sydney's train network. Other modes of transportation have also received attention. In April 2017, Infrastructure Australia, the statutory body responsible for overseeing national-level infrastructure projects, released its list of the 100 highest-priority projects. Three of the top-ranked projects were located in Sydney: a second airport, the Western Sydney Airport in the suburb of Badgerys Creek, which is scheduled for construction between 2018 and 2026; the addition of capacity and traffic management technology to the M4 motorway in western Sydney; and the WestConnex project to construct 21 miles of additional highways in the city. In the longer term, Infrastructure Australia also recommended that the governments of New South Wales and neighboring Victoria work together to acquire land for an eventual rail link between Sydney and Melbourne.

Improvements to the city's transportation infrastructure can create additional challenges. In western Sydney a lack of coordination between housing development and supporting infrastructure, including transportation, has limited residents' access to transit and other options. Conversely, construction of additional public transit services has led to localized decreases in housing affordability because prices rise in and around transit corridors. Road construction projects can also be controversial. Toll roads throughout Sydney have been criticized as regressive, since people pushed to live far from their work by the city's inflated housing market then face high tolls as they commute. The WestConnex highway project has been met with a range of objections, including its organization as a toll road, its high costs, and damage to neighborhoods and the environment. Opponents also challenge the project's rationale by citing an established body of data showing that due to induced demand, adding traffic capacity does not reduce congestion in the long term.

Sara C. Jorgensen

See also: Energy and Sustainability: Melbourne, Australia: Toward a Greater Reliance on Alternative Energy; *Schools:* Sydney, Australia: Making International Education a Thriving Sector of the Economy

Further Reading

Australian Associated Press. 2016. "Sydney Apartment Building Boom Fails to Ease Rental Affordability Crisis." *Guardian*, November 22. https://www.theguardian.com/australia-news/2016/nov/23/sydney-apartment-building-boom-fails-to-ease-rental-affordability-crisis.

Bleby, Michael, and Su-Lin Tan. 2016. "Why Housing Demand in Sydney Is So Strong." *Financial Review*, August 27. http://www.afr.com/real-estate/residential/nsw/why-housing-demand-in-sydney-is-so-strong-20160825-gr0sks.

Cadman, Emily, and Matthew A. Winkler. 2017. "Housing Costs Are Pushing People Further Out of Sydney." *Bloomberg*, April 9. https://www.bloomberg.com/news/articles/2017-04-09/sydney-s-price-of-success-sky-high-housing-costs-long-commutes.

Cox, Wendell, and Hugh Pavletich. 2017. "Thirteenth Annual Demographic International Housing Affordability Survey, 2017: Rating Middle-Income Housing Affordability." Belleville, IL: Demographia. http://www.demographia.com/dhi.pdf.

Hoh, Amanda. 2017. "Sydney Squeeze: Is Rent Control the Answer to the Housing Affordability Crisis?" ABC Radio Sydney, March 20. http://www.abc.net.au/news/2017-03-21/sydney-squeeze-affordable-housing-rent-control-options/8370364.

Infrastructure Australia. 2015. *Australian Infrastructure Audit: Our Infrastructure Challenges*, vol. 2. Sydney: Infrastructure Australia. http://infrastructureaustralia.gov.au/policy-publications/publications/Australian-Infrastructure-Audit.aspx.

Martin, Chris, Hal Pawson, and Ryan van den Nouweland. 2016. "Housing Policy and the Housing System in Australia: An Overview." Sydney: City Futures Research Centre, University of NSW Australia.

McIlroy, Jim. 2016. "Waterloo Housing Tent Embassy: 'Re-block, not Knock Down.'" *Green Left Weekly*, July 8. https://www.greenleft.org.au/content/waterloo-housing-tent-embassy-re-block-not-knock-down.

McIlroy, Jim. 2017. "Campaign against WestConnex Continues." *Green Left Weekly*, August 12. https://www.greenleft.org.au/content/campaign-against-westconnex-continues.

Menadue, John. 2017. "Housing Affordability Is Not Just a Supply Problem." The Committee for Sydney, May 1. http://www.sydney.org.au/housing-affordability-is-not-just-a-supply-problem.

Pawson, Hal. 2017. "If You're Serious about Affordable Sydney Housing, Premier, Here's a Must-Do List." *Conversation*, January 23. http://theconversation.com/if-youre-serious-about-affordable-sydney-housing-premier-heres-a-must-do-list-71791.

Pickering, Callam. 2014. "Why Australia Is Floored by Sky-High House Prices" *Australian*, June 13. http://www.theaustralian.com.au/business/business-spectator/why-australia-is-floored-by-skyhigh-house-prices/news-story/e3c3bdc672f62bc03f03217e97ed13aa.

Spencer, Andrew, Jeremy Gill, and Laura Schmahmann. 2015. "Urban or Suburban? Examining the Density of Australian Cities in a Global Context." State of Australian Cities conference paper. http://apo.org.au/node/63334.

Worthington, Andrew. 2012. "The Quarter-Century Record on Housing Affordability, Affordability Drivers, and Government Policy Responses in Australia." *International Journal of Housing Markets and Analysis* 5, 3: 235–52. http://hdl.handle.net/10072/50001.

Zhou, Naaman. 2017. "Sydney's Last Stand: The Residents Holding Out against Gentrification." *Guardian*, January 31. https://www.theguardian.com/cities/2017/feb/01/sydney-last-stand-gentrification-public-housing-sirius.

Touba, Senegal: A Spiritual Solution to Affordable Housing

Touba, Senegal's second-largest agglomeration, is an Islamic holy city. It is a relatively new city and has special autonomous status within the country, being administered by a Sufi religious order rather than by the usual state agencies. Touba's special spiritual and administrative status has fostered innovative housing solutions for its residents that are unique to it. In particular, two major constraints of urbanization in Africa, access to affordable housing and to safe drinking water, have largely been resolved in Touba. Touba is reputed to be a city without shantytowns, a rarity on the continent.

The holy city of Touba was founded in a clearing in the wilderness of central Senegal in 1887 by a mystic named Sheikh Ahmadu Bamba Mbacké (1853–1927), founder of the Murid Sufi order. However, actual construction of the city, starting with its Great Mosque, only got under way after the founder's death. The mosque was completed in 1963, at which point Touba still had less than 5,000 inhabitants. The growth of Touba as a city really dates from that event (Ross 2006, 97). According to the 2013 census, Touba had 753,313 inhabitants (Republic of Senegal 2015). Along with the neighboring town of Mbacké (77,256), today it forms an agglomeration of nearly a million people.

Touba does not have the administrative status of a municipality. It is recognized as an "autonomous rural community," which allows it to remain under the effective jurisdiction of the Murid religious authorities. The equivalent of the municipal council is designated by the calif-general of the Murids (a descendant of Sheikh Ahmadu Bamba Mbacké) and is responsible to him rather than to the local electorate. This arrangement has allowed the Murid Sufi order to develop unique urbanization policies not found in Senegal's other cities. All aspects of urbanization in Touba, from the laying out of housing subdivisions to the provisioning of drinking water and the administration of markets, are controlled either by the order's central religious authority (the calif-general and his administration) or by subordinate institutions within it (lineage heads, ward heads) (Guèye 2002).

Touba's first major distinction relative to housing is access to land. Touba was founded in a sparsely populated forested landscape used mostly for grazing. Beginning in the 1880s, the Murid order embarked on a campaign of agricultural colonization of the area. Trees were felled and land was brought under cultivation. Numerous villages were founded all around the holy site where the city would later develop. These agricultural villages and the fields around them fell under the jurisdiction of various sheikhs (religious teachers and Sufi masters) of the Murid order. They effectively owned the land (by "right of the ax" for having cleared it), which was worked by their students and disciples. As the city of Touba has expanded since the 1960s, formerly agricultural land under the control of the sheikhs has been progressively reallocated for urban use, with no recourse to real estate markets or hindrance from cumbersome land-rights disputes and prior zoning regulations.

As is the case with Senegal's other Sufi orders (Mbacké 2005), there is an internal economy within the Murid order. Students and disciples regularly make "gifts" in money or in kind to their sheikh (spiritual master, teacher), each in accordance with his/her means. In return, the sheikhs provide material and social support to their disciples according to their needs. After many years of devoted service, disciples are likely to receive a plot of land from their sheikh. This might be agricultural land so that they can start their own farm, or it might be a plot in Touba on which they can build a town house.

Outright ownership of the land in Touba remains with the Murid institution, represented by its calif-general. However, use of the land and ownership of the house built upon it lies with the disciples who received it as gifts. (Guèye 2002) This peculiar form of land tenure explains how, despite Touba's rapid demographic growth—which has varied in recent decades from at least 5 percent to over 10 percent per annum (Ross 2006, 97)—the provisioning of housing has kept pace with demand. Where shantytowns have formed around Touba they have been temporary transitional places, pending completion of new housing subdivisions. By comparison, approximately 30 percent of the urbanized area of greater Dakar consists of shantytowns, some of which have been in existence since the 1950s (Cissé et al. 2012, 11).

A second major problem for African cities, the reliable provisioning of safe drinking water, has also largely been solved by the Murid Sufi order. The order supplies piped water to each house free of charge. This policy is based on the religious premise that water is a necessity of life and that it is illegitimate to make people pay for it. The water is pumped from the water table beneath the city from a number of wells located on its outskirts. Water pressure in the system is low, and the taps often run dry in the course of the day. Most houses, however, have reservoirs, either on their roofs or sunken below ground, that fill at night when pressure improves. Good hygiene in these storage facilities is difficult to maintain, but the local authorities run annual cleanup campaigns aimed at preventing epidemics of water-borne disease. Touba's water system is severely strained during the annual pilgrimage, called the Grand Magal (on the 18th of the Muslim month of Safar), when upwards of a million pilgrims visit the city. Outbreaks of cholera in particular have occurred during these events. Not only are the city's water reservoirs cleaned in preparation for the pilgrimage, but the cesspits are emptied. As in most of Senegal's urban areas, Touba has no piped sewerage system. Houses have cesspits. The waste is dumped in designated natural depressions outside of the city.

As both land and water are obtained freely in Touba, the minimal conditions for decent urban housing are created. Much of the city's demographic growth has been fed by rural-urban migration. Especially in the last few decades, as agricultural conditions in Senegal's countryside have deteriorated and the national population has grown, villagers have been moving to cities in search of better living conditions. Those who are affiliated to the Murid order have preferred to move to Touba rather than elsewhere precisely because of ease of access to land.

For Murids, building a house in Touba is not just a personal ambition related to private life; it is also something of a religious duty. Touba's founder, Sheikh Ahmadu Bamba Mbacké, had urged his followers and successors to build the city as he had been prohibited from doing so by the colonial authorities in his lifetime. For the Sufi institution he established, building Touba has meant first of all erecting its Great Mosque and other monuments and infrastructure. For rank-and-file Murids, building Touba has meant building a family home there and perhaps even setting up a business. Over the past four decades, successive calif-generals have called on Murid disciples to come live in the holy city, and have striven to put in place the infrastructure and services necessary for this. Rural-urban migration to Touba is not necessarily a straightforward linear move. People may move to Touba during the dry season (November–May) when there is little work in the village but move back to the village each year for the agricultural season, effectively maintaining both a country home and a city house. In some cases, even the rural architecture "migrates" to Touba. People will build parts of houses, such as wattle walls and even entire roofs with frames and thatch covering, in their villages with traditional rural materials, and then transport these prefabricated pieces to Touba to install them in their town house.

For working-class Senegalese families, building a house is a lifetime endeavor. While the plot in Touba may be received as a gift from a sheikh, the building material (mostly cement bricks reinforced with steel rods, plus plumbing, roofing, and flooring) and the skilled labor must be paid for from the household budget. As a result, house-building is a slow process that proceeds as funds allow. The first thing to be built is usually the perimeter wall around the lot with a front gate that can be locked. Inside this compound, the owner will then erect individual rooms, either single or strung together two or three in a block (typically a living room with a bedroom at each end), sometimes fronted by a veranda. The kitchen is mostly an open-air area behind the buildings. Most of the compound inside the perimeter wall will not be built over. It will remain an open courtyard where many family activities take place: entertainment of guests, children's play, household chores, etc. Houses are rarely ever "finished" in the sense that additional rooms and floors will be added as funds are set aside and as the family grows over the years. As children grow to adulthood, for example, they will move into rooms separate from their mother's house but within the family compound.

Having a house in Touba accomplishes a number of objectives. As in other Senegalese cities, it establishes the family within the public sphere of the city and guarantees it a future there (Melly 2010). A house in Touba is also a resource for the extended family. For families who live in other Senegalese cities, or abroad, it serves as a second home. Having a house in Touba means not only that one's family has a place to stay during the Grand Magal pilgrimage; it means that during that event one will be able to accommodate visiting family members and guests. Murids often send their children to Touba to study as the holy city has a reputation for sound Islamic instruction, and many Murids build a house in Touba because they intend to move there when they retire.

The configuration of houses in Touba differs significantly from urban housing elsewhere in Senegal. House lots tend to be very large. The subdivisions laid out in the 1970s and 1980s had building lots 625 square meters in size (Guèye 2002, 194). This stands in stark contrast to the 150 square meters per lot allocated on average for working-class housing in government-planned subdivisions in other Senegalese cities. In the last few decades, average lot sizes in Touba's newer subdivisions have been reduced to 500 square meters or less. Still, these lots are much larger than the norm elsewhere. The large size of Touba's houses has implications for family life. Senegalese families tend to be polygamous, multigenerational, and extended (Ross 2008). Touba's houses are able to accommodate such families much more comfortably than can those of other cities, which are designed for small nuclear families according to international norms but which do not correspond to Senegal's social realities. Each wife in a polygamous household will have her own room,

---

Grand Magal

The annual pilgrimage called the Grand Magal is the clearest manifestation of Touba's religious function. Held on the 18th day of the Islamic month of Safar, the event commemorates the day in 1895 when Touba's saintly founder, Sheikh Ahmadu Bamba Mbacké, was condemned to exile by the colonial regime. Holding the Grand Magal each year requires the concerted effort of the entire Murid Sufi order, which has sole authority over the city. Preparations include a general cleanup of the city's streets and empty lots, the emptying of cesspits, the disinfection of domestic water tanks, the installation of public drinking water containers and portable toilets, last-minute roadwork and repairs of religious monuments, and the installation of sound and light systems at numerous public venues throughout the city. Major national agencies such as the ministries of health and of transportation as well as state security forces contribute substantial resources. As commerce booms during the Grand Magal, Touba's markets and stores stock up to meet the demands of pilgrims. Traffic congestion in the city and on all the roads that lead to it are a major concern. Much of Touba's street network was laid out in order to meet the needs of the Grand Magal, which now attracts over a million out-of-town pilgrims. There are no hostels or hotels in Touba. Pilgrims stay with family members who have houses there—another benefit of Touba's generously sized residential allotments—or else are accommodated in tents set up in the compounds of their sheikh. Feeding these guests over several days is a major undertaking. Thousands of tons of rice are donated to the religious authorities while flocks of sheep, cattle, and camels are brought to Touba on-the-hoof or by truck to be slaughtered.

rooms for her children, and her own kitchen, though all will be built within the large compound. Furthermore, many families in Touba maintain rural lifestyles and practice such agricultural activities as raising farmyard livestock (poultry and sheep) and sorting and storing grain. These activities easily find appropriate space in their large city houses. Touba's large houses also permit growing multigenerational families to continue to live together. As sons marry and start families of their own, they are able to do so comfortably in their parents' compounds, by building an additional house or adding a floor to an existing one. Houses in Touba's older neighborhoods have now been occupied by three successive generations of adults. Because of the small size of houses in other Senegalese cities, families must scatter as they grow.

Because of the generous house sizes, residential density in Touba is currently very low, ranging from 26 to 42 people per hectare (Ross 2006, 87). By contrast, population density in working-class neighborhoods of greater Dakar can reach as high as 200 per hectare. Yet densification of the urban fabric is in progress. Multi-story buildings are being erected in older compounds to house growing extended families. The city's major arteries are developing into commercial thoroughfares, lined with multistory apartment buildings with businesses on the ground floor.

If Touba's housing is linked to rural-urban migration, it is also increasingly linked to transnational migration. According to a 2007 World Bank study, Senegalese citizens working abroad send nearly US$1 billion of remittance back to Senegal each year (Lessault et al. 2011, 201). This represents 7 percent of the country's GDP. Much of this foreign income is channeled directly into household budgets, paying for things like schooling, health care, clothing, etc. Some of it, however, serves as capital, being invested in start-up businesses or in real estate and house construction. Murid disciples are particularly active in Western Europe, North America, West Africa, and the Middle East. Everywhere they settle they bring the holy city of Touba with them, establishing religious associations and small businesses that bear its name (Ross 2011). As much of the family lives and business activities of Murids revolves around Touba, the flow of remittances from abroad is contributing in no small measure to sustaining the city's economic growth generally and its home construction sector in particular.

Eric S. Ross

See also: Migration and Demographic Changes: Kinshasa, Democratic Republic of the Congo (DRC): Reaching for Demographic Dividend; *Traffic and Transportation:* Casablanca, Morocco: Will a Change in Lunch Habit Improve the Town's Traffic?; *Waste Management:* Dakar, Senegal: Peri-Urban/Urban Agriculture and Urban Waste Management

Further Reading

Cissé, Oumar, Seydou Sy Sall, El Housseynou Ly, Aly Ngouille Ndiaye, and Al Assane Samb. 2012. *Profil du secteur du logement au Sénégal.* Nairobi: United Nations Human Settlements Program.

Fall, Abdou Salam. 1998. "L'accès au logement à Dakar: Les réseaux sociaux." *Africa: Rivista trimestrale di studi e documentazione dell'Istituto italiano per l'Africa e l'Oriente* 53, 4: 505–29.

Guèye, Cheikh. 2002. *Touba: la capital des mourides.* Paris and Dakar: ENDA-Karthala-IRD.

Lessault, David, Cris Beauchemin, Papa Sakho, and Catriona Dutreuilh. 2011. "International Migration and Housing Conditions of Households in Dakar." *Population* 66, 1: 195–225.

Mbacké, Khadim. 2005. *Sufism and Religious Brotherhoods in Senegal*. Translated by Eric S. Ross and edited by John Hunwick. Princeton, NJ: Markus Wiener Publishers.

Melly, Caroline. 2010. "Inside-out Houses: Urban Belonging and Imagined Futures in Dakar, Senegal." *Comparative Studies in Society and History* 52, 1: 37–65.

Republic of Senegal, Ministère de l'économie, des finances et du plan, Direction des statistiques démographiques et sociales, Division du recensement et des statistiques démographiques. 2015. *Rapport Projection de la Population du Sénégal 2013–2063*. Dakar.

Ross, Eric S. 2006. *Sufi City: Urban Design and Archetypes in Touba*. Rochester: University of Rochester Press.

Ross, Eric S. 2008. *Culture and Customs of Senegal*. Westport, CT: Greenwood.

Ross, Eric S. 2011. "Globalizing Touba: Expatriate Disciples in the World City Network." *Urban Studies* 48, 4: 2929–52.

Vienna, Austria: Making Access to Public Housing Equitable

According to a well-known saying, "Vienna is a place where angels rest." Indeed, the capital of Austria is considered to be one of the best cities to live in. According to the "Quality of Living City Ranking" rating published by Mercer Human Resources Consulting, Vienna, for five consecutive years, continues to be first among 230 participating cities (2016). The city's cozy atmosphere, cultural scenery, well-developed transportation systems, high standards of health care and education, as well as affordable housing make Vienna very comfortable. Not surprisingly, its inhabitants are generally very happy and satisfied. Given those advantages, it is certainly not accidental that Vienna hosts many international organizations (e.g., United Nations Industrial Development Organization, International Atomic Energy Agency, United Nations High Commissioner for Refugees, Organization for Security and Co-operation in Europe, Organization of the Petroleum Exporting Countries, International Centre for Migration Policy Development, Council of Europe International Bank for Reconstruction and Development, etc.). People from around the world look at the Austrian capital as an example to follow in many aspects. Among other things, the affordable housing program is undeniably one of Vienna's most amazing achievements.

HISTORY OF HOUSING IN VIENNA

Vienna has not always been a city as comfortable as it is today. In the second half of the 19th century, the capital of the Austro-Hungarian empire attracted many people from all corners of the dominion. As a result, within a very short period of time, the metropolis's population significantly increased (from approximately

400,000 to over 2 million). Like most European cities of that time, the majority of houses were in poor condition, lacking proper heating, bathroom facilities, or kitchens. The unemployment rate was high, and crowds of homeless people roamed the streets in search of food and shelter. Many of them could only sporadically afford to spend a night in a house.

Those with moderate income often lived in small apartments and shared the accommodations. In fact, according to some scholars, Vienna's housing situation was the worst in Europe. Since the miserable conditions frequently prompted demonstrations or civil unrest, the city authorities had to pay close attention to the problem. In 1918, a law forbidding arbitrary rent increases was passed. That edict can be considered the beginning of significant transformations in the Viennese housing market. The law protected the tenants, and they could no longer be arbitrarily evicted from the houses where they lived.

In 1919, when the Social Democratic Party came to power, the issue of housing became one of the most central. A new taxation system was introduced, according to which small apartments were taxed at very low rates, while more luxury houses paid a higher property tax. In addition, developers of communal houses received preferential treatment. Thus, it became more profitable to build public houses and rent them.

By 1934, Vienna had over 60,000 apartments in almost 350 apartment complexes. Nearly 10 percent of the entire population lived in those publicly owned houses. The city council, however, decided not only to improve the supply, but also to make the municipal housing more attractive for the general public. Well-known architects often were invited to design new projects. The complexes additionally included schools, kindergartens, shopping centers, parks, libraries, laundry facilities, etc. In other words, it became logistically very convenient to live in such complexes. Furthermore, unlike in many countries, Vienna did not reserve its public houses strictly for the poorest. It was decided not to overemphasize income thresholds, and mixing people of different social classes was encouraged.

By the end of the 1930s, the Nazi regime had attempted to alter the Viennese approach to housing, but after the Second World War, it was fully restored. Nowadays, Vienna's municipal housing continues to thrive and develop further.

HOUSING DEMAND TODAY

Currently, almost 60 percent of Vienna's citizens live in subsidized apartments. Annually, approximately 6,000 new residences are built. As in the past, the newly built houses are of very high quality, close to amenities, affordable, and ecologically friendly. It is not surprising, then, that city dwellers strongly prefer to reside there.

The down side of these housing policies is, surprisingly, their very popularity. Because it is so successful in this area, Vienna attracts more and more people, and its population is constantly growing. The housing demand consequently continually increases, and the city has to invest more and more into the housing infrastructure. With the influx of immigrants and refugees in the last two years, the population of the city has dramatically expanded, with most of the newcomers looking for inexpensive houses. According to Michael Ehlmaier from property company EHL, since 2016, Vienna's housing demand has been on the rise, reaching approximately 11,000 new apartments annually. The developers, therefore, encourage the government to spend more on the programs.

Despite the very low return on investment rates and a tenant-protected market, foreign investors are attracted to Austrian real estate due to the laws that protect private property. According to the Property Right Index, Austria scored 90 because the government guarantees private property rights, courts effectively enforce contracts, and the justice system punishes any attempt to illegally confiscate or seize private property. Because corruption is almost nonexistent in Austria, the likelihood of expropriation is very low ("Property Rights"). Certainly, such high security makes the country a popular choice for investors. That is why, although most of the real estate (60 percent) is still owned by Austrian nationals, in recent years, many wealthy Eastern Europeans (especially Russians and Ukrainians) have found in Austria a quiet harbor for their investments, a fact that prompted the Austrian government to introduce certain legal restrictions.

HOUSING SUPPLY

According to Statistics Austria, Vienna has 164,746 buildings and 983,840 conventional dwellings (2011). In 2015, there were additionally 7,271 new buildings completed. In 2017, the Viennese government plans to build on average 13,000 new houses, which is significantly higher than the current level.

In Vienna, most people reside in multistoried buildings. Generally, Austria's home ownership rates are lower in comparison to other European countries. Vienna, for example, has the highest percentage of renters (approximately 75 percent). The virtual absence of tax incentives for homeowners makes buying a house a relatively unattractive option.

HOUSING POLICIES

As indicated above, what makes the housing market in Austria in general, and Vienna in particular, special is the high number of municipally owned buildings. While in many other countries municipally owned houses are often viewed as the residences for the poorest, Vienna's vast majority live in such houses, and those people by no means belong to the bottom of the society. In his study "Social Housing in Austria," Christoph Reinprecht notes:

> There is a general political consensus that society should be responsible for housing supply, and that housing is a basic human need that should not be subject to free market mechanisms; rather, society should ensure that a sufficient number of dwellings are available. (Reinprecht 2007, 41)

Indeed, following this approach, the municipality invests a great deal into the housing market. Nearly 25 percent of all the houses belong to the city government. These social houses are built in different parts of the city, so that islands of poverty are not formed. The policy of geographic dissemination ensures a mixture of social classes, and ghettoization is avoided. Moreover, because private landlords have to compete with the municipality in a densely saturated market, rental costs remain relatively low throughout the entire city. Unlike in other countries, the inhabitants of Vienna are not ashamed to live in subsidized houses, since that is the option for the majority.

The federal government generously funds different housing programs. Roughly 80 percent of Viennese houses are constructed with the assistance of public money. Only luxurious and second homes are not eligible for subsidy. Given that the government is essentially the largest builder, it has an opportunity to involve the best architects in the planning process. Open tenders also keep prices reasonable prices and help cut costs.

Despite the fact that Vienna has achieved amazing results, the government faces certain challenges. First, as mentioned above, the opportunity to have an affordable home attracts more and more people every year. Essentially, the better the program becomes, the more pressure it has to withstand. Second, even though the government encourages spreading the population around the city, newer houses, which are slightly more expensive, attract more affluent people, while poorer individuals, immigrants, and refuges tend to live in cheaper older houses. Third, although the government invites many different agencies to participate in design or construction of the new dwellings, there is very little involvement on the part of the common citizens. The latter, therefore, feel somewhat alienated.

Yet, despite these problems, the housing situation in Vienna is far better than in many other developed nations. Although the Viennese experience might not be appropriate for all the countries, some lessons can be learned, and the benchmark practices of the Austrian government can perhaps be selectively adopted.

Mykola Polyuha

See also: *Housing and Infrastructure:* Sydney, Australia: Struggle for Affordable Housing

Further Reading

Bergren Miller, Anna. 2014. "Public Housing Works: Lessons from Vienna and Singapore." Shareable, June 9. http://www.shareable.net/blog/public-housing-works-lessons-from-vienna-and-singapore.

Blau, Eve. 1999. *The Architecture of Red Vienna*. Cambridge, MA: MIT Press.

Förster, Wolfgang. n.d. "80 Years of Social Housing in Vienna." https://www.wien.gv.at/english/housing/promotion/pdf/socialhous.pdf.

"Property Rights." 2019. *2019 Index of Economic Freedom*. The Heritage Foundation. http://www.heritage.org/index/property-rights.

"Quality of Living City Ranking." 2016. https://www.imercer.com/content/mobility/quality-of-living-city-rankings.html.

Reinprecht, Christoph. 2007. "Social Housing in Austria." In C. Whitehead and K. J. Scanlon, eds. *Social Housing in Europe*. London: London School of Economics and Political Science, 35–43. http://vbn.aau.dk/files/13671493/SocialHousingInEurope.pdf.

Statistics Austria. http://statistik.at/web_en/statistics/index.html.

Migration and Demographic Changes

OVERVIEW

International migration on a massive scale is arguably the hallmark of the 21st century. At the city level, the challenges that result with this largely reflect global characteristics. According to the United Nations, international migration since the late 1990s shows a number of trends. From a geographical perspective, more migrants from the global South migrate to the global North. Most of the international migrants tend to choose 10 countries as their destinations: the United States, Russia, Germany, Saudi Arabia, the United Arab Emirates, the United Kingdom, France, Canada, Australia, and Spain. With respect to demographic structure, the origins of international migrants have become more diverse. For example, between 1990 and 2013, Chinese migrants living in North America, Africa, Europe, and Oceania tripled in number. During the same years, the number of Mexicans and Filipinos living in another country doubled. A noticeable change among international migrants is that approximately 50 percent are women, indicating that women are now more likely to seek employment opportunities abroad in domains previously dominated by men. Economic reasons continue to be the strongest driving force for migration. Overall, the majority of migrants originate from low-income countries, and nearly half are born in Asia. The age of migrants in countries of origin and destination is changing as well. Globally, 7 out of 10 international migrants are of working age (20 to 64 years). They contribute to reducing the old-age dependency ratio in destination countries. Old-age dependency in developed countries is projected to continue to rise. "Net migration" has become a new concept driving immigration policies in more developed regions (UN 2013 and 2016).

At the city level, we see multiple dynamics at work. For most immigrants, the top reason to migrate is to pursue a better life, a better job, a better education, and a safer environment. On the other hand, migration can also be caused by natural disasters, pollution, inequality, and war. Migration can be a new source of contribution to the target city, but it can also raise new challenges. The articles in this section provide an analysis of how various cities handle these challenges.

Too Fast Too Soon

One major challenge is that destination cities are simply unprepared to handle large waves of immigrants. Kinshasa, the capital city of the Democratic Republic of Congo (DRC), has a population of 11.5 million. In this impoverished country, economic development is concentrated in just a few large cities. As such, Kinshasa attracts hundreds of thousands of migrants from rural areas and small towns. Refugees from neighboring countries further inflate the migrant population. Unbeknownst to many, some 10,000 Chinese workers are also part of the flow of migrants. The challenge is that Kinshasa does not have adequate resources to support the sudden influx. Sprawling slums are already densely populated, making parts of the city "rurban" rather than urban. High inflation and social unrest widen the economic gaps. Jorgensen indicates that the situation in Kinshasa represents the pattern of many large African cities—the urban growth is a demographic change fueled more by involuntarily displacement than by economic development. Hence, the solution is presumably in creating more jobs. Some experts recommend urban agriculture as practiced in Latin American countries; others propose a secondary city be built next to the primary one to accommodate the influx, following the model of some Chinese cities. However, governmental corruption, absence of economic backing, and chaos in social policies prevent any fast-paced improvement from happening.

When influx happens too fast, it overwhelms resources in the target city. Lima is the capital and the largest city of Peru. Its population was 6 million in 2005, rose to 8.4 million in 2007, and 10 million in 2016. Within 50 years, Peru's urban population had gone from 25 percent urban to 75 percent urban. The drastic change was fueled by the worsening living conditions in rural areas. Johansen argues that global warming played a determining role in Lima's migration: the melting glaciers that imperiled water supply, frequent hurricanes causing severe damage to crops, and the warmer and wetter weather giving rise to mosquito-borne diseases. Massive rural-to-city migration has always hit largest cities first, as these cities possess more resources than medium and small-sized cities. Lima, however, is not ready to accommodate a population of 10 million in a short period. New urban settlements fail to provide adequate jobs, urban sanitation fails to catch up, and electricity falls short due to diminishing glaciers that supply water to hydroelectric centers. The country's tropical glaciers that power 70 percent of the country's energy generation are melting away. As a result, Lima has to invest in desalination of seawater to remedy the water shortage. Moreover, the situation triggers social conflicts: migrants find themselves victimized by discrimination.

The crisis is not limited to a shortage of economic backing; inexperience in handling new demographic and cultural changes can also make urban management difficult. Guangzhou is China's largest platform for international trade. Tens of thousands of traders arrive all year round, and almost every large international company has a presence in Guangzhou. As a result, more foreigners become long-term residents. Statistics show that the total number of long-term residents is above 80,000. A new sociocultural phenomenon is that ethnic enclaves, similar to the Chinatowns in the United States, have surfaced in Guangzhou. Two well-known communities are Korean Town and Little Africa. These communities perform multiple functions: they assist new arrivals in adapting to the local environment and provide a wide range of services in the residents' native language. Furthermore, these ethnic enclaves allow the residents to maintain a certain distance from the local Chinese. From the Chinese perspective, serving international ethnic communities is a new learning experience. The lack of a transparent immigration policy and shortage of management personnel with training in foreign languages and cross-culture communication skills often make managing efforts an uphill battle. Moreover, on the spiritual front, the foreign societies challenge China's Confucian-communist morality and cultural protocol. Impacts of cultural clashes are an area that increasingly attracts academic interest.

In some cases, the solution is in making the society more open and more tolerant. Tehran, the capital of Iran, is also the country's largest industrial base and center of higher education and research. Most of Iran's industries are headquartered in Tehran. As such, Tehran has become the top destination for internal migration. Tehran is also the most culturally diverse city in Iran, compared to other Iranian cities, with the highest population of minorities. The existence of a large number of minority enclaves in Tehran is believed to be due to the city's higher level of safety and security and its more liberal social environment. Tehran's population of 8.7 million is more than 10 percent of the country's population. Despite the Iranian society's increased openness, however, women's social status remains low. Women's job participation rate is less than 15 percent, compared to over 60 percent for men. On the other hand, women's unemployment rate is twice as high as men's. The Tehran government appears to be paying more attention to improving gender inequality. More government positions are offered to women, and more attention is paid to addressing working women's needs. Tehran's 20-year outlook is aimed at building a global city demonstrating strength in Islamic culture and identity, a green and sustainable environment, equality among citizens, and in being a world-class political, cultural, and economic urban center.

Developing an open and equitable society is a challenge not only faced by Tehran; Western cities are also struggling with this. Buenos Aires, the capital and most populous city of Argentina, has a demographic structure that reflects the country's history of migration with racial preference. The Spanish conquest in the name of "cross and sword" has had a long-lasting impact. The conquerors who achieved glory and wealth established a government that served the colonizers first and marginalized the indigenous. As such, racism was ingrained from the start through hierarchies, class, religion, and race. Since the 19th century, Argentina has been reaching out to European countries, encouraging Europeans to migrate. The dominant proportion of European population in Buenos Aires is reflected in the great number of European communities, indicating that a race-based tradition continues in the city today. The tradition, however, is increasingly failing to sustain Argentina's development as educated people tend to emigrate to countries where they can enjoy equal treatment and local migration brings in people from underdeveloped local economies. The migration trend is believed to be further boosted by free-trade agreements. In Buenos Aires, communities of the wealthy and the poor not only constitute a visual contrast, but they are also a source of sociopolitical conflicts. Any hope of improvement requires a cultural change, according to Donahue, one that will give new immigrants an equitable status.

Immigration Is a Solution

Immigrants are more often perceived as liability than asset. But history has shown that immigration is an invaluable source of strength, both in the long run and in the short term. In developed countries today, population aging has become a pressing issue. Los Angeles, California, has a population of 10.1 million. Two million more will be added in the next 40 years. As Cumo explains, the slow growth rate has much to do with the tightening of immigration policy and the recovery of the economy in Mexico. The trouble is, by 2040, 40 percent of the population of Los Angeles will be over 65. Senior care and services will be in high demand, and the economy will depend on a continued supply of qualifying labor force to sustain. Cumo indicates that in the 19th and the 20th centuries, a fast rise in immigration from European, Asian, and Latin American countries made Los Angeles a leader in economic creativity in the world as well as a melting pot of diverse cultures; solutions to the future will once again depend on a favorable immigration policy.

In making immigration a powerful growth engine, Vancouver, Canada, has much to share. In 2017, Vancouver had the largest Asian community in the Western world. Out of the population of just above half a million, almost half are of Asian origin. A high percentage of Asian immigrants are young people pursuing academic opportunities. The largest group is Chinese, representing one-third of the demographics. Globally, large cities in the West with a high percentage of Asian populations are Metro Toronto (35 percent), Los Angeles (33 percent), Calgary (23 percent), London (21 percent), and Sydney (19 percent). Johansen observes that Canada embraces in-migration, in contrast with the stance of the U.S. government, and has prospered from the contribution from immigrants. Immigrants not only bring in their assets; they also develop business connections with their countries of origin. The multifold increase over the years of export to China by companies in British Columbia serves as a good example.

Not every city, however, adopts Vancouver's path. Tokyo, the capital of Japan, has a population of over 38 million, which represents more than a quarter of the country's population. The challenge Tokyo faces, as Jorgensen indicates, is population aging. In 2017, Japan's birth rate ranked 199 out of 201 countries in the world. Tokyo's fertility rate is below 1 child per woman, while the replacement level is 2.1 child per woman. By 2050, 1 percent of the Japanese population will be centenarians. Jorgensen observes that while multiple factors may be blamable for the current low-fertility crisis, the most important one may be the high work pressure. Japanese women typically choose career over family; Japanese men are known to work long hours, and have little time to spend with the family. Moreover, due to the traditional stress on marriage, fewer children are born out of wedlock than in the West. Measures taken by Tokyo and the Japanese government include improving child-care facilities and increasing spending to allow more women of childbearing age to freeze their eggs so they could have children at a later time. A more effective solution, Jorgensen suggests, would be to relax the immigration policy and welcome short-term immigrants, including health-care workers, to join the workforce. For immigration reform to take place, however, the conservative attitude of Japanese society toward immigration—based on fear of a dilution of their culture—must be changed first.

For some cities, immigration policy is hardly plannable for the long term. London, the largest city in the United Kingdom, has a population of 8.7 million. London's population is expected to reach 10 million by 2036, increasing at twice the national urban average rate. A demographic characteristic is that migration has been going in both directions, with international immigration outpacing the exit population, in general. Jorgensen believes that London's primary challenge is to keep up with the demographic changes. Top source countries include India, Poland, Pakistan, Bangladesh, and Ireland. To accommodate the new immigrants, more primary and secondary schools must be built, traffic congestion must be resolved, and housing rents have to come down. The city must come out with all sorts of plans to help people solve the immediate challenges. The future of London's demographics will also depend on the outcomes of Brexit, observes Jorgensen. Brexit is expected to affect the city's international business presence, and as a result, its demographic structure as well.

Vibrancy of Small Towns

Williamsport, Pennsylvania, is located about 200 miles west of New York City and about the same distance to the north of Philadelphia. Here, the impact of influx is minimal. The quiet quasi-rural city in the eastern United States has a population of approximately 30,000. Williamsport was revered as the "Lumber Capital" of the world in the late 1800s. The population rose to 45,000 in the 1950s, at its peak time. As modern industries headed toward precision manufacturing and services, small cities like Williamsport have slowly faded to the background. However, these cities are playing an important function in modern society—their close-to-the-nature environment and low-cost living make them ideal places for "time-rich" artists, scientists, engineers, and computer programmers working on their next innovative project, argues Andrews. Williamsport is supportive of artistic creativity and identifies itself as an "art town." Media technology connects professionals with the rest of the world market just as conveniently as in New York City. Understandably, however, local residents expect the place to generate more employment opportunities. In Williamsport, that expectation is being met by the upcoming hydro fracturing to the area. The population is increasing again with the arrival of workers and their families.

Further Reading

UN. 2013. "Trends in International Migration." http://www.un.org/en/development/desa/population/publications/pdf/policy/InternationalMigrationPolicies2013/Report%20PDFs/g_Ch_1.pdf.

UN. 2016. "Migration Report 2015." http://www.un.org/en/development/desa/population/migration/publications/migrationreport/docs/MigrationReport2015_Highlights.pdf.

Buenos Aires, Argentina: Impact of European Migration

The matter of migration and demographics in La República Argentina (the Argentine Republic) in general and in Buenos Aires in particular can be divided into four separate discussions: the Spanish Conquest of the Americas, the early policies of the independent Argentine Republic (Argentina), the political and economic problems that have tainted Argentina since the mid-20th century, and the current status of regional migration.

The history of migration relative to the New World in general and to Argentina and Buenos Aires specifically goes back several centuries, yet the narrative is fairly straightforward. In an attempt to draw the connection between the initiation of the narrative and its status today, some historical background is necessary.

To begin, let us address the name *Argentina* (derived from the Latin *argentum*, "silver") and the similarly named estuary *Río de la Plata* ("River of Silver") on which the city rests. These names (and others like them that identify a number of locations throughout Latin America) harken back to the famed lust for wealth that led European explorers to the area in search of gold and silver. Legend held that Río de la Plata was a gateway leading to mountains of silver that lay inland. Thus, the name Argentina is a literal representation of what led colonizers to it.

Following the Encounter (aptly named by Chastain), which represents the first historically recorded movement of people to and from the area, it was Spain that colonized what is now known as the Argentine Republic. Historically speaking, the colonization was conducted for the two principal reasons that are succinctly conveyed with a phrase that captures the essence of the Spanish conquest of the Americas: *la cruz y la espada* ("the cross and the sword"). The aim of the Spanish was to conquer territory in the name of the Spanish monarchs and to evangelize heathens in the name of the Catholic religion (which was largely represented at the time by the power of the Spanish crown).

We are best served here by acknowledging the more authentic underlying aspiration of the conquistadors, hidden just beneath the call to conquer on behalf of their monarch and to convert in the name of their God: they sought wealth (or mere livelihood, if immediate wealth was not to be had) by means of military conquest. By the early 16th century, there existed in Spain an entire class of professional soldiers whose prospects for earning a living in that territory (or coming into possession of the land required to do so) had been exacerbated by the end of the *Reconquista* (Reconquest). Islamic Iberia had dominated the peninsula since the eighth century CE and had stimulated one of the highest representations of Islamic civilization the world has known. But after 700 years of yielding their control of the peninsula, battle by battle, Islamic Iberia finally bequeathed its last kingdom (Granada) in 1492. Christian Iberia had limited options for fully incorporating the warring conquistadors who had earned their existence for centuries by means of almost constant warfare. For these warriors, the appeal of remaining in their homeland, which offered little opportunity, paled before the temptation to seek fortune in the recently discovered Americas, where their best opportunity to secure a new means of providing for themselves lay.

So, Argentina is named for the greed of its conquerors, a greed that was rooted in the absence of opportunities for prosperity in Spain. Another hallmark of

Spanish society at the time the Americas were colonized was the Spanish sense of honor (captured most descriptively in the *comedia* of Spain's *Siglo de Oro*): the preservation of the integrity (purity) of the family bloodline was inextricably tied to the preservation of family wealth and family social standing. In addition to being a notably classist society, the Spanish culture that was transplanted to the New World became thus an inherently racist one. Indigenous peoples who survived the initial impact of the Encounter became a quickly marginalized segment of society. Even the *Criollo*—fully Spanish by heritage but American by birth—was a second-class citizen under such societal protocol. Having already mentioned the cause of religion in the Conquest, we can move forward from the great migration resulting from the Encounter with the understanding that significant hierarchies of the new American society were inherited directly from its virtually medieval colonizers. These are the hierarchies of class, religion, and race.

Today's Argentina, along with most of the former Spanish colonies in the Americas, claimed independence from Spain in the early part of the 19th century. The newly established republic set itself to the task of resolving some internal conflicts regarding how to move forward as a sovereign state and clearing itself of local rivalries with the newly formed nations that surrounded it. By 1861, Argentina had defined boundaries, general consensus regarding its form of government, and a plan for generating growth and prosperity: immigration. Article 25 of the Constitution of 1853 renders that "the Federal Government will encourage European immigration, and it will not restrict, limit or burden with any taxes the entrance into Argentine territory of foreigners who come with the goal of working the land, improving the industries and teach[ing] the sciences and the arts."

Boasting one of the most liberal policies on immigration in the world, Argentina entered at this time into the area's second important moment of migration, receiving significant waves of European immigrants (mostly Italian and Spanish) in the mid-19th century. The government went so far in the latter part of the 19th century as to pay the cost of passage for some Europeans in order to spur the immigration that they imagined would further civilize the newly founded nation.

The policy was a success. By 1914, almost 30 percent of Argentina's population was foreign born. and immigrants represented nearly half of the population of the city of Buenos Aires (Bastia and vom Hau 2014). While the nationalities of immigrants to Argentina vary widely, Italy and Spain still represented the highest numbers of immigrants, with Germany and Russia also providing significant numbers. Both Argentina at large and Buenos Aires in particular have well-known, established communities and neighborhoods made up of a variety of European nationalities. Thus, we see that immigration played an important role in the development of Argentina's economy, which by the early 20th century ranked highly among the world's economies. However, as demonstrated by Bastia and vom Hau, the planned immigration was not as liberally grounded as the wording of the Constitution of 1853 suggests. The idea of immigration was tied to the concept of the *civilización* (civilization): the immigration of Europeans was intended not only to populate the newly formed Republic, but to make it as European (i.e., civilized) as possible. The notions of race and class were, if not explicitly stated, implicitly embedded in the Argentine construct of immigration:

Political elites did not want to attract just any European immigrant. The aim was to promote the immigration of "white" Anglo-Saxon immigrants from Northern Europe. . . . Argentinian elites drew an intrinsic connection between the racial identity of these migrants, their supposed habits and biological dispositions, and their capacity for progress. In other words, migrants of these origins were deemed to be especially suitable for eliminating the negative characteristics which were at the time associated with what were considered to be "lower races," that is, indigenous people and the *gauchos*, who were found in the sparsely populated interior of the country. (Bastia and vom Hau, 478)

The liberal immigration policy embraced by Argentina was put to the test in the mid-20th century. Political, social, and economic strife arose, all of which led to a series of military dictatorships. Prior to the military's seizure of power, the populist President Juan Perón had garnered the widespread support of the working class in Argentina. "Peronism envisioned migrant workers from the interior, often of darker skin colour, as an integral part of the national community" (Bastia and vom Hau 482). Workers migrated from rural areas to Buenos Aires with the promise of work and housing. These workers, referred to as *cabecitas negras* ("little black heads") by those opposed to the policy, were housed in neighborhoods that came to be referred to as *villas miserias* ("impoverished neighborhoods"). The *villas*, and the predetermined separation of them (based on race and class) from the city's established inhabitants, lend clear credence to the notion that the hierarchies brought

A busy pedestrian crossing on the Avenida de Mayo in Buenos Aires, Argentina, 2013. The city's European-style architecture reflects Argentina's history of welcoming European migrants. (Peek Creative Collective/Dreamstime.com)

over by the civilization of the conquistadors were still a part of the Argentinian's imagining of their nation as late as the mid-20th century.

While Argentina is still an appealing destination to some European immigrants, the political, social, and resulting economic turmoil that plagued the country from the mid-20th century onward (and which has not yet fully ceased) has led to the tapering off of "old" (north-south) immigration patterns, along with noticeable emigration of educated professional Argentinians (many of European heritage) toward more stable and financially promising areas of the world. "New" (south-south) migration to Argentina now comes in large part from neighboring South American countries whose residents are seeking better employment opportunities than those that are available to them in their home countries with less developed economies. According to the CIA's *World Fact Book*, "in 2015, Argentina received the highest number of legal migrants in Latin America and the Caribbean. The majority of its migrant inflow came from Paraguay and Bolivia." The rise in regional immigration can be considered in part to be due to Argentina's liberal immigration policies, but it has been spurred considerably in recent decades by the Mercosur free trade alliance. The Mercosur trading block consists of full members Argentina, Brazil, Paraguay, Uruguay, Venezuela (currently suspended), and Bolivia (currently in the process of incorporation). Most of the remaining South American countries are considered to be associate members. Jachimowicz (2006) notes that "Uruguayans have the highest proportion of immigrants living in metropolitan Buenos Aires, mainly due to the high-skilled profile of this immigrant group and geographic proximity. The remaining neighboring immigrants who settle in Buenos Aires, predominantly Paraguayans and Bolivians, fill low-skilled service occupations such as domestic workers."

While regional migration does not lead wholly to Buenos Aires—immigrants from neighboring countries tend to stay close to their respective countries—the capital's need for low-skilled service workers has drawn in recent decades more immigrants than it is able to integrate successfully. The regional immigrants find work, but they also find significant challenges in securing affordable housing in a capital city that was developed along class and race lines. These lines are real, not fictitious. Lucrecia Martel, acclaimed filmmaker associated with the *Cine Nuevo Argentino* (New Argentine Cinema), a neorealist film movement that arose during the early years of the 21st century when Argentina was in deep financial trouble, lists among her credits a poignant 2006 short film titled *La ciudad que huye* (The Fleeing City). It is a spontaneous documentation of an elitist, gated Buenos Aires enclave shamelessly plotted amid a string of low-income neighborhoods. The film spontaneously yet piercingly captures the stark contrast that exists in Buenos Aires between the wealthy and the impoverished.

To close this essay, let us refer to an incident in December 2010 that crystallizes the status of new migration trends in Buenos Aires that have been developing since the late 20th century. In 2010, a need arose for housing for 500,000 people, while 150,000 people were already living in *villas miserias* throughout the city (Jastreblansky 2010). Some of the *villas* are planned neighborhoods; others arose out of mere necessity outside of the jurisdiction of the city. One particular conflict came to a boil over the use of one of the city's parks, Parque Indoamericano, located in the southwest parcel of the city. This park, with a history of disuse, had become an unofficial gathering place for many of the city's regional immigrants, particularly those from Bolivia and Paraguay, who hosted soccer tournaments, celebrated national festivals, and convened socially on weekends. After efforts by the city to control and to formalize the use of the otherwise unused park by the city's new immigrants, continued conflicts over its use led to its closure. Protest by the immigrant communities ensued. Beginning on December 10, 2010, thousands of immigrants squatted in the park for four days, while tensions among the squatters, city officials, and nearby residents rose, resulting in the unfortunate death of three squatters. The protests allowed the squatters to formally register their complaint of lack of adequate housing in the city. City officials negotiated, tentative agreements were reached, and squatters abandoned the park with the understanding that modifications to housing requirements in the city were going to begin to be remedied. The extent to which the agreements have been kept is still unknown. What is clear is that Argentinians are finding themselves challenged to live up to the liberal tone of the nation's immigration policy. Will Argentina be able to move away from its notion of "old" immigration and embrace the its "new" immigrants? I find it appropriate to give Bastia and vom Hau the final word: "Until the imagery of the nation is expanded to include the more recent arrivals and their descendants, as well as those Argentines who do not fit the dominant ideal of Argentina as a white nation, there is little hope that their everyday lived experience will improve" (Bastia and vom Hau 2014, 488).

Christopher J. Donahue

See also: Energy and Sustainability: Rio de Janeiro, Brazil: A City with a Passion for Conservation and Renewable Energy; *Housing and Infrastructure:* Caracas, Venezuela: Will Informal Settlement Be Forever?; *Traffic and Transportation:* Mexico City, Mexico: Improving Governance Is Key to Solving Traffic Challenges; *Violence, Corruption, and Organized Crime:* Mexico City, Mexico: Crime, Corruption, and Violence Have Deep Roots

Further Reading

"Argentina's Constitution of 1853, Reinstated in 1983, with Amendments through 1994." *Constituteproject.org.* Oxford University Press. p. 7. Article 25. https://www.constituteproject.org/constitution/Argentina_1994.pdf?lang=en.

Bastia, Tanja. 2015. "Transnational Migration and Urban Informality: Ethnicity in Buenos Aires' Informal Settlements." *Urban Studies* 52, 10: 1810–25.

Bastia, Tanja, and Matthias vom Hau. 2014. "Migration, Race and Nationhood in Argentina." *Journal of Ethnic and Migration Studies* 4, 3: 475–92.

Canelo, Brenda. 2016. "Migración y políticas públicas desde el margen. Acciones y omisiones estatales en un parque de la Ciudad de Buenos Aires" (in Spanish). *Migraciones Internacionales* 8, 3: 125–53.

Chastain, John Charles. 2016. *Born in Blood and Fire: A Concise History of Latin America.* New York: W. W. Norton.

La ciudad que huye. 2006. Film. Directed by Lucrecia Matel.

Jachimowicz, Maia. 2006. "Argentina: A New Era of Immigration and Immigration Policy." *Migration Information Source. Online Journal of the Migration Policy Institute.* February 1. https://www.migrationpolicy.org/article/argentina-new-era-migration-and-migration-policy.

Jastreblansky, Maia. 2010. "Claves y cronología de un complejo conflicto" (in Spanish). *La Nación,* December 10. https://www.lanacion.com.ar/1332425-claves-y-cronologia-de-un-complejo-conflicto.

Slater, Elizabeth. 2011. "Argentina Opens Its Doors." *World Policy Blog.* November 15. https://www.worldpolicy.org/blog/2011/11/15/argentina-opens-its-doors.

The World Fact Book. http://www.cia.gov/library/publications/resources/the-world-factbook/geos/ar.html. Accessed February 11, 2019.

Guangzhou, China: Foreign Communities Facing Challenges of Adaptation

Guangzhou is the largest city in China's Pearl Delta Region (PDR), and the capital city of the Guangdong Province. Located next to Hong Kong and Macau, Guangzhou has always been a frontline city connected to world economies. In 2016, its GDP exceeded 19 trillion yuan, ranking it #3 among all cities in China, after Shanghai and Beijing. The service industry alone contributed 77 percent of the city's GDP, followed by the share of manufacturing and construction. Guangzhou's demographic changes reveal a rapid influx. In 2016, the total population reached 14 million, representing an increase of more than half a million from the previous year. Approximately 40 percent of the population are migrants, and 86 percent reside in the metropolitan area (GCSB 2017).

Guangzhou is also a multicultural city, home to more than 80,000 long-term foreign residents (Ding 2017). During the Guangzhou Fair seasons in spring and fall, the number of foreign residents could reach 120,000. The top two countries that contribute the most residential citizens are South Korea and Japan. When taking account of continents as contributing sources, approximately 60 percent of foreign residents come from Asian countries and 14 percent from African countries (Ding 2017). Some sources indicate that Guangzhou's foreign population is bigger than that of Beijing or Shanghai, due to the city's role as the top contributor to China's export business. Historically, large ethnic-based enclaves of foreign nationals were rare. The largest foreign civilian community in recent history was arguably Shanghai's Jewish District at *Hongkou,* with over 20,000 Jewish residents who escaped Nazi-occupied Europe between the 1930s and the 1940s (Griffiths 2013). Overall, statistics indicate that Guangzhou's foreign population parallels China's unprecedented internal migration. Hosting 80,000 foreign residents, however, is not only a milestone in China's migration history, but also a challenge that Guangzhou is struggling to deal with.

ETHNIC ENCLAVES

Cultural enclaves have long been an important topic of urban studies. Ethnicity-based enclaves in large cities typically serve as ports of entry providing shelters and initial work environment to new immigrants, and helping them integrate into the local society (Burgess 1925). In the process of migration and demographic changes, support circles like these are critical for facilitating social mobility and cultural adaptation. Immigrants tend to congregate with compatriots who are relatives or fellows from the same home country to form a support network. Chinatown in New York City and the "Fellow-countrymen villages" (mostly province-origin-based organizations) in Chinese cities are support networks of this nature. Additionally, cultural enclaves also have business functions, due to their translocation nature. A garment business owner, for example, may draw on native place-based resources through strong connections to his/her hometown to exploit business opportunities. Moreover, enclaves are able to more resourcefully and better than what individuals could achieve in handling challenges from local authorities who impose unfair restrictions on their activities due to misunderstanding or even discrimination (Ye et al. 2015). Foreign residents with large concentrated populations in Guangzhou have successfully set up their living and commercial communities, such as Korean Street, Japanese Street, and Little Africa. Reports by the media and academic studies have shown that integration can be a challenging experience for any group due to language and cultural differences.

KOREAN TOWN

By 2017, Korean residents from South Korea (*Hanguo ren*) constitute the biggest foreign population of about 10,000 members (Cheng 2017). Most of the residents are businesspeople, and some work in diplomatic and educational services. Yuan Jing Road is popularly known as Korean Town in Guangzhou where visitors get a taste of authentic Korean foods, tour shopping malls, and enjoy services offered in the Korean language. It should be mentioned that South Korean residents are not the only members of Korean Town; they are joined by migrants from Chinese Koreans from the Jilin Province and the Yanbian Korean autonomous Prefecture in northeastern China.

A recent study titled "Shallow Integration and Deep Separation: Cultural Adaptation of South Korean Residents in Guangzhou" (Zhou and Yang 2014) reveals several distinct socio-demographic characteristics of the Korean group. The most noticeable seems to be the group's integrative presence among the Chinese locals. Unlike most foreign groups, Korean families blend into Chinese neighborhoods, living next door to Chinese neighbors without being noticed as "foreign." In some cases, a number of families share an apartment building, forming a small Korean neighborhood. Such housing arrangements do not segregate the Korean families from local Chinese, at least in appearance. The study indicates, however, that the language barrier seems to form a boundary around the Korean communities. Few South Korean residents speak Chinese fluently. Quite to the contrary, other than those who work in diplomatic functions and college students, most South Koreans have a low level of Chinese proficiency, and some do not speak Chinese at all. Wealthy merchants often depend on Chinese Koreans to interpret for them. However, most South Koreans in Guangzhou actively engage in learning the Chinese language. South Korean students typically have studied Chinese for three years before coming to China. Additionally, Korean communities make efforts to improve cultural communication. For example, they offer Korean-language classes to Chinese learners; organize social events, such as cooking and outing events, to Chinese acquaintances; and use the media to introduce Korean culture and society.

The researchers of the above study note, however, that the South Korean residents' immersion in Chinese society is limited to utility purposes; and an ethnocultural centrism runs deep in the group. The clichés "body and homeland are at one" (*shentu bu er*), "maintaining distance at deep level" (*shen ceng quge*), and "fateful bonding (with homeland" *yuanfen zhuyi*) are believed to represent an ethnocentric mentality. These beliefs generate, on the one hand, a pragmatic short-term approach rather than an in-depth involvement with sociocultural events in the broader community, and on the other hand, closed friends' circles. The religious practice is seen as a typical example. Approximately 80 percent of South Koreans in Guangzhou are Christians who frequent approximately 20 Korean churches in the city. Worshippers are required to show passports at the entrance for admission. Chinese Koreans may be selectively admitted without the national ID; however, Chinese locals are generally not admitted (Zhou and Yang 2014). It is noted that, bringing passports to social events is a common practice among Koreans. Moreover, the Korean ecosystem of support and services is comprehensive enough to cover virtually every aspect of life, from shopping to daycare to medical care. The mentality of maintaining a distance is reported in multiple studies (Kim 2012; Baker 2008). However, these studies also suggest that young people do not embrace ethnocentric concepts as strongly as their parents do.

ADAPTATION OF JAPANESE RESIDENTS

Guangzhou's Japanese population has increased significantly during the past three decades, and now ranks only behind South Koreans as the second-largest foreign community. Most of the Japanese citizens are company executives and technical personnel employed by major Japanese auto and electronics firms. The majority of Japanese families live in the downtown area in rented apartments, with a higher concentration in seven urban districts: Huadu, Guangyuan Road, East Belt Road, Tianhe North Road, Zhujiang New Town, Ersha Island, and Panyu (Liu et al. 2010). Districts with a larger foreign population, such as Tianhe North Road, tend to have more Japanese residents. However, there is not a road or urban location in Guangzhou that is named after Japanese presence. In their survey, Liu et al. (2010) found that, in general, Japanese participation in Guangzhou's social networks is more limited in breadth compared to South Koreans. Language is considered a notorious barrier that, in conjunction with Japanese ethnocentrism, is believed to pose a major hindrance to adaptation and involvement. It's been observed that Japanese residents in Guangzhou tend to hold social events within their own ethnic circles, go to Japanese hairstyle shops and restaurants, talk to taxi drivers with a note card, and have fewer than 20 percent in their friends circle that are Chinese. Moreover, women's mobility is even more confined—most stay home taking care of children and cooking, or travel within an area of less than one kilometer in radius, if they have to (Liu et al. 2010).

Separate studies corroborate Liu et al.'s assumption that ethnocentrism and the language barrier negatively impact on Japanese residents' social participation. In other studies, ethnocentrism is believed to affect the success rate in foreign-language learning by the Japanese. According to Reischauer (1981), Japanese ethnocentrism is more about feeling different and special. Additionally, Japanese cultural traits encouraging reticence to speak out (Matsumoto 1994) may encourage such perception by other groups. Reischauer observed, for example, that "Japanese as a whole are less inclined than Westerners to enter into casual contacts and are likely to seem forbiddingly formal in any new encounters" (pp. 143–144). Tanaka and Tanaka (1995) state that Japanese people feel more comfortable within their own group, but not outside of the group. Miller (1982) indicates that there is a widespread belief among the Japanese that their language can't be mastered by non-Japanese, because it embodies a spirit and sincerity that no one but they can truly understand, which makes them believe that foreign languages are exceptionally difficult to learn. Results of a study on ESL learning by adult Japanese conducted by Hinenoy and Gatbonton (2000) support the hypothesis that certain social factors such as Japanese ethno-specificity and Japanese language-specificity do somewhat influence language learning outcomes.

Among restrictive factors, researchers also indicate that other elements, such as flare-ups of anti-Japanese sentiment in Guangzhou and in the broader Chinese society, and the underdeveloped security system, may cause safety concerns to Japanese residents (Liu et al. 2010). Commemorative events for World War II are held multiple times over the year. During these events, the nationalist mood typically runs high. In the early 2000s, anti-Japanese sentiment has been occasionally magnified by the on-going tensions over territorial disputes in the South China Sea.

XIAOBEI ROAD—"LITTLE AFRICA"

Since the 1990s when China intensified development of trade and diplomatic relationships with African countries, more and more migrants from African countries have been coming to Guangzhou. The recent "One Belt, One Road" mega trade plan announced by President Xi Jinping is expected to boost the relationships to a higher level. Most of Guangzhou's African residents come from Nigeria, Egypt, and Mali. China's shrinking working-age population has been a factor driving more deals with Africa where the demographics are similar to China's 35 years ago (*MacauDaily* 2016). The majority are traders who purchase clothing in bulk, such as jeans, shoes, and jerseys, and bring them back to their home country. By early 2017, the official count of African migrants in Guangzhou was 10,344 (Cheng 2017), representing a decline of 50 percent since 2009 (Watts 2013; Xinhuanet 2009). Most African migrants live in Xiaobei Road, giving the 10-kilometer street as the name of "Little Africa," or "African Town." Early migrants were attracted to Xiaobei for a simple reason: the Muslim restaurants here serve proper Muslim dishes.

Adapting to Guangzhou's life has been a challenge. Most African migrants come from French- and English-speaking countries and do not speak Chinese at all. Sunday masses at Shishi Catholic Church is attended by thousands of African migrants, and by Chinese worshippers as well. As Christianity gains more popularity in Guangzhou, its services offer a platform of communication between

Chinese and foreign nationals. Some migrants have successfully settled down in Guangzhou, thriving in business and in some cases marrying Chinese women and raising a family. The majority, however, feel excluded. "My family has asked me what I have seen in China, and I say I have only seen jeans and black people," says one African businessman (Fauna n.d.). "Though we've tried hard to fit in this city, we can feel people look at us with a different eye. It's harder for us to get a taxi than for the locals, many of us got refused . . . or extorted," says an African resident (Watts 2013).

Language barrier is not the only difficulty. Cultural differences may lead to more frictions. Local residents complain about some African art forms for being rowdy, and interpret certain behaviors as disruptive or aggressive. Many migrants are staying on an expired visa; a visitor's visa lasts only 30 days. Since 2009, the crackdown on "illegal border crossing, illegal employment, and illegal stay" has intensified and sometimes resulted in violent conflicts. Some immigrants have had their homes raided, and been forced to pay heavy fines; some even served jail terms. Drug trafficking and robberies have been reported happening in African communities, particularly during the downturn of the global economy. Crackdown on illegal status has resulted in nearly 10,000 African migrants leaving Guangzhou and moving to other Chinese municipalities. African migrants, however, do not seem to attribute such treatment to racial discrimination, but rather, view it as urban residents discriminating against rural people who have no money nor know rules (Fauna n.d.). A Nigerian resident states, "It's still easier to make a living here than in Nigeria. But it's a frightening place to be" (Mackenzie and Moxley 2009).

Jing Luo

See also: Employment and Jobs: Shenzhen, China: Struggle to Leave Shanzhai Behind; *Housing and Infrastructure:* Chongqing, China: Chongqing's Ingenuity in Providing Public Housing for a City of 33 Million; Dandong, China: One Bridge, Two Islands; *Migration and Demographic Changes:* Vancouver, Canada: The Most Asian City in the Western World

Further Reading

Baker, Don. 2008. "Koreans in Vancouver: A Short History." *Journal of the Canadian Historical Association* 19, 2. https://www.erudit.org/fr/revues/jcha/2008-v19-n2-jcha3329/037752ar.

Burgess, Ernest Watson. 1925. "The Growth of the City: An Introduction to a Research Project." In Robert E. Park, Ernest W. Burgess, and R. D. McKenzie, eds. *The City.* Chicago: University of Chicago Press. http://prelim2009.filmbulletin.org/readings/09-Urban/Burgess.pdf.

Cheng, Jingwei. 2017. "Number of Africans in Guangzhou Decreases to 10,344, Lowest Level in Recent Years." *China News Service.* http://news.sina.com.cn/o/2017-03-13/doc-ifychavf2645633.shtml.

Ding Wenlei. 2017. "Guangzhou Hosts Approximately 80,000 Regular Foreign Residents." *ChinaNews Website.* http://www.chinanews.com/sh/2017/03-05/8166068.shtml.

Fauna. n.d. "Africans in Guangzhou: Opportunities and Discrimination." *ChinaSMACK.com.* https://www.chinasmack.com/africans-in-guangzhou-opportunities-discrimination.

Griffiths, James. 2013. "Shanghai's Forgotten Jewish Past." *The Atlantic.* November 21. https://www.theatlantic.com/china/archive/2013/11/shanghais-forgotten-jewish-past/281713/.

Guangzhou Statistics Bureau (GCSB) Website. http://www.gzstats.gov.cn.

Hinenoya, Kimiko, and Elizabeth Gatbonton. 2000. "Ethnocentrism, Cultural Traits, Beliefs, and English Proficiency: A Japanese Sample." *Modern Language Journal* 84, 2. http://onlinelibrary.wiley.com/doi/10.1111/0026-7902.00064/pdf.

Kim, Gabrielle. 2012. "Korean Americans and Multiculturalism: Beyond the Demographics." *Global Tides* 6. http://digitalcommons.pepperdine.edu/cgi/viewcontent.cgi?article=1050&context=globaltides.

Liu Yungang, Tan Yuwen, and Zhou Wenting. 2010. "Japanese Migrants in Guangzhou, Their Living and Environment" (in Chinese). *ACTA Geographical SINCA* 65, 10. doi: 10.11821/xb201010003.

Mackenzie, Tom, and Mitch Moxley. 2009. "China's 'Little Africa' Is under Pressure." *GlobalPost*. https://www.pri.org/stories/2009-02-23/chinas-little-africa-under-pressure.

Matsumoto, Kazuko. 1994. "English Instruction Problems in Japanese Schools and Higher Education." *Asian Pacific Communication* 5: 209–14.

Miller, R. A. 1982. *Japan's Modern Myth: The Language and Beyond*. New York: Weatherhill.

Reishauer, Edwin O. 1981. *The Japanese*. Cambridge, MA: Harvard University Press.

Staff Writer. 2016. "Human Resources Focus in Next Cycle of China-Africa Economic Cooperation." *MacauDaily*. http://macaudailytimes.com.mo/human-resources-focus-next-cycle-china-africa-economic-cooperation.html.

Tanaka, S., and H. Tanaka. 1995. "A Survey of Japanese Sources on the Use of English in Japan." *World Englishes* 14: 117–36.

Watt, Louise. 2017. "PRD and Macau Are 'Land of Opportunity' for African Traders." *MacauDaily*. http://macaudailytimes.com.mo/prd-macau-land-opportunity-african-traders.html.

Watts, Elleka. 2013. "A 'Little Africa' in Southern China." *Diplomat*. http://thediplomat.com/2013/08/a-little-africa-in-southern-china.

"Xiaobei, Black Community in Guangzhou, China." *Liveleak.com*. https://www.liveleak.com/view?i=75e_1330624296.

Xinhuanet. 2009. "Nearly 20,000 Reside in Guangzhou, Putting China's Foreign Resident Management Policy to Test" (in Chinese). http://archive.is/uyfX.

Ye Liu, Zhigang Li, Yuqi Liu, and Hongsheng Chen. 2015. "Growth of Rural Migrant Enclaves in Guangzhou, China: Agency, Everyday Practice and Social Mobility." *Urban Studies* 52, 3086–3105. http://journals.sagepub.com/doi/pdf/10.1177/0042098014553752.

Zhou Daming, and Yang Xiaoliu. 2014. "Shallow Integration vs. Deep Segregation: Cultural Integration of Koreans in Guangzhaou" (in Chinese). *Ethno-National Studies* 2014002. http://qk.laicar.com/M/Content/977203.

Kinshasa, Democratic Republic of the Congo (DRC): Reaching for Demographic Dividend

Kinshasa, the political and economic capital of the Democratic Republic of the Congo (DRC), is a rapidly expanding megacity with an estimated population of over 11 million people. By far the largest city in a still-rural African country, Kinshasa attracts internal and external migrants as well as expanding through natural increase, leading to an annual population growth rate of around 4 percent per year.

This pattern of rapid growth poses challenges beyond the basic problem of providing sufficient infrastructure, services, and employment for an increasing population. The DRC is an impoverished, politically unstable, and war-torn state with little capacity to provide support or stability for Kinshasa and its people. Any solution to the challenges of rapid growth must take this national context into account, and the city may lack the ability to channel its growing population toward social stability and economic expansion.

OUTLINE OF KINSHASA'S DEMOGRAPHIC AND MIGRATION PROFILE

In the absence of reliable fine-grained data, any demographic profile of Kinshasa's population is necessarily a sketch based on estimates. It is clear, however, that Kinshasa is one of the most rapidly expanding cities in Africa. Its population in 2018 was estimated at around 11.5 million people (Index Mundi 2018). This figure was more than a fourfold increase over that provided by the last DRC census in 1984, which enumerated the city's population at 2.664 million (Piermay 1997, 226). Along with Cairo and Lagos, Kinshasa is one of three African cities to have reached megacity status, with a population of over 10 million people. It is projected to reach 15 million residents by 2025.

Kinshasa's high rate of population growth reflects the combination of its internal growth rate and the impact of in-migration. Every year some 390,000 Congolese relocate to the capital, a number equivalent in itself to the population of a mid-sized city (Iazzolino 2016). The DRC is a young country, demographically speaking; its median age for males in 2018 was estimated as 18.3 and for females as 18.8 years old (Index Mundi 2018). National population has been growing rapidly since the country achieved independence in 1960, increasing from around 20 million residents to an estimated 67 million in the mid-2010s (Trapido 2016, 67). It is also among the nine countries in which, due to high birth rates, half of the world's population growth between 2015 and 2050 is projected to occur. The average fertility rate for Kinshasa province, which is dominated by the city, was 4.2 children per woman in 2013, significantly lower than the national average of 6.6 children per woman (Demographic and Health Survey 2014, 3). However, childhood mortality is lower in the DRC's urban areas than its rural regions, with an average of 96 deaths before age five per 1,000 live births in the cities versus 118 per 1,000 in rural areas (Demographic and Health Survey 2014, 7).

Kinshasa is more than five times larger than the DRC's second-largest city, Huambo. Standing alone as the country's leading city, it attracts a wide range of migrants seeking education, employment, stability, or refuge. Migration within the DRC is primarily urban-to-urban; a 2007 survey found that roughly 40 percent of internal migrants to Kinshasa came from other large cities in the DRC, and 44 percent came from small towns, with 16 percent of surveyed migrants coming from rural areas (Corker 2013, 14–15). The DRC is a large country, with an area of 905,400 square miles (about two-thirds the size of Western Europe). But few roads or railroads tie its regions together, and although it is officially a Francophone country—and Kinshasa is technically the world's largest French-speaking city—the country is multilingual. Most internal migrants to Kinshasa come from the nearby provinces, which share the city's common languages of Lingala, a lingua franca used along the Congo River, and the regional language Kikongo.

Kinshasa's population also includes refugees from inside and outside the DRC, as well as some other immigrants. Civil wars in the DRC between 1997 and 2003 displaced more than a million Congolese, many thousands of whom took refuge in the capital. Additionally, Brazzaville, the capital of the neighboring Republic of Congo (ROC), is located directly across the Congo River from Kinshasa, and due to strained diplomatic relations between the two countries tens of thousands of DRC nationals residing in the ROC were expelled from that country during the mid-2010s. Many of them were rehoused in refugee camps surrounding Kinshasa. However, although the eastern part of the DRC has intermittently been engulfed in conflict since 2008, most refugees resettle in areas closer to their homes and easier to reach than the distant national capital. War and unrest in the DRC have also limited Kinshasa's appeal as a destination for international immigrants who are not refugees, but the city is home to a community of somewhere around 10,000 Chinese migrants, whose presence reflects the country's courting of Chinese investment as it seeks to recover from its recent turmoil.

THE CHALLENGE OF THE BUILT ENVIRONMENT

Kinshasa's rapid population growth has exacerbated the already daunting challenge of accommodating its people—known as the Kinois—within its deteriorating and poorly managed infrastructure. The city's roots lie in the DRC's colonial past. Established as Léopoldville by the Belgians in 1881, it became the capital of the Belgian Congo in 1926. It is located along the southern bank of the Congo River alongside Malebo (formerly Stanley) Pool, which was historically an important trading center. Like most colonial outposts, it developed as two parallel and segregated urban zones. The European city of business, administrative, and residential districts was located along the river, and African residential districts were located inland. The European settlement enjoyed paved roads, water, and sewage service, but none of these amenities were developed in the African areas, which also suffered from flooding and outbreaks of infectious diseases. Nonetheless, the city's overall population grew rapidly. It had reached 50,000 people by the outbreak of World War II, and by 1959, a year before the Belgian Congo was granted independence, it had some 300,000 residents (Trapido 2016, 61). The city, which remained the capital after the Belgian Congo became independent, was rechristened Kinshasa in 1966.

Tens of thousands of refugees arrived during the turbulence and civil war that followed independence. Its population continued to grow rapidly during the long regime of Mobutu Sese Seko (1965–97), with growth peaking at an annual rate of 9.4 percent in 1970 before subsiding to an average rate of roughly 4 percent per year (Trefon 2004, 8). Refugees and other newcomers initially took over the colonial city's underdeveloped African districts, while government officials and members of the social and economic elite occupied the districts that had previously been reserved for Europeans. By the end of the 20th century, however, newcomers were creating sprawling new slum districts on the city's eastern and southern outskirts.

During the same period, the municipal and national governments lost the ability to support and regulate this burgeoning population. In the 1980s the DRC's economic and political institutions began to deteriorate, leading to the emergence of a "survival" (*débrouille*) economy in Kinshasa. In the early 1990s, catastrophically high inflation rates, measuring some 8,000 percent annually, and waves of looting and civil unrest destroyed much of its remaining formal economy and infrastructure. By the mid-1990s, only 5 to 10 percent of Kinois were participating in the formal economy (De Boeck 2015, S148), a figure that remained low into the mid-2010s. The city formerly known as "Kin la Belle" (Kinshasa the beautiful) came to be described as "Kin la Poubelle" (Kinshasa the trash bucket) due to the uncollected refuse that was a visual indicator of its social and political disorder. Kinshasa's growth patterns in the early 21st century echoed its colonial past: in the mid-2010s, wealthier residents clustered in the planned sections of the historic city and in new, often limited-access private developments, while poorer people settled on the city's periphery where there was very little planning and few if any services provided.

The city continues to struggle with the shape of its development, although by the early 2010s there were some signs of economic recovery including the re-emergence of a road network after a low point in the early 2000s when paved roads effectively disappeared, provision of basic bus service, and the emergence of a cellular network. However, Kinshasa's spatial structure is itself ill-suited for its growing population. Over time, the city has spread eastward along the river and southward into the interior, but the central business district, where public functions and access to informal business opportunities are clustered, is still located near the river at the northwestern edge of the city. The fastest-growing residential areas are far to the east, where there are few jobs and no roads or access to utilities. Residents of these neighborhoods must walk more than 15 miles to the center in search of jobs and services. Some 5 million people, almost half of the city's population, are estimated to live in these circumstances.

Suggested responses to these challenges often hinge on the regularization of Kinshasa's informal built environment as a means of integrating the outskirts and their residents into the city fabric. A partnership composed of the urban design firm Citilinks and China's Tongji University has proposed that Kinshasa should develop a second urban center along the river at the eastern end of the city as a way of integrating that region into the urban fabric and encouraging its economic development. This group also suggested the development of a bus rapid transit network to link Kinshasa's many isolated residential areas with economic centers and provide their residents with access to necessary goods and services (Patel 2015).

Because the poor migrants who have established themselves on the city's periphery often engage in subsistence farming in order to support themselves, the structure of parts of the city has become "rurban" rather than truly urban. A program called Pro Huerta ("Pro Garden"), which could provide a model for Kinshasa, was developed in Argentina in 2003 and has also been employed in Haiti, Brazil,

Guatemala, Venezuela, and Colombia. It supports gardens and small-scale agriculture as a means to economic and food self-sufficiency, as well as encouraging small-scale entrepreneurship in poor areas and creating entry points for health workers and other service professionals to engage with isolated communities (Solheim 2016, 328–29).

THE DEMOGRAPHIC DIVIDEND AND THE CHALLENGES FACING THE DRC

The growth of cities in 21st-century Africa has been described as a demographic phenomenon rather than an economic phenomenon, meaning that it is driven by the arrival of people who are concerned with issues such as the need to escape conflict, lack of services in rural areas, or difficulties caused by the climate, not economic opportunities or greater productivity. In 2012, the level of urban poverty in the DRC was estimated at 61.6 percent, unusually close to the rural poverty level of 64.9 percent (Bello-Schünemann and Aucoin 2016, 17), indicating that Kinshasa was then an especially strong example of this pattern. But because the city has a declining fertility rate, it is potentially in a position to benefit from what demographers refer to as a "demographic dividend"—a release of resources that would have been necessary to provide for the health and welfare of young dependents, which in their absence become available for economic development.

However, while a declining fertility rate creates the potential for a demographic dividend, Kinshasa lacks the qualities that would allow the city to benefit from it. In order for available resources to be channeled into economic development, a city must be able to generate additional jobs, a difficult task in Kinshasa's mostly informal economy. The corruption that is endemic in Kinshasa and the DRC as a whole also undermines the city's chances of harnessing a demographic dividend, as do the absence of clear and effective economic and social policies on the part of the country and the city. Kinshasa has strong demographic momentum, but its infrastructure and economic momentum are atrophied, making continued slum development and poverty for the city and its growing population a more likely trajectory than a shift toward patterns that encourage and reward economic growth.

Sara C. Jorgensen

See also: Migration and Demographic Changes: Lima, Peru: Migration and Demographic Changes Driven by Climate Changes

Further Reading

Bello-Schünemann, Julia, and Ciara Aucoin. 2016. "African Urban Futures." *African Futures* Paper 20. Institute for Security Studies. https://issafrica.org/research/papers/african-urban-futures.

Burke, Jason. 2017. "Face-off over the Congo: The Long Rivalry between Kinshasa and Brazzaville." *Guardian*, January 17. https://www.theguardian.com/cities/2017/jan/17/congo-rivalry-kinshasa-brazzaville-river-drc.

Corker, Jamaica. 2013. "Internal Migration to Kinshasa 1970–2007: Investigating Migrant Characteristics in Times of Insecurity and Economic Crises." Unpublished conference paper, IUSSP Conference, Busan, South Korea.

De Boeck, Filip. 2015. "'Poverty' and the Politics of Syncopation: Urban Examples from Kinshasa (DR Congo)." *Current Anthropology* 56, S11: S146–S158.

Democratic Republic of Congo Ministère du Plan et Suivi de la Mise en oeuvre de la Révolution de la Modernité (MPSMRM), Ministère de la Santé Publique (MSP) and ICF International. 2014. *Democratic Republic of Congo Demographic and Health Survey 2013–14: Key Findings*. Rockville, MD: MPSMRM, MSP, and ICF International.

Gondola, Didier. 2012. "Kinshasa: Confluence of Riches and Blight." In Aran MacKinnon and Elaine MacKinnon, eds. *Places of Encounter: Time, Place and Connectivity in World History*. Boulder, CO: Westview Press, 195–210.

Iazzolino, Gianluca. 2016. "Once upon a Time It Was Kin la Belle." *IRIN*, March 3. https://www.irinnews.org/special-report/2016/03/03/once-upon-time-it-was-kin-la-belle.

Index Mundi. 2018. "Congo, Demographic Republic of the, Demographics Profile 2018." http://www.indexmundi.com/democratic_republic_of_the_congo/demographics_profile.html.

Makungu, Nuah M. 2012. "Is the Democratic Republic of Congo Being Globalized by China? The Case of Small Commerce at Kinshasa Central Market." *Quarterly Journal of Chinese Studies* 2, 1: 89–101.

Patel, Neel V. 2015. "The Future of Kinshasa: A City with a Destination and Transport Problem." *Inverse*, July 1. https://www.inverse.com/article/4224-future-kinshasa-africa-prediction.

Piermay, Jean-Luc. 1997. "Kinshasa: A Reprieved Mega-City?" In Carole Rakodi, ed. *The Urban Challenge in Africa: Growth and Management of Its Large Cities*. Tokyo: United Nations University Press, 223–51.

Solheim, Kristina. 2016. "Pro Huerta: Urban Agriculture and Food Security in a Changing World." In Lisa Mastny, ed. *State of the World: Can a City Be Sustainable?* Washington, DC: Island Press, 328–29.

Trapido, Joe. 2016. "Kinshasa's Theatre of Power." *New Left Review* 98: 57–80.

Trefon, Theodore, ed. 2004. *Reinventing Order in the Congo: How People Respond to State Failure in Kinshasa*. London: Zed Books.

United Nations Department of Economic and Social Affairs, Population Division. 2017. "World Population Prospects: The 2017 Revision." Last modified June 21, 2017. https://www.un.org/development/desa/publications/world-population-prospects-the-2017-revision.html.

Lima, Peru: Migration and Demographic Changes Driven by Climate Changes

Lima's population has risen from 6 million in 2005 to 8.4 million in 2007, and to more than 10 million in 2016. Part of the increase is due to high reproduction rates, but a sizable part of it stems from rural in-migration, which has been plagued by severe poverty and violent political conflict. Migration from rural to urban areas has accelerated over several decades due to a lack of economic opportunities. Conditions in rural areas have been desperate enough to lure millions of people into urban areas despite acute competition for employment there. Climate change also has made life more difficult in both rural and urban areas. Within 50 years, Peru has transformed from three-quarters rural to more than 75 percent urban. Most of

The Cerro San Cristobal neighborhood in Lima, Peru, 2017. As Lima's population grows, immigrant families tend to settle in "informal" neighborhoods on the outskirts of the city. (Dvrcan/Dreamstime.com)

the urbanization has taken place in Lima and Arequipa, Peru's two largest cities. Lima alone was home to one-third of the country's roughly 30 million people in 2017.

Once in urban areas, immigrants establish "informal" or "popular" settlements, also known as *pueblos jovenes* (young towns) or *asentamientos humanos* (human settlements). A few people build shanties with whatever materials they can get, without power, sewers, water, or the sanction of city governments. Services come, if at all, much later. In this manner, the cities expand, as new informal neighborhoods spring up elsewhere. Such patterns of development are common throughout Latin America, from Mexico City to Sao Paulo and Buenos Aires, each of which now contains more people than New York City.

Residents typically improve their dwellings as they become established in the city. "Land tenure may also eventually be granted or sold to residents providing greater security and a sense of inclusion into the formal city," wrote Richie Dean for Helping Overcome Obstacles Peru (HOOP) (2016). "The rate of change and the transformation of informal settlements and when and whether this happens, however, varies enormously depending on the city and the area, with economic stagnation and enduring social issues common across many young urban areas" (Dean 2016).

Eventually, many of these communities receive city zoning, a place on maps, and urban infrastructure. Until that occurs (it can require 10 to 20 years), residents are forced to acquire water for cooking and sanitation, as well as electricity and waste removal, by any means necessary. Unpaved roads are dusty during droughts and muddy during heavy rains. New settlements typically offer very few jobs, so residents are forced to commute long distances around an urban area that has continually expanded as more people move in from rural areas. Migrants also face discrimination from longer-term city residents. This may be doubly true if they are indigenous peoples, who "commonly experience racial discrimination and find themselves relegated to a lower status in the social and cultural hierarchy of the city" (Dean 2016).

Climate change has caused additional stress. Global warming enhances the potential for increasing disease among migrating populations. More rapid climate changes, including El Niño (a warming of the equatorial Pacific Ocean west of Peru) and La Niña (which cools the ocean near Peru's coast) cycles, are playing havoc with the country's agriculture, forcing farms to be abandoned, with massive migration to cities, mainly to the Lima metropolitan area. Melting glaciers have imperiled Lima's water supply as well, at the same time that population is increasing.

According to William Checkley, who works in Baltimore at the Johns Hopkins School of Public Health as a specialist in epidemiology and disease control, admissions to the oral rehydration unit at Lima's Children's Health Institute, Peru's largest public children's hospital, doubled during the El Niño that occurred during the winter of 1997–98. This pattern was repeated during another severe El Niño event in 2015–16. "It changed winter into summer," said Checkley, the unexpected warmth permitting the growth of bacteria and parasites. He estimated that the El Niño of 1998–99 caused 6,225 cases of diarrhea, the treatment of which cost $277,000 (Fraser 2009).

Rising temperatures also have played a role in increasing populations of disease-carrying sand fleas, which cause young children to experience Carrion's disease, with its bleeding sores and high fevers. These outbreaks coincide with warm, humid El Niño conditions that occur more frequently as average temperatures rise. "The disease, readily cured with antibiotics, must be treated early, as later stages render patients extremely vulnerable to potentially fatal secondary infections. Illnesses such as malaria and diarrhea hit children particularly hard and can leave long-term, debilitating effects that extract a high cost from tropical countries" (Fraser 2009). Fleas and mosquitoes usually reproduce more quickly and live longer in warmer, more humid weather. "Researchers in Lima found a similar correlation with hospital admissions for diarrheal illnesses, especially among children in the shantytowns ringing the sprawling capital," wrote Barbara Fraser in *Scientific American* (2009).

Warming temperatures also bring more intense rainstorms during El Niño periods, increasing damage from floods, especially in shantytowns. Warm, humid conditions also increase mosquito-borne diseases such as dengue fever and malaria, especially in densely packed shantytowns. "As crops dry up and farmers migrate to urban shantytowns lacking clean water and basic sanitation, the burden is amplified," Fraser wrote (2009).

"It's really complicated to sort out how much is attributable to climate change," said Mary Wilson, associate professor of global health and population at the Harvard School of Public Health. Nevertheless, "many infections, including dengue, yellow fever, hanta virus, bartonellosis and leishmaniasis, are very sensitive to climate and to temperature, humidity, and rainfall" (Fraser 2009).

In the long run, melting glaciers provoked by rising temperatures may be the most ominous threat to urban Peru, where the water supply in an overwhelmingly dry climate depends on regular snowfall in the Andes. Growing urban areas and declining glacier runoff are on a collision course that will constrict water supplies in the Lima urban area. Lima already has a large and steadily increasing water shortage, in a dense urban area of more than 10 million people "living in what is essentially a desert with little rainfall and therefore heavily reliant on water from glacial melt" (Fraser 2009).

Peru has the world's largest number of tropical glaciers, which are rapidly melting. In the short term, rapid ice melt can overwhelm rural irrigation systems. In the longer term, the eventual exhaustion of glaciers will cause debilitating water shortages in both cities and countryside. More than 99 percent of the world's tropical glaciers are in South America and 71 percent of those are found in Peru (Fraser 2006). With 70 percent of Peru's energy from hydroelectric sources, variations in water supply can pose major problems. One river, the Mantaro, generates about 40 percent of Peru's electricity (Fraser 2006).

During three decades (1970–2000), Peru's glaciers lost almost a quarter of their 1,225-square-mile surface (Wilson 2001, A-1). Rapid glacial retreat has been observed all along the spine of the Andes and on adjacent high plateaus. The 18,700-foot-high Quelccaya ice cap in the Andes of southeastern Peru has been steadily shrinking at an accelerating rate, losing 10 to 12 feet a year between 1978 and 1990, up to 90 feet a year between 1990 and 1995, and 150 feet a year between 1995 and 1998. The glacier retreated between 100 and 500 feet, depending on location, between 1999 and 2004. Melting has continued after that. By 2015, according to the Peruvian National Commission on Climate Change, Peru had lost all of its glaciers below 18,000 feet. Within 30 years, all of Peru's glaciers may vanish except for isolated patches on the very highest peaks.

Within 25 years ending in 2012, 1,600 years' worth of ice had melted in the Peruvian Andes, according to scientists' measurements of the Quelccaya ice cap, at 5,670 meters (about 18,000 feet) above sea level, the largest surviving ice cap in tropical regions of earth. The scientists have been unearthing remains of plants that were buried under advancing ice thousands of years in the past. By dating the decay rate of the plants, the scientists can gauge the ice sheet's movements. Using these calculations (Thompson 2013, 945), the scientists estimated that the ice cap is now smaller than it has been for at least 6,300 years. Radiocarbon dating of the plants offers an extremely precise way of discovering the history of the margins of the ice sheet. This dating method measures a type of carbon in the plants that decays at a known rate. Douglas R. Hardy, a researcher at the University of Massachusetts who works in the region, said, "How much time do we have before 50 percent of Lima's or La Paz's water resources are gone?" (Gillis 2013). Drinking water is already drying up in parts of Bolivia.

"The effects are appearing much more rapidly than we can respond to them, and a reservoir takes five to seven years to build. I'm not sure we have that long," said Edson Ramírez, a Bolivian glaciologist who has documented and projected the glaciers' retreat for two decades. The Chacaltaya glacier, at 17,500 feet, until recently expected to last until 2020, disappeared in 2009. The area had been a ski area until 2005, when it closed as the ice and snow retreated. In 2009, the ski lodge still stood, mute and empty, stocked with rental gear (Rosenthal 2009).

> *Drought, Deluge, and Confusion*
>
> Many people in Peru and elsewhere have trouble understanding the language of climate-change science, especially when it seems to be calling for floods and droughts as part of the same pattern. Such is the case in Peru, where short-range changes in ocean temperatures can cause major changes in ocean currents that shape wind patterns, alternating droughts and downpours.
>
> El Niño causes airflow to reverse over the Andes, from the usual downslope east-west to upslope west-to-east, which pushes moisture off the water, bringing flooding rains to areas adjacent to the Pacific Ocean that are usually very dry. La Niña does the opposite. "More intense El Niños hit the Peruvian economy hard," according to a report by Peru Support. "In 1998, it caused damages worth an estimated 4.5 percent of gross domestic product (GDP). Infrastructure on the coast, not designed to withstand heavy rains, was in many places destroyed by floods and landslides. Lost crops amounted to 204,000 hectares in 1997–98. El Niño also brings adverse effects on human health. The 1998 episode saw an increase in malaria and cholera cases" (Fraser 2006). Similar damage occurred during another intense El Niño in 2015–16.
>
> In the longer run, many people also are confused by forecasts of devastating droughts at a time when rivers are running high because of melting glaciers in the Andes. Every drop of excess water, however, is a portent of a thirsty future when snowpacks run out.

As Barbara Fraser wrote in *Scientific American* (2009): "Peru's largest cities are on the arid west side of the Andes, and water systems are already insufficient to meet the growing demand spurred by migration. Projects are already in the works to build channels from sources in the sparsely populated but water-rich Amazon basin, while tropical regions are seeing increased migration from the highlands. That will likely increase deforestation, further disrupting the hydrological cycle, which could exacerbate the water crisis."

Solutions to Lima's looming water crisis may be elusive, given the global nature of climate change. The city's water utility has been involved in planning for a desalination plant that would tap the Pacific Ocean. Another, less expensive source of supply may be the Amazon Valley, using an upgrade of pre-Inca technology that would involve grouting ancient canals. The canals, known locally as *amunas*, were built by the Wari culture between 500 and 1000 CE. According to Fred Pearce, writing in the *New Scientist* (2015), "The canals captured water from rivers in the mountains during the rainy season and took it to places where it could infiltrate rocks that fed year-round springs further down the mountains, so maintaining river flow during the dry season."

Bruce E. Johansen

See also: Migration and Demographic Changes: Buenos Aires, Argentina: Impact of European Migration; Kinshasa, Democratic Republic of the Congo (DRC): Reaching for Demographic Dividend

Further Reading

Dean, Richie. 2016. "The Story of Urban Migration in Peru." Helping Overcome Obstacles Peru (HOOP). January 15. http://www.hoopperu.org/2016/the-story-of-urban-migration-in-peru.

Fraser, Arabella. 2006. "The Cost of Climate Change: Peru Feels the Heat of Global Warming." Peru Support. November 30. http://www.perusupportgroup.org.uk/article-174.html.

Fraser, Barbara J. 2009. "Climate Change Impacts Revealed: Disease in Peru." *Scientific American,* May 11. https://www.scientificamerican.com/article/climate-change-disease-peru.

Gillis, Justin. 2013. "In Sign of Warming, 1,600 Years of Ice in Andes Melted in 25 Years." *New York Times*, April 4. http://www.nytimes.com/2013/04/05/world/americas/1600-years-of-ice-in-perus-andes-melted-in-25-years-scientists-say.html.

Pearce, Fred. 2015. "Pre-Inca Canals May Solve Lima's Water Crisis." *New Scientist*, April 9. https://www.newscientist.com/article/dn27311-pre-inca-canals-may-solve-limas-water-crisis.

Regaldo, Antonio. 2005. "The Ukukus Wonder Why a Sacred Glacier Melts in Peru's Andes." *Wall Street Journal*, June 17. A-1, A-10.

Rosenthal, Elisabeth. 2009. "In Bolivia, Water and Ice Tell of Climate Change." *New York Times*, December 14. http://www.nytimes.com/2009/12/14/science/earth/14bolivia.html.

Thompson, L. G., E. Mosley-Thompson, M. E. Davis, V. S. Zagorodnov, L. M. Howat, V. N. Mikhalenko, and P.-N. Lin. 2013. "Annually Resolved Ice Core Records of Tropical Climate Variability over the Past ~1800 Years." *Science* 340 (May 24): 945–50.

Wilson, Scott. 2001. "Warming Shrinks Peruvian Glaciers; Retreat of Andean Snow Caps Threatens Future for Valleys." *Washington Post*, July 9, A1.

London, United Kingdom: Facing the Challenges of Population Growth

London is a cosmopolitan, fast-growing city. By far the largest city in the United Kingdom, its 2016 population was an estimated 8.7 million, and it is expected to reach 10 million by 2036 (GLA Economics 2016, 226). Between 2011 and 2015, its growth rate of 5.7 percent was almost twice the national UK average of 2.9 percent (Osborne 2016b). London's primary demographic challenge is keeping up with this rapid growth. The booming population has contributed to high housing prices, leading city government bodies, business, and nonprofits to explore how to increase the supply. Rising numbers of people have also put pressure on services and the built environment. In addition, London must face the challenge of an unsettled future. Since the 2016 Brexit vote for the UK to leave the European Union (EU), its economic and demographic prospects have become less certain. It remains to be seen how departure from the EU will affect the demographics of a city with a population built on immigrants.

COMPONENTS OF LONDON'S DEMOGRAPHIC PROFILE

London's population is growing and becoming younger. This differentiates it from the United Kingdom as a whole, which has an aging population. Between 2011 and 2015, births outnumbered deaths in London, contributing a 4 percent increase to the city's overall population, and young adults in their 20s migrated from other parts of the UK to London in large numbers, almost 35,000 per year. Overall, however, London loses more people to the rest of the UK than it gains. Enough adults in their 30s and older moved away from London between 2011 and 2015, along with their children, to result in a net average loss of 63,200 people per year to the rest of the country (Office for National Statistics 2017).

This decrease is offset by positive international net migration to London, meaning that the city attracts far more people from outside the UK than leave it for non-UK destinations. The 2011 UK census recorded that 36.7 percent of London's population was foreign-born. The number of foreign-born people living in London in 2015 was 3.2 million, comprising 36.8 percent of the UK's total immigrant population (Migration Observatory 2018). As of 2015 India, birthplace of about 267,000 Londoners, was the greatest source of immigrants, with Poland (around 135,000), Pakistan (113,000), Bangladesh (126,000), and Ireland (112,000) also part of the top five (GLA Economics 2016, 244).

Internal and international migration also form patterns of movement within London. Greater London, usually referred to simply as "London," is overseen by the Greater London Authority (GLA) and has a mayor and council, but basic municipal and social services are provided by its 33 local governments. For purposes of analysis, it is divided into Inner London—the 12 boroughs that are contiguous with the historic city of London as it existed in the early 20th century, plus the City of London (the ancient part of London, whose local government dates to medieval times)—and Outer London, the 20 boroughs that were added when Greater London was created in 1965. Migrants from outside the UK tend to settle in Inner London. People are more likely to move from Inner London to Outer London than vice versa, and people from Outer London are more likely to leave London for other parts of the UK than those from Inner London. In contrast, migrants from other parts of the UK divide evenly between Inner and Outer London.

CHALLENGES OF POPULATION GROWTH

Greater London is prevented from expanding outwards by the Metropolitan Green Belt, a low-density zone that forms a ring around it. The GLA, the boroughs, and other stakeholders therefore face the prospect of providing additional housing and services within a set amount of space. For example, it is estimated that by 2025, London will need an additional 60,000 primary school slots and 10,400 secondary school slots to meet demand (GLA Economics 2016, 237). Services of this type may prove difficult to support, however, because of the limited funds available to the borough governments that are responsible for them. The government of Greater London has limited powers, but the areas in which it can make policy include housing and transit, both of which respond directly to the challenge of population growth.

One element of this issue is the need to combat congestion, a persistent problem. In 2003, London's mayor instituted a congestion charge in central London, a fee to drive through the dense, crowded central part of the city that was intended to decrease traffic in the area by 20 percent. But while the zone was initially successful, over time congestion has again crept upwards, due in part to increases in commercial traffic and new options like ride sharing, and in part to the reuse of some roadway space for other purposes such as cycle highways (dedicated bike lanes).

Greater London is also working to expand its public transportation network. A new line for its tube (subway) system, the Elizabeth Line, was constructed during the 2010s, running through the city from east to west and linking distant suburbs to the city center. In the mid-2010s, the city also considered extensions to existing lines that would contribute to its development goals. One possible project was an extension of its Bakerloo tube line, linking designated "opportunity zones" slated for development into the tube network. Another possibility was the extension of the Overground network of heavy-rail public transport to an area in East London in which development of over 10,000 new homes, plus businesses and services, had been approved. These plans were designed to take advantage of opportunities for growth within London's current boundaries.

Population growth has created a need for additional housing. London is projected to have 4.3 million households by 2036, an increase of 25 percent or 856,000 households from 2016 (GLA Economics 2016, 258). Yet between 2009 and 2014, fewer than 30,000 new homes were added in any given year, although the mayor's London Plan set an annual goal of 42,000. London is less dense than other European cities like Paris and Madrid, leading to suggestions that increasing density levels in areas with low density but good transit links could contribute to a solution. Other possibilities that have been suggested include easing regulation on the redevelopment of brownfield areas and opening parts of the greenbelt to development, although the latter is very controversial.

The housing crisis is also a housing-cost crisis, because the cost of housing in London has risen much more quickly than have incomes. Between 2011 and 2014, average house prices in London increased by 47 percent; at the end of 2014, the average London house cost £465,000, 14 times the average London income (Tanaka 2015; Osborne 2016b). Rental costs were also high. In January 2014, the average monthly rent for a London apartment was £1,211 (versus £665 for the UK as a whole), and by April 2016, it had increased to £1,543 (versus £764 elsewhere in the UK) (Osborne 2016a; Osborne 2014). This aspect of the housing issue has the potential to influence the evolution of London's demographic profile. The "squeezed middle"—a term that can refer either to the middle class in general or to mostly young, potential first-time homebuyers who can't afford down payments because of high rents and housing costs—is being pushed out of London, contributing to the pattern of net internal migration to other parts of the UK. Within London, residential patterns are also shifting as people who can no longer afford expensive areas in Inner London are moving to some of Outer London's traditionally suburban boroughs. Outer London has begun to house more immigrants and young workers, and its poverty rates are rising; Inner London, in contrast, is becoming wealthier.

One response to this challenge was put forward by the mayor in a five-year plan covering 2016 to 2021. The plan outlined three types of housing subsidy, funded by the UK government: a London Living Rent, set at 35 percent of income, available for those saving for their first homes; a London Affordable Rent designed for those with low incomes; and a London Shared Ownership program in which residents buy shares of their home over time, ideally ending with 100 percent ownership. Critics of such programs note that "affordable rent," often set at 80 percent of market rates, is itself not always affordable for target populations. The Greater London Council has also provided funding to private developers to build small, minimalist houses marketed specifically to first-time buyers seeking to remain in their home boroughs.

Other cities have addressed their own challenges in ways that could apply to parts of London's housing dilemma. The Metropolitan Green Belt has an analog in the American city of Portland, Oregon, which is ringed by an Urban Growth Boundary that was created in 1980 as a measure to curb urban sprawl. Unlike London's greenbelt, the Portland boundary was not designed to be static. It has been expanded more than 20 times, and Portland's Metro government is legally required to maintain a 20-year supply of land for residential development within its boundaries. While Portland has expanded, it remains surrounded by a strictly enforced greenbelt. Because the boundary undergoes periodic reviews, Portland is able to respond to current conditions; in 2015, it chose not to expand the boundary because housing needs were being met.

The issue of affordable rental housing has been addressed by the German city of Berlin. In 2015, Berlin, where 85 percent of the population rents, enacted a law to counteract unpredictable, quickly rising rental rates that had the potential to create social instability. Under the law, an outside "rental observatory" determines typical rents for a range of apartment conditions and amenities in each area, and almost all new rents are not allowed to exceed the stated rate by more than 10 percent during the next five years. In 2016, Berlin also enacted a law prohibiting the short-term rental of entire units. The implementation of the rent rules has been criticized due to a lack of city enforcement, which has encouraged landlords to ignore its limits. Nonetheless, this approach differs strikingly from that of London.

CHALLENGES LINKED TO IMMIGRATION POLICY

At this writing, it is not known how the UK's exit from the EU will unfold, or what immigration policies will replace freedom of movement among EU nations. While migrants come to London from around the world, Europeans are by far the largest group, with Asians a distant second. New restrictions on immigration would alter London's demographic profile and, by doing so, impact the city's economy and social fabric. At the beginning of 2017, 960,000 immigrants from Europe were members of London's workforce, contributing at all economic and social levels (O'Sullivan 2016). A steep decline in their numbers could leave gaps in London's social structure; for example, 11 percent of London's professional caregivers for the elderly are immigrant non-citizens (Lyons and Hill 2017). Some industries will also be specifically affected. The city of London is a hub of the financial services industry, which relies on an international workforce as well as the ability to do business across national boundaries. Potential obstacles to immigration, as well as other aspects of Brexit, led companies in this category to begin moving their operations to other countries soon after it became final.

Increased obstacles to immigration could also influence London's overall demographic trajectory, given that its current demographic pattern is a net loss of population to the rest of the United Kingdom. London's population, which has been increasing consistently since the early 1970s, could begin to decline if the number of immigrants admitted decreases significantly, or if current immigrant residents leave the UK. Conversely, reductions in congestion and competition for housing and services could reverse the trends of internal migration within the UK and maintain London's recent history of growth.

Sara C. Jorgensen

See also: Employment and Jobs: London, United Kingdom: Brexit, the Known Unknown; *Energy and Sustainability:* London, United Kingdom: Improving Mobility Can Save Energy

Further Reading

Duncan, Emma. 2012. "On a High." *Economist*, June 30. http://www.economist.com/node/21557528.

GLA Economics. 2016. "Chapter 6: London's People 2016." Draft Economic Evidence Base 2016. February 20. https://www.london.gov.uk/sites/default/files/chapter6-draft-eeb-2016.pdf.

Greater London Authority. 2017. "The Current London Plan." https://www.london.gov.uk/what-we-do/planning/london-plan/current-london-plan.

London Datastore. 2015. "London Housing Market Report." March 18. https://data.london.gov.uk/housingmarket.

Lyons, Kate, and Amelia Hill. 2017. "Hard Brexit Means Retiring Later, Britons Warned." *Guardian*, January 15. https://www.theguardian.com/uk-news/2017/jan/15/hard-brexit-means-retiring-later-britons-warned.

The Migration Observatory. 2018. "Migrants in the UK: An Overview." October 15. https://migrationobservatory.ox.ac.uk/resources/briefings/migrants-in-the-uk-an-overview/.

O'Brien, Oliver. 2014–15. "CRDC Maps: London." Consumer Data Research Center. https://maps.cdrc.ac.uk/#/metrics/countryofbirth/default/BTTTFTT/10/-0.1500/51.5200.

Office for National Statistics, 2017. "Population Dynamics of UK City Regions since Mid-2011." https://www.ons.gov.uk/peoplepopulationandcommunity/populationandmigration/populationestimates/articles/populationdynamicsofukcityregionssincemid2011/2016-10-11.

Osborne, Hilary. 2014. "Renting in London 'Costs Twice as Much as Elsewhere.'" *Guardian*, January 27. https://www.theguardian.com/money/2014/jan/27/renting-london-costs-twice-elsewhere.

Osborne, Hilary. 2016a. "Rents Continue to Rise across the UK and in London." *Guardian*, May 5. https://www.theguardian.com/money/2016/may/05/rents-continue-rise-uk-london.

Osborne, Hilary. 2016b. "London Population Growth Rate Twice That of UK, Official Figures Show." *Guardian*, October 12. https://www.theguardian.com/uk-news/2016/oct/12/london-population-growth-twice-that-of-uk-official-figures-show.

O'Sullivan, Feargus. 2016. "For London, 2017 Could Be the Year That Makes or Breaks the City's Future." *Citylab*, December 29. http://www.citylab.com/politics/2016/12/brexit-effects-on-london-jobs-housing-politics-mayor/511778.

Tanaka, Adam. 2015. "Democracy and the Challenge of Affordability: London's 'Squeezed Middle.'" *Challenges to Democracy*. Kennedy School, Harvard University. November 12. https://medium.com/challenges-to-democracy/democracy-and-the-challenge-of-affordability-londons-squeezed-middle-32db64cad5d2.

World Population Review. 2017. "London Population 2017." http://worldpopulationreview.com/world-cities/london-population.

Los Angeles, United States: A Dynamic Demographic Mix

Migration to Los Angeles, California, is not a recent phenomenon. Peoples of various Amerindian groups migrated to the area in pre-Columbian times. These migrations did not cease with European contact but only accelerated as people began coming to the region from nearly all parts of the Old World. True, there was migration from east to west across North America, but before the advent of railroads such treks were difficult. It was easier in many cases to come across the Pacific Ocean, and from the late 18th century and through the 19th century, people came to Los Angeles from East and South Asia. In more recent times, migrants have come to Los Angeles from parts of Africa, Mexico, and Central America. These migrations caused important demographic changes. Among the most notable was the initial contact between Amerindians and Europeans, the latter bringing with them Old World diseases to which the native peoples were vulnerable. Illness, epidemics, and death claimed large numbers of Amerindians in one of the most dramatic and terrible demographic changes in human history. Economic opportunities likewise created demographic changes. Since the 1990s, difficult economic times have caused still more demographic changes to Los Angeles. The one constant in Los Angeles appears to be change.

PRE-COLUMBIAN MIGRATIONS

Even before Los Angeles became a city, it was a destination for migrants in pre-Columbian times. These aboriginal peoples gave what would become Los Angeles a pre-European identity. The first migrants into Los Angeles may have been the people who spoke dialects of a language now classified as Hokan. These people arrived in Los Angeles possibly as early as 6500 BCE, at the beginning of what is known as the Milling Stone Period. The Tongva Amerindians appear to have displaced the Hokan speakers sometime during prehistory. Drought in the Great Basin may have hastened these migrants to settle Los Angeles. The Tongva Amerindians named Los Angeles *Yaa* in their Uto-Aztecan language. By the 18th century CE, the period of European contact, as many as 5,000 Native Americans inhabited what is today Los Angeles. The point is that Los Angeles was not a pristine wilderness when the Spanish came upon it, but a thriving community of Amerindians of various languages and lifeways. The Spanish named the principal peoples they encountered the Gabrielinos and the Fernanenos. The Gabrielinos called what would become Los Angles *Yaanga*. These people appear to have been the dominant group of migrants in the town.

THE SPANISH AS MIGRANTS

The earliest European thrust into the area that is now Los Angeles came in 1542 when Spanish naval officer Juan Rodriguez Castillo entered the region. He did not stay, and a later Spanish incursion in 1602 likewise produced no lasting trail of migrants. In 1777, Spain's governor of California (California was then a Spanish possession as part of Spanish Mexico), Felipe de Neve, ushered in a period of Spanish migration into Los Angeles. Neve wanted to shape Los Angeles into a region of farms and small businesses to attract more migrants. The original Spanish contingent of migrants into Los Angeles in 1777 included 22 adults and another 22 children. This Spanish influx did not mean the end of Native American migrants, though it signaled a diminution in Amerindian populations as the aboriginal inhabitants of Los Angeles were vulnerable to Old World diseases and perished, sometimes in horrific numbers. The death of the native peoples from these diseases ushered in a sweeping period of demographic change in the composition of the population of Los Angeles. At the same time, not all Native Americans perished, so that some of the Spanish intermarried with these peoples and had children of mixed ancestry.

LOS ANGELES BECOMES PART OF THE UNITED STATES

Spain's hold on Mexico and with it California was tenuous, and in 1821 Mexico declared independence from its former imperial power. The 1820s, with an expansion in farming and ranching, attracted new migrants from Mexico to Los Angeles. Yet Mexico could not hold California and Los Angeles any more securely than had Spain. The Mexican-American War brought California and Los Angeles into the orbit of the United States, with California becoming a state in 1850. Patterns of migration drove this change as Americans came to Los Angeles during the 19th century, if not initially in large numbers. The journey across North America from the Eastern Seaboard and the Midwest was perilous as it involved the crossing of arid, mountainous, inhospitable lands. The discovery of gold in California in the late 1840s quickened the pace of migration into many parts of the region including Los Angeles. The thrust of this migration was European as people of German, English, Scottish, and even Irish ancestry came to Los Angeles in hopes of growing rich. This pattern of migration made Europeans an important component of Los Angeles.

European migration into Los Angeles created the need to bridge eastern and Midwestern settlements with the Far West. The railroad emerged as the solution to this problem, and in 1869, the Los Angeles and San Pedro Railroad began to attract migrants from other parts of the United States and East Asia because it provided jobs. In many ways, before the completion of a network of railroads east and west across the United States, migrants from Asia had an easier time reaching Los Angeles than their American counterparts. In the age of the steamship, the Pacific crossing could be managed with comparative ease. Chinese migrants came in especially large numbers to work on the Los Angeles and San Pedro Railroad, but African Americans coming from the South also entered Los Angeles in search of work. Between 1900 and 1930, the African American population in Los Angeles leapt from 2,000 to some 40,000.

In the early 20th century, other migrants came to Los Angeles, notably from Japan and Vietnam, then part of French Indochina. The Japanese came to work on the farms near Los Angeles, though they were quick to aspire to land ownership and to develop their own farms specializing in vegetables and fruits to feed the other residents of Los Angeles. These crops, along with milk and cheese from Japanese-owned dairy farms, fetched premium prices, spurring even more people from East Asia to risk the Pacific crossing to Los Angeles. The Vietnamese came in large numbers after the Vietnam War, when the United States accepted them as refugees. About 20 percent of Vietnamese migrants to the United States settled in Los Angeles after 1975, making the city the largest Vietnamese enclave in America. In smaller numbers have come Filipinos, Koreans, and even Indians across the Pacific Ocean. Many wanted a quality university education and a new life in Los Angeles. At the end of the Cold War, refugees from Eastern Europe, Central America, South America, and Africa provided even more migrants to Los Angeles into the 21st century. Outside of legal channels came undocumented migrants from Mexico and Central America, people intent on a better life in Los Angeles. As with the lure of agriculture and the railroads in the 19th century, migrants have come to Los Angeles in the 21st century in search of prosperity. As long as Los Angeles creates jobs, migrants will seek advancement in the city through employment.

THE REACTION TO MIGRATION

As Los Angeles became a city of migrants of many ethnicities, discord, racism, and xenophobia came to the fore. The Zoot Suit Riots came to symbolize these attitudes of intolerance. These riots derived their name from the zoot suit, a type of baggy garment worn by Mexicans, often those in poor neighborhoods where ethnic tensions were already high. Some African Americans likewise adopted this style of dress, though it was most closely associated with the Mexicans of Los Angeles. The media, police, and other agencies of government harassed Mexicans and African Americans who wore such clothes. Matters might have remained tense but largely uneventful but for America's entry into World War II. The war heightened patriotism and an aversion to anyone perceived as a foreigner. Mexicans, African Americans, and the Japanese of Los Angeles were all targets of bias. This discrimination escalated into violence as U.S. military personnel began to attack these putatively foreign elements in 1943, less than two years after America's entry into the war. African Americans joined Mexicans in organized protests against violence, but these actions seemed only to embolden the perpetrators. Riots exploded after the highly charged and probably false conviction of nine Mexicans from Los Angeles for murder. The police responded to these riots by arresting hundreds of Mexicans and African Americans. The police did not respect civil liberties and arrested people even when they had no connection to the riots. The status of being Mexican or African American was sufficient to warrant arrest. Although the riots ended, tensions have remained in Los Angeles between the police and minorities. The people who migrated into Los Angeles did not always find the opportunities they sought for advancement.

DEMOGRAPHIC CHANGES

We have seen that demographic changes were pronounced with the arrival of Europeans and the Old World diseases they spread to the native populations. Demographic changes have not ceased but have been a constant in Los Angeles's history. We noted how economic opportunities brought migrants to Los Angeles beginning in the late 18th century. In recent decades, the pace of economic growth has slowed. In fact, the recession of the 1990s hit Los Angeles with great force even as other parts of the United States prospered. Just as prosperity attracted migrants to Los Angeles, hard times have chased them away. A notable demographic effect has been a slowing of the birth rate in Los Angeles. About 2005, the birth rate sufficed to allow demographers to forecast that Los Angeles's population, which stood at about 10.1 million people, would increase to 12 million by 2030. By 2016, it had become clear that the birth rate had slowed enough to delay this increase likely until after 2060. This problem has afflicted the rest of California, which in 2010 did not gain any congressional representatives for the first decade in its history. The population and birth-rate boom appear to have abated. As the birth rate has slowed, so has migration to Los Angeles. Bereft of a rapidly expanded economy, Los Angeles is no longer a magnet for migrants seeking a better life.

The change in migration patterns has been notable. The economic expansion in Los Angeles that had characterized the 1970s and 1980s halted and even reversed

---

Hokan Languages

The original Amerindians to settle California may have spoken Hokan, the putative first language from which all Native American languages in California and parts of the American Southwest and Mexico derive. In 1913, American anthropologists Roland Burrage Dixon (1875–1934) and Alfred Louis Kroeber (1876–1960) hypothesized that the native peoples who came to California perhaps 20,000 years ago must have spoken a single language. Over time and migration to different parts of the American West and Mexico, Hokan diversified into many languages in the way that a single tree trunk yields many branches as it grows. This proposal makes sense if the original migrants came in a single wave. But anthropologists now believe that migrants came in many groups over thousands of years. Such diverse peoples likely spoke different languages even before crossing the Bering land bridge from Asia to North America. The story of Amerindian language must therefore be more complex than Dixon and Kroeber had supposed.

in the 1990s. Adding to the difficulties that migrants faced on the economic front, authorities in Los Angeles and California at large began to patrol the U.S. and Mexican border with greater vigor after 2000. With construction jobs in decline in Los Angeles, authorities did not want a new wave of migrants to compete with the city's residents for a shrinking pool of jobs. Moreover, the Mexican economy revived after 2000 so that fewer Mexicans decided to risk the crossing into Los Angeles and other areas in Southern California. With fewer Mexicans coming to Los Angeles, this fecund group has contributed fewer births to the city, with the resulting slowing of the birth rate that we noted earlier. Today, about 35 percent of Los Angeles' residents are foreign born, a figure that is expected to hold steady through 2035. Nonetheless, Latinos will probably be the majority of Los Angeles's residents by 2020. Since 2001, about 60 percent of babies born in Los Angeles have been to Latino parents, a rate that is about 10 percent greater than in the rest of California. With the decline in the birth rate, the proportion of very young children in Los Angeles is declining. Between 2000 and 2013, the percentage of Los Angeles's population under age 10 declined by 18 percent. Part of this decline stems from the fact that baby boomers are at the end of their reproductive cycle. Moreover, Latinos are exiting Los Angeles in search of jobs elsewhere. With their exit has gone a fertile population. Whereas Los Angeles recorded about 204,000 births in 1990, the number dropped to 134,000 in 2016. As the proportion of very young people is declining, the old increase, a trend that seems destined to continue. In 2016, about 20 percent of Los Angeles's population was over age 65, a figure that is expected to double by 2040. The need for senior care and other services seems certain to increase.

Christopher Cumo

See also: *Migration and Demographic Changes:* Tokyo, Japan: Sustainable Growth Calls for Immigration Reform

Further Reading
Gerston, Larry N. 2012. *Not So Golden after All: The Rise and Fall of California*. Boca Raton, FL: CRC Press.
Qadeer, Mohammad Abdul. 2016. *Multicultural Cities: Toronto, New York, and Los Angeles*. Toronto: University of Toronto Press.

Tehran, Iran: Toward a More Open and Tolerant Society

In 1786, Agha Muhammed Shah founded the Qajar Dynasty in Tehran, and the city has been the capital of Iran since then. It is also the capital of the Tehran Province. The city's geographical layout includes a high altitude of between 5,600 feet above sea level in the north and 3,600 feet in the south. Mount Damavend and the Caspian Sea offer stunningly beautiful scenery that is often compared by tourists, as seen in blogs on TripAdvisor, to Mount Fuji in Japan and many other beautiful mountains in the world. Tehran has 22 districts, each administered by its own district head who reports to the mayor of metropolitan Tehran. Today, Tehran is not only Iran's political, industrial, and financial center, but also the country's most important gateway to the world.

Until the late 18th century, Tehran was inhabited by agrarian communities. Its urbanization began with the expansion of the city's political and economic status. At an early stage of the city's development, traditional industries, such as shoe-making and hosiery-making, gradually gained footing. By the time Nassar Ed-Din Shah (1848–96) was in power, Tehran had become a major commercial center. After 1925, Reza Shah's aggressive pursuit of industrialization laid the foundation for the growth of private and public industries in the 1940s. By the 1960s, Tehran had nearly one-third of the country's manufacturing facilities and one-fourth of its workforce (Firoozi 1974). By the 1970s, industrialization brought further changes to the originally agrarian society, bringing more openness to the conservative cultural and ideological tradition. An economic downturn in the 1970s, however, became a stepping-stone for conservative political forces. Eventually, Ayatollah Ruhollah Khomeini led the 1979 Revolution that toppled Mohammad Reza Shah Pahlavi. The revolution resumed many traditional practices, suppressed Western influence, re-enforced dress codes, and removed many newly established familial and marriage-related rights for women. Today, after more than three decades since the 1979 Revolution, Islamic fanaticism has weakened. Globalization is once again winning over puritanism, and propelling Tehran to be more open to the world.

Today, more than half of Iran's industries are based in Tehran, including automobiles, electronics, military weaponry, textiles, sugar, cement, chemical products, and oil refineries. The city is also a center for the sale of carpets and furniture. Economic growth requires powerful transportation capability, and as a result, Tehran has become the hub of the country's railway network. More than 30 percent of the Iranian workforce in the public sector are employed in the capital city. Migrant populations have brought cultural diversity to Tehran; there are more churches, synagogues, mosques, and Zoroastrian fire temples around the capital than anywhere else in the country. The city is also known for abundant museums and art centers, in addition to palace complexes.

DEMOGRAPHICS

Tehran is the most populous city of Iran. Its population is 8.7 million (City Population 2016), which is about 10 percent of the total population of the country. The Iranian population is largely urban: of 79.9 million citizens, about 74 percent reside in urban areas (SCI 2016). As more and more people have access to education and employment, household size has shrunk measurably. Since 1976, the average household size in urban areas has dropped from 5.2 to 3.3 members (SCI 2016).

The Province of Tehran has over 16.6 percent of the nation's population, or approximately 13.3 million, making it the largest province in Iran. The population of the Tehran province has the highest literacy rate of 92.9 percent. According to the 2011 census, nationally, the Province of Tehran attracts the most migrants. Close to a million people moved to the capital between 2006 and 2011 (SCI 2016). Clearly, the capital city and its immediately surrounding province concentrate most of Iran's employment and educational opportunities.

MINORITIES

The majority of Iran's population is Muslim. The 2011 census shows the country's population by religions as follows: out of 75.2 million total population, there were 74.7 million Muslims, 117,704 Christians, 25,271 Zoroastrian, and 8,756 Jews. The "other" category contained 49,101, and 265,899 belonged to "not stated" (SCI 2011). According to the UN's estimate of 2014, however, the Christian population is approximately 300,000, the majority being Armenian and Assyrian Christians. Likewise, the population of Jews in Iran is estimated to be 25,000, and the Zoroastrians 60,000 (DOS 2014).

Iran's constitution declares Ja'afari Shia Islam the official state religion, and all laws and regulations must be based on the "Islamic criteria" and official interpretation of Sharia law. The constitution, however, does allow Sunni Muslims—who represent 9 percent of the population, mostly consisting of Turkmen, Arabs, Baluchis, and Kurds—to practice their worship and hold ceremonies (DOS 2014). The constitution recognizes Zoroastrians, Jews, and Christians as the only religious groups with legitimate rights to practice their religious rituals (DOS 2014).

Most minority religious groups traditionally reside within the boundaries of the capital city. In the 1970s, Tehran was home to 65.42 percent of Iranian Jews, 47.12 percent of Zoroastrians, 66.52 percent of Armenians, 49.77 percent of Assyrians, 53.50 percent of other Christian denominations, and 39.6 percent of other religious affiliations (DOS 2014; Firoozi 1974). Minorities are drawn to Tehran for historical, social, and economic reasons. The top reason, however, is that Tehran has a more tolerant social atmosphere than elsewhere. In contrast with religious fanaticism in the provinces, the higher degree of tolerance makes Tehran more suitable for minorities. For example, rather than being viewed as oddities, Tehran's cultural and ethnically diverse citizens make clothing, diet, and physical appearance an integral part of the social life. Moreover, minority groups tend to live in the vicinity of government compounds to take advantage of protection by the governmental apparatus. One example is the Jewish enclave in the Siroos Avenue area. Additionally, many occupations that minorities typically engage in, such as banking and trade, are urban-based operations. In contrast, many service areas that typically provide abundant employment opportunities, such as food service, are inaccessible to minorities in Iran due to religious reasons (Firoozi 1974).

WOMEN

According to a report in the *Tehran Times* titled "Iranian Women Shoulder to Shoulder with Men," as a result of the Islamic Revolution in 1979, women gained more access to education and the job market. According to the report, women make up 27 percent of the workforce today. The new Family Law, according to the report,

Women in Tehran cross a street beneath a mural of the Ayatollah Ali Khamenei, Iran's supreme leader (left), and Ruhollah Khomeini, founder of the Islamic Republic of Iran, 2012. In Tehran and elsewhere, gender inequality continues to widen in the workplace, despite government reports to the contrary. (Ali Mohammadi/Bloomberg via Getty Images)

changed Muslim marriage to a contractual relationship, allowing women more independence in marriage. They can negotiate with their future spouse and jointly work out a schedule for education. Another law issued in 1992 requires the man who divorces his wife to pay back her wages for her work for the duration of the marriage:

> Muslim housewives are entitled to wages for housework (*ojrat ol-mesal*). Presently, a man who intends to divorce his wife without proving fault on her part must first pay housework wages for the duration of the marriage. The law does in a way signify that women, their labor and contribution, should not be taken for granted in any way. (*Tehran Times* 2011)

While Tehran's official media tend to praise the 1979 Revolution for its contribution to civil liberty, opposite opinions hold that the revolution dialed back civil liberties and the country's openness by more than a decade. Nevertheless, it is widely viewed that women's position in Iran has been notably improved, particularly since the 1990s. In Tehran, there are more office jobs in government agencies occupied by women. Additionally, many of these agencies reportedly pay attention to working women's needs by opening day-care centers. Women also form their own trade associations of women lawyers, nurses, and teachers. In academia, the female-to-male ratio has reached 60 to 40 percent. More women postpone marriage in order to complete their education. Iranian women are also more participative in politics, according to the report, contributing to decision making at government, urban, and rural levels. More female politicians are serving at the highest state level—the first female vice president, Masoumeh Ebtkar, served the administration of President Mohammad Khatami (1997–2005); and Marzieh Vahid-Dastjerdi, a former university professor, served as minister of health and medical education in the administration of President Mahmoud Ahmedinejad (*Tehran Times* 2011).

Despite the civil rights gained, however, Iranian women are fighting for more ground in equality. According to the *Financial Tribune*, an influential economic newspaper in Iran, the participation rate of women in the job market in the 2016–17 fiscal year was 14.9 percent, much lower than the rate of employment for men at 64.1 percent. In the same period, the unemployment rate was 11.6 percent in Tehran Province. More women lost jobs than men: 10.5 percent of working men were unemployed versus 20.7 percent of working women (*Financial Tribune* 2016); and one out of every three women with a bachelor's degree was unemployed (Iran Primer 2017). Clearly, fighting gender inequality remains a top challenge for the Iranian society.

THE YOUTH AND MODERNIZATION

In technology, the city of Tehran takes the lead, being home to more than 50 major colleges and universities. More young people receive a college education. In 2009, 34 percent of Iranians went to university; the number climbed to 55 percent in 2012. Tehran-based Azad University, for example, now operates over 100 campuses and has 1.5 million students enrolled. Moreover, development of higher education has boosted scientific research. Iran's scientific output has increased by 570 percent in about a decade's time (*Economist* 2014). Likewise, the demand for information has been on the rise. Reports indicate that Tehran is more open to the Internet than many in the West could imagine. Facebook and Twitter are ubiquitous, according to one report, and mobile penetration is more than 120 percent, meaning people have more than one phone per person. The government operates dozens of incubators around the country in agriculture, banking, security, education, and infrastructure, catching up with the most advanced emerging markets in the world (Schroeder 2015; *Economist* 2014).

A great push for modernization comes from the youth population born after the monarchy regime, and mostly after the 1979 Revolution. They are better educated, and free from their parents' mentality marked by goals, fears, and nationalism. The younger generation also embraces globalization. Pursuit of individual freedom is reflected in the creative arts and entertainment activities. One example is *parkour*, a sport that has gained popularity among the youth, who sees in it an expression of individual freedom. Tehran's fashion shows represent another platform where young people find their expression. As a commentator wrote: "Fiery reds, flashy yellows, bright blues and brassy greens are replacing the dark, drab and dreadful—and defying rigid dress restrictions that have inhibited Iranian women from showing their shapes or individuality since the 1979 revolution" (Noori 2013).

TOWARD MORE OPENNESS

The municipality has set forth a 20-year outlook: the city will promote Islamic genuineness and identity, to build a knowledge-based global city, to develop a green and sustainable environment, to reduce the economic gap among its citizens, and to build a world-class political, cultural, and economic urban center (Tehran Municipality n.d.c). These goals demonstrate that Tehran is dedicated to achieving sustainable urban development together with the other cities in the world.

Jing Luo

See also: Green Spaces: Abu Dhabi, United Arab Emirates (UAE): Building a Greener City with a More Open Culture

Further Reading

Chalabi, Mona. 2014. "Tehran in Numbers: Crowded, Low-Cost and Fashion Cons." *Guardian*, January 30. https://www.theguardian.com/cities/datablog/2014/jan/30/tehran-in-numbers.

City Population Website. "Iran: Tehran." https://www.citypopulation.de/php/iran-tehran.php.

Ebrahimi, M. Hassan. n.d. "Whatever Happened to Urban Knowledge in Downtown Tehran? Effects of Rural Domination of Urban Society." http://n-aerus.net/web/sat/workshops/2010/pdf/PAPER_ebrahimi_h.pdf.

Economist. 2014. "The Revolution Is Over." *Economist*, October 30. https://www.economist.com/news/special-report/21628597-after-decades-messianic-fervour-iran-becoming-more-mature-and-modern-country.

Financial Tribune. 2017. "Iran Unemployment Rate at 12.4%." March 15. https://financialtribune.com/articles/domestic-economy/61550/iran-unemployment-rate-at-124.

Firoozi, F. 1974. "Tehran: A Demographic and Economic Analysis." *Middle Eastern Studies* 10, 1: 60–76. http://www.jstor.org/stable/4282511.

Iran Primer Website. 2017. "Report: Women Face Bias in Workplace." May 25. http://iranprimer.usip.org/blog/2017/may/25/report-women-face-bias-workplace.

Noori, Maral. 2013. "Youth in Iran Part 3: The Politics of Fashion." *Iran Primer*, August 19. http://iranprimer.usip.org/blog/2013/aug/19/youth-iran-part-3-politics-fashion.

Schroeder, Christopher. 2015. "American CEOs Eye Iran." *Iran Primer*, May 6. http://iranprimer.usip.org/blog/2015/may/06/american-ceos-eye-iran.

Statistical Center of Iran (SCI). 2011. *Statistical Yearbook 2011–2012*. https://www.amar.org.ir/english/Iran-Statistical-Yearbook/Statistical-Yearbook-2011-2012.

Statistical Center of Iran (SCI). 2016. "Population and Housing Censuses." https://www.amar.org.ir/english/Population-and-Housing-Censuses.

Tehran Municipality. n.d.a. "Tehran, Environment & Geography." http://en.tehran.ir/Default.aspx?tabid=97.

Tehran Municipality. n.d.b. "Atlas of Tehran Metropolis." http://atlas.tehran.ir/Default.aspx?tabid=227.

Tehran Municipality. n.d.c. "The Ideals of the Prospect of the Long Term Development of Tehran." http://en.tehran.ir/Default.aspx?tabid=87.

Tehran Times. 2011. "Iranian Women Shoulder to Shoulder with Men." August 17. http://www.tehrantimes.com/news/302986/Iranian-women-shoulder-to-shoulder-with-men.

United Nations. 2015. "The State of Asian and Pacific Cities 2015—Urban Transformations Shifting from Quantity to Quality." http://www.unescap.org/sites/default/files/The%20State%20of%20Asian%20and%20Pacific%20Cities%202015.pdf.

U.S. Department of States (DOS). 2014. "Iran 2014 International Religious Freedom Report for 2014." https://www.state.gov/documents/organization/238666.pdf.

Tokyo, Japan: Sustainable Growth Calls for Immigration Reform

Tokyo is the world's largest city. The population of this megacity—which includes, in addition to Japan's Tokyo Prefecture, three neighboring prefectures (administrative districts)—reached an estimated 38,241,000 people in 2017 (World Population Review 2017a). More than a quarter of the country's population now resides in Greater Tokyo, which has become a magnet for young people throughout Japan. However, the city has a very low fertility rate and, like the rest of Japan, an aging population.

Japan has a shrinking population and a fertility rate well below the replacement standard of 2.1 children per woman. Both the city and the country are working to address the complex challenges created by this situation. Their goals include balancing the needs of the elderly with support for the working-age population; in addition, resources must be found for child care, education, and family support if the country hopes to increase its birth rate. Another challenge is the need to increase the size of Japan's workforce, leading the city and the country to seek policies that facilitate participation by women and elderly people. Finally, Japan, which in recent decades has been very reluctant to accept significant numbers of immigrants, is beginning to grapple with the question of how immigration might help to resolve its demographic crisis.

THE FRAMEWORK OF TOKYO'S DEMOGRAPHIC CHALLENGES

The beginnings of the crisis can be traced as far back as the 1970s. Between 1971 and 1974, Japan experienced a brief "echo boom" as the members of its post–World War II baby boom began to have children. Since 1975, however, Japan's birth rate has been decreasing. Nineteen seventy-four was also the first year that the fraction of Japanese people under the age of 30 fell below half, where it has remained ever since. This was an early sign that Japan's population was beginning to age.

At the start of 2017, Japan's crude birth rate, the number of births per 1,000 people, was 8.124, ranking it 199 out of 201 countries tracked by the United Nations. Its total fertility rate, the number of children a statistically representative woman would have during her reproductive life, was 1.443 children per woman. Japan also had the second-oldest population among the 201 countries, with a median age of 48.3 for women and 45.6 for men, and a life expectancy of 80.569 years for men and 87.026 for women. Japan was the first country to reach the benchmark of 30 percent of its population over the age of 60, and it is predicted that by 2050 nearly 1 percent of its people will be centenarians. The convergence of these two trends meant that Japan's population growth rate turned negative between its 2005 census, which placed the rate at .12 percent, and its 2010 census, when the rate was −.05 percent. Its decline has accelerated and was expected to reach −.24 percent in 2017. Total population continued to grow for a few more years, reaching 127,319,802 people in 2010, but by 2015, it had reversed for the first time, shrinking to 126,572,481. This decline is expected to continue (World Population Review 2017b).

Japan's aging population and negative growth reflect broad trends within the developed world, but Japan is leading the way in both categories due to its very low fertility rate. The average age of marriage is rising. Because there are relatively few unmarried mothers in Japan, this trend reduces the window of time available for childbearing. The material cost of raising children is high, and Japan provides less support to young families than many other developed countries. Japanese women want meaningful careers, but employers have been slow to accommodate working mothers. Many women respond by choosing career over family; in 2009, only 13 percent of Japan's population were children, the lowest rate among a group of 30 industrialized countries (Kingston 2011, 44). Japanese work culture has also traditionally assumed that men would put in very long hours and privilege work commitments over family responsibilities, another obstacle in the way of parenthood.

Tokyo shares these issues, but it also makes a unique contribution to Japan's declining population. In the early 1960s, young Japanese began to migrate from

Mothers with their babies in the Asakusa District of Tokyo, Japan, 2016. Japan faces a low birthrate and an aging population. Some believe that immigration could be a solution to Japan's declining numbers, but others worry it would erode the Japanese way of life. (Witaya Ratanasirikulchai/Dreamstime.com)

the countryside to cities like Osaka, Nagoya, and Tokyo for education and employment. But by 2014, Tokyo had become the destination for people throughout Japan, even pulling them away from other cities. Overall, the largest group of migrants to Japan is younger than the average age of migrants in OECD countries (OECD 2017). With Tokyo's total fertility rate even lower than that of the rest of Japan, below one child per woman, the city's magnetic draw contributes to Japan's overall demographic crisis (Worldometers-Japan 2019).

DEMOGRAPHIC CHALLENGES AND RESPONSES IN THE JAPANESE CONTEXT

Responses to Tokyo's demographic challenges can emerge at local, regional, or national scale. Tokyo has no unified government. The Tokyo Prefecture is overseen by the Tokyo Metropolitan Government, but it includes 23 "special wards" covering the historic city of Tokyo, as well as dozens of other municipalities with their own local governments. The other three prefectures within Greater Tokyo have similar systems. Many of these regional and local governments, as well as businesses and nonprofit groups, have developed plans to solve parts of the problem.

In 2014, the Tokyo Metropolitan Government released a long-term plan for the city. Much of it focused on preparation for Tokyo's upcoming 2020 Olympic Games, but the plan also reiterated several common approaches to the demographic crisis. It called for increased access to child care and family-friendly housing, and supported the goal of keeping seniors in their communities. It also reiterated the importance of expanding labor force participation by the elderly and, especially, women. This solution to Japan's shrinking workforce has also been embraced by the national government.

Since 1994, Japan has officially supported gender equality, which in this context refers to "joint participation of men and women" (*danjo kyōdō sankaku*)—a society where individual choice is equally available to all (Schad-Seifert 2006, 8). The "Abenomics" economic revitalization initiative introduced in 2013 by Prime Minister Shinzo Abe included a "Womanomics" component, with pledges of child care and increased access to leadership roles. One obstacle is the expectation in traditional Japanese marriages that the burden of household and caregiving responsibilities will rest on women; as long as that pattern persists, the goal of increasing the birth rate will be at odds with the goal of increasing women's labor force participation. Both the Tokyo plan and Womanomics call for better work-life balance, including men becoming more involved in family responsibilities. Japan has also developed programs to support the elderly, rather than leaving this task entirely to family caregivers who are almost always women. In 2000, the country introduced a long-term care insurance program to streamline and contain the cost of health care for the elderly. It was advertised as a shift from care by the family to care by society.

On a smaller scale, public and private actors have developed initiatives designed to meet some of these general goals. The Tokyo-based Lawson convenience store chain has responded to the desire of older Japanese to work as long as they can, raising the age limit for its franchisees and developing a program of limited part-time work for elders who want to work but cannot perform a regular job. Other programs focus on the solitary elderly; some Tokyo municipalities have developed programs that reach out to people over 70 who are not receiving long-term health services. Others emphasize fitness and preventative care.

Child care is an important aspect of the campaign to increase fertility rates, and in 2015, Tokyo's Metropolitan government amended a noise ordinance to exempt children's playing from its otherwise strict limits, since applications for new child-care facilities were being denied because of complaints that they would violate the law. Other cities have been more creative. In 2016, Urasuyu unveiled a plan to cover 80 percent of the cost of freezing eggs from women aged 25 to 34, so they could more easily have children in the future. Urasuyu has also attempted to encourage marriage and childbearing with municipally sponsored matchmaking, shopping subsidies for larger families, and bans on working late.

One area where Japan has empowered its city governments is improving the built environment. Some of these needs reflect the country's declining population, like the need to address housing abandoned when its owners die or can no longer maintain it. Such houses, including many in suburban parts of Tokyo, are often owned by heirs who don't want them but can't find buyers. Municipalities have been given the power to repair, reuse, or tear down these structures; in Tokyo, one proposal was to reuse some of them as child-care facilities. Revitalization of declining parts of the megacity is another area of concern. Parts of a development in southwestern Tokyo Prefecture called Tama Old Town fall into this category, with hilly terrain and walk-up buildings that are unsuitable for elderly tenants. Attempts to retrofit these areas showed the limits of this strategy: regardless of improvement, it will always be competing with newer, more desirable locations for a limited pool of potential residents.

Another Japanese city, Toyama, responded to the problems of sprawl and social isolation with what they called a "dumpling and skewer" model of development. The city center and pockets of dense development (the dumplings) are connected to one another and areas of low-density residential development by public transportation (the skewers). This approach allows the city to encourage residents to use the amenities and services of the central hub, and holds the city together despite its shrinking population.

Tokyo's challenges cannot be resolved at the local level, however; it also faces the constraints imposed by Japan's national economic situation. The shrinking population means that fewer workers are available to support each person over 65 by paying taxes; in the 1950s, there were about 11 workers per retiree, while in 2013 that number had shrunk to fewer than 2.5 (Below 2016). Furthermore, the collapse of a real estate and stock market bubble in the early 1990s sent the country's economy into a decades-long recession. This encouraged the undermining of Japan's social contract between employers and employees, in which employees were expected to devote themselves to their work but in return could expect comfortable salaries, benefit packages, and job security. Employers began to hire more contingent, temporary, or contract workers, who could be paid less and were not eligible for benefits. Some who found themselves in this situation joined the ranks of the "freeters"—atypical workers who either are not seeking regular full-time employment or cannot find it. Since Tokyo has a high cost of living, growing numbers of freeters and other contingent workers are less likely to be able to afford families. Tokyo's 2014 plan included the ambitious goal of cutting the number of people stuck in irregular positions by half, from 167,100 people in 2012 to a projected 83,000 in 2022 (Tokyo Metropolitan Government 2014, 60). However, attempts to solve the problem through regulation have been met with resistance from employers.

One potential solution to the demographic crisis has proven controversial. Immigration could increase Japan's workforce, solving the problem of too few workers supporting too many retirees, as well as helping to reverse its long-term population decline. The Abe government has facilitated short-term immigration by categorizing participants as limited-term "trainees," and admitted healthcare workers to meet specific shortages. In general, however, the Japanese public remains opposed to immigration that could dilute what they consider the essential nature of their society and culture. Immigrants comprised less than 2 percent of the population in 2008, but according to the United Nations, Japan would have to attract 17 million immigrants, bringing them and their descendants to about 22.5 million people by 2050, in order to restabilize its population at its 2005 level (Kingston 2011, 181). This outcome, while potentially more effective than Japan's efforts to encourage work-life balance and recruit women and the elderly into the workforce, would require a major cultural shift as a prerequisite.

Sara C. Jorgensen

See also: Green Spaces: Tokyo, Japan: Making the City More Livable; *Schools:* Tokyo, Japan: The *Yutori* Educational Reforms; *Violence, Corruption, and Organized Crime:* Tokyo, Japan: Violence, Corruption, and Organized Crime

Further Reading

Adomaitis, Kasparas. 2014. "Transformation of Japanese Cities." *Euromonitor International Market Research.* http://blog.euromonitor.com/2014/10/the-demographic-transformation-of-japanese-cities.html.

Below, Bill. 2016. "The Case of the Shrinking Country: Japan's Demographic and Policy Challenges in 5 Charts." *OECD Insights: Debate the Issues.* http://oecdinsights.org/2016/04/11/the-case-of-the-shrinking-country-japans-demographic-and-policy-challenges-in-5-charts/.

Coulmas, Florian, et al., eds. 2008. *The Demographic Challenge: A Handbook about Japan.* Leiden: Brill.

Kingston, Jeff. 2011. *Contemporary Japan: History, Politics and Social Change since the 1980s.* Chichester, UK: Wiley-Blackwell.

Muramatsu, Naoko, and Hiroko Akiyama. 2011. "Japan: Super-Aging Society Preparing for the Future." *Gerontologist* 51, 4: 425–32.

Noda, Yumiko. 2016. "From Urbanization to Aging Society: Lessons from Japan." PWC Japan Group. http://www.pwc.com/jp/en/japan-knowledge/thoughtleadership.html.

OECD. 2017. "How's Life in Japan?" https://www.oecd.org/statistics/Better-Life-Initiative-country-note-Japan.pdf.

Schad-Seifert, Annette. 2006. "Coping with Low Fertility? Japan's Government Measures for a Gender Equal Society." Tokyo: German Institute for Japanese Studies Working

Paper 06/4. https://academic.oup.com/gerontologist/article/51/4/425/599276/Japan-Super-Aging-Society-Preparing-for-the-Future.
Tokyo Metropolitan Government. 2014. "Creating the Future: The Long-Term Vision for Tokyo." http://www.metro.tokyo.jp/ENGLISH/ABOUT/VISION/index.htm.
Worldometers. 2019. "Japan Population (live)." http://www.worldometers.info/world-population/japan-population/.
World Population Review. 2019. "Tokyo Population 2019." http://worldpopulationreview.com/world-cities/tokyo-population.

Vancouver, Canada: The Most Asian City in the Western World

Vancouver, British Columbia, by 2017 had become home to the largest Asian community in the Western world, comprising almost half of its population within city limits. Unlike the United States, "south of the border," with anti-immigrant rhetoric stoked by President Donald J. Trump, Vancouver and Canada's liberal federal government has been welcoming in-migration, which has been a source of urban vitality, diversity, and prosperity—as well as conflict.

The proportion of Asian or Chinese population in Vancouver depends upon which area one examines. The city of Vancouver itself contained 631,486 people, according to Canadian census records for 2011. About 28 percent were Chinese, 6 percent south Asian, 6 percent Filipino, 3 percent Southeast Asian, 1.7 percent Japanese, 1.5 percent Korean, and 1.2 percent West Asian. For the urban area of roughly 2.5 million that envelops Vancouver proper, the Asian proportion was lower, on the order of 15 to 20 percent.

Worldwide, according to Douglas Todd, writing in the *Vancouver Sun*, "the only major cities outside Asia . . . that come close to Metro Vancouver for their portion of residents with Asian backgrounds are San Francisco (33 percent Asian), London, England (21 percent), Metro Toronto (35 percent), Calgary (23 percent) and Sydney, Australia (19 percent)." Todd continued: "Observers from Asian and non-Asian backgrounds predict that as a result of Metro Vancouver's unique demographics, residents should expect more changes; adjustments that will create opportunities and richness, as well as tension and difficulties."

Chinese immigration to Vancouver and British Columbia is not a recent phenomenon. It began in 1858 as Vancouver became a trans-shipment point for a gold rush in northern and central parts of the province. By the 1880s, about 6,500 Chinese were employed by the Canadian Pacific Railway as tracks extended throughout the nation's west. Tensions also stem from the early days, when some white workers asserted that "the yellow peril" were stealing their jobs. Canada's federal government in 1885 enacted a "head tax" of $50 per immigrant. Between 1923 and 1947, Chinese immigration to Canada was banned completely, under the federal Chinese Exclusion Act.

The present immigration surge into Vancouver began during the 1980s and 1990s involving, according to a British Broadcasting Company (BBC) report, "a largely wealthy class of Hong Kong Chinese who snapped up homes in the priciest neighborhoods, sent their children to the best schools, and kicked off a construction boom

Migration and Demographic Changes

which transformed downtown Vancouver into a Hong Kong-style city of skyscrapers" (Bhatty 2012). "Their sudden impact brought a sharp backlash. Polite Vancouver society was aghast at the 'monster houses' being built in the old-monied communities of Shaughnessy and Kerrisdale, often demolishing character homes and tearing down trees. . . . Newspaper headlines and some politicians warned of an 'Asian invasion' while the bitter elite coined the phrase 'Hongcouver' to express their dismay at the perceived Asian-isation of their city" (Bhatty 2012).

The increase in Asian population has brought with it several majority Asian neighborhoods, newspapers, magazines, and television stations publishing or broadcasting in a variety of Asian languages, retail stores, and artistic events. Ninety percent of immigrants to the Vancouver area between 2001 and 2011 were born outside of Canada, about 70 percent of whom arrived from Asia.

Many affluent Chinese also have also bought property in Vancouver, without (yet) actually moving there, which puts substantial upward pressure on housing prices. This is also an issue in Seattle and San Francisco, both of which have substantial populations that share Chinese, Filipino, East Indian, and other Asian ethnicities, including South Korea, Pakistan, Iran, Vietnam, Singapore, Afghanistan, Lebanon, and elsewhere. However, Seattle's proportion of Asian population, at 13 percent in 2016, was less than 30 percent of Vancouver's (Todd 2017).

The economic boom in China was thus elevating the prices of rather modest single-family homes. For many affluent Chinese, a house in Vancouver is a hedge

Millennium Gate in Chinatown in Vancouver, British Columbia, Canada, 2007. Vancouver is home to the largest Asian community in the West. The city's open immigration policy reflects an appreciation of the economic and social value of immigrant communities. (Deymos/Dreamstime.com)

against possible political and financial instability at home, as well as a potential escape should anti-capitalist sentiment provoke expropriation of assets. It is also an expression of a preference for less crowding, clean air, and personal freedom than China offers the upwardly mobile.

Demographia's 2014 survey indicated that the median house price in Vancouver was $670,000, the highest in Canada, while the median household income at the time was only $65,000, among the lowest of all major Canadian cities. The disconnect between wages and the rising cost of mortgages was severely restricting home ownership. During the next three years, average sale prices for homes in Vancouver spiked upward to almost $1.4 million early in 2017, before subsiding to $1,185,000 Canadian (about US$1 million) by August of that year.

The Asian demographic surge, most pronounced first among college-age students, has become more family-oriented over time. According to a report published by Canadian immigration lawyer Richard Kurland, "Visas being processed by Canada's embassy in Beijing [indicate that] kindergarten-to-grade 12 students made up 37 percent of all study permits issued in China last year [2015], a sharp rise from 18 percent just six years ago [2009]. In B.C., there were 1,094 Chinese students enrolled in K-12 in 2009; by 2014, that figure had quadrupled to 4,306" (Chiang 2016). Sending children ahead as students improves parents' chances for Canadian-residency permits.

Vancouver's swift demographic changes have not come without controversy. Farid Rohani, of the Laurier Institution, said that immigrants should integrate into local culture more quickly, "since for the most part they have benefited from leaving behind Asian countries buffeted by instability, pollution and low wages." Rohani, an importer-exporter of Asian goods, said that members of some large Asian ethnic groups "isolate themselves by forming cultural, language and moral silos, which work against the principles of liberal democracy." Regent College professor Edwin Hui, who immigrated to Vancouver from Hong Kong in 1974, said that he has "noted tensions between the formerly European-oriented host culture of Metro Vancouver and some Asian newcomers, particularly the wealthy. There has also been conflict, he says, among Asian ethno-cultural groups themselves" (Todd 2017).

Canadian scholar Ludovic Rheault, an expert in politics and immigration, said that one-third of Asian immigrants speak or write little or no English. "Nothing guarantees that the economic and cultural integration of Vancouver's Asian communities will go smoothly," he said (Todd 2017). While Rohani acknowledges that high immigration rates place burdens on the city's infrastructure, he holds onto his dream that the immigration of Chinese and other Asians "will, in the end, make Vancouver a much more cosmopolitan and culturally rich city" (Todd 2017).

One report (Hiebert 2012) warned that "Vancouver and Toronto are likely to see racial enclaves with segregation approaching that between whites and blacks in the United States" (Young 2013), as Canadian whites' proportion slips to minority status by 2031. The 2012 study, which was titled "A New Residential Order?," anticipated that increasing Asian populations in three major Canadian cities (Vancouver, Montreal, and Toronto) will segregate themselves racially, rather than assimilating into general Canadian culture.

Daniel Hiebert, a geographer at the University of British Columbia, concluded this report by saying that the two cities "are likely to have a social geography . . . of 'ethno-cultural enclaves' . . . that is entirely new to Canadian society" (Young 2013). Hiebert's study focused on the Vancouver suburb of Richmond, where, as Ian Young wrote in the South China Morning Post (2013), "ethnic Chinese already outnumber the white population, creating the most Chinese city in North America." Hiebert forecast that populations of Vancouver and Toronto will explode by 60 to 67 percent within 25 years (comparing census figures for 2006 with his forecasts for 2031), as residents whose family histories run two generations or more into the past will shrink to a quarter or less of overall populations, due to in-migration and "the fertility of immigrants." Hiebert concluded that "There is no significant European city with anything like this demographic structure, nor will there be by 2031" (Young 2013).

"The wealth of the newcomers was an irritation to some in the local community," said historian John Douglas Belshaw, a professor at the University of Victoria. But attitudes soon began to change, he said. "The elite said, 'Our bread's buttered on this side. We can sell a ton of real estate to this community and they're kind of like us. These people like their whiskey straight'" (Bhatty 2012).

Richmond, adjacent to Vancouver, once a village of fishermen and farmers, has become known for its Asian shopping mall, Aberdeen Centre, and its Lamborghini dealership, Chinese restaurants, and live-fish grocery stores, as well as ice-cream shops selling flavors such as green tea and lychee. The *Vancouver Sun* has a Mandarin edition. Auto insurance in British Columbia is sold in 170 languages, with Mandarin and Cantonese among the most popular (Bhatty 2012). By 2011, British Columbia had more trade with nations of the Pacific Rim than with the United States. British Columbia exports to China increased 500 percent in 10 years, between 2001 and 2011 (Bhatty 2012).

By Canada's 2016 census, more than 74 percent of Richmond's 200,000 residents were of Asian heritage. It also had become "a one-stop paradise for lovers of Asian food" (Grescoe 2018). Vancouver International Airport, a 15-minute train ride from downtown Richmond, had become North America's leading departure and transfer point for flights to Asia. Fernando Medrano, who came to Richmond with his parents from the Philippines in 1976, said that in Richmond, Asian cooking techniques have been enhanced with some of the New World's best ingredients. "People often say the Chinese food you get here is superior to what you get in China, where everyone is concerned about pollution. A lot of Richmond is still protected farmland, which means there's great bok choy, gai lan—all the Chinese greens. And we're right on the Pacific, so we have access to some of the freshest seafood in the world" (Grescoe 2018).

The influx of affluent Chinese young people has even spawned a reality television show. As described by Wayne Leidenfrost in Canada's *National Post*: "Chelsea Jiang is young, beautiful and smart. An ethnic Chinese woman living the high life in Vancouver, she's more than willing to display her wealth. This qualifies her to star on a local reality show [on YouTube] that's attracting millions of viewers at home and abroad, especially in China. Subtle, it is not. Presented in snappy 12- to 15-minute segments, 'Ultra Rich Asian Girls' puts a lens

> **Urban Ethnic Enclaves**
>
> In an increasingly diverse world, many cities are home to a vast array of ethnic communities. Vancouver's Asians are only one example. In the United States, most medium-sized and large cities have distinct Asian areas, as well as Latino barrios and others. New York, Boston, Los Angeles, San Francisco, and Seattle all contain well-established Asian communities with their own business districts.
>
> Some ethnic neighborhoods have been largely dismantled by economic changes. Seattle's Central Area, for example, long mainly African American, has been gentrified to a point where it will be 90 percent non-minority within a decade or two. The main cause here is a technology boom that has raised housing prices to levels that most Central Area residents cannot afford. Neighborhoods that once contained affordable housing have now become very expensive, dispersing residents into suburbs 20 to 30 miles away from downtown. Whereas housing was once less expensive near the city's core, the opposite is now the case. The same trend has also taken place in other cities, such as Washington, D.C., where the city center is now more affluent in some neighborhoods, as immigrant communities cluster in suburbs such as Annandale, Virginia, where Vietnamese immigrants and their children have gathered.

on Ms. Jiang and three female contemporaries, as they swan about their adopted city" (Leidenfrost 2014).

Between 2005 and 2012, according to Statistics Canada, 37,000 Chinese millionaires arrived in British Columbia as permanent residents under the short-lived Immigrant Investor Program (IIP), a federal government program that offered wealthy immigrants fast-track entry into Canada as a quid pro quo for low-interest loans to provincial governments (Leidenfrost 2014).

Linkage of preferences for wealthy immigrants extends to British Columbia's flagship university. "At the University of British Columbia, the province's largest post-secondary institution," wrote Wayne Leidenfrost in the *National Post*, "Students worry about precious resources being directed to a new college under construction on their campus. Vantage College is meant for the exclusive use of 1,000 international students who can afford its $50,000 annual tuition and accommodation fees. There are already 19,100 students from China enrolled in B.C. universities, more than the number of foreign students from the United States, Korea, Japan and India combined, according to provincial government statistics" (Leidenfrost 2014).

By 2016, Canada's liberal government was planning to double or triple the number of offices in China from which it could issue visas. Canadian Immigration Minister John McCallum said in 2016 the Liberal government wanted to increase the number of immigrants, just as Vancouver city officials enacted a property-transfer tax for foreign buyers of homes in the city, a reaction to soaring prices (Johnson 2016).

Bruce E. Johansen

See also: Employment and Jobs: Shenzhen, China: Struggle to Leave Shanzhai Behind; *Migration and Demographic Changes:* Guangzhou, China: Foreign Communities Facing Challenges of Adaptation

Further Reading

Bhatty, Ayesha. 2012. "Canada Prepares for an Asian Future." British Broadcasting Company (BBC) News, May 25. http://www.bbc.com/news/world-radio-and-tv-18149316.

Chiang, Chuck. 2016. "Chinese K-12 Students a Booming Demographic for B.C. Schools." *Vancouver Sun*, May 25. http://vancouversun.com/news/local-news/chinese-k-12-students-a-booming-demographic-for-b-c-schools.

Grescoe, Taras. 2018. "The Best Asian Food in North America? Try British Columbia." *New York Times*, June 4. https://www.nytimes.com/2018/06/04/travel/richmond-bc-asian-chinese-food-restaurants.html.

Hiebert, Daniel. 2012. "A New Residential Order? The Social Geography of Visible Minority and Religious Groups in Montreal, Toronto, and Vancouver in 2031." July. Citizenship and Immigration/Canada. http://www.cic.gc.ca/english/resources/research/residential.asp.

Johnson, Lisa. 2016. "Canada Wants More Chinese Workers, Students and Tourists, Says Immigration Minister." Canadian Broadcasting Corporation (CBC) News, August 17. http://www.cbc.ca/news/canada/british-columbia/chinese-immigration-canada-china-1.3725202.

Leidenfrost, Wayne. 2014. "Vancouver Being Transformed by New Wave of Brash, Rich Asians Looking for a Safe Place to 'Park Their Cash.'" *National Post* (Canada), December 12. http://nationalpost.com/news/canada/vancouver-being-transformed-by-new-wave-of-brash-rich-asians-looking-for-safe-place-to-park-their-cash.

Todd, Douglas. 2017. "Vancouver Is the Most 'Asian' City Outside Asia." *Vancouver Sun*, March 27. http://vancouversun.com/life/vancouver-is-most-asian-city-outside-asia-what-are-the-ramifications.

"Vancouver Housing Prices." 2017. Zolo, August. https://www.zolo.ca/vancouver-real-estate/trends.

Young, Ian. 2013. "Chinese Numbers in Vancouver, Toronto to Double by 2031." *South China Morning Post,* April 6. http://www.scmp.com/news/world/article/1207878/chinese-numbers-vancouver-and-toronto-double-2031-study-says.

Williamsport, United States: A Quiet Town in Deep Pennsylvania

Walking down the tall and narrow hallways of the Pajama Factory, the space feels like any other art studio building in New York City. The building was constructed in the late 1800s; it is five-stories of brick, steel, and glass and has 300,000 square feet (91,440 square meters) of floor space taking up two city blocks. The building is 40 percent complete, leaving 60 percent currently empty to build more living, studio, and retail spaces. The 110,000 square feet of occupied space contains a diverse mix of tenants from artists, artisans, engineers, programmers, to organic gardening and soap makers. The intent of the building's design is to provide an ideal environment for creative types of people: large raw space, cheap rent, all within an inspired community. Over 100 of the studio spaces are occupied, and there is a waiting list for more studios. But here is the catch: the Pajama Factory is not located in New York City, it is in Williamsport, Pennsylvania, about 200 miles

(322 km) west of NYC. In a small city that has a population of 30,000 and a regional population of 120,000, who are the creative people that are playing a part in the transformation of this small city?

THE CITY

In the late 1800s, Williamsport, Pennsylvania, was named the lumber capital of the world. The economic boom lasted from the late 1800s to the 1920s, and at that time there were more millionaires per capita in Williamsport than anywhere else in the world. The population of the town peaked at 45,000 in the 1950s and has been in a slow decline ever since. Williamsport is like a number of small cities on the East Coast suffering from brain drain. "Brain drain" is used to describe the inability for a region or town to hold onto its young, intelligent, and motivated people who move away to find better opportunities in other large cities across the United States. Although the city of 30,000 maintains two colleges, two hospitals, light industry, and the Little League Baseball World Series, there was the perception that there was little opportunity for growth. In 1999, downtown Williamsport was slowly dying through economic neglect and brain drain. Then a revival of the downtown began to take shape in the early to mid-2000s. The factors that prompted this revival can be attributed to a shift in economics, the Internet, and philosophy of life.

THE ECONOMICS

Williamsport's generally low cost of living, easy access to nature and outdoor activities, and proximity to New York City, Philadelphia, Pittsburgh, and

The "Pajama Factory" is an old industrial building in Williamsport, Pennsylvania, that was converted into an art complex. The space contains artists' studios and offices for small businesses and startups. Williamsport's rural setting and low cost of living appeals to artists and entrepreneurs. (Illustration by Chad Andrews)

Washington, D.C., places it in the middle of nowhere and yet ideally located between these four major metropolitan areas. In 2000, the Williamsport First Friday event (part of a national trend) formed to promote the arts and attract families to downtown on the first Friday of every month. Local businesses participate by being open late and use their storefronts and sidewalk to become galleries showcasing local artist, artisans, and musicians. The city's interest in and support of the arts is a direct attempt to create a new identity for Williamsport as an "art town." An art town can be defined as a city or town whose economic health is partly dependent on a large number of the population being involved in the arts. In an effort to attract more artists and art enthusiasts to the area, the city commissioned a few public artworks for downtown and in 2003 hired a muralist, Michael Pilato, to paint *Inspiration: Lycoming County*. This mural was a multiyear project that was promoted heavily throughout the region and was paid for through public and private funds. The mural project heightened awareness of the arts and energized the region as a creative place. Williamsport is not an art town, but the arts have become more prominent downtown with two contemporary art galleries, art businesses, a few new murals, and a little west of downtown, the Pajama Factory.

The biggest factor in the economic revival of the Williamsport area is the natural gas boom from the Marcellus Shale deposit. During the late 2000s and early 2010s, the natural gas industry came to the region and began hydro fracturing the shale deposit. The hydro-fracturing process continues to be a highly controversial natural gas extraction process, but the immediate economic impact did bring numerous investors, workers, and their families to the Williamsport area. The construction of new hotels, businesses, roads, and other infrastructure started immediately all over the city and across the region. There has been talk about building arts studios in what is now called the Pajama Factory, but nothing has worked. But combine the First Friday events, the mural project, installation of public artworks, with the population increase from the economic boom of the gas industry, and Williamsport was now primed for a studio arts building.

THE PAJAMA FACTORY

In 2007, just about the time when the gas industry was moving in all over the region, investors from New York City purchased a mostly abandoned 300,000-square foot industrial complex and began turning it into an art complex now called the "Pajama Factory." The Pajama Factory is a privately funded project and has attracted artists, musicians, actors, designers, and small start-up businesses to the area from all over the country. The economic plan is to provides cheap rental space that gives start-up businesses an affordable space near other start-up businesses and hope for collaborations to form. The Pajama Factory's business model captures a current trend of "makers space," a do-it-yourself movement where designers, engineers, programmers, and other creative people meet in a space to explore ideas and share knowledge. At the Pajama Factory, it is not uncommon to walk into Way Cool Beans, an independent coffee roasting and brewing shop, to find a programmer tweaking the coffee shop's personal server before teaching a nine-year-old how to program or build a basic circuit board. Across the hall, a hair stylist is exchanging a haircut for a painting from an artist who is about to drive her new artwork to a gallery in Washington, D.C. Upstairs an artist is working with a master printer hand-printing the CD cover for his newest soundscape that will be part of an exhibition happening in downtown Williamsport. Numerous other activities like this happen all the time throughout the building because of the proximity and diversity that are allowed to cross-pollinate within the building. On First Fridays, visitors from all over the region and some well beyond roam freely through the Pajama Factory halls visiting studios and stores.

THE INTERNET

The reason for living in New York used to be for making connections, learning new technologies, and "being part of the conversation," a phrase used to indicate that your work is part of what is currently in style. Connections to other artists, galleries, museums, and opportunities within the arts community are now being served digitally. Sites like Hyperallergic (https://hyperallergic.com) or Inliquid (https://inliquid.org) provide commentary on current issues in contemporary art as well as job, exhibition, and other opportunities for artists. Open-source and freely exchanged information through the Internet have had enormous impact and influence on the creative class, giving them more options to choose ideal locations of operation. Williamsport's location once kept it isolated or buffered from the opportunities in New York and other major cities. Not only does the Internet allow artists access to what is happening in New York City, but it provides them access to any city in the world. This is compounded by social media sites that give the feeling of personal and immediate connectedness with artists who are willing to share their creative experiences. Artists now have access to endless art reviews, articles, art chatrooms, exhibitions, grant opportunities, and philosophical arguments—all available at their fingertips. This connectedness lets artists avoid making art in a vacuum, without being aware of what others in the field are doing. No longer hampered by being disconnected from the art world through distance, artists are able to conduct a majority of their research and business online.

THE CREATIVE CLASS

Visiting Williamsport, one finds an upbeat downtown that has an independent bookstore, coffee shops, galleries, ceramic studios, chocolate shops, jewelers, restaurants, and other small local businesses. There is a renewed vibrancy in the city that is attractive enough for new people while keeping locals from moving away. The renewed economic growth combined with a focus on the arts and access to nature has resulted in a noticeable increase of young artists and entrepreneurs moving to or staying in Williamsport to open studios and businesses.

What makes Williamsport attractive to the young creative class? The ability to become "time rich," of having the time to create, is an important factor. Living in an area where the cost of living is high often demands too much time in a job(s) that only supports the living cost but leaves little time and money for much else.

Living in a big city and having access to everything one desires seems ideal at first, but having too much access to everything can become a burden because of the time and money it takes to satisfy desires. The choice of having more time to create and building an enriching life without conveniences is why creative people tend to move to impoverished areas where rental space is cheap. In discussions with millennials, there is interest in forgoing the quest for material wealth; having experiences is an important value to their lives. In a conversation with a young theater director, she said one of her reasons for moving from New York City to Williamsport was that in New York she could assist in a play's production, but in Williamsport she can write, direct, and produce a play.

PHILOSOPHICAL OUTLOOK

The revitalization of Williamsport relied on a number of independent factors. A small group of people began working on promoting the arts as an identity for the city in hopes that the arts would provide vibrancy and excitement to attract new businesses and entrepreneurs. But the First Fridays, murals, and public art would not have been enough to make the small post-industrial city a viable place to live and work. It was the gas industry that played a vital role of infusing money and jobs into the region at the right time to jump-start the optimism for what is possible in Williamsport. It brought investors from New York to create the Pajama Factory, which is now a flagship for the arts in the region. The Internet and social media transformed the idea of connectedness and opportunities available to anyone, anywhere, and made Williamsport's central location to major cities infinitely more attractive to the creative class. Williamsport is not officially an "art town," but the arts now play a much greater part in its cultural and social identity. There is now a group of preservationists who are advocating for Williamsport to be branded as a "river town." The city's identity cannot be defined by preexisting labels; it will become what the new creative entrepreneurs make it. The rise of the creative class and the experience-oriented mindset of the millennial generation now make the city of 30,000 more of an attractive place to live and work.

Chad Andrews

See also: Migration and Demographic Changes: Los Angeles, United States: A Dynamic Demographic Mix

Further Reading

Federowicz, Jeffrey Allen. 2007. "Williamsport Mural Depicts Lycoming County's Colorful History." *Daily Item,* May 24. http://www.dailyitem.com/news/entertainment/williamsport-mural-depicts-lycoming-county-s-colorful-history/article_12796dbf-6608-5e55-9b4d-0391455a4751.html.

Florida, Richard. 2014. *The Rise of the Creative Class—Revisited: Revised and Expanded.* New York: Basic Books.

Geology.com. 2017. "Marcellus Shale: Appalachian Basin Natural Gas Play." http://geology.com/articles/marcellus-shale.shtml.

Lutz, Ashley. 2012. "Why the 'Creative Class' Is Taking Over the World." *Business Insider,* July 28. http://www.businessinsider.com/why-the-creative-class-is-taking-over-the-world-2012-7.

Makerspaces.com. 2017. "What Is a Makerspace?" https://www.makerspaces.com/what-is-a-makerspace.

New Hampshire Department of Environmental Studies. 2010. "Well Development by Hydro-fracturing." https://www.des.nh.gov/organization/commissioner/pip/factsheets/dwgb/documents/dwgb-1-3.pdf.

The Pajama Factory. 2017. http://www.pajamafactory.net.

United States Department of Labor. 2017. "Economy at a Glance: Williamsport, PA." https://www.bls.gov/eag/eag.pa_williamsport_msa.htm.

Villani, John. 2005. *100 Best Art Towns in America*. Woodstock, VT: Countryman Press.

Williamsport First Friday. 2017. http://williamsportfirstfriday.org/about.

Williamsport/Lycoming Chamber of Commerce. 2017. http://williamsport.org/

Index

Note: **Bold** indicates volume numbers; *italicized* page numbers indicate illustrations; page numbers followed by *t* indicate tables.

Abe, Shinzo, **1**:291; **2**:158, 232, 293
Aboriginal Australians, **1**:236
Abu Dhabi, United Arab Emirates (UAE), green spaces, **1**:130, 131–35
Adelstein, Jake, **2**:234
Afghanistan, violence, corruption, and organized crime, **2**:178, 207–11, *209*
Aggarwal, Rajiv, **2**:264
Aguascalientes, Mexico, green spaces, **1**:128–29, 135–39
Ahmed, Azam, **2**:217
Ahmedinejad, Mahmoud, **1**:287
Air pollution
  Baku, Azerbaijan, **2**:2–3, 6–10, *7*
  Karachi, Pakistan, **2**:4, 23–27, *24*
  Kolkata, India, **2**:142–43, 144
  Krakow, Poland, **2**:3, 28–32, *29*
  New Delhi, India, **2**:4, 33–38, 34*t*
  Pittsburgh, Pennsylvania, **1**:106–10
  Rome, Italy, **2**:5–6, 39–43
  Sao Paulo, Brazil, **2**:3, 45–48
  Seoul, South Korea, **2**:2, 52–53
Air transportation, Osaka, Japan, **2**:156–58
Al-Ali, Zaid, **2**:188, 189
Alberta, Canada, waste management, **2**:240, 251–56, 253*t*, 255*t*
Aleppo, Syria, violence, corruption, and organized crime, **2**:178, 182–86, *185*
Almaki, Sarah, **2**:189–90, 192
Almaty, Kazakhstan, housing and infrastructure, **1**:188, 189–94
Almukhtar, Sarah, **2**:188, 191–92
Al-Nahyan, Crown Prince His Highness Sheikh Mohammed bin Zayed, **1**:132

Amari, Akira, **2**:233
Amazon.com, **1**:50, 51
Ambrose, Jerry, **2**:18
Amerindians, **1**:279–80
Amin, Muhammad, **2**:245
Anaerobic co-digestion (AC), **2**:295–96
Anaerobic digestion (AD), **2**:295
Anderson, Lars Bo, **1**:77
Araujo Vormittag, Evangelina da Motta Pacheco de, **2**:45
ArcelorMittal Factory, **2**:31–32
Argentina
  immigration, **1**:255–58
  migration and demographic changes, **1**:251–52, 254–58, *256*
Arnold, Carrie, **2**:57
Asahara, Shoko, **2**:232
Assad, Bashar al-, **1**:232; **2**:182
Atia, Sabah, **2**:242
Atwani, Atwan al-, **2**:243
Aum Shinrikyo, **2**:232
Australia
  energy and sustainability, **1**:66, 92–96, *94*
  housing and infrastructure, **1**:185, 233–38, *234*
  schools, **2**:65, 91–95
Austria, housing and infrastructure, **1**:186–87, 244–47
Automobile industry, **1**:213, 214–15
Azerbaijan, air and water pollution, **2**:2–3, 6–10, *7*
Azikiwe, Abayomi, **1**:218

Baden-Wuerttemberg, Germany, **2**:169
Bagasse, **1**:93

Baghdad, Iraq
  violence, corruption, and organized crime, **2:**177–78, 187–92, *190*
  waste management, **2:**237–38, 241–45, *242*
Baku, Azerbaijan, air and water pollution, **2:**2–3, 6–10, *7*
Baltic Sea, **1:**58
Bamako, Mali, schools, **2:**62–63, 67–71, *70*
Banna, Niran, **2:**190
Barrio adentro, **1:**198–99
Bastia, Tanja, **1:**255, 258
Beauchamp, Edward, **2:**101–3
Beijing, China
  energy and sustainability, **1:**65–66, 70–74, 72*t*
  traffic and transportation, **2:**119–20, 124–29, *126*
  violence, corruption, and organized crime, **2:**179, 193–97
  water shortage, **1:**65–66, 70–74, 72*t*
Belgium, violence, corruption, and organized crime, **2:**179, 197–202, *199*
Bell-Jefferson, Jackie, **2:**58
Belshaw, John Douglas, **1:**297
Bengaluru, India, **1:**21
Benz, Karl, **2:**165
Beouinde, Armand, **2:**83
Berlin, Germany
  housing and infrastructure, **1:**277
  schools, **2:**64, 72–77, *74*
Berlin Wall, **1:**228
Berlusconi, Silvio, **2:**275–76
Berman, Ethan, **2:**80
Bertolaso, Guido, **2:**275
Bhada-Tata, Perinaz, **2:**284, 285
Biking
  Casablanca, Morocco, **2:**133
  Copenhagen, Denmark, **1:**76–78, *77*
  Zurich, Switzerland, **2:**174
Biocell landfill, **2:**252–53
Biofuels, India, **1:**101
Biomass
  Frankfurt, Germany, **1:**84
  Melbourne, Australia, **1:**92–93
Bioreactor landfill, **2:**252
Black (2016), **2:**201
Black Clothes Gang, **2:**196
Bo Xilai, **1:**201, 204–5
Bonaparte, Joseph, **2:**214
Bonaparte, Napoléon, **1:**165; **2:**214
Bono, **1:**180

Boston, Massachusetts
  schools, **2:**66, 78–82, *79*
  water pollution, **2:**1–2, 11–15, *13*
Boyle, Kevin, **1:**214
Braiterman, Jared, **1:**180
Brazil
  air pollution, **2:**3, 45–48
  energy and sustainability, **1:**68, 111–15, *112*
Bremer, L. Paul, **2:**188
Brexit, **1:**4, 16–18
Brillembourg, David, **1:**197
British Columbia, Canada, migration and demographic changes, **1:**252, 294–98, *295*
Brussels, Belgium, violence, corruption, and organized crime, **2:**179, 197–202, *199*
Bryant, William Cullen, **1:**161
Buenos Aires, Argentina, migration and demographic changes, **1:**251–52, 254–58, *256*
Building insulation, Copenhagen, Denmark, **1:**78
Burkina Faso, schools, **2:**63, 83–86
Bush, George H. W., **2:**217
Byrnes, Mark, **1:**106

Cairo, Egypt, waste management, **2:**238–39, 246–50, *248*
Calderón, Felipe, **2:**217
Calgary, Alberta, Canada, waste management, **2:**240, 251–56, 253*t*, 255*t*
California
  migration and demographic changes, **1:**252, 279–83
  waste management, **2:**239–40, 288–92, *290*
Campania, **2:**275
Canada
  energy and sustainability, **1:**68–69, 120–24, *122*
  green spaces, **1:**128, 140–46, 141*t*, *142*
  migration and demographic changes, **1:**252, 294–98, *295*
  waste management, **2:**240, 251–56, 253*t*, 255*t*
Caracas, Venezuela, housing and infrastructure, **1:**188, 195–99
Carbon dioxide emissions
  Copenhagen, Denmark, **1:**75–76
  London, United Kingdom, **1:**88–89
  Melbourne, Australia, **1:**66

Carbon tax, **2:**48
Carpooling, Stuttgart, Germany, **2:**168–69
Casablanca, Morocco, traffic and transportation, **2:**122, 130–33
Castro, Fidel, **1:**187, 222, 223
Castro, Raúl, **1:**223
Cathay Glory Association, **2:**98
Catholic schools, **2:**69–70
Centres d'animation pédagogiques (CAP), **2:**68
Chaebol, **2:**225
Charles I, King, **2:**15
Charles River, **2:**1–2, 11–15, *13*
Charles River Watershed Association (CRWA), **2:**13–14
Chávez, Hugo, **1:**195–96, 198
Checkley, William, **1:**271
Cheonggyecheon Stream Restoration Project, **2:**53–54
Cheung Bing-leung, Anthony, **1:**151
Chicago, Illinois, violence, corruption, and organized crime, **2:**181, 202–6
Chikan (subway groping), **2:**181, 232
China
   employment and jobs, **1:**5–6, 52–57, *54*
   energy and sustainability, **1:**65–66, 70–74, *72t*
   green spaces, **1:**127–28, 147–52, *148,* 162
   housing and infrastructure, **1:**186, 188–89, 200–205, *203,* 206–11
   migration and demographic changes, **1:**250–51, 259–63
   schools, **2:**62, 111–16, 113*t*
   traffic and transportation, **2:**119–20, 124–29, *126*
   violence, corruption, and organized crime, **2:**179, 193–97
Choi, Jang Jip, **2:**220–21, 222
Choi Soon-sil, **2:**220, 224
Chongqing, China, housing and infrastructure, **1:**186, 200–205, *203*
Chun Doo-hwan, **2:**221–22, 223
Chung Yoo-ra, **2:**224
Chunmei, W., **2:**265
Clairton, Pennsylvania, **1:**108–9, 110
Climate change
   Peru, **1:**271–73
   Syria, **2:**184–86
Climate vs. weather, **2:**186
Coal, Singapore City, Singapore, **1:**119
Cogeneration systems, Frankfurt, Germany, **1:**83

Cohen, Sharon, **1:**215
Coleman, Vernal, **1:**49
Columbus, Christopher, **1:**41, 115
Community Energy Planning (CEP), **1:**121
Commuter rail system, Casablanca, Morocco, **2:**133
Composting
   Dakar, Senegal, **2:**258
   Singapore, **2:**295–96
Congestion, traffic. *See* Traffic and transportation
Conniff, Ruth, **1:**218
Conocarpus erectus, **2:**26
Copenhagen, Denmark, energy and sustainability, **1:**66–67, 74–79, *77*
Copernicus, Nicolaus, **2:**28
Copycat manufacturing, **1:**55–56
Corruption. *See* Violence, corruption, and organized crime
Cosa Nostra, **2:**226
Cuba, housing and infrastructure, **1:**187–88, 220–25, *221*
Cybriwsky, Roman, **2:**231

Dakar, Senegal
   landfill, **2:**260
   waste management, **2:**238, 257–61, *258*
Dak'art, **2:**261
Dandong, China, housing and infrastructure, **1:**188–89, 206–11
Danish, Jamil, **2:**210
Dawood, Qasim, **2:**243–44
Dean, Richie, **1:**270
Dearborn STEM Academy, **2:***79,* 79–80
Decentralized home power stations, Frankfurt, Germany, **1:**83
Deibert, Michael, **2:**217–18
Delhi, India
   employment and jobs, **1:**20–21
   landfills, **2:**264–65, 265–66
   waste management, **2:**239, 262–66
   See also New Delhi, India
Democratic Republic of Congo (DRC), migration and demographic changes, **1:**250, 264–68
Demographic changes. *See* Migration and demographic changes
Deng Xiaoping, **1:**53, 202, 208, 211; **2:**116
Denmark, energy and sustainability, **1:**66–67, 74–79, *77*
Detroit, Michigan, housing and infrastructure, **1:**186, 213–19, *216*

Dharavi, neighborhood (Mumbai, India), **1:**22
Díaz, Porfirio, **1:**136; **2:**215
Dipiao system, **1:**203
District energy (DE) systems, **1:**124
Diwali, **2:**38
Dixon, Roland Burrage, **1:**282
Dongan, Thomas, **1:**160
Droughts, Syria, **2:**183–84
Dry-tomb landfills, **2:**252
Duda, Andrzej, **2:**31
Duggan, Mike, **1:**216
Dumpling and skewer model of development, **1:**292
Durning, Alan, **1:**50
Dutch disease, **1:**196

Ebtkar, Masoumeh, **1:**287
Eco-villages, **1:**134
Education. *See* Schools
Eetbaar Rotterdam (Edible Rotterdam), **1:**171–72
Egan, Tim, **1:**48
Egypt, waste management, **2:**238–39, 246–50, *248*
Ehlmaier, Michael, **1:**246
Eichstaedt, Peter, **2:**58
Eiffel Tower, **1:**166
El Centro de la Raza, **1:**50
El Niño, **1:**271, 273
Electrical vehicles, **1:**84, 85
Electricity consumption
  Frankfurt, Germany, **1:**83
  Mumbai, India, **1:**98–100
Employment and jobs
  Lagos, Nigeria, **1:**1–2, 6–10, *8*
  London, United Kingdom, **1:**4, *12,* 12–18
  Mumbai, India, **1:**2–3, 19–23
  New York City, New York, **1:**24–29, 25*t,* 27*t*
  overview, **1:**1–6
  Paris, France, **1:**5, 31–35, *32,* 34*t*
  Riyadh, Saudi Arabia, **1:**3, 36–40
  San Juan, Puerto Rico, **1:**2, 41–46, *44*
  Seattle, Washington, **1:**4, 48–51
  Shenzhen, China, **1:**5–6, 52–57, *54*
  Stockholm, Sweden, **1:**3–4, 58–63, *59*
Energy and sustainability
  Beijing, China, **1:**70–74, 72*t*
  China, **1:**65–66
  Copenhagen, Denmark, **1:**66–67, 74–79, *77*
  Frankfurt, Germany, **1:**68, 79–85
  London, United Kingdom, **1:**67–68, 86–90
  Melbourne, Australia, **1:**66, 92–96, *94*
  Mumbai, India, **1:**67, 97–102
  overview, **1:**65–70
  Pittsburgh, Pennsylvania, **1:**69–70, 106–10, *107*
  Rio de Janeiro, Brazil, **1:**68, 111–15, *112*
  Singapore City, Singapore, **1:**69, 116–19
  Toronto, Ontario, Canada, **1:**68–69, 120–24, *122*
Energy-efficient buildings
  Rio de Janeiro, Brazil, **1:**111–13, *112*
  Singapore City, Singapore, **1:**116–17
Engineering is Elementary (EiE), **2:**82
Environment, New York City, New York, **1:**28–29
Erdogan, Ercep Tayyip, **2:**138
Esser, Daniel, **2:**209, 211
Ethnic enclaves, **1:**259–60, 298
European Green Capital Award (EGCA), **1:**80–81
Eye Opener Program, **2:**66, 81

Finance and construction enterprises (FCEs), **1:**204
Fish, Robert, **2:**104
Flexi-jobs, **1:**22
Flint, Michigan, water pollution, **2:**4–5, 16–21
Food waste
  Norway, **2:**279–80
  Singapore, **2:**241, 293–97, 297*t*
Ford, Henry, **1:**213
Ford, Richard, **1:**108–9
Forsberg, Carl, **2:**210–11
France
  employment and jobs, **1:**5, 31–35, *32,* 34*t*
  green spaces, **1:**130, 164–68, *167*
Franco, Francisco, **2:**214
Frankfurt, Germany
  energy and sustainability, **1:**68, 79–85
  green space, **1:**81–84
Fraser, Barbara, **1:**271, 273
Fridell, Julia, **1:***59*
Frisch, Max, **1:**231
Fu Zhenghua, **2:**197

Gallagher, John, **1:**218
Gangs
  Beijing, China, **2:**196
  Brussels, Belgium, **2:**200–201

Chicago, Illinois, **2:**203
Sicily, Italy, **2:**228
Garbage disposal. *See* Waste management
Gardens
    Paris, France, **1:**164–68
    Tel Aviv, Israel, **1:**173–77
Garner, Jay, **2:**188
Gatbonton, Elizabeth, **1:**262
Germany
    energy and sustainability, **1:**68, 79–85
    housing and infrastructure, **1:**189, 226–32, *227*
    immigration, **1:**228–32
    schools, **2:**64, 72–77, *74*
    traffic and transportation, **2:**121, 165–69
Gilbert, Dan, **1:**217
Goto, Shinpei, **1:**180
Grand Magal, **1:**242
Grands taxis, **2:**132
Granholm, Jennifer, **2:**17
Grant, Julie, **1:**108
Green spaces
    Abu Dhabi, United Arab Emirates (UAE), **1:**130, 131–35
    Aguascalientes, Mexico, **1:**128–29, 135–39
    Beijing, China, **1:**162
    Copenhagen, Denmark, **1:**75
    Frankfurt, Germany, **1:**81–84
    Halifax, Nova Scotia, Canada, **1:**128, 140–46, 141*t, 142*
    Hong Kong, China, **1:**127–28, 147–52, *148*
    Moscow, Russia, **1:**129–30, 154–58, *157*
    New York City, New York, **1:**128, 159–63
    overview, **1:**127–31
    Paris, France, **1:**130, 164–68, *167*
    Rotterdam, the Netherlands, **1:**129, 169–72
    Tel Aviv, Israel, **1:**130–31, 173–77
    Tokyo, Japan, **1:**129, 178–81, *181*
Greenblatt, Sharon, **1:**175
Greenhouse gas, **1:**95
Greenhouse gas emissions, Toronto, Ontario, Canada, **1:**122–24
Gropius, Walter, **2:**187
Group of Twenty (G20), **1:**39
Guangzhou, China, migration and demographic changes, **1:**250–51, 259–63
Gulabzoi, Najibullah, **2:**210

Guo Shoujing, **1:**71
Gutcher, Laine, **2:**210
Gymnasium, **2:**75–76

Hagwon, **2:**90
Haiti, waste management, **2:**238, 281–87, *283, 284t, 285t, 287t*
Haiti earthquake (2010), **2:**286
Halifax, Nova Scotia, Canada, green spaces, **1:**128, 140–46, 141*t, 142*
Hall of Princes, **2:**196
Handshake buildings, **1:**162
Hannssen, O. J., **2:**280
Hardy, Douglas R., **1:**272
Hashimoto, Toru, **2:**156
Hauptschule, **2:**74, 76
Havana, Cuba, housing and infrastructure, **1:**187–88, 220–25, *221*
Haysom, Simone, **2:**208–9
Hiebert, Daniel, **1:**297
Hinenoya, Kimiko, **1:**262
Hiroshi, Chiba, **2:**268
Hokan languages, **1:**279, 282
Home Energy Loan Program (HELP), **1:**121
Hong Kong, China
    employment and jobs, **1:**53
    green spaces, **1:**127–28, 147–52, *148*
Hoornweg, Daniel, **2:**284, 285
Household responsibility system, **1:**202
Housing and infrastructure
    Almaty, Kazakhstan, **1:**188, 189–94
    Berlin, Germany, **1:**277
    Caracas, Venezuela, **1:**188, 195–99
    China, **1:**149–52
    Chongqing, China, **1:**186, 200–205, *203*
    Dandong, China, **1:**188–89, 206–11
    Detroit, Michigan, **1:**186, 213–19, *216*
    Havana, Cuba, **1:**187–88, 220–25, *221*
    London, United Kingdom, **1:**276–77
    Munich, Germany, **1:**189, 226–32, *227*
    overview, **1:**185–89
    Sydney, Australia, **1:**185, 233–38, *234*
    Touba, Senegal, **1:**187, 239–43
    Vienna, Austria, **1:**186–87, 244–47
Huang Qifan, **1:**203–4
Huang Teng, **2:**114, 115
Huaqiangbei Electronics Market, **1:***54,* 54–56
Huffelen, Alexandra van, **1:**171
Hugo, Victor, **1:**165

Hukou system, **1:**202, 203–4
Hussein, Adnan, **2:**192
Hussein, Saddam, **2:**177, 187, 189, 191, 238, 243
Hwang, Kyung Moon, **2:**222–23
Hydroponics farming, Tel Aviv, Israel, **1:**176

Illinois, violence, corruption, and organized crime, **2:**181, 202–6
Immigration
  Argentina, **1:**255–58
  France, **1:**34–35
  Germany, **1:**228–32
  London, United Kingdom, **1:**253
  Los Angeles, California, **1:**252
  Tokyo, Japan, **1:**252
  United Kingdom, **1:**277–78
  Vancouver, British Columbia, Canada, **1:**252, 294–98
Incineration, Singapore, **2:**295
India
  air pollution, **2:**4, 33–38, 34*t*, 142–43, 244
  employment and jobs, **1:**2–3, 19–23
  energy and sustainability, **1:**67, 97–102
  traffic and transportation, **2:**122–23, 140–44
  waste management, **2:**239, 262–66
Infrastructure. *See* Housing and infrastructure
Inose, Naoki, **2:**233
Iran, migration and demographic changes, **1:**251, 283–88, *286*
Iraq
  violence, corruption, and organized crime, **2:**177–78, 187–92, *190*
  waste management, **2:**237–38, 241–45, *242*
Ishihara, Shintaro, **2:**234
Iskandar, Leila, **2:**249
Islamic Iberia, **1:**254
Islamic schools, **2:***70,* 70–71
Israel, green spaces, **1:**130–31, 173–77
Istanbul, Turkey, traffic and transportation, **2:**123, 134–38, *136*
Italy
  air pollution, **2:**5–6, 39–43
  violence, corruption, and organized crime, **2:**179–80, 226–30
  waste management, **2:**240, 272–76, *274*
Ivan the Great, **2:**105

Jachimowicz, Maia, **1:**257
Jackson, Betsy, **1:**215, 216, 218–19
Jameson, Sam, **2:**232
Jang Song-thaek, **1:**211
Japan
  green spaces, **1:**129, 178–81, *181*
  immigration, **1:**252
  migration and demographic changes, **1:**252, 289–93, *290*
  schools, **2:**66, 100–105, *104*
  traffic and transportation, **2:**121, 154–58, *155*
  violence, corruption, and organized crime, **2:**181, 230–34
  waste management, **2:**241, 267–71, *270*
Japanese Street, **1:**261–62
Jardin des Champs Élysées, **1:**164–66
Jardin du Champ de Mars, **1:**165–66
Jeanneret, Charles-Édouard (Le Corbusier), **1:**191
Jensen, Frank, **1:**75
Jiang, Chelsea, **1:**297–98
Jobs. *See* Employment and jobs
John Paul II, Pope, **2:**28
Johnson, David, **2:**233
Jones Act of 1917, **1:**42–43
The Jungle (Seattle, Washington), **1:**49
Jus sanguinis, **1:**230
Jus soli, **1:**230

Kabul, Afghanistan, violence, corruption, and organized crime, **2:**178, 207–11, *209*
Kahn, Albert, **1:**213
Kansai International Airport, **2:**157–58
Karachi, Pakistan, air pollution, **2:**4, 23–27, *24*
Karzai, Hamid, **2:**210, 211
Kato, Hoei, **2:**157
Kazakhstan, housing and infrastructure, **1:**188, 189–94
Keegan, John, **2:**189
Kelley, Colin, **2:**183, 184
Kelly, Jim, **1:**109
Khameinei, Ayatollah Ali, **1:***286*
Khan, Sadiq, **1:**17, 88
Khashoggi, Jamal, **1:**37
Khatami, Mohammad, **1:**287
Khomeini, Ayatollah Ruhollah, **1:**284, *286*
Khrushchev, Nikita, **1:**191, 192
Khrushchevkas, **1:**191
Kibbutzim Movement, **1:**177

Kim Chae-kyu, **2:**221
Kim Dae-jung, **2:**222, 223
Kim Jong-un, **1:**208, 211, 209
Kim Young-sam, **2:**223
Kingsland, A. C., **1:**161
Kingston, Jeff, **1:**181
Kinshasa, Democratic Republic of Congo (DRC), migration and demographic changes, **1:**250, 264–68
Koban, **2:**181, 231
Kobe, Japan, waste management, **2:**241, 267–71, *270*
Koike, Yuriko, **2:**233
Kokichi, Mikimoto, **1:**131
Kolbert, Elizabeth, **2:**183
Kolkata, India
  air pollution, **2:**142–43, 144
  traffic and transportation, **2:**122–23, 140–44
Korean Town, **1:**251, 260–61
Kosmowski, Daniel, **1:**217
Krakow, Poland, air pollution, **2:**3, 28–32, *29*
Krakowski Alarm Smogowy, **2:**32
Kroeber, Alfred Louis, **1:**282
Kulbachevsky, Anton, **1:**154, 156
Kumar, Ashwani, **2:**263
Kurland, Richard, **1:**296
Kurtz, Ed, **2:**17
Kwon-Hein, Jaok, **2:**223

La Linea Verde, **1:**137–39
Lagos, Nigeria, employment and jobs, **1:**1–2, 6–10, *8*
Lake Zurich, **2:**174
Landfills
  Calgary, Alberta, Canada, **2:**252–53
  Dakar, Senegal, **2:**260
  Delhi, India, **2:**264–65, 265–66
  Haiti, **2:**285
  Naples, Italy, **2:**273–76
  Singapore, **2:**294
  United States, **2:**247
Law 116: Sterilization Law, **1:**43
Le Corbusier, **1:**191
Leary, Margaret, **1:**215, 216, 218–19
Lee, Anton King-wah, **1:**150
Lee, Jay Y. (Lee Jae-yong), **2:**224, 225
Lee Myung-bak, **2:**223
Leidenfrost, Wayne, **1:**297, 298
Lem, Stanislaw, **2:**28
Leung Chun-ying, **1:**149

Li, Zhen-shan, **2:**265
Liang Ke, **2:**196
Lima, Peru, migration and demographic changes, **1:**250, 269–73, *270*
Lincicome, Mark, **2:**101
Little Africa, **1:**251, 262–63
Liu Yungang, **1:**261
London, United Kingdom
  employment and jobs, **1:**4, *12,* 12–18
  energy and sustainability, **1:**67–68, 86–90
  housing and infrastructure, **1:**16, 276–77
  migration and demographic changes, **1:**253, 274–78
London Living Wage program, **1:**15, 16
Lopez Rivera, Oscar, **1:**42
Los Angeles, California, migration and demographic changes, **1:**252, 279–83
Louis XIV, King, **1:**164, 165
Louis Philippe, **1:**165
Lu, Professor, **1:**211
Luo, Michael, **2:**237–38, 241–45, *242*

MacBride, Samantha, **2:**291
MacLehose, Murray, **1:**147
Madrigal, Alexis C., **1:**106
Maduro Moros, Nicolas, **1:**196, 199, 197
Maestas, Roberto, **1:**50
Magistris, Luigi de, **2:**276
Mali, schools, **2:**62–63, 67–71, *70*
Mamadou, Sibalo, **2:**85–86
Marco Polo, **2:**6
Martel, Lucrecia, **1:**257
Martin, Richard, **1:**98
Marzolini, Pio, **2:**170
Mass transit, Karachi, Pakistan, **2:**26–27
Massachusetts
  schools, **2:**66, 78–82, *79*
  water pollution, **2:**1–2, 11–15, *13*
Massachusetts Institute of Technology (MIT), **2:**66, 78–79
Masuzoe, Yoichi, **2:**233
Matsu, Ichiro, **2:**156
Mayeur, Yvan, **2:**201–2
Mbacké, Sheikh Ahmadu Bamba, **1:**239, 241, 242
McCallum, John, **1:**298
McChrystal, Stanley, **2:**211
Mckean, Cameron Allan, **1:**180
Médersas, **2:***70,* 70–71
Medrano, Fernando, **1:**297

Meiji years (Japan), **2:**101–2, 103
Melbourne, Australia, energy and sustainability, **1:**66, 92–96, *94*
Merkel, Angela, **1:**81, 229, 231
Metcalfe, Victoria, **2:**208–9
Mexican Revolution of 1910, **2:**214–15
Mexico
  green spaces, **1:**128–29, 135–39
  traffic and transportation, **2:**123–24, 145–49, *147*
  violence, corruption, and organized crime, **2:**180–81, 213–19, *217*
Mexico City, Mexico
  traffic and transportation, **2:**123–24, 145–49, *147*
  violence, corruption, and organized crime, **2:**180–81, 213–19, *217*
Michigan
  housing and infrastructure, **1:**186, 213–19, *216*
  water pollution, **2:**4–5, 16–21
Micro-districts, **1:**191
MicroFIT solar photovoltaic programs, **1:**124
Micro-gardening, **2:**258, 259
Migration and demographic changes
  Buenos Aires, Argentina, **1:**251–52, 254–58, *256*
  Guangzhou, China, **1:**250–51, 259–63
  Kinshasa, Democratic Republic of Congo (DRC), **1:**250, 264–68
  Lima, Peru, **1:**250, 269–73, *270*
  London, United Kingdom, **1:**253, 274–78
  Los Angeles, California, **1:**252, 279–83
  overview, **1:**249–53
  Tehran, Iran, **1:**251, 283–88, *286*
  Tokyo, Japan, **1:**252, 289–93, *290*
  Vancouver, British Columbia, Canada, **1:**252, 294–98, *295*
  Williamsport, Pennsylvania, **1:**253, 299–303, *300*
Miles, Nelson A., **1:**41
Miller, R. A., **1:**262
Ministère de l'Education Nationale (MEN), **2:**68, 70–71
Ministry of Education, Sports, Culture and Technology (MEXT), **2:**101, 103–5
Minuit, Peter, **1:**24
Mobutu Sese Seko, **1:**266
Mohammed, Abbas, **2:**245
Montesquieu, **1:**164
Moon Jae-in, **2:**225
Morocco, traffic and transportation, **2:**122, 130–33
Moscow, Russia, green spaces, **1:**129–30, 154–58, *157*
Mottainai spirit, **2:**268
Mubarak, Hosni, **2:**249
Muggah, R., **2:**218
Muhsin, Haider, **2:**245
Mumbai, India
  employment and jobs, **1:**2–3, 19–23
  energy and sustainability, **1:**67, 97–102
Munich, Germany, housing and infrastructure, **1:**189, 226–32, *227*
Munich Wall, **1:**189
Municipal solid waste (MSW). *See* Waste management
Murid Sufi order, **1:**239–43
Murray, Ed, **1:**49
Museum of Science, Boston, **2:**81–82

Naeif, Salama Dhaeia, **2:**244
Naples, Italy
  landfills, **2:**273–76
  waste management, **2:**240, 272–76, *274*
Napoléon, **1:**165; **2:**214
Navajo nation, **2:**5, 55–59
Near-urban wilderness, Halifax, Nova Scotia, Canada, **1:**141*t*, 141–46
Netherlands, green spaces, **1:**129, 169–72
Neve, Felipe de, **1:**280
New Delhi, India, air pollution, **2:**4, 33–38, 34*t*. *See also* Delhi, India
New Mexico, radioactive pollution, **2:**5, 55–59
New Yalu River Bridge, **1:**206–8, 209, 211
New York City, New York
  employment and jobs, **1:**5, 24–29, 25*t*, 27*t*
  green spaces, **1:**128, 159–63
  traffic and transportation, **2:**122, 150–53, 151*t*
Niayes, **2:**257–59
Nichols, John, **1:**218
Nigeria, employment and jobs, **1:**1–2, 6–10, *8*
Nilsson-Wright, John, **2:**223
Nixon, Richard, **2:**218
North Korea, **1:**188–89, 206–11
Norway
  food waste, **2:**279–80

waste management, **2:**240, 276–80, 278*t*
Nova Scotia, green spaces, **1:**128, 140–46, 141*t, 142*
Nuclear power
   Germany, **1:**81
   Singapore City, Singapore, **1:**118–19

Obama, Barack, **1:**42, 45; **2:**19
Oil industry, Baku, Azerbaijan, **2:**2–3, 6–10, *7*
One belt one road (OBOR) initiative, **2:**116
Ontario, Canada, energy and sustainability, **1:**68–69, 120–24, *122*
Open source philosophy, **1:**56
Open-air dumps, **2:**285
Operation Bootstrap, **1:**43
Operation CeaseFire, **2:**205–6
Organized crime. *See* Violence, corruption, and organized crime
Orr, Kevyn, **1:**215, 217
Ortega, Estela, **1:**50
Ortega Douglas, Luis, **1:**136
Osaka, Japan, traffic and transportation, **2:**121, 154–58, *155*
Oslo, Norway, waste management, **2:**240, 276–80, 278*t*
Ouagadougou, Burkina Faso, schools, **2:**63, 83–86

Pahlavi, Mohammad Reza Shah, **1:**284
Pajama Factory, **1:**299–300, *300,* 301–2, 303
Pakistan, air pollution, **2:**4, 23–27, *24*
Papachristos, Andrew, **2:**204
Paris, France
   employment and jobs, **1:**5, 31–35, *32,* 34*t*
   green spaces, **1:**130, 164–68, *167*
Park Chung-hee, **2:**89, 221, 223
Park Geun-hye, **2:**180, 220, 222, 223–25, *224*
Parking, Beijing, China, **2:**127
Parks, New York City, New York, **1:**160–63
Partido Revolucionario Institucional (Institutional Revolutionary Party, PRI), **2:**215–16
Passive houses, **1:**83–84
Payind, Alam, **2:**211
Pearce, Fred, **1:**273
Pearling industry, **1:**131–32

Peña Nieto, Enrique, **2:**217
Pennsylvania
   energy and sustainability, **1:**106–10, *107*
   migration and demographic changes, **1:**253, 299–303, *300*
People's Communes, **1:**201–2
Pérón, Juan, **1:**256
Persian Gulf War, **2:**187–88
Peru
   climate change, **1:**271–73
   migration and demographic changes, **1:**250, 269–73, *270*
Petits taxis, **2:**131–32
Pfiffner, James, **2:**188
Phillips, Ted, **1:**216
Photovoltaics, Frankfurt, Germany, **1:**84
Piano, Renzo, **2:**157
Pilato, Michael, **1:**301
Pittsburgh, Pennsylvania, energy and sustainability, **1:**69–70, 106–10, *107*
Plaza Roberto Maestas, **1:**50
Pohlmann, Markus, **2:**223
Poinsett, Joel Roberts, **2:**215
Poland, air pollution, **2:**3, 28–32, *29*
Pollution, **2:**1–6. *See also* Air pollution; Radioactive pollution; Water pollution
Polytechnic University of Bobo-Dioulasso (UPB), **2:**84
Port-au-Prince, Haiti, waste management, **2:**238, 281–87, *283,* 284*t,* 285*t,* 287*t*
Portland, Oregon, **1:**277
Prodi, Romano, **2:**275
Public transportation
   Casablanca, Morocco, **2:**132–33
   Copenhagen, Denmark, **1:**78
   Istanbul, Turkey, **2:**136–37
   Kolkata, India, **2:**143–44
   London, United Kingdom, **1:**88, 276
   Mexico City, Mexico, **2:**147–48
   Saint Petersburg, Russia, **2:**161–62
   Toronto, Ontario, Canada, **1:***122,* 122–23
   Zurich, Switzerland, **2:**171–74
Puerto Rico, employment and jobs, **1:**2, 41–46, *44*
Puerto Rico Oversight, Management, and Economic Stability Act (PROMESA), **1:**45
Putin, Vladimir, **1:**39

Radioactive pollution, Shiprock, New
    Mexico, **2:**5, 55–59
Railroads, **1:**280–81
Ramírez, Edson, **1:**272
Rashid bin Saeed Al Maktoum, Sheikh,
    1:132
Reagan, Ronald, **2:**217
Realschule, **2:**74–75, 76
Recycling, Calgary, Alberta, Canada,
    2:255–56
Reeve, James, **1:**37
Reilly, Edward, **2:**234
Reinprecht, Christoph, **1:**246
Reishauer, Edwin O., **1:**262
Renewable energy, Melbourne, Australia,
    1:93–96
Resource curse, **1:**196
Reza Shah, **1:**284
Rheault, Ludovic, **1:**296
Rhee, Syngman, **2:**221
Richtel, Matt, **2:**288
Ring roads, **2:**125–26
Rio de Janeiro, Brazil, energy and
    sustainability, **1:**68, 111–15, *112*
Riots, **1:**281–82
Ripley, Amanda, **2:**90
Riyadh, Saudi Arabia, employment and
    jobs, **1:**3, 36–40
Rodriguez Castillo, Juan, **1:**280
Roh Moo-hyun, **2:**223
Roh Tae-woo, **2:**223
Rohani, Farid, **1:**296
Rome, Italy, air pollution, **2:**5–6, 39–43
Roosevelt, Franklin D., **1:**161
Rotterdam, the Netherlands, green spaces,
    1:129, 169–72
Roxbury Latin School, **2:**66, 80–81
Ruiz Cortines, Adolfo, **1:**136
Rumpshakers, **1:**213
Russia
    green spaces, **1:**129–30, 154–58, *157*
    schools, **2:**63–64, 105–10
    traffic and transportation, **2:**120,
        160–65, *161*
Russian Federation Transport Strategy
    2030, **2:**164

Sadek, Wathek, **2:**243
Sadr, Moqtada al-, **2:**192, 243
Saint Petersburg, Russia, traffic and
    transportation, **2:**120, 160–65, *161*
Sale, Murray, **2:**232
Salinas de Gortari, Carlos, **1:**136
Sall, Khalifa, **2:**259
Sami, Ola, **2:**243
Sami, Sabah, **2:**244
San Francisco, California, waste
    management, **2:**239–40, 288–92, *290*
San Juan, Puerto Rico, employment and
    jobs, **1:**2, 41–46, *44*
Sanitary landfill, **2:**285
Santa Anna, Antonio López de, **2:**214–15
Sao Paulo, Brazil, air pollution, **2:**3, 45–48
Saudi Arabia, employment and jobs, **1:**3,
    36–40
S-Bahn, **2:**173–74
Schellnhuber, Hans Joachim, **2:**184–85
Schmitt, Eric, **2:**217
Schools
    Bamako, Mali, **2:**62–63, 67–71, *70*
    Berlin, Germany, **2:**64, 72–77, *74*
    Boston, Massachusetts, **2:**66, 78–82, *79*
    Ouagadougou, Burkina Faso, **2:**63,
        83–86
    overview, **2:**61–66
    Seoul, South Korea, **2:**65–66, 87–90
    Sydney, Australia, **2:**65, 91–95
    Taipei, Taiwan, **2:**64–65, *96*, 96–100
    Tokyo, Japan, **2:**66, 100–105, *104*
    Vologda, Russia, **2:**63–64, 105–10
    Xi'an, China, **2:**62, 111–16, 113*t*
Schulz, Sebastian, **2:**190
Science, technology, engineering, and
    math (STEM), **2:**66, 78–82
Sea Forest, **1:**179–80
Seager, Richard, **2:**183–84
Seattle, Washington, employment and
    jobs, **1:**4, 48–51
Seine Valley, France, **1:**31–32
Sekundarschule, **2:**76
Senegal
    housing and infrastructure, **1:**187,
        239–43
    waste management, **2:**238, 257–61, *258*
Seoul, South Korea
    air pollution, **2:**2, 52–53
    schools, **2:**65–66, 87–90
    violence, corruption, and organized
        crime, **2:**180, 220–25, *224*
    water pollution, **2:**2, 50–52, *51,* 53–54
Seth, Michael, **2:**87–88, 222
Set-Setal movement, **2:**261
Sewage treatment plants, Kobe, Japan,
    2:269

Shah, Agha Muhammed, **1:**283
Shah, Nassar Ed-Din, **1:**284
Shakespeare, William, **2:**182
Shanghai, China, **1:**21
Shanzhai industry, **1:**55–56
Shen Baozhen, **2:**96
Shenango Coke Works, **1:**108
Shenzhen, China, employment and jobs, **1:**5–6, 52–57, *54*
Shiprock, New Mexico, radioactive pollution, **2:**5, 55–59
Shuey, Chris, **2:**56
Sicily, Italy, violence, corruption, and organized crime, **2:**179–80, 226–30
Singapore City, Singapore
    energy and sustainability, **1:**69, 116–19
    waste management, **2:**241, 293–97, 297*t*
Six-party talks, **1:**210
Skyline alleys, **1:**162
Slums, **1:**197–98
Small and medium-sized enterprises (SMEs), **1:**9–10
Smith, John, **2:**15
Smith, Stephen J., **2:**156
Snyder, Rick, **1:**215; **2:**16–17, 19
Social housing, Australia, **1:**236–37
Solar panels
    Melbourne, Australia, **1:***94*, 95
    Rio de Janiero, Brazil, **1:**113–14
    Singapore City, Singapore, **1:**117–18
South Korea
    air pollution, **2:**2, 52–53
    schools, **2:**65–66, 87–90
    violence, corruption, and organized crime, **2:**180, 220–25, *224*
    water pollution, **2:**2, 50–52, *51,* 53–54
Soviet-Afghan war, **2:**207–8
Spanish colonization of the Americas, **2:**213–14
Special economic zone (SEZ), **1:**208–9
Special education, Taiwan, **2:**98–99
Spencer, John, **2:**189
Stadtbahn, **2:**167–68
Steel, Pittsburgh, Pennsylvania, **1:**106
Steele, Jonathan, **2:**207
Stensgård, A. E., **2:**280
Stephens, Kathleen, **2:**225
Sterilization program (Puerto Rico), **1:**43–44
Stockholm, Sweden, employment and jobs, **1:**3–4, 58–63, *59*
Strategic Subject List, **2:**204–5, 206

Streetcars, Zurich, Switzerland, **2:**172–73
Stuttgart, Germany, traffic and transportation, **2:**121, 165–69
Subways, New York City, New York, **2:**122, 150–53, 151*t*
Sugarcane, **1:**115
Sugrue, Thomas, **1:**214, 215, 218
Sullivan, Tim, **2:**210–11
Summer Olympics (Mexico City, 1968), **2:**216
Sustainability. *See* Energy and sustainability
Sweden, employment and jobs, **1:**3–4, 58–63, *59*
Switzerland, traffic and transportation, **2:**121–22, 170–74, *171*
Sydney, Australia
    housing and infrastructure, **1:**185, 233–38, *234*
    schools, **2:**65, 91–95
Syria, violence, corruption, and organized crime, **2:**178, 182–86, *185*
Syrian War, **1:**232
Szymborska, Wislawa, **2:**28

Taipei, Taiwan, schools, **2:**64–65, *96,* 96–100
Taiwan, schools, **2:**64–65, *96,* 96–100
Talbot, Margaret, **1:**110
Taliban, **2:**208, 209–10
Talyan, V., **2:**263
Tanaka, H., **1:**262
Tanaka, Kakuei, **2:**233
Tanaka, S., **1:**262
Tang, Bo-Sin, **1:**150
Taxis, **2:**131–32
Tehran, Iran, migration and demographic changes, **1:**251, 283–88, *286*
Tel Aviv, Israel, green spaces, **1:**130–31, 173–77
Terán Market, **1:**138
3D printing, **1:**27–28
Three R's (reduce, reuse, and recycle), **2:**240, 252, 269
Todd, Douglas, **1:**294
Tokyo, Japan
    green spaces, **1:**129, 178–81, *181*
    migration and demographic changes, **1:**252, 289–93, *290*
    schools, **2:**66, 100–105, *104*
    violence, corruption, and organized crime, **2:**181, 230–34

Tongva Amerindians, **1:**279
Too Good to Waste Strategy, **2:**254
Toronto, Ontario, Canada, energy
    and sustainability, **1:**68–69, 120–24, *122*
Toronto Green Standard, **1:**120–21
Total trihalomethanes (TTHM), **2:**19, 20
Touba, Senegal, housing and
    infrastructure, **1:**187, 239–43
Tower of David, **1:**197–98
Traffic and transportation
    Beijing, China, **2:**119–20, 124–29, *126*
    Casablanca, Morocco, **2:**122, 130–33
    Istanbul, Turkey, **2:**123, 134–38, *136*
    Kolkata, India, **2:**122–23, 140–44
    Mexico City, Mexico, **2:**123–24, 145–49, *147*
    Mumbai, India, **1:**100
    New York City, New York, **1:**28–29; **2:**122, 150–53, 151*t*
    Osaka, Japan, **2:**121, 154–58, *155*
    overview, **2:**119–24
    Saint Petersburg, Russia, **2:**120, 160–65, *161*
    Stuttgart, Germany, **2:**121, 165–69
    Zurich, Switzerland, **2:**121–22, 170–74, *171*
Tramlines
    Casablanca, Morocco, **2:**133
    Istanbul, Turkey, **2:**136
Transportation. *See* Traffic and transportation
Trees
    Karachi, Pakistan, **2:**25–26
    Moscow, Russia, **1:**154–55, 156–58, *157*
    Tokyo, Japan, **1:**179
Trittin, Jürgen, **1:**81
Trolleybuses, Zurich, Switzerland, **2:**173
Trotsky, Leon, **1:**191
Trump, Donald, **1:**39, 218, 232, 294
Tung Chee-hwa, **1:**149
Tunnels, Istanbul, Turkey, **2:**136–37
Turkey, traffic and transportation, **2:**123, 134–38, *136*
Turner, Duncan, **1:**56

Uber, **2:**128–29, 132
Umi no Mori (Sea Forest), **1:**179–80
United Arab Emirates (UAE), green spaces, **1:**130, 131–35

United Kingdom
    Brexit, **1:**4, 16–18
    employment and jobs, **1:**4, *12,* 12–18
    energy and sustainability, **1:**67–68, 86–90
    migration and demographic changes, **1:**253, 274–78
United States
    employment and jobs, **1:**4, 5, 48–51
    energy and sustainability, **1:**69–70, 106–10, *107*
    green spaces, **1:**128, 159–63
    housing and infrastructure, **1:**186, 213–19, *216*
    migration and demographic changes, **1:**252, 253, 279–83, 299–303, *300*
    radioactive pollution, **2:**5, 55–59
    schools, **2:**66, 78–82, *79*
    violence, corruption, and organized crime, **2:**181, 202–6
    waste management, **2:**239–40, 247, 288–92, *290*
    water pollution, **2:**1–2, 4–5, 11–15, *13,* 16–21
University of Koudougou (UK), **2:**84
University of New South Wales (UNSW), **2:**92, 93–94
University of Ouagadougou (UO), **2:**84
University of Technology's Sydney (UTS) Institute for Public Policy and Governance, **2:**94–95
Uranium mines, **2:**5, 55–59
Urban forestry, Karachi, Pakistan, **2:**25–26

Vahid-Dastjerdi, Marzieh, **1:**287
Vancouver, British Columbia, Canada, migration and demographic changes, **1:**252, 294–98, *295*
Veisten, Knut, **1:**77
Venezuela, housing and infrastructure, **1:**188, 195–99
Verkehrsbetriebe Zurich (VBZ), **2:**172
Verkehrs-und Tarifverbund Stuttgart (VVS), **2:**167
Vermicomposting, **2:**296
Viberg, Rebecka, **1:***59*
Vienna, Austria, housing and infrastructure, **1:**186–87, 244–47
Vilalta, C., **2:**218
Violence, corruption, and organized crime
    Aleppo, Syria, **2:**178, 182–86, *185*

Baghdad, Iraq, **2:**177–78, 187–92, *190*
Beijing, China, **2:**179, 193–97
Brussels, Belgium, **2:**179, 197–202, *199*
Chicago, Illinois, **2:**181, 202–6
Kabul, Afghanistan, **2:**178, 207–11, *209*
Mexico City, Mexico, **2:**180–81, 213–19, *217*
overview, **2:**177–81
Seoul, South Korea, **2:**180, 220–25, *224*
Sicily, Italy, **2:**179–80, 226–30
Tokyo, Japan, **2:**181, 230–34
Vologda, Russia, schools, **2:**63–64, 105–10
Vologda Multidisciplinary Lyceum, **2:**108–9
Vologda State University, **2:**109–10
Voltaire, **1:**164
Vom Hau, Matthias, **1:**255, 258

Wade, Abdoulaye, **2:**259
Wang, Hao, **2:**265
Wang Yi, **1:**210
Washington, George, **1:**24, 160
Washington (state), employment and jobs, **1:**4, 48–51
Waste management
 Baghdad, Iraq, **2:**237–38, 241–45, *242*
 Cairo, Egypt, **2:**238–39, 246–50, *248*
 Calgary, Alberta, Canada, **2:**240, 251–56, 253*t*, 255*t*
 Dakar, Senegal, **2:**238, 257–61, *258*
 Delhi, India, **2:**239, 262–66
 Kobe, Japan, **2:**241, 267–71, *270*
 Naples, Italy, **2:**240, 272–76, *274*
 Oslo, Norway, **2:**240, 276–80, 278*t*
 overview, **2:**237–41
 Port-au-Prince, Haiti, **2:**238, 281–87, *283*, 284*t*, 285*t*, 287*t*
 San Francisco, California, **2:**239–40, 288–92, *290*
 Singapore City, Singapore, **2:**241, 293–97, 297*t*
 United States, **2:**247
Watanabe, Teresa, **2:**232
Water pollution
 Baku, Azerbaijan, **2:**2–3, 6–10, *7*
 Boston, Massachusetts, **2:**1–2, 11–15, *13*
 Flint, Michigan, **2:**4–5, 16–21

Seoul, South Korea, **2:**2, 50–52, *51*, 53–54
Water shortage, Beijing, China, **1:**65–66, 70–74, 72*t*
Weather vs. climate, **2:**186
Wen Jiabao, **1:**207
Wiarda, Jan-Martin, **2:**75
Williams, Brian Glyn, **2:**208
Williams, Phil, **2:**191
Williamsport, Pennsylvania, migration and demographic changes, **1:**253, 299–303, *300*
Wilson, Mary, **1:**271
Wing, Paul, **2:**189
Women
 Iran, **1:**285–87
 Japan, **1:**291
 Saudi Arabia workforce, **1:**38
Wong, Siu-Wai, **1:**150
Woodhull, C. S., **1:**161
Worms, **2:**296
Wowereit, Klaus, **2:**77
Wright, Frank Lloyd, **2:**187
Wyant, Dan, **2:**17, 19

Xi Jinping, **1:**209, 262; **2:**116, 193, 196
Xi'an, China, schools, **2:**62, 111–16, 113*t*
Xi'an International University, **2:**114, 115
Xiaobei Road, **1:**262

Yakuza, **2:**233–34
Young, Bob, **1:**49
Young, Ian, **1:**297
Yutori, **2:**66, 101, 103–4

Zabaleen, **2:**249–50
Zagorin, Edmund, **1:**216
Zayed bin Sultan Al Nahyan, Sheikh, **1:**132
Zero waste, **2:**288–92
Zero Waste Building Program, **1:**123–24
Zero Waste National (Singapore), **2:**296
Zhao, Yan, **2:**265
Zhou Yongkang, **2:**196–97
Zones touristiques internationales (ZTI), **1:***32*, 32–34, 34*t*
Zoot Suit Riots, **1:**281
Zurich, Switzerland, traffic and transportation, **2:**121–22, 170–74, *171*